FOR THINGS YOU CAN'T DO IN A BOOK: **i•claim visualizing argument** offers a new way to see argument, with six tutorials, an illustrated glossary, and more than seventy multi-media arguments.

ORDER   *Seeing & Writing* **+ free i•claim** CD-ROM using ISBN 0-312-62457-3

PREVIEW   **i•claim visualizing argument** at bedfordstmartins.com/iclaim

Teaching *Seeing & Writing 4*

Teaching
Seeing &
Writing 4

Prepared by

Kim Haimes-Korn
Southern Polytechnic State University

Dan Keller
University of Louisville

Anne Kress and Suellyn Winkle
Santa Fe Community College

Bedford / St. Martin's
Boston ◆ New York

4 3 2 1 0
e d c b a

For information, write: Bedford/St. Martin's,
75 Arlington Street, Boston, MA 02116
(617-399-4000)
bedfordstmartins.com

ISBN-10: 0-312-57188-7
ISBN-13: 978-0-312-57188-7

Instructors who have adopted *Seeing & Writing 4*
as a text book for a course are authorized to duplicate
portions of this manual for their students.

Preface

Many teachers collaborate when teaching with *Seeing & Writing*—discussing material, formulating approaches to it, sharing assignments and syllabi. Some of the material is challenging to teach, but that's also what makes *Seeing & Writing 4* fun to pick up and to share with new students and fellow teachers, year after year. We hope that *Teaching SEEING & WRITING 4* helps you to teach critical reading and writing more effectively, and to keep the challenging from becoming difficult.

Much of our focus in this edition was to make *Teaching SEEING & WRITING* more user-friendly. When we thought of the audience for this book, we imagined busy, creative, innovative teachers—real teachers. Some teachers are considering this topic for the first time, while others of you have incorporated visual literacies into your curriculum in creative ways for years. This guide should help you both begin and extend your teaching strategies in this area.

Many of you will use the guide as you develop your courses, but we also like to imagine you bringing the guide with you to class to act as a touchstone for classroom activities and points for discussion. We picture you glancing down and being able to visually process these ideas and implement them on the spot. We see you directly using the questions with students to create discussion, generate group work, and inspire writing. Part of this revision involved working with the document design of the book to make the assignments and reading selections both readable and scannable. This fits in with the redesign of *Seeing & Writing* to present a "more composed and accessible text." This means a more "simplified design," such as bulleted lists for discussion questions and a consistent look and feel throughout the many submissions.

Our newest feature, Visualizing Composition: Teaching and Composing Visually, includes essays introducing some of the language and philosophies of visual literacy forms. There are so many new technologies, visual and virtual spaces, and definitions that are currently taking shape within our culture. Students and teachers need to understand terms like *new media*, *graphic novels*, and *interactive games* and the ways we might incorporate them in our curriculum. We have pulled together authors who focus on particular areas of expertise or unique perspectives to help us and our students situate ourselves in this visual world. This emphasis addresses several purposes for teachers. The first is to help them introduce students to genres and mediums—their definitions, conventions, perspectives, presence, and impact. The second is to help them understand the ways they are both consumers and producers of visual texts. In other words, along with analysis, students can compose in these alternate forms, and "acts of composition" transcend forms when brought to students' attention.

Nearly all of the features from the first three editions of *Teaching SEEING & WRITING* remain the same. Instructional resources are included for each selection and special feature, organized under four categories: Possibilities for Discussion, Reflection, and Journaling; Additional Writing Topics and Classroom Activities; Connections with Other Texts; and Suggestions for Further Reading, Thinking, and Writing. Each contains clusters of questions and further instructions and provides an opportunity to thicken and widen the instructional impact of the visual and verbal materials you might choose to work with in your classes. Suggestions for Further Reading, Thinking, and Writing for each selection can prompt additional instructional activities in which students work with other materials drawn from print, web-based, and audiovisual media.

In addition to these resources, *Teaching SEEING & WRITING 4* includes the voices and the pedagogical practices of many teachers. Integrated throughout the manual are Surefire Classes and Assignments for many of the selections in the fourth edition. You'll hear from many first-rate teachers who are part of the *Seeing & Writing* community and who have contributed to this edition. These are passionate and accomplished teachers, and their voices and their perspectives on teaching make this book pedagogically rich. Each of us is but one member of a large community of instructors who enjoy teaching with this book, and we are delighted to have our voices linked with theirs.

We trust that you will find in this edition of *Teaching SEEING & WRITING* not only a wide range of teaching possibilities but also a great deal of flexibility about how best to adapt these materials to the particular instructional circumstances and challenges your students bring to each class. We invite you to visit the *Student Center for Seeing & Writing* online at bedfordstmartins.com/seeingandwriting4. There you'll find free tutorials on analyzing visuals, interviews with artists and writers from *Seeing & Writing*, videos, checklists, and much more to support *Seeing & Writing 4*. We would be most grateful to hear from you about which exercises worked most effectively for you in the classes you teach.

We have designed every aspect of *Seeing & Writing 4*, including what you will find in this guide to teaching the book, with one overarching goal in mind: to improve the ability of each student to read and think more critically and to write more effectively.

Donald McQuade
Christine McQuade
Kim Haimes-Korn
Dan Keller

Contents

Introduction to Teaching SEEING & WRITING

I started using *Seeing & Writing* many years ago with the very first edition, and have contributed assignments to previous editions of *Teaching SEEING & WRITING*. I was very excited to extend this work through editing this edition. Many books come with teaching guides, but I stand by my feeling that this one is truly different because of the many voices and ideas represented. Rather than mere summaries of reading selections or the perspective of a single author, this guide collects innovative teaching practices and classroom assignments from teachers across the country who feel strongly about incorporating visual literacies into their classes. I find that the most productive work in the teaching of composition is through this kind of exchange and sharing. Over the years, I have enjoyed experimenting with creative assignments and have learned much through this form of teacherly exchange. In this edition, like the editions before it, contributors share innovative composition assignments and theories that ask students to both analyze and create visual texts in the writing classroom. It is with this collaborative spirit in mind that I add to the fine work of Dan Keller and others who envisioned such a teaching community through this book.

As director of a writing program responsible for teacher training, I have shared my excitement about *Seeing & Writing* with other teachers who are interested in incorporating visual literacies into their composition classes. Today, the job of the writing teacher is much different than it was years ago as we realize that "acts of composition" involve more than print on a page. Increasingly, our classrooms are melting pots of different personae, ethnicities, cultures, and skill sets. To meet this challenge as composition teachers, we need to formulate assignments to meet the diverse communities of student learners we serve. Our students are inundated with hundreds of visual images daily. We must develop writing assignments and composition classes that combine rhetorical strategies with participant-centered learning through connecting the textual and the visual, moving outside the walls of academia and into the real and virtual worlds that our students occupy.

Visual literacy, loosely defined, is the ability to understand and communicate with visuals of any kind. It can involve the interpretation and analysis of a painting, an image, an advertisement, or a film. It also might involve students producing in and through these means, through digital photography, document design, or video projects. It is the interacting with visual and contextual situations to motivate critical thinking and writing.

In 2003, the National Council of Teachers of English (NCTE) passed resolutions on media literacy skills as practices in our classrooms. And according to Scott Sullivan of National-Louis University, co-editor of *Media Literacy: Finding a Foothold in the English Classroom*, "using media as an additional text in English class is a surefire way to increase the level of involvement for even the most reluctant students."[1] In fact, in 2007 *Time* magazine named "You" its Person of the Year, and *Newsweek* described such sites as Flickr, MySpace, Craigslist, Digg, and YouTube as "putting the 'We' in the Web." Media theorist Henry Jenkins, in his *Chronicle of Higher Education* article, coined the term *YouNiversity* to describe "a new academic setting in which the student is at the center and [in] which information is displayed in more public ways." In the 2009 NCTE report, *Writing in the 21st Century*, Kathleen Blake Yancey reviews the roles and expectations of our composition students. She acknowledges that with "digital technology . . . writers are *everywhere*" and recognizes that there is more of what Deborah Brandt calls "self-sponsored writing" than ever before, "a writing that belongs to the writer, not an institution, with the result that people — students, senior citizens, employees, volunteers, family members, sensible *and* non-sensible people alike — want to compose and do — on the page and screen and on the network — to *each other*." All of these are indicators that students have a stronger sense of interest and agency through these emerging

---

[1] Mary T. Christel and Scott Sullivan, *Lesson Plans for Creating Media-Rich Classrooms* (NCTE, 2007), xv.

discourse communities and that we, as composition teachers, need to revisit and rethink the ways our students compose.

For those of us who work in academia, it is clear that college students today are constantly searching for ways to understand themselves and their fast-changing and ever-evolving communities. We must work to keep our assignments relevant to our students' lives in this very visual culture, and still remain focused on teaching solid rhetorical strategies and communication skills. So how might we, as composition teachers, work with these challenges that our students face and bring reality, understanding, and valuable critical thinking skills into the writing classroom? One of the best ways to incorporate these ideas into our own teaching philosophies and pedagogies is to create invigorating and relevant assignments that involve our students in areas where they feel most comfortable, and these areas, without a doubt, involve visual literacies. Thus we must expand our notions of what it means to compose in these new spaces.

Enter the conversation and join us in creating dynamic writing classrooms that engage students through connecting the textual and the visual. Engage as a twenty-first-century teacher of writing in which composing takes on a whole new perspective. Try a couple of assignments, or design a full curriculum that focuses on visual literacies. However you use this book, know that you are an important part of the ways our students visualize composition in a changing world.

Kim Haimes-Korn

Voices from the *Seeing & Writing* Community

A rhetorician, I take it, is like one voice in a dialogue. Put several voices together, with each voicing its own special assertion, let them act upon one another in cooperative competition, and you get a dialectic that properly developed, can lead to the views transcending the limitations of each.

—Kenneth Burke, from "Rhetoric—Old and New" (1950)

Kenneth Burke's famous reference to the "parlor" invites other rhetoricians to join a philosophical conversation to draw from and extend upon the voices that have preceded their participation. The teaching of writing is often also talked about as an ongoing conversation in which teachers share their ideas and build on the ideas of others. This teaching guide has encouraged us to enter this conversation and join voices of others to "transcend the limitations" of our individual vision and be part of a larger community. From the very first edition, *Teaching SEEING & WRITING* has been about these kinds of conversations—conversations where teachers share their best classroom practices with others. This book is built on the excitement of teachers engaging in this kind of collaboration through the sharing of their ideas for teaching composition in a visual world.

What makes this instructor's manual (IM) different is what you'll see in the following pages: the *Seeing & Writing* community, passionate teachers who enjoy teaching with *Seeing & Writing* and who use the textbook in creative ways. They are teachers who are determined to keep their classrooms relevant and purposeful for our changing students. In the following teacher profiles, you'll be introduced to a group of teachers, their programs, and their reasons for choosing *Seeing & Writing*. As evident in their statements, *Seeing & Writing* offers challenging and unusual readings in both print and visual forms. It is these characteristics of the readings that, at least in part, inspire the sense of community around this textbook.

Although you regularly access this community in your office hallway, on your department blog, or at the Student Center for *Seeing & Writing*, the community has been extended into these pages. Throughout the text of the IM, in the Surefire Classes and Surefire Assignments, you will find "tested" materials, activities, and assignments that instructors have found effective and gratifying. The Surefire Classes are in-class activities that often address more than one work in a chapter; the Surefire Assignments are writing prompts or seeing prompts that usually focus on one specific work.

As author of this work, you will hear my voice throughout the IM. I enjoyed learning more about visual literacies and thinking through the many creative ways to work with the selections in the text. I drew upon years of teaching, student feedback, experimentation, and many conversations with others to come up with assignments and directions for discussion. The work in here is part of an ongoing conversation for all the teachers and students I have known and all that I have yet to meet. I have had the privilege of working with many creative teachers who value student engagement and innovative assignments— teachers who are not afraid to take risks and allow students to create their own meanings through discussion and writing. Much of my motivation in taking on this project was to celebrate these teachers and their collective years of experience in writing classrooms across the country.

This section gives you a sense of the people behind the ideas and the contexts for their assignments. The profiles provide a bit of background information as well as insights into the kinds of students and schools for which they work. It is our hope that you will become part of this community of teachers who value the connections between seeing and writing—the textual and the visual. We are pleased to highlight some of these teachers in this section and to welcome you into the *Seeing & Writing* community.

Profile: Susan Al-Jarrah

Susan Al-Jarrah
*Southwestern Oklahoma
State University*
(Surefire Assignment, p. 229)

ABOUT ME

I currently teach freshman composition, secondary English methods, and numerous Spanish courses at Southwestern Oklahoma State University in Weatherford. I serve as a university supervisor for student teachers and resident-year teachers throughout the state. I hold a master's degree in English education and am certified as a public school teacher by the Oklahoma State Department of Education in the areas of middle school language arts, secondary language arts, English literature, American literature, English grammar, and Spanish. I have taught English, Spanish, and humanities in Butler and Arapaho high schools; and I previously taught English as a second language in Saudi Arabia and Jordan. Intrigued by the processes that have allowed me to develop fluency in English, Spanish, and Arabic, I've worked with the Oklahoma State University Writing Project, the National Writing Project's Rural Sites Network, and English Language Learners Network, to examine the recursive way learners develop proficiency in listening, speaking, reading, and writing—not only in their native language but in foreign languages as well. I live in Weatherford during the school year and spend my summers at my second home, in Al-Mazar, Jordan.

ABOUT MY PROGRAM

Southwestern Oklahoma State University, located in rural western Oklahoma, is one of twenty-six institutions in the Oklahoma State System of Higher Education and is one of six state-supported regional universities governed by the Board of Regents of Oklahoma Colleges. The approximately 5,000 students come from western Oklahoma, from urban areas, from other states, and from several foreign countries. The freshman composition program at SWOSU is made up of two general education requirements—English 1113 (Freshman Comp I) and English 1213 (Freshman Comp II)—and serves a community of about 850 freshmen, with an average age of 20, predominantly from ranching and farming backgrounds in western Oklahoma. English 1113 emphasizes expository essay writing, and English 1213 emphasizes research-based writing.

WHY I USE *SEEING & WRITING*

I have found *Seeing & Writing* to be a wonderful textbook for introducing students to making connections, not only between visual images and written words, but also between those images and words and the culture surrounding them.

Profile: Rebecca Burns

ABOUT ME

I teach composition and literature at St. Louis Community College, Meramec. Prior to accepting my full-time faculty position at STLCC, I taught at Lewis and Clark Community College and Southern Illinois University Edwardsville where I earned my MA in English and started my teaching career. In

Rebecca Burns
*St. Louis Community
College, Meramec*
(Surefire Class, p. 183)

addition to teaching, I am actively involved in a number of projects and committees on campus. I co-chair the Technology Committee and serve on the Academic Service-Learning/Civic Engagement Committee; I participate with my colleagues in Teaching Squares; and I just completed writing instructions on using Blackboard 8.0's integrated version of *Turnitin* for the college's Center for Teaching and Learning.

As much as possible, I implement what I advocate in class: I write, I revise, and I write some more. Along with my three Technology Committee members, I co-author "Technology Tips," a monthly newsletter written for our department, and another colleague and I are co-writing an e-book. On my own, I've published several articles and a poem.

ABOUT MY PROGRAM

STLCC has four campuses that serve over 28,000 students. Over 40% of those students attend the Meramec campus. Our English Department offers two pre-college level writing courses (English 020 and 030), two college composition courses (English 101 and 102), two honors composition courses (English 104 and 105), and one workplace writing course (English 103). Because we serve a diverse international population, we also offer a six-course ESL program to prepare students for their composition courses. To further assist students, our campus provides a fully-staffed writing

center whose faculty assists both day and evening students. Those students who wish to enroll in composition must pass the prerequisite with a C or better, provide an ACT composite score of 21 or higher, or an SAT English score of 500 or higher, or be placed according to the college's ACCUPLACER assessment test.

The college is also committed to service-learning. In fact, many courses—in all disciplines—contain a service-learning component, and each year nearly 2,000 STLCC students work more than 10,000 hours with our community partners to assist those in need while developing a sense of civic responsibility. Most semesters I teach at least one service-learning composition course. In November 2008, over forty of my students served as election judges, and during the Spring 2009 semester, one of my classes worked with the Kirkwood Landmarks Commission to design brochures to help local residents identify their homes as Sears Houses. At the end of the semester, the Commission honored my students at a special award ceremony. This project was especially enjoyable because not only did the students perform an important service for the community, but they were also given the opportunity to write for a real audience and purpose, which helped them realize that we really do write beyond the composition classroom.

WHY I LIKE *SEEING & WRITING*

As a visual learner, I was immediately attracted to the hundreds of images in *Seeing & Writing*, and I knew that many of my students would be as well. After all, this generation of students is engaged with images more than any generation to-date.

Profile: Jeff Cravello

Jeff Cravello
California State Polytechnic University, Pomona
(Surefire Assignment, p. 270)

ABOUT ME

I was born in Los Angeles but was raised and educated in the desert communities of California and Arizona. After seeing *Star Wars: A New Hope* in 1977, I closely identified with Luke Skywalker's looking into the twin suns of Tatooine and longing for anything or anywhere else. As soon as I finished high school, I began college in metropolitan Los Angeles, and I've never completely left education or Southern California since then.

Because of finances and personal restlessness, college was a stop-and-go process for me. Part-time jobs became full-time jobs, and I'd drop out of one university only to return to another one in a year or two. I have no regrets.

My itinerant education included many fascinating experiences outside formal education. I have worked variously as a typesetter, a proofreader of phonebooks, a theme park ride operator, a hotel manager, an electrical components salesman, and a corporate trainer. All of these occupations, however mundane or enthralling, offered distinctly new lessons, which I have found invaluable and consistently applicable.

Ultimately, I discovered that my true passion was training and education, and, as a result of a recession, I found myself back in college, pursuing my master's degree in English to completion. Upon graduating, I was quite fortunate in being added to the English and Foreign Language Department's lecturer pool at California State Polytechnic University, Pomona, my alma mater. At the same time, I was hired by the Cal Poly English Language Institute to teach in its advanced studies program for international students. I have been an adjunct faculty member at Cal Poly Pomona for fourteen years now, and I am grateful to say that I have never had to suffer as a "freeway flyer."

I truly enjoy teaching and the constant flow of new faces and personalities. Of course, I've considered quitting at least a dozen times, but I can't imagine another profession that would suit my idiosyncrasies. I've never had any other goal than to attempt to leave the world a bit better for my having been here. Often, I doubt whether anyone or anything is better as a result of my efforts or if I'm on the right track. This keeps me on my toes.

ABOUT MY PROGRAM

California State Polytechnic University, Pomona, is located on the western edge of Los Angeles County. Although the university is composed of students from all parts of California and the world, most of the roughly twenty thousand students come from metropolitan Los Angeles.

Cal Poly Pomona is one of twenty-three California state universities and one of six national polytechnic universities. As the name implies, the university focuses primarily on the applied sciences and a few other specialty programs.

The English and Foreign Languages Department offers both a bachelor's and a master's degree, but the program is relatively small compared with others in the university, so the department's primary task is supporting the various colleges in the university with general education. For the most part, this includes remedial and college-level composition courses. Within the department, we are encouraged to be innovative in our course design while ensuring that our end result is proficient student writing across the disciplines.

The text appeals to our natural preference toward images while also challenging that inclination. We can learn that seeing is not necessarily believing and that images warrant much scrutiny.

Profile: Kirk Lee Davis

Kirk Lee Davis
University of Michigan–Ann Arbor
(Surefire Class, p. 111)

ABOUT ME

I often invite students to discuss the relationship between the making of writing and the making of other things: a good pizza, for example, or music playlist or painting. I find that when students in the writing classroom contemplate what sets apart impressive creations in other realms, they are prone to construct parallels to the way written texts are made. I find art objects and images to be especially useful in the writing classroom because they can serve simultaneously as complex problems and mnemonic devices.

I have taught a range of courses in rhetoric, literature, and professional and creative writing at the University of Michigan's Sweetland Writing Center, and in the school's Department of English. I have also taught at Siena Heights University and served as a Jay C. and Ruth Halls Poetry Fellow at the University of Wisconsin–Madison during the 2004–2005 academic year. My own writing has appeared in *The Concher*, the *DIAGRAM III* anthology, and was selected by Mark Doty for inclusion in *The Academy of American Poets College Prize* anthology.

ABOUT MY PROGRAM

Undergraduates at the University of Michigan may opt to take a Writing Practicum course, offered through the university's Sweetland Writing Center. In addition to in-class instruction, each student meets with his or her instructor (a member of the Writing Center staff) on a regular basis throughout the semester. This intensive class allows students to cultivate college-level writing skills without risk to their grade point averages, and often serves as a stepping-stone to the required freshman-level composition course.

These Practicum classes contain a significant proportion of special-needs students, including nonnative English speakers and students admitted to the university primarily for their nonacademic strengths. The students may be aspiring engineers or botanists; they are also often musicians, athletes, or visual artists. And although the larger student body at Michigan comes primarily from upper-middle-class backgrounds, students in the Writing Practicum comprise a conspicuously heterogeneous group in terms of socioeconomic makeup. As a consequence, the knowledge base these students bring to the class varies widely.

WHY I LIKE *SEEING & WRITING*

I use *Seeing & Writing* because it highlights the ways that students' writing lives overlap with their other lives better than any other textbook I've encountered.

Profile: Kim Haimes-Korn

Kim Haimes-Korn
*Southern Polytechnic
State University*
(Surefire Class, p. 214)

ABOUT ME

After a first career in advertising, I returned to school to earn a master's and a PhD in rhetoric and composition from Florida State University in 1996, birthing a son along the way (Garrett, the "thesis baby"). Thereafter, I got a position at Southern Polytechnic State University in Marietta, Georgia, where I have been for the past fourteen years. Along the way, birthing a daughter (Maggie, the "tenure baby"), taking care of a family (mostly my husband, Larry), watching students come and go (many of whom graduated), I've expanded my ideas through conferences, books, and presentations. I am currently a professor and director of the First Year Writing Program at Southern Polytechnic State University, teaching classes in first-year composition, literature, rhetoric, and communication.

Much of my scholarship in the field focuses on classroom inquiry and draws upon student voices to understand writing theory and practices. I write on portfolios, response theory, collaborative learning, visual literacies, and multicultural pedagogies. My writing work is directed toward a teacher audience to help improve classroom practices in the teaching of writing. I am interested in the multiple layers of language and experiences students bring to their writing lives. My most recent project, *Teaching SEEING & WRITING 4* has given me opportunities to reflect upon a long held interest of mine involving connections between the textual and the visual. It has given me the opportunity to share many years of successful classroom activities and assignments with others and to bring together the voices of many of the awesome teachers I have met along the way.

ABOUT MY PROGRAM

Southern Polytechnic State University is a mid-size, comprehensive state university in the University of Georgia system. Located in the metro-Atlanta area, the school attracts students from within the state and also boasts a large number of international students ranging from Africa, India, and China. Although we have many majors in architecture, engineering, and computer science, our department offers several English degrees (a BS and a BA) with a technological twist. The degrees in professional and technical writing and media arts draw heavily on writing for electronic spaces and multiple purposes. Students learn to write for the fields of journalism, professional writing, digital media and graphics, and technical communication. Beyond first-year writing, much of my work focuses on these degree programs and the ways students bring together the textual and the visual. This experience culminates with our capstone course, Project Portfolio, in which students pull together and visually represent their work across their degree program for the job market or graduate school.

Our first-year writing courses approach writing from a rhetorical perspective and often ask students to engage in reading and writing through visual means. Our writing courses are taught mostly in computer writing classrooms and also include online components. This works well for our students who are definitely "plugged in" and "wired." Like most students today, they can be found close to their phones, computers, or other media.

We have many dedicated, innovative, and creative writing teachers who work to understand the connections between seeing and writing and have used this textbook since its very first edition. In fact, many of our teachers have contributed to this and earlier editions of *Teaching SEEING & WRITING*. In our program we see composition as a deeply theoretical subject that is constantly taking on new shapes and strategies. Although we have some foundational principles in our program, teachers are encouraged to find their own way and bring their own mark to their writing classrooms. We often get together to share teaching ideas and connect through professional development opportunities and collaborative scholarship. It is this dynamic teaching community that allows us to create a composition program that is purposeful, interesting, and current.

WHY I LIKE SEEING & WRITING

I like *Seeing & Writing* because STUDENTS like *Seeing & Writing*. The visuals help students to communicate both critically and creatively.

Profile: Charles Hood

ABOUT ME

Charles Hood
Antelope Valley College
(Surefire Assignments, pp. 80, 169, and 209)

I teach at Antelope Valley College near Los Angeles, where I have been Scholar in Residence and Composition Coordinator for our Arts & Letters Division. Before that, among other things, I was an Artist in Residence with the Center for Land Use Interpretation, a Fulbright scholar, a lecturer at UC Irvine, a freeway flyer, a ski instructor, and a dishwasher.

My most recent book is *Bombing Ploesti* (2008).

Before I stopped counting, I had seen more than four thousand species of birds in the wild and four hundred kinds of mammals, from voles to whales to dholes. The nature thing is nice and all, but I am an English teacher more than anything. Language remains deeply powerful, deeply thrilling, more so than I ever thought possible.

ABOUT MY PROGRAM

Antelope Valley College is a 15,000-student community college located near Edwards Air Force Base, the high desert test center made famous in *The Right Stuff*. The average student age is twenty-nine. The students are a varied bunch: Among them are those on the cusp of transferring to UC Berkeley, ranch hands, suburban skateboarders trying to figure out what the hell to do with their lives, and undocumented workers—and some students are all of these things. The college has two levels of developmental composition, both essay-based, a standard English 101 semester-long course (three hours a week, no lab), and various advanced rhetoric and intro-to-lit courses. Teachers select their own textbooks. Since I discovered and started using the first edition of *Seeing & Writing,* it has become the most commonly selected anthology in the English Department sequence.

WHY I LIKE SEEING & WRITING

One thing that works for our instructors is the "not your typical burger" look of the book. More important, for now anyway, this book says, "English isn't boring, and this class will *not* be like anything you have ever done before." This is a sharp looking book and a new kind of book, and also—Dare I admit it?—a fun book.

Profile: Debbie Jacob

Debbie Jacob
*International School
of Port of Spain*
(Surefire Assignment, p. 73)

ABOUT ME

Reading a book really can change your life. I'm proof of that. More than twenty years ago I read the novel *Miguel Street* by Trinidadian writer and Nobel laureate V. S. Naipaul. I packed my bags, quit my job as a technical writer at Boeing Commercial Airplane Company in Mukilteo, Washington, and came to see if the people on the island of Trinidad were really like the carefree characters in Naipaul's book.

They were, so I settled in the middle of a sugar cane field that reminded me of my father's wheat fields on the farm where I was born and raised in Lexington, Ohio.

One year after arriving in Trinidad I began working as a journalist and script writer. My six-part television drama series, *Sugar Cane Arrows,* aired throughout the Caribbean and in England. It became one of the pioneering programs in local television and was the first Trinidadian drama series shown in the United States.

When the International School of Port of Spain (ISPS) opened in 1994, I was hired to start the English Department and teach every child in Grades 7 through 12. As head of the English Department at ISPS, I have developed courses in English and the media. I am currently the librarian at ISPS.

Over the years I have combined theory from my academic background—a BA in anthropology from Ohio State University and a master's in education from Framingham University—with my own experiences in writing to create nontraditional ways to conceptualize the writing process. My students learn to transform abstract ideas into a visual, concrete framework that makes writing come alive.

In turn, my experiences in the classroom offer new directions for my own writing. My first book, a folktale called *Legend of the St. Ann's Flood*, was released in 2005. I am currently working on study guides for books on the Caribbean Examination Council's reading list and a teaching text that uses calypso music as a model for writing.

ABOUT MY PROGRAM

ISPS offers students in Trinidad and Tobago an alternative education to the traditional, British-based system. The school has an American-based curriculum with an international philosophy designed to meet the academic needs of local students and foreign students whose parents work in one of the many international companies here.

Grades 9 and 10 provide survey courses in literature on the AP English literature track, while Grade 11 offers students the alternative of pre-AP or Composition via Visual Texts, a course that uses *Seeing & Writing* along with supplementary materials. In Grade 12, students can advance to AP English Literature or English and the Media.

My Composition via Visual Texts class targets a variety of interests and learning needs by using visual/concrete methods to create alternate methods for structuring writing. Students use the photographs in the textbook and exercises at the end of each selection to connect the text to their own life experiences. All exercises include comparisons between fiction and nonfiction sources, and visual and written texts.

Visual images in literature, film, and print media and the school celebration of Carnival serve as models for creating theme, transitions, and overall basic essay structure.

This course is an exciting alternative for those who enjoy English and want to experience a different method of writing. Students pursuing careers in art, media, and English education, along with students who want to improve their writing, are encouraged to take this course. Students who struggle with language or abstract thinking and have not been able to master basic writing skills using traditional methods of teaching by Grade 11 are required to take this course. Composition via Visual Texts can also be taken as an elective.

WHY I LIKE SEEING & WRITING

Students who have mastered English enjoy the challenge of a different vision for writing, while students who struggle with the writing process find success in creating structure through visual imagery.

Profile: Dan Keller

ABOUT ME

Dan Keller
University of Louisville
(Surefire Assignment, p. 265)

I recently maxed out my university library card. As the librarian scanned in my stack of finds, the computer made a series of small, disagreeable bleeps. "You've reached your limit," he said, eyebrows raised.

I raised my eyebrows in return. "There's a limit?"

I suppose reading a lot isn't unusual for someone in this field, especially while studying for PhD examinations and preparing a dissertation. But I have a habit (for over ten years now) of reading three different books at once, placing them in different rooms of the house. I'm intrigued by the promise of what books hold, and of what I can learn next, so I have a hard time reading books in a one-after-the-other fashion. And the three-at-a-time selections usually vary in genre: I might read a novel, a history of science, and some philosophical text at one point, and then replace them with books of three other genres. I manage to read and absorb quickly, so having a sizable rotating stack is always a good idea.

My accepted publications include chapters on multimodal composition and video games: One's a cultural examination of video games; the other links learning principles of video games to classroom pedagogy. I get to research and write about literacy practices, new media, pedagogy, and popular culture. And, of course, working on the instructional supplements for the second and third editions of *Seeing & Writing* was a pleasure since they gave me the opportunity to think pedagogically about a wide variety of texts in a detailed, sustained way.

When I'm not exceeding my library limit, I hike, I walk, I run. I go to see movies, plays, concerts, museum exhibits. I travel and I look for strange tourist sites. Everyone needs a break from reading now and then.

ABOUT MY PROGRAM

The University of Louisville is a state-supported research university located in metropolitan Louisville. Most of the 21,000 students are in-state, which means that nearly all of the students coming into English 101 are familiar with the writing process and the portfolio system (sometimes painfully so, if it's been taught badly). They tend to be around eighteen years old, and they reflect the hard-to-pin-down, ever-shifting mix of scared, eager, cautious, irreverent students you would expect in an introductory college course in which the teacher actually gets to learn about students' lives.

Despite the metropolitan setting, most of my students have been Caucasian. Female students usually outnumber male students, and they usually do better as both students and writers (reflecting the national trend). While male and female students seem equally comfortable with in-class discussion, the classroom disparities in race and ethnicity sometimes lead to lopsided conversations, some voices being heard more than others—at least, that's how it seems to me— and I try harder and harder to overcome such disparities, but not always successfully. I love learning, I love teaching, and I want to reach as many students as possible.

While I've taught a variety of composition and literature courses, I've used *Seeing & Writing* mainly in introductory composition courses. English 101 and 102 are required freshman composition courses dealing primarily with expository writing, with an emphasis on research in 102. Some teachers do special topic courses—war, urban legends, film—but I usually organize the courses around student writing, supplementing their material with helpful readings. I like introducing students to rhetorical concepts and helping them apply such concepts to a variety of texts.

My students don't claim to read much outside of school, but they don't consider Internet reading to be reading; of course when you take instant messaging, e-mail, message boards, blogs, and hypertext navigation and creation to be reading, that's a fantastic amount of reading. And they turn out to be good readers of print texts, too—despite claims about that national trend. When I look at my classes, I don't see students who need back-to-basics or reading-is-fundamental training. I see students who have skills and knowledge that haven't been acknowledged by and adapted into school curriculums. My program gives teachers a lot of pedagogical freedom, and for that I am grateful.

WHY I LIKE *SEEING & WRITING*

I'm drawn mainly to the unusual selections. Students like the book, too, which is even more important. I see them leafing through it before and during class. I can't think of any other text that has garnered requests from students.

Profile: Rich Lane

Rich Lane
Clarion University
(Surefire Assignment, p. 130)

ABOUT ME

I began my teaching career after receiving a BA in literature and secondary education at American University in Washington, D.C., in 1983. I taught high school in various capacities for eight years, at Archbishop Carroll High School in D.C. and Sidwell Friends School in D.C. During this time I also received my master's in literature from AU. I moved on to complete my PhD at Miami University, where I worked with Susan Jarrett and Lu Ming Mao, among others. While at Miami, where I discovered a passion for composition and rhetoric, I was chosen for a team that developed an epistemic approach to first-year composition, an approach that was adopted and used for approximately eight years. My dissertation concerned composition theory, teacher training, and a critical/historical look at composition pedagogies and their influence on beginning teachers over three decades. After leaving Miami, I taught composition and directed the English education program at Murray State University. After two years at Murray, I moved to Salt Lake City to codirect the English education program at the University of Utah. There I taught advanced composition courses, as well as English education courses, and it was there that I first used *Seeing & Writing*, in both advanced composition and advanced theory/humanities courses. Also while at Utah, I was named the Lowell Bennion Public Service Professor for Service Learning, and, with my classes and colleagues, developed a family literacy center that serves the community of Salt Lake City. After four years in Utah, I moved back East to teach both graduate and undergraduate courses in composition at Clarion University, where I continue to use *Seeing & Writing*.

I have published in *Essays on Canadian Literature* and *The Writing Instructor*, and have contributed essays to the collections *Miss Grundy Doesn't Teach Here Anymore: How Popular Culture Has Changed the Composition Classroom* (1997) and, most recently, *Rhetorical Education in America* (2004).

ABOUT MY PROGRAM

The first-year composition program at Clarion is a two-course sequence, English 110 (Writing I) and English 111 (Writing II). Clarion is a state university, and many of its students come from Pennsylvania. The student population consists largely of working-class people and is evenly split between entering and continuing college students. A large percentage of the first-year students are of typical college age, although some returning adult students also take first-year courses.

English 110 is designed to introduce or reintroduce students to the processes of academic writing. The course addresses the creation, drafting, and revision of compositions in various genres. Although instructors determine their own approach, all share two goals: to give students practice in the fundamentals of writing and to guide students in the discourse of academic writing.

English 111 continues the work started in English 110. However, English 111 introduces students to the more critical modes of reading and writing that are essential to success in both academic and nonacademic environments. This course concentrates on the skills of critical thinking and reading, research, analysis, and argument.

WHY I LIKE *SEEING & WRITING*

Seeing & Writing presents composition as both a verbal and visual form of communication. This concept is crucial in the changing landscape of "writing" in the twenty-first century.

Profile: Maureen Ellen O'Leary

ABOUT ME

I was born and raised in Massachusetts and received my BA in English from the University of Massachusetts, Boston. After living and working in Paris for a while, I migrated to California to attend graduate school (and apparently to live out my adult life—I raised my two children in California and am happily settled in Oakland with my husband). I received my MA and my PhD (1988) from the University of California, Berkeley. I remained at Berkeley for a few years after earning my doctorate, teaching (primarily freshmen) in the College Writing Program (formerly Subject A).

In 1992, I became a full-time member of the English Division at Diablo Valley College, a community college in Pleasant Hill,

Maureen Ellen O'Leary
Diablo Valley College
(Surefire Assignment, p. 126;
Surefire Class, p. 193)

California. Although I had concentrated on the Victorian novel in my graduate studies, I embraced the opportunity our division offers to teach a variety of courses—women's literature, the short story, creative writing, and so forth. I fell in love with Shakespeare again and used a sabbatical to write a text with a workbook component, one that invites students who are diverse in all respects to fully engage with the wonders, complexities, and fun of the plays. Along with literature, I teach developmental reading and composition courses at many levels.

I write as well as teach writing, and a number of my personal essays have appeared in various northern California publications.

WHY I LIKE *SEEING & WRITING*

It is enormously easy for students to draw connections between the content of this text and the content of their own lives. *Seeing & Writing,* in short, inspires good teaching, good writing, good learning, and good fun.

Profile: Jean Petrolle

Jean Petrolle
Columbia College Chicago
(Surefire Assignment, p. 253)

ABOUT ME

While receiving a BA and MA in English from Southern Connecticut State University and Southern Illinois University, respectively, I gathered considerable experience teaching writing, film, and literature, and produced my first publications. As a result I obtained a tenure-track position at Columbia College Chicago, a four-year arts and communications school in Chicago's South Loop. I earned my PhD in English at the University of Illinois while on the tenure track and while serving as basic writing coordinator and, later, director of composition. These multiple demands turned me into an efficient writer myself—fast, focused, effective. My experiences as a writing teacher and writing program administrator enabled me, of course, to interact with many writers, and this interaction changed my life as a writer. My writing has benefited most from my contact with struggling student writers in basic writing classes. They have taught me again how to get lost in a piece of writing, how to make a journey toward an intellectual destination that could not be imagined at the beginning of the writing process. With my students as models, I exchanged some speed and efficiency in writing for an increased sense of discovery and authenticity. Teaching writing is a wonderful way to facilitate one's own growth as a writer!

ABOUT MY PROGRAM

The composition program at Columbia College Chicago consists of three courses—Introduction to College Writing, Composition I, and Composition II. Introduction to College Writing, a basic course in essay writing with intensive individualized attention, prepares students for Composition I. Composition I strengthens students' ability to write essays of moderate length that feature clear controlling ideas, plentiful illustration, effective organization, and appropriate usage. Composition II is a course in researched writing: Students develop original ideas to explore through primary and secondary research and through the composition of sustained and considerably detailed pieces of writing. With all these courses, students have multiple themes and/or methodologies from which to choose. In Composition II, for instance, we offer sections that use ethnographic, inquiry, and visual rhetoric approaches to the composing process. All of our courses include significant amounts of reading, emphasize workshop-style participation, and enable students to pursue personally meaningful writing projects.

WHY I LIKE *SEEING & WRITING*

Seeing & Writing, because it is packed with images and full of references to contemporary popular culture, is an easy sell to students: It appeals to their interest in images and popular culture.

Profile: Priscilla Riggle

Priscilla Riggle
Truman State University
(Surefire Class, p. 276)

ABOUT ME

I teach first-year writing, creative writing, cultural studies, and world literature at Truman State University, a small public liberal arts university in semi-rural Missouri.

ABOUT MY PROGRAM

We require one course in the first year, Writing as Critical Thinking, and a writing-intensive interdisciplinary course in the junior year. Instructors for these courses select their own textbooks and design their own course syllabi. Because most of our students arrive well versed in the fundamentals of academic writing, we are able to focus on using writing to explore various topics and issues. Within the English major, we also offer a track for students interested in writing, and several courses are offered as electives within that track.

WHY I LIKE *SEEING & WRITING*

I especially like *Seeing & Writing* because it allows me to teach my class using whatever approach works for that course's particular objectives, unlike many composition texts that have a rigid design that almost dictates a course syllabus and schedule.

Profile: Joyce Stoffers

ABOUT ME

I primarily teach composition: Fundamentals of English, and English Composition I and II. I also regularly teach Introduction to Literature and have taught Creative Nonfiction, Writing for Business and Industry, Bible as Literature, and Romanticism. Introduction to Editorial Assisting and Nature Writing are two courses I have offered for independent study. My other major responsibility at SWOSU has been editing for the school's literary journal, *Westview*. I have been the managing editor and currently am the journal's nonfiction editor.

I enjoy participating in various university and community projects and activities. During Weatherford's centennial celebration, I was one of the editors of a history of the

Joyce Stoffers
*Southwestern Oklahoma
State University*
(*Surefire Assignment*, p. 123)

town. A departmental committee membership has been particularly rewarding: Our Writing Emphasis Committee helped institute a writing-emphasis minor for students who wanted an alternative to a literature-emphasis minor. As a result, we are able to offer a wider variety of writing courses, and we are teaching students from across disciplines rather than just our usual general education and English majors.

Before coming to SWOSU, I taught in New York at Broome Community College and Binghamton University (where I had received my MA in English). In addition I have held managerial and curatorial positions in such diverse institutions as the Roberson Museum and Science Center (Binghamton, New York), the Glebe House (Woodbury, Connecticut), and the American Clock and Watch Museum (Bristol, Connecticut). My interdisciplinary background is probably what first drew me to a text titled *Seeing & Writing*; its success in the classroom is what keeps me using it.

ABOUT MY PROGRAM

We serve about 850 freshmen, most of whom come from western Oklahoma. Their average age is twenty. Under our general education requirements, students must have an ACT of at least nineteen to enroll in the composition sequence of English Composition I (1113) and English Composition II (1213). Fundamentals of English is offered for those with an ACT below nineteen. The course focuses on skill building at the sentence and paragraph level, leading to essay writing by mid-semester. English Composition I emphasizes expository essay writing, requiring five to six major essays and numerous exercises and/or journal writings. We look for the following learner outcomes:

1. Students will demonstrate that they can organize their thinking for a logically written presentation.

2. Students will demonstrate that they can communicate their ideas clearly in writing, using effective sentences and paragraphs.

3. Students will demonstrate that they can revise and improve drafts of papers.

English Composition II focuses on the research element of expository writing and requires four to five major essays. A number of classes are held in the campus library, where the library staff teaches the latest technological research tools. The objectives of this course are as follows:

1. Students will demonstrate the ability to use parenthetical citations according to MLA style documentation.

2. Students will demonstrate the ability to construct works-cited entries according to MLA style documentation.

3. Students will demonstrate the ability to correctly paraphrase and quote information from sources without plagiarizing.

4. Students will demonstrate the ability to distinguish the elements of argumentation—for example, the use of evidence in the form of facts, statistics, and expert opinion; the acknowledgment of opposing arguments; and logical presentation.

WHY I LIKE *SEEING & WRITING*

With the proliferation of all types of media today, I'd be doing students an injustice by not incorporating visual literacy into the course.

Profile: Jason Stupp

Jason Stupp
West Virginia University
(Surefire Class, p. 93)

ABOUT ME

I teach composition and introductory literature courses at West Virginia University, where I have just finished the required coursework for the doctoral program in English. My research interests include critical race studies, performance theory, and twentieth-century American literature, and much of my work focuses on race, social justice, and incarceration. In the fall of 2009 semester, I started teaching a section of English composition that questions the nature of concepts such as "justice" and "punishment" while encouraging students to become active in the community. Working with the Center for Civic Engagement at WVU, the class explores options available to students who want their written work and research to become more than just a requirement for a grade. Students work on projects that in some way serve imprisoned people in West Virginia and surrounding states, and at the end of the semester, they present their research in an open, public forum. I strongly believe that a community-centered approach to the classroom not only helps motivate students who might otherwise have little interest in writing but also shows how the composition classroom can be a place where ideas and action come together to promote positive change.

ABOUT MY PROGRAM

The composition program at WVU involves students in a sequence of two courses (English 101 and 102) designed to introduce and polish the skills students need to become active thinkers and writers both in and out of class. The stress on such concepts as close reading, reflection, peer revision, and process-based writing (through portfolio submission) allows students to see how their writing can have an impact on the community level as well as on their grade for the course, and allows them to gauge their progress consistently through revision and instructor feedback. Because class sizes are small, instructors often get to know students and their writing very well throughout the course of the semester and can extend individualized support and conferencing to those enrolled. Also, the Center for Writing Excellence, which oversees the composition program, encourages both faculty and graduate teaching assistants to be creative in their approaches to the composition classroom. Because of this, the composition program at WVU is characteristically interdisciplinary and is relevant to students of diverse backgrounds, goals, and interests.

WHY I LIKE *SEEING & WRITING*

I've found the choice of material to be both relevant and intellectually stimulating, while my students prefer *Seeing & Writing* because the focus on introductory composition courses means that the readings won't be dry or "too academic."

Profile: James M. Wilson

ABOUT ME

I received my PhD in creative writing from the University of Louisiana at Lafayette.

Currently, I teach composition, creative writing, and American literature at Flagler College, in St. Augustine, Florida, where I

James M. Wilson
Flagler College
(Surefire Assignment, p. 232)

directed the composition program for five years. I co-direct the Florida Literary Arts Coalition "Other Words" Conference, held each year at Flagler College. I am also working on a novel called *Giving It Away* and am excited about my recently published nonfiction article for sixth-grade readers about caving.

ABOUT MY PROGRAM

Flagler College's composition program requires students to take two semesters of composition. Our courses are capped at twenty students per section. We serve about five hundred freshmen per year. The first-semester course does not require research. In my ENG 101 courses, where I use *Seeing & Writing*, I require that my students *do not* do any research for their writing. The college's composition program wants students to cultivate a desire for self-directed inquiry and an awareness that "authority of experience" is one basis of a relationship with audience.

WHY I LIKE *SEEING & WRITING*

About eight years ago I realized that my students needed to better analyze visual texts. I began to integrate photos, magazines, and web sites into my class discussions. Therefore, I was very pleased to find *Seeing & Writing* when it came out.

PROFILES

Visualizing Composition: Teaching and Composing Visually

What do we mean when we talk about visualizing composition? What does this mean for us in terms of our writing classrooms? How can we possibly keep up with the rush of information to remain current in our composition classes? Much of the early work in the area of *visual literacies* and composition focused on the analysis of visual texts — perhaps the analysis of photographs, painting, advertisements, or film. Our composition classrooms addressed interpretive reading strategies where students learned to analyze alternate, visual texts along with the written word. They helped us teach close reading, research strategies, and strong critical thinking skills. Although many of these skills are still an essential part of understanding visual rhetoric, we are now moving toward another phase in which we need to focus equal attention on the composition of visual texts. We are in an exciting time of shifting ideas, new definitions of composition, and more access to technologies to make many things possible that we might not have ever previously considered.

Acts of composition now span across mediums as we consider our purposes, audiences, and subject matter. Students can use visuals to support and communicate new ideas in conjunction with written texts or compose exclusively in these modes to communicate meaning. Everything that we teach about style, clarity, persuasion, or voice has a place here as well. Research is enriched as we analyze, interpret, and synthesize visual forms. Visuals can inspire invention, extend meaning, and initiate critical thinking. They can help generate revision and encourage collaboration. The inclusion of visual rhetoric does not have to be something we teach *outside* the teaching of writing; instead we can find ways in which it can reinforce and extend what we believe is important about writing and communication.

Many of our students are already very comfortable composing in these ways and use technologies such as digital photography, video, and other forms of multimedia to communicate their ideas within their own discourse communities. Although our students have an intuition about how to compose visually, there is a definite lack of direct instruction in these areas. The learning curve is still vast, and teachers are often uncomfortable venturing into areas that involve new technological skills or unfamiliar terms. Rather than resist, it is important that teachers embrace this opportunity—especially in a time when motivation is high because students are actively composing in these forms on their own.

It is this focus and need that prompted the following articles—our newest feature to this edition of *Teaching SEEING & WRITING*. These articles all address either a *visual literacy genre*—such as digital photography, comic illustration and graphic novels, or popular culture—or a *perspective*—college student, artist, interactive game designer—that help you understand the ways that we are both consumers *and* producers of visual texts. Each essay includes an introduction that provides a short definition of the genre or perspective. The essays also serve a pedagogical purpose, with assignments for students to practice composing in the various forms across themes and chapters in *Seeing & Writing*.

Featured Authors and Article Summaries:

Welcome to My World: Living and Writing in Visual and Virtual Spaces (p. 26) by Garrett Korn, author and university student, on visual culture from the student's perspective. Korn writes about a day in his visual/virtual life as well as his role as a communicator in these spaces. This essay aims to help teachers immerse themselves in the worlds of our students to better understand the ways they already compose in these spaces and how we might extend on this communication in our writing classes.

The (Social) Medium Is the Message: Digital Rhetoric and Media Literacy (p. 28) by Mark Nunes, English and new media studies teacher, on new media. Our individual and cultural identities are redefined through interaction with new media. The author focuses on social media such as the Internet, Facebook, and Twitter as means of communication along with the shaping of virtual identities.

Visual Re-Vision: Seeing Again through Digital Photography, Video, and Other Art Forms (p. 33) by Kim Haimes-Korn, English and communication teacher, on photography and video. This essay explores how digital and multimedia technologies can be used in conjunction with writing assignments to capture contemporary life and explore rhetorical contexts through visual rhetoric. The author discusses composing strategies and includes assignments using digital photography, YouTube videos, and other visual representations.

Zap! Snikt! Bamf!: Comics in the Classroom (p. 38) by Jeffrey David Greene, teacher and novelist, on the graphic novel. This essay presents terms such as *graphic novels*, *comics*, and *sequential art* to help us realize the teaching potential of these forms. Greene also references particular texts in *Seeing & Writing 4*, such as *Persepolis* by Marjane Satrapi and Peter Arkle's graphics on the writing process.

We're So POPular: Turning Composition Students ON with TV, Film, and Advertising (p. 42) by Ann Parker, English teacher. This essay focuses on popular culture created through what we see on television, in movies, and in advertisements. Parker provides multi-genre assignments that draw on these forms and the ways we read these alternate texts.

Saying What You See, and Seeing What You Say: Visuals and Information Design Strategies (p. 46) by Betty Oliver, teacher and artist, on information design. An artist herself, Oliver introduces us to some of the basic principles of visual rhetoric and information design.

All the Virtual World's a Stage: A Sense of Place through Interactive Game Environments (p. 50) by Jeff Voeltner, interactive game designer, on interactive gaming. Gaming creates an entire virtual world within which gamers interact. Here, Voeltner discusses the ways that he constructs environments to create compelling spaces for visitors, and what writers and designers need to do to achieve *virtual immersion*.

Garrett Korn, *Welcome to My World: Living and Writing in Visual and Virtual Spaces*

Garrett Korn is a student at Georgia College and State University. He lives a real and virtual life through images, music, and words. Like many other young people today he is deeply immersed in these worlds through personal, social, and academic experiences. He enjoys writing, philosophy, and psychology.

As I attempt to write this article, I find myself constantly distracted by my surroundings. The Internet, just a *minimize* and a *click* away, finds its way to conquer my interests and the computer screen every five minutes. Can you blame me, though? It's an infinite source of information and mind-numbing entertainment. I can check what my friend's uncle's barber's brother-in-law had for breakfast on Facebook, or I can find out the score of a little league cricket game in Poltava, Ukraine, in just three simple clicks. My cell phone, which never leaves my side, catches more glances than necessary, and I find myself flipping aimlessly through channels on my television set, stopping only on the ones that have the ability to snag my attention, usually through means of explosions and/or nudity, in the 1.56 seconds that I give them before I'm on to the next one. The struggle with writing this article, and the reason it falls so low on the priority list, is that it makes me think, while all these other entertainment sources are thinking for me. This is the trap of today's visual and virtual culture, although this isn't the only aspect of it. On the contrary, the Internet and other sources can be great outlets for creative and critical thinking. The web is an amazing tool that allows any and all to research and publicly speak their minds to larger audiences. There just happen to be more passive observers letting the active participants fill their minds.

As the visual culture continues to grow exponentially, it carries with it both huge benefits and huge drawbacks. Convenience is at an all-time high, but does this put work ethic at an all-time low? In some ways, definitely. There are so many sources of captivating entertainment that less time is devoted to productive behavior. Would Thomas Jefferson have had time to write the Declaration of Independence if he had been an avid player of the computer game World of Warcraft, a game that has taken over the lives of so many individuals? Would Jesus Christ have spread his message if he had been too busy texting to actually listen to what God was saying to him? Who knows what repercussions modern technology might have had on the great figures of history, and who knows what kind of potential it is stifling in the present day.

But let's look at the positives. Maybe Thomas Jefferson could have used an online survey to determine which phrases to include in the Declaration of Independence. Perhaps Jesus could have sent a mass text to people explaining his religious philosophy, avoiding a good bit of bloodshed in future centuries. We have found ways to communicate on a massive scale, and this seems to be connecting us in ways no one thought possible. With sites like eBay and Craigslist, we can get what we want, pretty much when we want it. Evite and Facebook make getting our friends together for a party almost effortless. These sites eliminate the effort spent in sending a message, thus allowing us to improve on the actual message itself. Today's technology can be used as a shortcut to productivity. Unfortunately, it also has the potential for abuse and can easily turn into a veered, scenic route to the promised land, assuming we get there at all.

This new aspect of culture has intruded into our personal and intimate lives. The popular social networking site Facebook has added a whole new dynamic to relationships. It has infiltrated itself into the rulebook of dating and even friendships. When once it was common to just ask a girl for her number and then go on a date, it is now necessary to befriend a girl via Facebook, write on her wall, ask her on a date, and then, to make it an official relationship, post our affiliation on Facebook. This gives us several chances to initiate interaction, but it is also allows us to retouch and manipulate our image. A Facebook interaction offers none of the subconscious, nonverbal cues that we give off when we are face-to-face. It's almost like cheating the conversation. We should not use Facebook as a substitute for real relationships. It creates artificial relationships that allow us to feel socially connected while avoiding the deep, sometimes troubling, yet always satisfying, waters of actual intimate relationships.

Another huge convenience of today's visual culture is the information overload supplied by the Internet. It is frighteningly easy to obtain information on just about anything thanks to the web monster Google, or any other popular search engine. Twenty years ago, when a curiosity popped into your head, such as Napoleon Bonaparte's favorite kind of cheese, you had two options. You could take a twenty-minute ride to the library, look for books on cheese, realize that you really needed a book on Napoleon, walk to the other side of the library, search dozens of books for any word on his cheese preference, and be satisfied when you found it or be disappointed when you didn't. Your second option was to simply force the curiosity out of your mind and go on with your life. The latter was the most likely route. Today, however, you can simply type "Napoleon's favorite cheese" into the Google search bar and find out that Valencia French goat cheese was in fact the winner. What would have taken several hours can now be figured out in a minute, literally. Although the Internet, which allows quick access to so much information, does seem to be devaluing the process of obtaining information, we can spend less time searching for answers and more time applying the information in effective ways.

Today's visual and virtual spaces have extreme advantages, along with some disadvantages. It really comes down to how we use them and how educators portray them. As long as we don't take them for granted and we use them as a creative outlet, then I'm sure they will prove beneficial to society as a whole. But if we use the Internet solely as a mind-numbing device and become too reliant on its many powers, then it could be quite detrimental. Teachers can encourage students to blog, write on message boards, research, start up web sites, post videos on YouTube, and any of the other endless options that the Internet has to offer. It won't take much to make students realize the potential of this source.

All students want to put their ideas out there. In order to confirm themselves and their ideas, they might just need a little push of motivation to show them the way. However, teachers have to make students understand that they still need to know how to obtain information the old-fashioned way and how to initiate relationships through face-to-face social interaction. Students need to learn how to shift back and forth between their real and virtual worlds. Teachers should still encourage library usage along with Internet findings as a supplement to and confirmation of online information. Teachers can't do much about the artificiality of Facebook relationships, but they can ask students to examine their Facebook relationships and to think or write about ways their virtual lives compare to their real ones.

To understand how to converse face-to-face, people need to have some forms of entertainment that do not involve electronic communication. If we, as a human race, forget these natural tasks, we might lose a huge dynamic that makes us human. The Internet is phenomenal, and its powers are literally endless, but if we continue to put all of our eggs into this one online basket, then we will devolve into a less effective race. Teachers can help students use and maintain all of their skills by asking students to regularly participate and communicate in both of these worlds. We can all have conversations that allow us to understand and spread our ideas, in a world where getting our words out there has never been so easy. Let's just hope that our natural attraction to mind-numbing laziness does not outweigh the need to be heard.

ADDITIONAL WRITING TOPICS

- In a writing assignment, ask students to compare their online profile pictures on sites such as Facebook with their actual image and personality. Then have them compare the friends they talk to just on Facebook with the friends they converse with in the real world.

- Ask students to focus on a historical event or figure, and have them predict how this event or figure might have been changed or influenced by modern technology. Students should extend their ideas through online research. They might also experiment with their writing style and take on the voice of the individual in the form of a letter, an online blog entry, or a chatroom conversation.

- Since many students go to Wikipedia as their first source for research, it is a good idea to talk about and experiment with this site. You can help students understand that it is an *open source* document and that research involves connection to other concepts. Give the class a subject that you wish to explore. It can be from a reading or chapter from the book. Ask them to go "five clicks in" and explore the ways this additional information helps them understand their subject. Talk about the connections between these various subjects and the significance of building information through different perspectives. Through small-group and full-class discussion, have students compare notes and ideas with one another. You could also have them write an analysis of this experience.

Mark Nunes, *The (Social) Medium Is the Message: Digital Rhetoric and Media Literacy*

It's a familiar scene. You walk into your composition classroom, and there are your students, eyes trained on the computer screen, fingers rapidly working their way across the keyboard, hard at work composing—their Facebook page.

For many of us confronted with this scene, our professorial impulses might lead us to redirect our students away from their social networks and toward the task at hand—composition. And perhaps for some very good reasons. While institutionally tolerated for the most part, "Facebooking" in class would technically fall outside of a strict interpretation of most universities' "acceptable use" policies. After all, those computers are in the classroom to support *instruction*, not socialization.

But what if Facebook were to become the scene of instruction?

Don't get me wrong. I am not necessarily suggesting that you "friend" each and every

Mark Nunes, PhD, teaches English and media studies courses at Southern Polytechnic State University. He is the author of Cyberspaces of Everyday Life (Minnesota, 2006). His most recent work includes an edited collection of essays entitled Error: Information, Control, and Noise in New Media Cultures (Continuum, forthcoming).

student in your classes. Facebook, after all, occupies that shadowy land of "what my students do with their lives outside of the classroom." Do you *really* want to know (and see pictures of) what your students were up to last night? Engaging Facebook as a scene of instruction and joining the countless many in social networking are two distinct activities. But it is important for instructors to realize that when confronting Facebook and other social networking sites, we are coming face-to-face with a scene of writing that is very much a part of everyday life for our students. While many of our students come to our classrooms declaring "I don't like writing," and all have come of age within an increasingly pervasive visual culture, our students are still very much tied to the word when given the need and opportunity to define themselves in relation to a larger community.

THIS IS YOUR CLASSROOM ON MEDIA

Professor Michael Wesch's 2007 survey of his Intro to Cultural Anthropology students provides a rather compelling Vision of Students Today (and an even more compelling YouTube video of the same name). Based on the response of 133 students, Wesch estimates that today's undergraduates produce more than ten times as much text outside of class than they do inside the classroom—more than five hundred pages of e-mail alone in a semester. That's not counting comments or "wall postings" on

Facebook, chat/instant messaging online, or what has become an increasingly dominant form of student-to-student social interaction: texting. Again, that professorial impulse kicks in. Yes, I understand we're teaching composition and rhetoric, not *chat*. Surely I'm not suggesting that what passes for writing through text messaging, with its SYLAs and ROFLs, should find its way into what is an already cramped Comp I syllabus of general education outcomes and course learning objectives!

I will leave that argument to the National Council of Teachers of English (NCTE). In the November 2007 issue of *The Council Chronicle*, Lorna Collier argues for "21st-century literacies" in high school English classes as a way of engaging students within the communications media that already occupy a major role in their everyday lives— and in the future, their workplace. To aid teachers in new media integration, the NCTE ReadThinkWrite web site includes lesson plan suggestions for topics such as "If a Body Texts a Body: Texting in *The Catcher in the Rye*" and "Texting a Response to *Lord of the Flies*." While these lesson plan titles may evoke a chuckle (or groan), IMHO, we do our discipline a disservice if we are not willing to confront new media for what they are: a scene of writing that occupies an increasingly central role in the lives of our students. Keep in mind that as a result of the availability of cheap, powerful new media interfaces, our students now live in a media environment that is radically different from the world in which most of us received our education and prepared for our careers as educators. Increasingly, our students are media producers as well as consumers. They live in what Henry Jenkins describes as a "convergence culture," in which audiences have a participatory role in defining and extending the production of cultural works. Our students don't merely "respond to" movies and television shows; they are producing texts and images in parallel production, in a vast "transmedia narrative" made possible by the social network that is the Internet.

MCLUHAN: (NEW) MEDIA/(NEW) LITERACIES

While much of the discussion of new media literacies has an eye toward the future, it is probably worth commenting, at this point, on the "newness" of new media. As Lisa Gitelman and Geoffrey B. Pingree note in their introduction to *New Media, 1740–1915*, "all media were once new media." While it would be hard to argue against this point, the "new" that concerns us here is marked by the shift from material network to electronic network that started in the nineteenth century with the telegraph and has accelerated throughout the past 150 years. As a term, however, *new media* is not quite that old, dating back a mere fifty years. The *Oxford English Dictionary* gives its earliest quotation as a 1960 article by Marshall McLuhan in the *Journal of Economic History* entitled "Effects of the Improvements of Communication Media," with specific reference to "globally gathered information, moved at electronic speeds"—some nine years before ARPANET, the Army Research Projects Agency network that would grow to become the Internet. But the *OED* misses a more relevant reference from that same year, namely McLuhan's 1960 project and accompanying report to the U.S. Office of Education, *Report on Project in Understanding New Media*. From these earliest writings, McLuhan's key point is that what makes today's media "new" is a shift in medium, from the visually oriented linearity of text to the tactile "allatonceness" of electrical media. Over the course of his career, McLuhan would elaborate on these ideas in a number of works, most notably *The Gutenberg Galaxy* and *Understanding Media: The Extensions of Man*.

McLuhan's insistence that "the medium is the message" provides an important point of contact for our discussion of new media as a scene of instruction. While the aphorism is certainly well known, its implications are often truncated in popular use of the phrase. To quote from his 1960 report, "Any medium based on any of our senses has the power of imposing its own assumptions"; or, as he would later write in *Understanding Media*: "The formative power in the media are the media themselves." McLuhan maintains that when we focus on "the content" of a medium (whether or not a particular kind of television broadcast—or online role-playing game, for that matter—is harmful), we are really missing the point. Our tendency to think in terms of content, he argues, is an assumption imposed on us by text-based culture. Rather than thinking of media as "encoding" content, McLuhan insists that we need to come to terms with the ways in which media *structure* sense perceptions, thought, and the possibilities for social interaction. This is not to drift into a "hard" technological determinism; rather, it is an approach that frames communication as an ecological concern. We find ourselves *situated* within a media environment, and that situation determines and delimits a range of possible ways of being and modes of social formation.

REMEDIATING THE COMPOSITION CLASSROOM

In the context of writing, then, social media such as Facebook provide us with an opportunity not to "convert" one medium into another—capture new media writing into the service of the composition classroom. Rather, our students' deep involvement in these networks as part of their everyday lives offers up an opportunity to take the rhetorical concerns of our discipline into a new medium. If many of our students are what John Palfrey has called "digital natives," then perhaps we need to "go native" ourselves. This is not an argument to abandon printed text for the screen. Rather, it is an attempt to define a media environment in which page and screen coexist and (to use Jay Bolter and Richard Grusin's term) "remediate" each other within the same ecological system. Teaching media literacy at a deep level—allowing students to understand media capabilities and the demands and assumptions of a given medium—will allow students to negotiate more effectively between these two very different media contexts.

Consider Facebook, then, as a rhetorical situation. This social networking tool presents opportunities for students to engage in critical reading and critical thinking. How do Facebook updates differ, for example, when comparing younger and older friends? Can students discern the rhetorical function of status updates in different contexts? What about wall postings? How do friends "read" social cues for what is or is not appropriate to post on a friend's wall? What sorts of audience issues are raised by a medium in which wall posts are both personal (intended for one recipient) and public (viewable by all friends)?

Facebook also has a number of functions that speak to a range of rhetorical concerns. On "cause" pages, how does Facebook establish *ethos* and/or *kairos*? In what ways does persuasion occur? At another level of analysis, does Facebook present an opportunity for "activism" in some form? How does the medium structure "involvement" in a cause, through networking, digital pamphleteering, and fund-raising? Issues of membership arise as well, not only on cause pages but on "fan" pages as well. In what ways do users position themselves by declaring (again, in a manner that is simultaneously public and private) a fan of a particular television show (*The Office*), a local restaurant (The Brewhouse), an action (sleeping late), or even an inanimate object (cast-iron cookware)?

Twitter provides another interesting opportunity for developing media literacy along with helping students think about how media create their own rhetorical demands on users. Twitter, of course, is the increasingly popular medium for status updates, limited to 140 characters, called "tweets." Users of Twitter can "follow" other users (and do so as uninvited observers). Sometimes referred to as microblogging, tweeting has been applied to a range of different uses, from the banality of "what I had for breakfast" to coordinating collective action, as in the post-election unrest in Iran. As a site for teaching and a scene of writing, Twitter provides a number of opportunities for students to explore the medium as a social networking tool. To what degree do 140 characters limit communication? How does the structure of followers/following, and the visual presentation of a real-time feed of tweets, structure the nature of discourse? To use the language of McLuhan, is this medium "hot" (high resolution, low involvement) or "cold" (low resolution, high involvement)? What sorts of community-structuring discursive practices does Twitter offer—for example, the practice of "retweeting" (RT) another user's status update as your own?

Of course, there is also the well-established world of blogging to consider. Having students think critically about the function of blogging as a medium provides important insight into media new and old. How, for example, do blog sites remediate "news"? If we can move beyond thinking of media as "encoding" or delivering content, we will instead have to think in terms of how media interact with and alter one another in a larger media ecology. Why does "objectivity" emerge as a dominant ideology in print-based journalism, but not so on blogs? How do blogs and talk radio differ, again not so much in content, but in the structuring of our understanding of public discourse? Do comments matter in blogs? How do author and commenter interact? Is this dialogue? Do "zero comments" on a blog signal a "failure to communicate," or, as Geert Lovink suggests, is it the linkages between blogs that matter the most to this medium?

DIGITAL RHETORIC

Much of what has been said here falls under the framework of what is increasingly labeled "digital rhetoric." As Elizabeth Losh notes, digital rhetoric covers a range of concerns, from "the conventions of new digital genres that are used for everyday discourse, as well as for special occasions, in average people's lives" to "mathematical theories of communication . . . which attempt to quantify the amount of uncertainty in a given linguistic exchange or the likely paths through which messages travel." Losh goes on to note that while the "conventional" and "mathematical" may seem worlds apart, everyday use of digital media is informed by implicit or explicit assumptions about the medium that are informed by the technical structuring of the medium itself. Understanding convention—and teaching students to think of media as making conventional demands on its users—provides a framework for understanding how these social media structure our assumptions about public discourse.

We would do well, then, to remember that when our students are writing, more often than not they are doing so within a new medium—the digital. Online, or on mobile phones, our students inhabit a media environment in which "the word" still occupies a very important place in constructing and maintaining social networks and a form of "imagined community." We would do well to consider the ways in which composition curricula can occupy this intersection of digital rhetoric and media literacy.

ADDITIONAL WRITING TOPIC

In my current class, students must make at least five journal entries over the course of the semester, each serving as an open-ended opportunity for reflection on the readings we have covered over the past couple of weeks. Each journal entry must be approximately five hundred words. The catch, however, is that each journal entry must be presented in a different medium. Students are encouraged to be as creative in their approach to the assignment as they can. Create a YouTube video journal entry. Stream a five-hundred-word podcast. Use Twitter to send a set of 140-character tweets. Mail me a handwritten letter.

Audience is always an issue, so you might want to consider how you will treat these journal entries. Do you want students to share them with the class as a whole, as an in-class publication on a course management site, or as one-to-one exchanges between student and instructor? Make your plans clear to students at the start of the semester. If you choose to keep journal entries as student-to-instructor correspondences (what does that mean for a YouTube video?), at minimum provide your students with an in-class and/or online opportunity to reflect on the process itself. Who knows? Perhaps they could even write an essay on the experience.

SUGGESTED READINGS

Bolter, Jay, and Richard Grusin. *Remediation*. Cambridge, MA: MIT Press, 1999. Print.

Bruett, Joyce. "Texting a Response to *Lord of the Flies*." *ReadWriteThink*. National Council of Teachers of English, 27 Jul. 2009. Web. 10 Sept. 2009.

Collier, Lorna. "The Shift to 21st-Century Literacies." *The Council Chronicle* Nov. 2007: 4–8. Print.

Digital Ethnography. "A Vision of Students Today." *YouTube*. YouTube, 12 Oct. 2007. Web. 10 Sept. 2009.

Filkins, Scott. "If a Body Texts a Body: Texting in *The Catcher in the Rye*." *ReadWriteThink*. National Council of Teachers of English, 1 Jul. 2009. Web. 10 Sept. 2009.

Gitelman, Lisa, and Geoffrey B. Pingree. *New Media, 1740–1915*. Cambridge, MA: MIT Press, 2003. Print.

Jenkins, Henry. *Convergence Culture*. New York: NYU Press, 2006. Print.

Losh, Elizabeth. *Virtualpolitik*. Cambridge, MA: MIT Press, 2009. Print.

Lovink, Geert. *Zero Comments*. New York: Routledge, 2008. Print.

McLuhan, Marshall. "Effects of the Improvements of Communication Media." *Journal of Economic History* 20.4 (Dec. 1960): 566–575. Print.

——. *The Gutenberg Galaxy*. Toronto: U of Toronto P, 1962. Print.

——. *Report on Project in Understanding New Media*. New York: National Association of Educational Broadcasters, Office of Education, U.S. Department of Health, Education and Welfare, 1960. Print.

——. *Understanding Media: The Extensions of Man*. Cambridge, MA: MIT Press, 1994. Print.

Palfrey, John. "Born Digital." *John Palfrey*. Berkman Center for Internet and Society at Harvard Law School, 28 Oct. 2008. Web. 10 Sept. 2009.

Wesch, Michael. "A Vision of Students Today." *Digital Ethnography*. Kansas State University, 12 Oct. 2007. Web. 10 Sept. 2009.

Kim Haimes-Korn, *Visual Re-Vision: Seeing Again through Digital Photography, Video, and Other Art Forms*

Kim Haimes-Korn, PhD, teaches English and communication courses at Southern Polytechnic State University and also directs the writing program. She has been instrumental in incorporating the teaching of visual literacies within the composition curriculum at SPSU. Much of her work in the field concentrates on portfolios, composition pedagogy, and visual literacies.

INTRODUCTION

"A picture is worth a thousand words"—a common cliché that is never more relevant than it is today. Not only is this concept important for students immersed in visual worlds in terms of analysis, textual interpretation, and critical thinking, but it also encourages students to participate as both consumers and creators of visual texts. The availability of visual images for our students is limitless, and the ways that images are used and shared continue to evolve. With the rise of sites such as Flickr, YouTube, and Facebook, our students are already composing regularly in these formats and communicating with more self-sponsored writing and images than ever before.

Consider asking students to re-see their ideas and words in ways that extend their thinking through engaging in visual dimensions. The use of visuals in the writing classroom asks them to engage in deep acts of composition and revision as they translate what they know about words, texts, and ideas into images. Visual assignments have the potential to draw students into traditional acts of composition such as invention, arrangement, style, and delivery. These assignments also get them to think deeply about their rhetorical situation—their purposes, audiences, subjects, and contexts. Although many classroom methods concentrate on the analysis of visual images, I like to extend that to include the production of visuals in conjunction with the written word.

We might rewrite the old cliché to read, "A word is worth a thousand pictures."

Digital Immigrants and Digital Natives

What does this mean for us as teachers? We might question the practicality, use, and availability of technology for this kind of endeavor. Years ago when I started using visuals in my composition classes, I would ask the question on the first day, "How many of you have access to a camera?" Only a few students would raise their hands, and many felt that picture taking was more closely related to their parents' generation. For the college student, photography meant expensive equipment, as well as time and money spent in developing film. We also did not have the immediacy afforded us today in viewing the images. Now, however, when I ask the same question, most (if not all) students have some sort of access to digital photography and video because of disposable cameras, cell phone technology (the inclusion of cameras in the most basic of phones), and other electronic resources. Although there is still a *digital divide*— the gap that addresses access in terms of economic, social, or cultural availability— students actually do have access to computers and other devices that allow them to participate in visual composition (obviously teachers working in these kinds of settings need to think of other means of accessing these resources). Teachers might also be concerned about the technological and communication skills associated with this kind of inclusion. Teachers of our generation are generally considered what Mark Prensky termed *Digital Immigrants*— "those of us who were not born into the digital world but have, at some later point in our lives, become fascinated by and adopted many or most aspects of the new technology." He compares them to our students, whom he considers *Digital Natives*, or "'native speakers' of the digital language of computers, video games, and the Internet." As Prensky states, "It's very serious,

because the single biggest problem facing education today is that our Digital Immigrant instructors, who speak an outdated language (that of the pre-digital age), are struggling to teach a population that speaks an entirely new language."

We need to ask ourselves, How can we recognize our instructional intentions and at the same time speak in a *language* that our students understand? Basically, we can rest a bit easier knowing that most of our students feel more comfortable producing in these formats than we do. Visit the Digital Native's web site at digitalnative.org to learn more about our students from this perspective. Technological instruction does not have to take too much time away from our teaching, although we can supplement it with online tutorials and other instructional technology sessions outside the classroom. The fact is that students have most likely been participating in some way in these forms and communities for most of their lives. This is an important factor to remember in reducing teachers' anxiety about teaching these students because of their own unfamiliarity.

Teachers sometimes feel as if they need to have mastery of photography or film in order to include these media in their classes. Our goals here do not necessarily involve expertise in these disciplines. It is actually all about emphasis. We are not necessarily emphasizing artistic technique and mastery. Instead we can focus on how images are rhetorically constructed to convey meaning and purpose, consider audience, substantiate claims, move beyond generalizations, communicate style and clarity, along with other concerns of the writing teacher. We, in essence, are working to get our students to better understand and communicate their ideas in different rhetorical situations. The image is a powerful rhetorical tool in today's cultural contexts.

Some Considerations for Writing Instruction

Where do we turn our attention as students use images as part of their composing processes? What does this mean for us in terms of research, drafting, and revision? Here are some of the ways we can help students when they use images in their composition:

- **Search procedures:** Although most students feel they are experts at searching the Internet, we can help them refine these skills through teaching them how to search for images and videos. Of course, we can guide them to databases and collections such as Flickr and YouTube, but they can also employ search engines such as Google Images and others. Like any kind of research, this type requires purposeful search terms, analysis and evaluation of sources, and the ability to develop right-brain thinking through the use of both concrete and abstract terms. For example, students might search for images to support a paper on the Vietnam War with images from newspapers and film reels, or they might use images to understand an abstract concept such as culture.

- **Ethical use of images:** Many students don't fully understand their responsibility to ethically use the images they pull off the Internet. This is a good opportunity to talk about the ethics of media communication and the ways images are still authored artifacts that deserve the same kind of treatment as textual sources. Images are voices within intellectual conversation and communicate meaning, philosophy, and purpose. You might address subjects such as ownership and images in the public domain, as well as the altering of images through software such as Photoshop and other photo manipulation software.

- **Documentation of electronic sources:** It is more important than ever that students learn the style and documentation procedures for visual images and other electronic sources. While our teaching of documentation often focuses mainly on proper citation of books and journals, most of our current sources—including images—are obtained through the Internet. Students often have the impression that the Internet is free and communally owned. We can show them that they have a responsibility to accurately give credit to the images they use.

- **Document design:** One of Aristotle's five canons in the composing process is arrangement. The inclusion of images is no exception. Students need to concentrate on the placement and layout of their images along with considerations such as clarity and communication. We might discuss how images act as rhetorical devices that need grounding, explanation (captions), and connection to the writer's ideas (text) as a whole. How they look on the page is a whole new consideration that writers must address. I usually have students address the visual rhetoric of their compositions and include it as part of peer response and revision.

Using Digital Images in the Writing Classroom

There are many ways to use digital photographs in our writing classrooms. Through the Internet, students can search and explore images with ease. The number of images available for interpretation is limitless.

Visual Internet searches: I ask students to go online and search for visual images that somehow represent their ideas about particular concepts or readings. For example, students were asked to collect images that helped them define their idea of "place."

They brought in pictures of vacation spots, neighborhoods, home pages from their high schools, imaginary places, sports fields, e-mail logos, the earth, the state of Georgia, and more. The variety of places allowed us to complicate and expand on this definition as a class.

Visual writing sequence: Teachers can design a visual/image sequence that accompanies the writing assignments in their existing curriculum. This often works best for a thematically based curriculum that has students writing through and about particular subjects. Many of the chapters in *Seeing & Writing 4* lend themselves well to this kind of treatment, such as Chapter 2, Coming to Terms with Place; Chapter 4, Projecting Gender; and Chapter 5, Examining Difference. You will see many image/writing assignments scattered throughout the textbook and in this teaching guide.

For example, if students are writing about a place that is significant to them, they might take or find six images that visually or conceptually represent that place. This kind of paired exercise helps them expand through critical thinking in unexpected ways. The assignments create a sequence that encourages students to question the ways they see the world around them through visual and textual analysis of their personal, social, and cultural experiences. The sequence involves them in photo assignments in which they are composing their own pictures, while other sequences have them working with found images on the Internet. This concept is useful at all stages of students' writing processes. These photos might inspire their writings, or the writings might inspire the photos.

Photoessays, albums, and galleries: In conjunction with their writings, students might take photos that address the subjects they pursue. Along with each writing assignment, I ask students to take several pictures (three to five) that represent their ideas. At the end of the sequence, students compose a photoessay that incorporates both their written and their visual texts and looks at the connections between the two. A colleague of mine also has students create photo albums or mount and display their images in an "art gallery" around our school for others to see and enjoy.

OTHER FORMS OF VISUAL INTERPRETATION

Although we are heavily immersed in digital culture, there are many other ways to get students to compose visually. I use hand drawing, collage, and other art forms for alternate modes of expression.

Visual representation: Students revise their written texts as visual texts in the form of visual representations. They might generate three-dimensional art that represents their ideas. Once they have finished drafting and revising a textual piece (such as an essay, a journal entry, or a research paper), I ask them to think about the ways they might represent their ideas visually. Students have created visual representations such as sculpture, painting, collage, video, and the display of found objects. They have used pictures, symbols, and words. I usually have a gallery day in which they display their representations along with an index card that has their name, title, and a short quotation from their accompanying paper.

This assignment does not require students to be master artists. Instead, it concentrates on the notion of representing and communicating meaning through different forms, thus recognizing the relationship between form and content. I usually have students follow up with a process statement in which they articulate their revision choices—an important part of the project.

Although this visual revision should take into account the essence of their written work, assure students that they do not have to include every word or idea. As a matter of fact, they don't necessarily have to include words at all. Get them to think carefully about the ways they might express their ideas in a different form. Encourage them to think creatively through this assignment. They might work with images that somehow symbolize their ideas, or they might incorporate parts (quotes or ideas) from their written texts. They can use the images they gathered as part of the revision. They might construct three-dimensional versions in which they use an assortment of objects to communicate ideas—they should not feel constricted to a flat page. They might combine visual and written text.

Visual metaphors: You can ask students to extend their ideas and draw metaphors for their ideas or their writing and thinking processes. They might visually represent their own process as a writer or draw and label concepts they are considering through their writing.

Charts and mapping: I often ask students to explore relationships between subjects, ideas, and experiences by charting them out. For example, I might ask them to list all the groups to which they belong (an invention activity toward an understanding of discourse communities) and then visually represent these groups, their overlaps, and their connections. Maps can also be used to illustrate concepts such as success or love. Or they might be used to demonstrate perception, scale, or emphasis. See Katharine Harmon's map and discussion about mapping in the textbook (Chapter 2, p. 179).

COMPOSING AND PRESENTING MULTIMEDIA PROJECTS

Slideshow presentations: Presentation software (such as PowerPoint) allows students to share their image work with others. I often create team projects that involve verbal/visual slideshows to express their ideas. I have asked students to create shows that explore a concept from the book such as *defining moments* or *sense of place*. I have them pull quotes from their writings along with images that represent their ideas. I also have them explicate literature or poetry through impressionistic slideshows. For example, I ask them to create visual interpretations of Robert Frost poems. You could also ask them to include audio in the form of music or narration.

Videos and short films: Students can "go viral" in the composition classroom through the creation of YouTube videos. This type of assignment allows them to explore rhetorical conventions in this visual space and both analyze and construct audience in new ways. For example, I ask them to create cultural critique videos in which they "read across" cultural influences, writings, and images and reflect on the connections among them. I ask them to select some (small) aspect of society they would like to critique or explore. They can brainstorm through interacting with other media such as radio (talk stations), newspapers, books, magazines, and the Internet. They have to produce a video, a class presentation, and an accompanying report on their project.

Web sites: I have asked students to compose web sites for many purposes in my classroom. They have created individual e-folios of their work across the class, along with full-class or small-group sites that display student work. Many schools provide web space for students to create and display these kinds of projects.

VISUALLY SPEAKING

Within these larger categories there are many possibilities for developing visual assignments. Never before have students taken on such active roles as composers in public spaces through the use of visuals.

They are already composing in both textual and visual ways on a regular basis. We can get them to understand that there are many ways to communicate meaning through analysis and production of visuals. This kind of analysis can only lead to sharper thinkers who are able to communicate through both the right and the left sides of their brains.

Jeffrey David Greene, *Zap! Snikt! Bamf!: Comics in the Classroom*

Jeffrey David Greene teaches English at Georgia Perimeter College in Atlanta, Georgia. He fosters a lifelong interest in comics and the comic book form. He has focused much of his work in composition on online teaching and distance learning, along with his own creative writing.

Many of us have encountered comics at some point in the past. Whether it was a Boondocks strip in the Sunday paper or a faded issue of *Daredevil*, we likely have enjoyed the medium but may not have given much thought to its complexity or rhetorical possibilities. Only in recent years has America truly begun to get "serious" about our superhero comics, manga, and indie graphic novels. Other countries, particularly France and Japan, are far ahead of us in this regard, and only in the last couple of decades have teachers used comics in the composition classroom as texts and inspiration for writing activities. This always makes me wonder: Why the long wait?

I think it's because comics are a medium that we often read unconsciously or one that we don't take seriously—as literature. In our gut we know the rules by heart: Unconsciously, we read the work from left to right (or right to left in other countries!), understand that the speech and thought balloons above characters' heads represent what they're saying and thinking, and recognize that the spatial relationship between the frames holding the artwork (the panels) suggests order and pacing. Rarely, though, do we intellectualize comics or spend much time trying to define them. Although traditionally they are not thought of as classic literature, this genre has taken on a new literary status through graphic novels and films that focus on important themes for critical thought.

WHAT COMICS ARE

Just what are comics anyway? What separates them from, say, a cartoon? Is the definition based on style or substance or something else? When pressed for a definition, many people mention the hybridization of text and artwork, and the sequential nature of the form. The *sequential* part of this definition is vital. Will Eisner, famed comic book author and artist of *A Contract with God and Other Tenement Stories*, coined the term *sequential art* to explain the ordered nature of comic panels and how we view them. In this medium we observe the art and read the text in a deliberate order supplied by the author. This process often helps form the narrative.

Comic books have been a great way to introduce students to writing about visuals as part of a narrative structure. I've specifically used comics as a catalyst for writing assignments and large-scale exercises, such as having students write about visual rhetoric and artistic symmetry in Alan Moore's opus, *Watchmen*. In my experience, students are at first hesitant to delve deeply into the visual minutiae of comics. They don't pay much attention to the significance of the sequential nature or focus on how complicated the form can be. But once they get into writing about comics, they quickly decode the visual complexities. Things that at first seemed innocuous—the shading (inking) of a character's face or the lack of white space—suddenly become a significant part of the story and narrative. These observations help students explore the interplay between visuals and text.

THE COMIC LEXICON OR THE ANATOMY OF A COMIC BOOK

To get students thinking and writing seriously about comics and graphic novels, it's important to supply them with a lexicon with which to discuss the medium, including the following terms:

- **Panel:** Panels are literally the windows that hold the artwork. Generally they have a border and are arranged in a deliberate order. Panels are often read much like text: left to right in American comics, for example, and right to left in Japanese manga. Comics are an interesting medium specifically because the layout is just as important as the content.

- **Gutter:** The white space between the panels is called the gutter.

- **Splash page or splash panel:** A splash page is generally a full-page artwork (that is, a single large panel on a page) at the front of a comic book. It commonly includes the title and credits. A splash panel is a larger (or the largest) panel on a page. Since it offers more room for an artist to offer detail and visual complexity, it is commonly used for narrative emphasis.

- **Caption:** Captions are narrative devices that provide information. They are commonly represented as colored boxes of text connected to panels.

- **Balloon (speech or thought):** A balloon is an artistic convention that allows attribution of dialogue or thoughts to a character in a panel. Speech balloons (also called speech bubbles) allow characters to speak, and thought balloons allow readers to see what the characters think through connecting the textual and the visual.

- **Writer:** In comics, a writer commonly composes a script for the artists to work from. This may seem like a simplistic term, but it's important to note that comic books and graphic novels are often (but not always) constructed by multiple artists and writers performing different functions on the same work.

- **Penciler:** A penciler produces the actual illustration of the comic. He or she draws the panels and all the artwork.

- **Inker:** An inker adds black ink to the penciled comic, providing shading and background to the images.

- **Colorist:** A colorist adds color to the comic (but not always—there are many black and white comics).

- **Letterer:** A letterer inscribes the words and text.

Each of these roles is vital to the medium, and understanding how all of these components—layout, artwork, text, shading, and so on—work together is a rich area for student discussion and writing.

After equipping your students with the language to discuss comic books, it's best to begin with something short as an introduction to the form. Peter Arkle's work can be found throughout the textbook, and the introductory foldout on the writing process is a great piece to start with. Not only does it give an amazing narrative of a student involved in the writing process, but it's also visually complex and entertaining.

After students read any comic book, graphic novel, or other sequential artwork, you may want to have them consider these characteristics as they apply them to comics or graphic novels. I find that this is a great way to spark discussion of comic books as a form. Students need to see that the art has purpose. It is meant to form some sort of a narrative, at least through its sequential nature. With each passing question, students are urged to try to analyze the rhetorical choices of the artists, writers, inkers, and editors. Hopefully this process will allow them to see comics as much more than simply stories told through pictures.

Discussing Sequential Art

I use the following questions to encourage students to consider the form and language of comics and graphic novels:

- **Who created the work:** Did a single artist or a group of collaborators (inker, writer, colorist, letterer, editor) create the work? What do you know about the author(s) of this text?

- **Analyze the layout:** Take a look at the individual frames and layout of the comic book. Are the panels large, small, or of varying sizes? Are there splash pages or panels? Do you see gutters? Are they thin or thick? Are panels isolated to individual pages, or do they sometimes stretch across two (or more) pages? Overall, how do the panels and layout affect the narrative structure or anything else in this work?

- **Analyze the penciling:** Look at the comic and try to describe the penciling. What is literally being drawn here? After defining the basics of the art, attempt to describe the visual style in detail (use specific examples from the text). Are characters and objects represented realistically (proportionate body parts, realistic scale, etc.)? Or are they hyper-realistic or surrealistic? Or are they cartoonish and outlandish? Does art appear in the foreground? in the background? Is there emphasis on anything through the penciling? Overall, how does the penciling affect your read-

ing of the narrative or anything else about this work?

- **Analyze the inking:** Look at the inking. Do you see shading and dark lines? or just a touch of black traces over characters and objects? How has the inker added (or not added) depth to the artwork? How does the inking affect your reading of the narrative or anything else about this work?

- **Analyze the lettering:** Look at the lettering. How are dialogue and the characters' thoughts represented in this work? Are there captions? Is there any special emphasis on the letters? Do they stand out? Are they in a sequential, readable form? What typefaces have been chosen? Are the letters large or small? How does the lettering affect your reading of the narrative or anything else about this work?

- **Analyze the coloring (optional):** Is the text in black and white, or is there color? Describe the colors. What colors do you see, and where are they being used? Are the colors vibrant and deep? raw and fiery? cold and dark? How does the coloring affect your reading of the narrative or anything else about this work?

Bringing Comics to Composition

Personally, I've had the most luck presenting students with graphic novels, possibly because these longer, bound comic books commonly give the impression that they should be taken more seriously. Often graphic novels are perceived as "grown-up" comics, but the very term *graphic novel* is actually somewhat of a misnomer. Trying to define what qualifies as a graphic novel and what doesn't is fairly complex because the term itself is nebulous. If it were based simply on length and how the work is printed and bound, then many collections of the serialized comic books that line bookstore shelves across the country would count. If it's not length, is it subject matter that separates comic books from graphic novels? Comics as a whole have been maturing for decades. To divide the works along such lines and then simply slap the "graphic novel" label on them seems a little hasty. There's a lot of scholarly writing on this subject, and it's a good topic for students to explore.

Comic books open up a composition classroom to some interesting ideas. Sequential art can be treated as an act of visual rhetoric, making it ripe for discussion of rhetorical strategies. You can deconstruct comic books as a visual narrative, looking at how images and text work together to tell a story. In addition, since many comic books are collaborative efforts that undergo numerous revisions with varied feedback from participants, analyzing sequential art is an interesting way to look at the role of peer review and editing.

Examining comics can also be a detailed study on genre and culture. Looking at American superhero comics in comparison to Japanese manga or Franco-Belgian comics serves not only as a way to introduce students to diverse forms of sequential art but also as a springboard for discussion of comics and culture. What do our comic books say about us? about our values? about our hopes?

And always, comics are a great place to explore the role of rhetorical choice and historical circumstance. I've used the superhero genre effectively in this regard: The content of comic books has been subject to serious attacks and censorship over the years, particularly during the mid-1950s with the rise of the CCA (Comics Code Authority), an organization that sought to censor comic books with material deemed "inappropriate." In my class, students have researched the Golden, Silver, and Bronze Ages of comics to see how (and why) comics have changed over the years, as they gradually broke away from the strictures imposed by the CCA.

I've also used graphic novels to explore deep social issues in new and interesting ways. Marjane Satrapi's *Persepolis* (2004) provides a great opportunity to discuss religion, culture, politics, and the function of the memoir. Craig Thompson's *Blankets* (2003) is a very accessible meditation on first love, growing up, and spirituality. Art Spiegelman's *Maus* (1991) allows students to explore the Holocaust, the function of memory and autobiography, and race and religion. Many graphic novels are also available as film versions, which are great for classroom use as well. Students can explore all three examples above in a multitude of ways: artistically, as a deep reflection on how the style and layout affect the narrative, and also along the lines of literary theory and theme.

SUGGESTED READINGS

Eisner, Will. *Comics and Sequential Art.* New York: Poorhouse Press, 1985. Print.

McCloud, Scott. *Understanding Comics: The Invisible Art.* New York: Harper Perennial, 1994. Print.

GRAPHIC NOVELS FOR THE CLASSROOM

Moore, Alan. *Watchmen.* New York: DC Comics, 1995. Print.

Satrapi, Marjane. *Persepolis.* New York: Pantheon, 2004. Print.

Spiegelman, Art. *Maus.* New York: Pantheon, 1991. Print.

Thompson, Craig. *Blankets.* Marietta: Top Shelf Productions, 2003. Print.

Ware, Chris. *Jimmy Corrigan, the Smartest Kid on Earth.* New York: Pantheon, 2000. Print.

Yang, Gene Luen. *American Born Chinese.* New York: First Second Books, 2006. Print.

Ann Parker, *We're So POPular: Turning Composition Students ON with TV, Film, and Advertising*

Ann Parker teaches English at Southern Polytechnic State University. She also regularly teaches Honors courses that involve service learning and active citizenship as part of their goals. Parker demonstrates these goals herself as a dedicated volunteer for an animal rescue organization. She is the recipient of many teaching awards and regularly incorporates visual literacies into her curriculum.

Visual literacy, media literacy, digital storytelling, multi-media, multimodal, YouNiversity, consumer culture . . . Okay, I'm confused, and I have to assume that I'm not alone when it comes to keeping up with the current terminology that revolves around how we, the general public, produce and consume information. As a teacher with a special interest in what I will call *visual literacy* for the sake of simplification, I often find myself asking "WHAT?" when it comes to yet another buzzword for the visual. Every time I think I've figured it all out, I find myself running to catch up with the latest philosophies on how to handle this overly visual world in which we live.

If I'm running, then what about my students? I think they're sauntering along. They have grown up in a culture that bombards them with visuals every minute of every day. Whether they are watching television, using the computer, or playing with their iPods and cell phones, our children are surrounded by visual images that directly or indirectly influence the decisions they make on everything from the clothes they buy to the colleges they attend. But they don't consider these actions in the terms I've mentioned above. For them, it's just a way of living.

According to Scott Sullivan, co-editor of *Lesson Plans for Creating Media-Rich Classrooms*, "the skills of composition, analysis, and interpretation that we associate with the traditional study of printed texts are beginning to be applied to a wide variety of media texts, and the crucial links of relevancy between the lives of students and the texts we teach are beginning to be made" (xix). He also notes that in a 2003 Harris Interactive and Teenage Unlimited Research poll, researchers found that the media "occup[y] 50.8 hours a week of our average student's life" (xvii). Can we imagine how that number has grown over the past seven years as more and more methods of information delivery emerge?

Keeping Sullivan's quote in mind, let's consider three forms of popular media—television, film, and advertising—and how we might use them in our English composition classrooms. If we ask students to think of *everything* as texts, then how do we help students critically consider and evaluate these texts? It has quickly become our job as teachers to introduce and reinforce interpretive reading strategies of multiple texts, and we can do this by incorporating popular media into our curricula. It's something our students see and use every day, so why not make use of what is readily available?

TELEVISION: PASS THE REMOTE

You will be hard pressed to find a college student who does not like to watch television, but what they watch and what you watch are most likely on opposite ends of the viewing spectrum. Adultswim? *Family Guy, King of the Hill*, and *Robot Chicken*? I don't watch these shows, but you better believe your students do. The fact that my students and I have such different television viewing habits is a great starting point for discussing audience, topic, and intended response. They love to tell me about all the great television that I'm missing when I stick to the major networks. I explain to them that I'm their parents' age; I'm not in the same target audience as young adults, and I generally don't have the same interests they do. (In other words, I'm old!) It then becomes easy for me to discuss the basic tenets of good composition—audience, content, intended response, and final product—when we can compare it to television. Whether the finished product is visual or written, they're both texts, and they both need to be fully considered in order to produce the intended outcome.

Using television in the classroom: Have your students watch television; require them to spend some time with their televisions, one of the easier assignments you can give. Students should record their observations and inferences (at least twenty). Encourage them to watch over a period of time or at different times of the day or night, using their remotes to see what is there. They should notice the program offerings and advertisements across the board and record observations and inferences in a double-entry journal. Have them complete a follow-up media analysis in which they investigate the ideas generated from their freewrite. This writing might produce a larger cultural analysis and particular patterns, ideologies, and values observed through this interaction with television. Or students might look at the patterns through reality shows, news programs, talk shows, or sitcoms. They might also look at character trends such as stereotypical portrayals or genres such as "cop shows" or "hospital dramas." You might also have them recognize audience trends and television advertising placement. Another perspective is to have students look at television shows from their past (or their parents' past) and discuss the ways these shows created

culturally defining moments in their lives. Have them analyze and compare particular examples. There are so many ways students can think critically through this medium.

Film: Dim the Lights

Along the same lines as television, we have the broader category of film, which is very easy to incorporate into a writing classroom. I start almost every class at the beginning of the week by asking, "Did anybody see any movies this weekend?" Again, a conversation readily erupts on all the great films I must see. The basic concepts associated with television come into play here as we discuss intended audience and content. *Tropic Thunder* was a must-see for most of my students in 2008, while I was much more interested in Sean Penn's portrayal of Harvey Milk in *Milk* (2008). Common ground is easy to reach, however, when it comes to movies in the classroom. I have used such varied films as *American Beauty*, *The Truman Show*, and the documentary *Born into Brothels* as a way to introduce theme into students' writing portfolios. For example, when we are discussing visual media and how we as consumers are asked to believe whatever the producers choose to show us, *American Beauty* and *The Truman Show* are excellent examples of what is real and what might be considered "make-believe." This ties in nicely with the portfolio that examines reality versus make-believe, what we believe about a topic compared with the actuality of the situation. Likewise, *Born into Brothels*, a film about children born to prostitutes in the red-light district of Calcutta, is a great way to introduce students to the concept of how we choose what to see and believe and how easy it is to turn our backs to the reality of others.

Using films in the classroom: You might ask your students to do the following when they view any movie you choose to include in your curriculum. I will use *The Truman Show* as an example from our unit on reality versus make-believe.

- **Step 1:** Have students take notes: As they watch the film, they should pay particular attention to anything in the movie that reflects our discussion of reality versus make-believe. This includes settings, characterization, time, colors/design, and script/language. The list should be lengthy. In addition to considering the theme of a film, students should examine other aspects of the rhetorical web as well. Any movie is a great starting point for discussing audience, purpose, and context. You might have students look at the detail in costumes and what those choices in color and style mean for the viewer. Likewise, setting can offer an interesting connection between the use of detail in writing and the use of detail in visual mediums. Set designers do not randomly place artifacts in a film without a specific purpose, so have students consider how the details they include in their own composition output serve a specific purpose.

- **Step 2:** Ask students to complete a film analysis: In writing, they should reflect on some aspect of the film that they found particularly intriguing. Students might consider how the film deals with the concept of what is real and what is constructed to appear real. For example, how are the film's characters manipulated into believing that Truman's world is actually a reality? How are setting, color, characterization, and costumes used effectively by the film's directors to influence their audience and to send the intended message? When students are writing or creating their own interpretation of a visual text, what should they include in order to reach the desired effect?

Other options: What about films that we don't see in movie theaters? Try YouTube!

YouTube offers more videos than we could ever expect to see in the theater, and best of all, they're free for the viewing. Pick a topic, and the choice is endless for finding an appropriate "movie" that you can use to discuss any of the components inherent in major motion pictures. You might even ask students to create their own videos for YouTube, and since most of our twenty-first-century students are very media and tech savvy, they love the opportunity to *have* a reason to make a video and put it online. Again, students need to consider all of the components they will include in the video they make: audience, purpose, setting, context, character, script. You can discuss how this video will be available worldwide and not just to their best friends, so this can take the act of making meaning to a new level when they are considering moving beyond the boundaries of the classroom walls.

ADVERTISING: TURN IT OFF?!?

The headline of an online Associated Press article from August 2009 screams, "But wait! There's more! Ads on TV, that is." Apparently, new technology is on the way that will allow advertisers to target their audience according to specific interests, and no longer will we, the consumers, be able to "TiVo" through those pesky ads. We'll be forced to watch, whether we want to or not, because the advertisers are showing us exactly what we want to see.

Advertising is a multi-billion-dollar industry in the United States, and, with respect to our students and our classrooms, it is an extremely easy medium to use as a teaching tool. I use advertising as a way to get students to examine how we as Americans respond to products that we may buy. Whether we like it or not, we are greatly influenced by advertising (on TV, the radio, the Internet), and we respond, either by buying the product advertised or by choosing to take a stand against the product because, usually, we object to the advertising. It is almost impossible to be a member of our society without somehow being influenced by advertising. According to M. F. Jacobson and L. A. Mazur in their book *Marketing Madness: A Survival Guide for a Consumer Society*, "the average American is now exposed to over three thousand ads each day and will spend approximately three years of his or her life watching television advertisements" (58).

I begin the discussion by casually asking the class of approximately twenty-four students if any of them feel they are *not* influenced by advertising. Usually one or two hands go up with claims that these particular students don't fall prey to the coercion of advertisers; they operate as *individuals*. Then I ask the students to take a look around the room. Who is wearing an article of clothing that sports a logo, an emblem, or a catchy phrase? Who is carrying a designer purse? wearing name-brand shoes? How about book bags and computers? Any way to tell the brand name of those? Of course! It quickly becomes clear to students that they are greatly influenced by the media in their choices of clothing, accessories, and even technology. Essentially, we are walking advertisements. Once we branch out from our clothes, we discuss *where* we see advertising, and an endless list of ideas spouts from students, everything from billboards on the interstate to—you guessed it—television and films.

Using advertising in the classroom: There are endless ways of including advertising in the classroom since, as mentioned above, we're inundated with it wherever we go. Some quick, in-class mini-projects I have used effectively include the following:

- **Print ad analysis:** I bring in a large variety of advertisements from various magazines and hand them out to pairs of students. I choose ads that offer students a chance to see the visuals from magazines they may not usually read. I then give students a list of basic questions that ask them to examine the ads from an elitist's versus a mass-appeal standpoint. We look at the composition of the ad, color, and written text (if any is available). This is a great exercise to get students to understand that nothing is random in advertising; every component of the ad has a distinct purpose.

- **Feminist advertising:** There are many DVDs on the market that examine the issue of male/female images in advertising. I use the DVD entitled *Killing Us Softly 3* by Jean Kilbourne. This particular film looks at how advertising devalues women compared to men, and it creates spirited discussion among the male and female students in the class. After watching the DVD, you might have students create collages of examples of how women and men are portrayed in current advertising. Students can find ads in magazines, online, or on television. This is a fun and eye-opening exercise for students, and again, it provides a great context for discussing how what we deliver visually (or in writing) is received by our audience.

- **Multigenre advertising project:** I end the semester by having students create a multigenre project that examines the evolution of the advertising of a particular product.

  - **Step 1:** Ask students to choose a product they are interested in learning more about. I encourage students to think about items they use regularly or a hobby they are really interested in. This will make their topics more appealing than if you assign specific products to the class. However, make sure students understand that they are researching the advertising of the product over the years, not just the product itself.

- **Step 2:** Students will create a multi-genre book: Give students the freedom to tell their audience about their chosen product using any genre of text they would like. Encourage creativity and experimentation; ask students to include a poem, song lyrics, a press release, an obituary. The list is endless. Asking students to write outside of the mold they have comfortably created for themselves over the years requires them to consider all the processes of composition.

- **Step 3:** Finally, students will create a visual component: Ask students to create their own visual representation that shows the audience how their product has been advertised to the general public over the years. Again, creativity and experimentation are key. If a student likes to create web sites or computer-generated projects, this is a great opportunity to combine technology with creativity to produce this visual representation. Artistic students who like to create with their hands might build a three-dimensional representation of the product and its ads. By including this final component, you successfully combine both aspects of visual literacy when you ask students to write about their chosen product and create a visual representation as well.

TUNING IN, NOT TUNING IT OUT

With the glut of visual texts so readily available to us as teachers, it is imperative that we find ways to blend these forms of popular media into our pedagogical practices. We cannot ignore the fact that we, students and teachers alike, are constantly influenced by what we *see* around us and that we need to interpret these alternate texts in ways that are beneficial. One way to do this is to help our students learn to read texts in all of their various forms, to assist students in critically analyzing what they see, and to connect texts as touchstones for critical thinking as well as sources for research and writing. In other words, students need to "tune in" rather than "tuning out" or blindly consuming popular culture artifacts. Although many think that these media are stripping creativity from our students' minds, in fact these media can enhance creativity in productive ways. No matter what genre of "text" we are reading, whether visual or written, all genres are forms of communication, and they require planning, creativity, and critical thinking skills in order to obtain an optimum result. And the best thing about incorporating visual literacy into your writing classroom? It's free and it's fun!

Betty Oliver, *Saying What You See, and Seeing What You Say: Visuals and Information Design Strategies*

"Art is not what you see, but what you make others see."

—Edgar Degas

INTRODUCTION

Visual literacy is not just understanding what we see; it's sharing what we see with others in a way that enables them to understand as well. Taking a stand on visual literacy means acknowledging the importance of the image of the composition and the image within the composition. It means promoting the importance of both the visual appearance of writing and the appearance of visuals within writing. It means acknowledging the importance of "whole brain" writing to enhance creativity. If we understand the design principles—proximity, repetition, alignment, and contrast—that control how readers perceive the writing, we can predict

Betty Oliver, PhD, teaches information design and art at Southern Polytechnic State University. In addition to her teaching responsibilities, Dr. Oliver enjoys the life of an artist herself and works in watercolor, illustration, and digital mediums. She continues to exhibit her watercolor paintings.

what they read first, control how they scan, aid in assimilation of information, and create and maintain interest. If we incorporate visuals within the writing, we can give directions, describe with accuracy, transmit information quickly, and teach difficult concepts by relating to simple ones. If we understand the need to incorporate visual, spatial, holistic right-brain operations with logical, sequential left-brain processes, we can increase creativity exponentially. By taking a stand on visual literacy, we acknowledge that writing is a whole-brain activity that involves both the logical, sequential left brain and the creative, visual, holistic right brain.

IMAGE OF THE COMPOSITION

Visual hierarchies: An integral part of visual literacy, and one that's frequently overlooked, is the image of the composition—the way the composition looks to the reader. To understand why this is important, we need to know how we "see." To make meaning out of the visual world, our brain first seeks out the largest, darkest object in its field of vision; then it starts "pattern-seeking" by searching for other objects that fit the same pattern (size, darkness). Thus similar large, dark objects automatically become associated with the first object; they form a group, which lets the brain relate the objects to one another. This is why we have headlines and subheads in articles and newspapers. The headline gives readers a starting point, and the subheads are markers that lead readers' eyes through the writing while the brain is creat-

ing a relationship between the headline and subheads. Readers use this grouping technique to scan the writing and form a general idea—a holistic overview—of the subject before they read the details in the text. Emphasizing the headline (or title) and subheads and pull quotes creates a visual hierarchy, telling readers where to begin, what the subject is about, and how the contents relate to one another. The visual information hierarchy gives readers a general overview of the information and creates a framework that will help organize the text that follows, making reading and comprehending both easier and faster. Without the framework of a hierarchy, readers have to read the entire composition while they struggle to organize the information in a way that "makes sense."

Utilizing white space: White (or empty) space plays an important part in the image of the composition. An adequate margin of white space around the text acts like a frame, isolating the text within its own separate reality by creating contrast between the information and the distracting world outside. A good rule of thumb is to leave a one-inch margin on both sides and at the top and bottom of the article or page. This white frame created by the margins helps the reader shut out distractions and focus on the text at hand. A good way to help students see the value of white space is to have them compare the margins of magazines with those of tabloids. They can easily see that the wider margins of the expensive magazines are there to frame the luxurious graphics, while cheaper tabloids economize by reducing margin size and printing on as much of the paper as possible. Another way to see the value of white space is to have students view magazine ads and compare those that use lots of white space with those that are crowded with images and text. An abundance of white space makes the reader focus quickly on a particular word or image.

An ad with less white space and more content has less immediate impact, because the reader has to search out the message from the text and images.

Textual arrangement and presentation: We organize text into columns to keep the lines of text short enough to scan quickly. The columns are placed in close proximity so that we see the columns as an organized whole. Newspapers provide good examples of text organized in easy-to-read columns. Have students search for articles on the Internet where lines of text are so long that you have to scroll back and forth to read the whole line. Discuss why reading a newspaper column is easier than reading these lengthy lines of text.

Even the type of paper used contributes visually to the impact of the writing. Lined composition paper suggests a draft—an unfinished composition; so does a paper written in pencil. A paper written in ink implies that the writer has already drafted and edited the message. Choice of paper forms the reader's first impression. Cheap newsprint sends a casual message, suggesting the temporary nature of the information; a good bond paper suggests a more formal and timeless one.

Writing and reading are left-brain functions, logical and sequential, but our pattern-seeking right brain allows us to form relationships and to see these related parts as a whole. Controlling the image of the composition—the way it looks—helps achieve whole-brain writing by helping us not only read the information but also see how the information is related.

IMAGES WITHIN THE COMPOSITION

The more familiar understanding of visual literacy is the use of images within a composition. There are three ways of incorporating images within a composition: by using real images (graphics), by using virtual images (descriptions), and by using implied images (metaphors).

Real images can be either photographic or abstract. Most photographic images are two-dimensional, although electronic media make it possible for us to use three-dimensional images that can be rotated and viewed from all directions. Photographic images give the reader the most information but sometimes depend on words and numbers for additional understanding. For example, a three-dimensional image of Michelangelo's *David* could lack reference points to indicate scale. It's possible, though, to give the reader too much information. For instance, using a photo of your own child to illustrate a point might lead the reader to the conclusion that your point applies only to children of that particular size, culture, or race. Using more generic or abstract images suggests that the image applies to a large group of similar but not identical objects or persons. For the same reason, a writer should use a more abstract diagram when illustrating an action or a set of instructions. Diagrams with few or no words can be much more efficient and effective than pages of words with no illustration. The reason? Because images are basically language-independent, they have greater communication possibilities than do words and numbers, which can be understood only logically and sequentially. Moreover, images can be rotated, flipped horizontally or vertically, superimposed, stretched, scaled, distorted, and so on.

Placement of images in text should be carefully considered. When the text refers to an image, the image should appear as close to that text as possible (using the design principle of proximity). This proximity strengthens the relationship between the image and its description or explanation. Either the image itself should be the width of the text column to strengthen visual alignment or, if the image is smaller, the text should wrap around the image with enough white space between to form a frame of white. Captions should always appear either directly under the image or beside the image, with the text aligned to the edge of the image. They should be informational and should also connect to the purposes of the paper. The captions of charts, graphs, tables, and diagrams are generally preceded by "Figure 1," "Figure 2," and so forth. This is especially important when the text refers to a graphic that can't be placed immediately following the text.

Virtual images—descriptions or word pictures—offer the reader a creative opportunity to experience a mood, view a landscape, or invent a character suggested by words but defined by the reader. How many of us have read the Harry Potter series and, through the descriptions of J. K. Rowling, created images of the characters and Hogwarts in our imaginations? When we saw the movies, the characters in our imaginations changed completely because we now had someone else's ideas replacing or adding to our own images. We have all been, at one time or another, disappointed in the movie version of a great book because the characters "just didn't seem quite right"—not like we imagined them in the book. Written descriptions invite reader participation in a way that is excluded by real images. Instructional description, on the other hand, requires that readers see things the same way. And of course, when the reader and the writer don't share the same language, visual literacy is compromised further. How many of us have thrown up our hands in despair when trying to hook up electronic equipment when the instructions are poor translations from another language? We quickly realize that written instructions need supporting graphic images. But again, how many of us are frustrated to find that the picture in the instructions doesn't match the equipment we're trying to put together? Wonderful examples of excellent instructions can be found with any product from

IKEA, and most of these instructions have almost no words. The best instructions usually pair both words and images.

Metaphors, or implied images, greatly enhance visual literacy. The right brain, the realm of metaphors, is capable of "all-at-once" thought, the ability to consider multiple meanings simultaneously. This ability enables us to compare a familiar object or process to an unfamiliar object or process and, as we do so, to transfer meaning from the familiar to the unfamiliar. As Keith C. Heidorn observes, "Metaphors jump to mind to explain scientific concepts that would be incomprehensible to the layperson. William Harvey described the heart as a pump; Niels Bohr described the atom as a tiny solar system with the nucleus in the centre and the electrons orbiting like planets around it" ("Expanding the Mind: The Metaphor"). Similarly, Leonard Shlain noted that "metaphor's cousins—similes, analogies, allegories, proverbs, parables—each in their own way allow multiple simultaneous means of interpreting one single set of words" (*Art and Physics*, 395). A great exercise for illustrating the power of metaphor is to have students deconstruct a poem or a song by rewriting it without the metaphors. Lyrics to "The River" by country singer Garth Brooks work well with this exercise, as do poems like "Mending Wall" and "The Path Not Taken" by Robert Frost. After rewriting and removing metaphors and similes, students can share their discoveries of how the implied images created by metaphors and similes can turn ordinary words and thoughts into extraordinary experiences.

All these images within a composition—metaphors or implied images, word pictures or virtual images, and real images—and the images of the composition—the visual hierarchy and the information hierarchy—are integral parts of visual literacy. And visual literacy is the art of understanding what we see and being able to share what we see with others. It's the art of creatively engaging both the logical left brain and the holistic right brain in the act of writing. Visual literacy is written communication at its best!

ADDITIONAL WRITING TOPICS

• **From ordinary to extraordinary:** Using a copy of William Carlos Williams's poem "This Is Just to Say," write the words (no title, no author's name) in your handwriting on lined notepaper. Ask students what they think they're looking at. Usually the answer is "some sort of refrigerator note about plums in the fridge." Ask students if they've ever shared a refrigerator with a roommate and had that roommate eat something that they were saving. This can be a really active and fun discussion. I usually share with the class my experiences of putting Post-it notes on food in the fridge to keep my two teenage sons from eating something intended for a special occasion. Then redirect the students back to the "note" and ask them to guess for whom the note was intended. Usual response: a roommate or family member (a specific person). Emphasize that the note specifically mentions plums. Now, show the class a book with the same poem (or a carefully formatted typeset version of the poem with the title and author included). Lead them in a discussion of what has happened to the refrigerator note ("Oh, it's a poem!" is usually the first response). Ask them how they know ("There's a title"; "The author's name is there"; "It's printed in a book"; "There's special formatting now"; "The punctuation is different"). How has the meaning changed? It's no longer just a tongue-in-cheek apology for eating a specific plum in a specific person's refrigerator; its message has been expanded to address anyone who might take something (not just a plum) from someone else—a tale of giving in to temptation. Conclude the discussion by observing that the special formatting has the power to transform the words from an ordinary note into an extraordinary poem.

• **Write it; do it!** Give one student several Tinker Toy pieces. In a limited amount of time—say, ten minutes—the student builds an object using all the pieces while another student carefully records how the object is assembled. These instructions, along with the same unassembled Tinker Toy pieces, are passed along to two other students in another room; their job is to assemble the exact same structure using the written instructions in ten minutes. It's amazing how quickly an exercise like this shows students how difficult it is to write good instructions.

Jeff Voeltner, *All the Virtual World's a Stage: A Sense of Place through Interactive Game Environments*

"We must not cease from exploration. And the end of all our exploring will be to arrive where we began and to know the place for the first time."

—T. S. Eliot

In the film *The Chronicles of Narnia: The Lion, the Witch and the Wardrobe* (the film adaptation of C. S. Lewis's classic children's novel), Peter, Susan, Edmund, and Lucy step through a wardrobe one day and enter a world beyond anything they had ever imagined, and they give us a great picture of what it's like to leave the world of the mundane and embark on a journey into a world of wonder, intrigue, and adventure. The four children are taken to a place that represents what we all hope to find throughout our lives,

Jeff Voeltner is an artist and designer in the entertainment industry, where he shapes environments and "worlds" for the land of fiction. Recently, his focus has been on designing and building environments for video games, which is akin to set design in movies. He has designed environments for games such as Call of Duty™: Finest Hour™; Legendary™; and Turning Point™: Fall of Liberty™ with Spark Unlimited in California. He is currently developing the city and social spaces for the massively multiplayer online (MMO) game Global Agenda™ with Hi-Rez Studios in Atlanta, Georgia, as well as the production design for a 3-D animated short film, Cattyswampus.

and my hunch is that this picture is just a *glimpse* of what we're trying to catch when we log onto the virtual world—a world much more intriguing than the world that (at times) we *seem* to be in.

What exactly are we doing when we go to the movies, visit an amusement park, or go on vacation—or even when we play a video game? The simple answer is that we're going to a *place*. However, whether consciously or unconsciously, we're looking to do something more; we're looking to experience a *sense* of place, a sense of belonging. Whether we want to quench a thirst for adventure or satisfy our need for rest and relaxation, we pursue such destinations with the hope that we're going to be taken someplace interesting, somewhere different and more exciting, perhaps, than the place we are coming from.

As an environment designer in the interactive game industry, I have the opportunity to shape the worlds that players enter to explore new places, go on missions and quests, fight and battle, and even socialize with others within the context of virtual spaces. Essentially, my job is to design and construct areas that draw visitors into an experience that is engaging, entertaining, inviting, and fun, with the hope that players around the world will be lured into them

time and time again. Creating a game or virtual world can be very rewarding and adventurous in itself, but quite a bit of design, planning, and collaboration go into constructing a place that people feel compelled to interact with and to return to. In studying the topic of *place*, let's consider relating this subject to the overwhelming popularity of virtual spaces and video games today, their relationship to the real world, and the impact that they have on each other and on people. And in order to do so, we first need to ask ourselves the question, *Why have virtual spaces and video games become so popular, and what makes them so compelling?* To create such spaces, we look to what works in the real world in order to find the inspiration and vision for creating within the *virtual* world.

THEME

Beyond establishing an area's *purpose*, theme is perhaps the single most important factor to consider. If you take a look at any new construction project, whether remodeling a child's bedroom or building a new restaurant, the first factors to be considered are purpose, location, visual style, and the desired end—in other words, user experience. All of these factors are important, but theme is the glue that binds them all together through setting the overall tone and context for people to experience. And to define the theme, you need to ask yourself a few important questions: How do you want to define the experience? Who is your audience? Who are your guests, and what are their preferences? These questions have to be asked before setting out to build a space, and they must be considered carefully. Theme plays a role in every new development, from home styles to the world's largest theme park. It establishes the entire experience by setting a major tone, and it provides the context from which everything else for that space will follow.

Take one step into Disneyland, and you will see the impact of theme. It's quite possible that nobody else knows how to lure people into space like the folks at the Walt Disney Company, for they have mastered the art of shaping real-world environments in order to transport people into vastly different "worlds." Their environments are completely drenched in theme, and every square inch of their parks has been planned as part of a larger experience we can enjoy as a result.

Spatial Layout

Las Vegas hotels and casinos also exemplify the use of theme, but they also pay close attention to layout. What exactly is layout? Layout can be defined as the arrangement of the objects in a space and the relationships among them as they relate to the design for the use of the space. The rhythm and flow of an area's layout is an extremely important factor in creating a successful space and is essential to creating a positive experience within it. And with casinos, developers do everything they can to encourage us to stay in the space for no other reason than the obvious—they want us to keep spending our money!

Setting

We often use the term *setting* in a general sense to convey an overall "mood" for a space. For example, when we imagine going somewhere for a vacation or eating at a nice restaurant, we often visualize our destinations from a "big picture" perspective and describe or imagine them with phrases such as "a sandy beach at sunset" or "a romantic candlelit dinner overlooking the city at night." These are indeed great settings; however, if we pay close attention to the details that make up these particular settings, the elements that make them successful are often very specific. The romantic candlelit dinner setting, for example, includes relatively little work or content, yet when properly set, the

environment can have a major impact on our mood, and, combined with dimmed lighting and delicious food, we can enjoy the space to its fullest.

Each of these three factors—theme, layout, and setting—plays a major part in creating places that ultimately produce a *positive* or *negative* experience. Many restaurants and businesses go to great lengths to ensure that they provide the best customer service; however, the most successful of them also consider the *surroundings* of their customers and provide them with an inviting and comfortable sense of place.

Now that we're familiar with some of the basic factors that play a role in our real-world settings, let's take a deeper look at our fascination with the virtual world, what factors go into making it so compelling, and why we devote so much of our time and attention to it. The major difference between the real world and the virtual world has to do with the epic sense of scale that we're able to experience when we are inside the virtual world. But how would we define this experience?

Immersion

One of the popular buzzwords in the field of entertainment design today, particularly within the game development community, is *immersion*. Immersion, as defined by Wikipedia, is "the state of consciousness where an immersant's awareness of physical self is diminished or lost by being surrounded in an engrossing total environment; often artificial." An experience that is "immersive" for players is one that transports them into a seemingly real and new world and temporarily removes them from their engagement to reality.

So why is the topic of immersion important? In order to experience life in a virtual space, we must feel that we are really in that place, and that cannot happen when a world has not been shaped with consistency to reality or when there is no consistency within the virtual world (enabling the suspension of disbelief). The purpose of creating such compelling spaces is to help players experience life as something far beyond what they are able to experience in real life.

Thankfully, we are now at a point where technology has caught up to what our creative minds are able to imagine, and the possibilities for creating new realities/new worlds are now, in large part, endless. Video and computer games are no longer made up of just simple blocks and shapes, as they were during the infant stages of technology. They are now fully engaging, lifelike experiences that play to our senses. We now have the ability to shape the most realistic experiences possible, mimicking everyday life, while also allowing us to experience the impossible, the fantastical. As game developers, when we discuss the vision for crafting a game experience, most importantly, we set out to create a world in which players feel as though they are a part of it and are experiencing it in a very real way. Whatever the visual direction might be, whether photorealistic or stylized/caricatured, game designers and artists alike try to define a look and an experience that are compelling and interesting enough to take a player into an immersing and entertaining experience. That is, these environments are meant to get players so involved that their senses are completely tuned *into* the experience and tuned *out* of the world in which they find their physical presence.

Whether your preference is to use a console or to sit at your personal computer, many different systems and entertainment devices can provide these experiences. And of course, with the availability of the Internet, millions of people around the globe are now spending hours of their lives inside these worlds, interacting with others, and, in some cases, spending more time inside these places than they are living and participating in the *real* world. Games such as World of Warcraft and Second Life now dominate many people's lives. According to Wikipedia, World of Warcraft, the massively multiplayer online role-playing game (MMORPG) by Blizzard Entertainment, had 11.5 million monthly subscribers worldwide by the end of 2008. That is a staggering number, and the game's potential impact on the world is impossible to ignore. In fact, at this time, if you type "world of" in the Google search engine, World of Warcraft will be the first item presented in the list. That is pretty impressive, and in order to answer the question of what makes virtual worlds so compelling, it seems appropriate to also ask, Why are we so drawn to them? I believe we find these virtual spaces compelling for three basic reasons:

1. We are given an opportunity to play a *role* that we often do not have a chance to play in real life. Whether playing the role of a beastly creature or the role of the hero, we want to be something more than we actually are.

2. We enjoy *puzzles* and problem solving. Life itself is full of problem solving. It's the guiding factor to our very existence, and, when we turn toward entertainment to fill our attention, games provide the opportunity to solve problems, with the added benefit of enjoyment and entertainment.

3. We have a need and a thirst for *adventure*. Adventure can take many shapes. For some, adventure entails some sort of epic quest, traveling to some distant, exotic, or dangerous location. But for others, an adventure might be something as simple as solving a whodunit. Adventure is a large part of our human makeup, and, in a world that has been overrun with concrete jungles and strip malls, virtual worlds allow us to escape to new experiences and new places.

On Role-Playing and Human Limitations

Let's face it, our human bodies are capable of doing only so much. We're not actually superheroes, nor are we some sort of advanced cybernetic creatures. Instead, we're the most amazing of creatures, with minds that can imagine extremely complicated machines and partake in advanced technological endeavors, yet we want to be so much more than we actually are. We want to do more than we can possibly ever do. Take a look at some of the outrageous stunts that humankind has attempted throughout the ages, starting with our never-ending flirtation with flight. A classic picture comes to mind that perfectly captures how I believe we think of ourselves at times. It's an old photo from the early 1900s of a man on a hillside making an attempt to fly, with wings attached to his arms. Needless to say, he wasn't successful in his endeavor, and it's safe to assume that his audience was amused and entertained, yet *disappointed* by the failed attempt. You see, we want to experience new things, and in the back of our mind, the ever-present voice of our childhood wonder holds out hope that we actually can do more. And now, the virtual world has finally made it possible for us to (in a way) experience the impossible. Experiences that in the past were possible only in our imagination are now suddenly a possibility through virtual places in which we can retreat into new experiences and unlimited realities.

On Puzzles and Problem Solving

In looking at the subject of games and virtual spaces, notice how many of them are geared toward solving a problem. Whether it be advancing to the end of a quest, collecting a given set of objects, or figuring out a whodunit, games almost always provide some form of a puzzle and problem-solving experience. It's human nature not to be satisfied unless there is something to be figured out; that's just how we're designed. We need to be *engaged*, doing something purposeful, and the makeup of the human brain seems to be geared to finding problems, even if none exist. I believe there are two reasons that games and virtual spaces focus primarily on problem solving. First, as technology has advanced, so have our options for advanced entertainment experiences. As technology continues to engage and push our imaginations, now, what we can imagine we can build, and the options given to us in the digital age provide an opportunity for us to "solve" so much more. Second, as the expediency of information and technology has streamlined the efficiency of our daily lives, the activities of our lives have also changed dramatically. I believe that we're simply becoming much more dissatisfied with life as it is, even as we spend significantly less time in doing physical and laborious work. We may feel as though we're busier than ever, yet we often find ourselves searching for more stimulating activities, and we demand to be engaged in doing *something*.

On Escape and Adventure

Virtual spaces allow for an easy escape and adventure. If we're honest with ourselves, we might say that we've become bored. Yes, bored! We're constantly looking to experience something new, to visit someplace more exciting than the "world" in which we find ourselves living. Many people don't take the opportunity to enjoy a daily adventure (an epic hike, an exploration of some faraway place, a vacation to an exotic, distant land), or even a weekly, monthly, or yearly adventure. And if the desire for adventure is such a large part of our human makeup, then *we must satisfy it through some other means*. As our lives and the world become so much more dependent on technology and efficiency, we neglect to care for some of the most essential desires we have in life, excusing them as "extras" or things that we'll do "one day." But what happens at the end of the day, when our work is finished, when school is out, when the responsibilities of our lives are put on pause? What do we do? Again, if we're honest with ourselves, we look to escape to somewhere more exciting. Whether it is watching television, surfing the Internet, playing the latest video game, or indulging ourselves within Facebook and MySpace, we're looking to escape to another *place*.

In the past, exploring new lands, visiting another country, and even the simple unknowns of what the next day was going to bring were worthy and fun adventures. Today, people still do enjoy and experience such things, but, I would argue, to a much lesser degree. The world in which we live now has become increasingly smaller and, in many aspects, much less interesting as a result of the availability of information, quick travel, and our fast food lifestyles. We often find that we're not really engaged in any sort of bigger adventure. Ironically, despite all the technology and all the amazing things we have at our disposal, we're intensely bored with the world that we have shaped for ourselves, and the *virtual* worlds to which we can escape become much more exciting when we realize all the things we can do in them.

APPLICATION

In the real world, as we pursue shaping a world and experiences that we can control, we must still ultimately answer to the ways of nature, the needs of our souls, and the unpredictable ways of the real world in which we live. Our natural surroundings will continue to remind us that we are in a much larger place and one filled with wonder and adventure. The question is: Will we choose to embrace it again?

If you notice, when nature builds something, it is organic, curved, and wild. Yet when humans build something, it is straight, perfected, controlled, and often plain. So much of the world that we have shaped for ourselves is purely functional. From our office cubicles to our classrooms and airline seats, much of the places that we must enter and interact with are indeed operating as they're designed to, yet we're dying to be somewhere else because we rarely consider the deepest needs and longings of our hearts, our minds, and our imaginations. We have closed off nature, the real world, and even other people as we are hell-bent on controlling the places around us. But, as real people, in the real world, we are impacted by the things that surround us. We have feelings, and we are impacted by what we see. We have no real choice as to whether or not the environment and our settings affect us. However, we do have the opportunity to improve and take care of our surroundings through shaping experiences that engage our senses.

We need to constantly remind ourselves about the importance of shaping places that cause us to interact on a physical level and the importance of designing areas that make us feel comfortable and remind us that we belong. The virtual world provides opportunities for us to interact with others and even to work as a team, but if we choose to let this world replace our own, then we'll detach from one another and lose the opportunity to experience the chance of a lifetime: to really know each other.

ADDITIONAL WRITING TOPICS

- On role-playing: If you could create a character in a virtual space that would reflect a character you would like to be in real life (superpowers and all), who/what would you be? Describe that character and/or design him/her/it through any visual medium (drawing, 3-D model, etc.). Think outside the box here and don't limit yourself to just the superheroes and characters that you are already familiar with.

- As Aristotle once said, "The soul never thinks without a picture." Think for a moment about some of the areas that you truly long to be in. Or perhaps think of a place that you have never visited (a distant or exotic country, hotel/resort, city). Now, find a picture from the Internet or a magazine that illustrates that place as you imagine it and place it somewhere that you do *not* enjoy being in. (Many people place these types of pictures on their computer desktop, but they're often very clichéd.) Choose a specific location, somewhere you *long* to be, and think about *why* you want to be there. Ask yourself why you're so drawn to this place. Why aren't you there now?

- A lesson in lighting: In your classroom, turn on all of the main lights normally used in the room. Note the mood or how you feel in that setting. Describe that feeling and then note how you would categorize it (positive or negative?). Now, turn off the lights and, if possible, close any shades or curtains on the windows or diffuse the incoming daylight. If you do not have any lamps in the room already, bring one or two into the class and light the room using only those lamps. Any lamps will do. The main goal here is to create a "softer" setting. With the room now lit only by the lamps, note how the mood or setting inside the room changes. What's the difference in the feeling created, and is it more comfortable? What are the advantages and disadvantages of this lighting scenario inside of a classroom setting?

Introduction: Writing Matters

Introductions teach themselves.

Well, that's what I used to think. The first time I taught with *Seeing & Writing,* I assigned the introduction without ever discussing it in class. And then I was mystified when the lessons of the introduction didn't show up in my students' work. Did they read the introduction carefully? Did they read it at all? Was this more evidence of the much-touted reading crisis? Or was this — gasp — poor pedagogy? The latter, I think. And discussions with other teachers revealed that I wasn't alone in how I taught (or did not teach) introductions.

Since then, the McQuades have drastically revised the introduction, and it's better than ever. It not only offers an interactive preview of the skills students will use throughout the book, but also does what many other textbooks — writing handbooks included — do not: It makes a case for the importance of writing. Students probably could read this material on their own and be fine; but I'd discuss some of it in class just to be sure.

The beauty of Writing Matters is that students can read and discuss most of it in one class period, and you can align its principles with your opening-day discussion of the writing process and your expectations for the class. Thankfully, my students are aware of the writing process and know the different forms writing can take; but they are less aware of how they read and of the type of reading they are expected to do in college. So in the first class, after talking about different forms of writing, we spend a few minutes on different kinds of reading. Once I list a few, students have no trouble coming up with other examples: skimming, scanning, reading boldface words, highlighting, retention reading, comprehension reading, critical reading, rereading, and so on. We talk about when each kind of reading is useful, and I describe the kinds of reading that will help students most in this class.

Before students read the introduction, ask them to look at the Peter Arkle illustration on page 2, which presents a major theme of the book—the relationship between word and image. Arkle points out that "drawings are just another form of writing." Since students will explore photographic images throughout the book, you could bring up photographs as another form of representation. How might photos be another form of writing? Writing, drawing, and taking a photograph are ways of representing what we see, but there may be other ways to view our experiences. You might ask students to consider the illustration in reverse, to see the words pouring up the faucet and creating the images coming out of the funnel. How does what we see influence our writing, our representation of the world? And then how do the forms of representation influence how we see? Using Arkle's illustration as a starting point, ask students "How does the word *snake* differ from a drawing of a snake or from a photograph of a snake?" The point is not to come to any definitive answers on these questions—raise them, explore them, and let students know that these will be issues to consider throughout the course.

After reading the opening text, students could freewrite about the title of the introduction: Why does writing matter? How does it matter to them not only academically but personally? The McQuades describe how seeing informs writing: "The more your eyes are open and alert . . . the more you will write with conviction and clarity" (p. 3). You might ask students to think about how seeing and writing feed into each other. How can writing help them see more clearly?

MAKING OBSERVATIONS (P. 6) AND DRAWING INFERENCES (P. 8)

The objective in these sections is to get students thinking about how "the sum total of [their] experience and . . . identity" (p. 6) affects the way in which they approach a text. Recognizing "predispositions" and "prejudices" is tough, even for instructors who have had the benefit of psychoanalytic theory (and possibly even psychoanalysis). You might start students down this path with a safe example—this book. Ask students about their first impression of *Seeing & Writing 4*. What observations can they make about the book—its design, its contents? What inferences can they draw from these observations? And, then, ask the students about their relationship to this textbook. What previous experiences—at school, at home, with friends—might influence their reading of this textbook?

DRAFTING (P. 12) AND REVISING (P. 14)

These sections provide a direct, honest account of the writing process. Writing is messy, and there is no one correct way to do it. Good writers figure out what works best for them. Ask students to write a description of their writing process. You might encourage them to try out different writing processes throughout the course and to keep track of how they write: Where are they when they write? Are there distractions? When do they write? Do they do any prewriting, or do they usually start with a blank screen? Do they revise as they go or at the end?

COMPOSITION TOOLKIT (P. 16)

I find it useful to assign this section as in-class group work or as homework that we then discuss in the next class.

1
OBSERVING THE ORDINARY

What does it mean to see? How is "seeing" connected to reading and writing? How, as writers, can students transfer the skills of observation and inference into their writing? These are the central questions of this chapter.

The introductory material for Chapter 1, Observing the Ordinary, asks students to acknowledge the acts of visual perception they perform every day and to become more aware of this very powerful and highly developed skill that they often take for granted. Discuss with students how we *actively* see new surroundings and people, whereas we tend to see those places and people *passively* after we become familiar with them. The key is to clarify what *observing the ordinary* means.

"Even if we all had the same object before us, our descriptions would likely be different, depending on who we are" (p. 27, para. 2). Some students will undoubtedly see different things in the classroom and/or name them in different ways. For example, how are the people in the room dressed? Fashion—clothing style and cut—is a major industry in Western culture. We are expert at "reading" clothing. But we are expert at reading body language and other visual cues as well.

We use observations to draw informed inferences. By accumulating visual data, concrete and specific observations about what we *see*, we can begin to make informed inferences about the meaning of what we see. To better understand the readings and images in this chapter of *Seeing & Writing 4*—and in the rest of the book—students need to understand the kinds of observations they can make about what is visible to them and how those observations come to-gether to create meaning.

This chapter also provides ways for students to understand that definitions are communally constructed and change based on situation and context. For example, you might discuss the differences between the terms *ordinary* and *extraordinary*. Students will inevitably arrive at the notion that these terms change through time, perspective, or vantage point. Something that was once considered extraordinary (such as a telephone) might change due to purpose, demand, and availability.

These skills naturally connect to discussions about writing and composition. In writing we talk about them in terms of narration, exposition, and the ways we write effectively by shuttling back and forth between these perspectives. Encourage students to understand that sight often equals insight and that writing can be a way to make these connections and communicate them to others.

This whole chapter lends itself well to the writing/reading strategy of double-entry journals, for all of the selections ask students to become more active readers through observation and inference. For any of the selections or assignments, ask students to divide their page into two columns. Under the first column, have them record observations of situations, readings, or the images presented in the book. Under the second column, ask them to extend through inferences about those observations. As students begin to see these side by side, they will better understand this critical reading strategy and incorporate it into their writing. Readers move between observation and inference while writers make these moves rhetorically through narration and exposition.

This chapter offers many opportunities for students to move from "passive looking" to "active seeing." Recognizing the ordinary trains students to focus on the details and think and write analytically as they become critical readers of their lives, or, as the textbook authors state, "If you devote attention to the ordinary you increase the likelihood of becoming someone on whom nothing is lost."

POSSIBILITIES FOR DISCUSSION, REFLECTION, AND JOURNALING

- In connection with the discussion of passive and active seeing, you might ask students to take a few moments to jot down a list of what they see in their classroom. Then ask them to read their lists aloud. Use what they've written as a springboard to a discussion of how and why people notice the things they do.

- Try to get students to move from their lists of concrete objects to what those lists imply about how they understand their classroom space. You may also want to point out that what they see probably depends on where they sit.

How does perspective from one physical position differ from another? How can they distinguish the instructor's space from their own? How do their backgrounds and experiences feed into their perspectives? What do they notice about the things in the room? Encourage them to move beyond noting color, which is often the first thing students mention when asked to describe an object.

- Have students look at the ways their classmates are sitting. What cues does body posture give? What do students bring with them to class? What does the instructor bring? What visual cues tell students they are in a classroom? How do they know which person in the room is the instructor? Ask them to "read" the classroom using only visual cues as their data.

- Does the concept of ordinary have to do with something being common or present, or with frequency of use? How does our connection to ordinary objects define us as a culture, a generation, or a group?

ADDITIONAL WRITING TOPIC AND CLASSROOM ACTIVITY

- **Ordinary/Extraordinary Objects:** This is a particularly good exercise to try early in the course as it is a great icebreaker and introduces the concepts of this chapter. It helps students with observation and inference-making along with developing stronger writing skills through definition and substantiation. You can also use this assignment as a springboard for writings throughout the chapter. For example, you can have students extend upon this assignment through Woiwode's "Ode to an Orange" (p. 48) and have them write an ode to their chosen ordinary object or have them research commercial representations of their objects like the Phone Home advertising series (p. 54).

  This particular version of the assignment takes two class periods, in which students expand their ideas:

  Day 1 — Ordinary Objects: Have students bring in an "ordinary object." Go around the class and have them introduce their objects and describe why they consider them ordinary. Students might bring objects such as pencils, cell phones, or car keys. Take discussion notes and create categories as you work together to define the term *ordinary* through the discussion of their objects. Ask them to write for a few minutes or make a list of reasons they identify this object as ordinary. Emphasize the connection between the ways they make their claims—"My lip balm is ordinary"—and the ways those claims are substantiated through the examples and explanation of their objects. Help them see multiple perspectives through comparing categories and complicating their definitions.

Day 2 — Extraordinary Objects: For this follow-up day, ask students to bring in an "extraordinary object." Encourage them to draw on the discussion about ordinary objects as they make their choices. Some students might even decide to bring in the same object they brought with them on the first day (but their perspectives might have changed). Have students meet in small groups and conduct a similar discussion as in Day 1. Ask them to share and explain their objects and work to construct a communal or group definition of *extraordinary*. Ask each group to choose one item from the group that they consider the most extraordinary. Share these with the full class along with their definitions, distinctions, and qualifications.

Tie this exercise back into composition strategies through an emphasis on attention to detail, writing to learn (inquiry), and the rhetorical situation. Here we might try to explain that words do not have single meanings that never change. Instead words are constructed by our connections to them, the ways their audience perceives them, and the ways they are socially understood. It is a good time to show that, as writers, it is our job to assess these situations and contexts and to find the best language to communicate our ideas.

Surefire Class: Observing the Ordinary

Winnie Kenney
Southwestern Illinois College

To the first class in this unit I bring a bag of oranges (or other seasonal citrus fruit), enough for each student.[1] With an orange, an ordinary object, as the *Seeing & Writing* chapter suggests, my class and I discover other invention methods.

In introducing this exercise I explain that before class, students likely would have thought writing an essay about an orange would be a daunting task. After all, how much can one person say or write about such an ordinary object. Then I explain that if students learn to observe closely from this activity, they will be so familiar with their particular orange that they will be able to distinguish it from everyone else's in class. I tell each class that when I used this activity my first semester as a TA, two student athletes, one a football player and another a wrestler, almost came to blows because one mistook the other's orange for his own. So I caution them to observe carefully. (Notice the connection to the overall concepts in *Seeing & Writing*.)

Students choose an orange at random from the bag and then spend a few minutes on each of the following invention strategies:

- **Description.** "Freewrite, noting all the characteristics of your orange, until time is called." Before they begin I give my students a couple of points of reference: that one end of the orange is the stem and that the other is the flowering end. I also allow time when they've finished freewriting for those who would like to share what they have written.

- **Comparison and contrast.** "In peer editing groups, decide whose orange wins the beauty contest and whose wins the Olympics." Each group selects the category winners among the members' oranges. Then we all compare the group winners and select the most beautiful and the most athletic oranges in the class.

- **Narrative.** "Tell the story of your orange, including how he or she came into your possession." Again I ask for volunteers to share what they have come up with. Some are very factual: "My orange grew up on a farm in Florida . . . until my instructor picked it up at the local grocery." Others are very inventive, giving their orange a name, a personality, and a life story.

Having prepared them with this tactile fun activity, for homework I have the students read Larry Woiwode's "Ode to an Orange" (p. 48) and the orange crate labels (p. 52) and ask them to begin an essay on an ordinary object by answering the following questions:

- What is the inanimate object you have chosen for the Observing the Ordinary essay?

- What is your background knowledge of the object?

- What are your preconceptions about this object?

- What observations will you need to make of or about the object for this essay?

- How will your perspective likely affect your thinking about the object?

---

[1] I have used this activity in several classes, through two editions of *Seeing & Writing*, and so far only one student has been allergic to citrus and had to have a classmate hold her orange.

The next class period, we discuss planning methods they have found effective in the past and ones they have learned from class (through either reading or activities) that they think will be helpful. And with the answers to the questions above, they begin their essays in earnest.

The completed essays that emerge from this unit include topics like these:

- The running shoes that others would consider trash but that helped me win awards at track meets

- The tree house I built with my father, which left me with lasting memories and a continued interest in woodworking

- The keyboard to my computer, one of my windows on the world

Portfolio: Menzel and D'Aluisio (p. 30)
Peter Menzel and Faith D'Aluisio, *The Hungry Planet*

Menzel and D'Aluisio's Portfolio, *The Hungry Planet*, provides a global look at the term *ordinary* through looking at people's common grocery choices over the course of a week in different countries. The photos show images of families standing by their week's supply of groceries and are accompanied by "ration and cost statistics." This series and textual pairing provides a good opportunity to have students look closely and observe the ordinary in a larger context. It can also help them realize the rhetorical notion of definition through comparison as they realize that the concept of the "ordinary" depends on variables such as situation and context, background, ideologies, nationality, and socioeconomic status.

POSSIBILITIES FOR DISCUSSION, REFLECTION, AND JOURNALING

• What kinds of cross-cultural connections can be made between the images and the texts?

• How do we define *ordinary*? What does our sense of the ordinary say about us as individuals and as a society? What observations and inferences might be made upon deep analysis of the images?

• What are the differences between the visual and textual treatments in the Portfolio? What do you get from the images that you can't get from the text, and vice versa? How do these two formats work together to create a full picture?

• How does our relationship with food represent our culture? How does packaging affect perception? How does food represent ethnicity? What are particular trends that students might recognize as they look at the connections between individual choices?

• How do students interpret the pair from the United States (a home culture for many)? Which items do they feel are representative of their own experiences, which ones seem different, and why? Do they think this represents a typical American family? What ideas and images do they consider typically American? Which particular cultural values are represented through items such as processed foods, packaging, or take-out pizzas? How do the "fast food" items found in the list add something that is not seen in the image?

ADDITIONAL WRITING TOPICS AND CLASSROOM ACTIVITIES

• **Double-Entry Journal:** Have students record their observations and inferences across the Portfolio (both the images and the texts). Have them divide their page into two columns. In the first column ask them to record *what they see or notice*—their observations. In the second column have them record *what they think the images and texts mean*—their inferences and interpretations. Encourage them to reflect on issues such as socioeconomic factors, values, and context drawn from the discussion questions. Use these observations to create a cross-cultural reading/writing in which they discuss and compare the images and texts. Students might share these journals in class or in small groups to recognize the connections between their observations and their inferences.

- These photographs and lists can make us think about how we represent ourselves through our grocery choices. Have students consider their own — or their family's — "grocery list for a week." Make lists and write about how these choices represent their values and their culture.

- **Image/Writing Assignment:** Have students take six images of their groceries and write about how those ordinary daily objects reflect their individual and cultural values. They might compose the images through staging the products like Menzel and D'Aluisio's Portfolio pieces or take them in their regular settings (the refrigerator, the pantry, the cabinet). Ask them to create a textual comparison for their images in which they catalog their groceries in a similar style to the accompanying list in the Portfolio.

CONNECTION TO ANOTHER TEXT

- After students have studied the *Hungry Planet* portraits, have them read the "portrait" of a single piece of fruit in Larry Woiwode's "Ode to an Orange" (p. 48). Discuss how each of these texts elicits a sense of place. Does the description of an orange in Woiwode's essay give a sense of North Dakota in the same way that the spreads of food in Menzel's photographs represent different countries?

SUGGESTIONS FOR FURTHER READING, THINKING, AND WRITING

PRINT

Menzel, Peter, and Faith D'Aluisio. *Man Eating Bugs: The Art and Science of Eating Insects.* San Francisco: Top Speed, 1998. Print.

———. *Material World.* San Francisco: Sierra Club, 1995. Print.

———. *Robo Sapiens: The Evolution of a New Species.* Cambridge, MA: MIT Press, 2000. Print.

———. *Women in the Material World.* San Francisco: Sierra Club, 1998. Print.

WEB

menzelphoto.com. Peter Menzel's official site. Contains more than ten thousand photographs taken over the course of his thirty-year career.

wfp.org. The United Nations' web site for the World Food Programme. Most of the rations displayed in the photograph of the Aboubakar family from Chad come from the program.

AUDIOVISUAL

King Corn. 88 min. 2009. DVD. From Mosaic Films Incorporated. In this documentary, friends Ian Cheney and Curtis Ellis buy an acre of corn in Iowa and track where their kernels go — and what they go into.

Pair: Newitz & Pillsbury (p. 44)

Annalee Newitz, *My Laptop*
Matthew Pillsbury, *Penelope Umbrico (with Her Daughters)*

Looking at Newitz's and Pillsbury's work brings to light the pervasive influence of technology in our lives — particularly the laptop computer. The laptop, once considered a luxury, something extraordinary, is now considered an ordinary object. It goes beyond the obvious presence of the machine and is actually a portal to the virtual worlds in which many of our students reside.

Newitz's essay expresses her satisfaction with her laptop and the ways it has enhanced her life and become part of her everyday thinking, her memories, and her identity. Pillsbury's photo shows "ghostlike figures" sitting together but also separate. It is particularly interesting to notice that the laptops are clearer than the people. This might prompt a discussion about how the concept of identity is blurred in light of this technology. The figures seem unaware of one another, emphasizing the idea that this technology not only brings us together in new social ways but also pulls us apart.

These two selections, when viewed as a pair, show two different perspectives on this same object, asking students to critically reflect on this "ordinary" object's complexity.

POSSIBILITIES FOR DISCUSSION, REFLECTION, AND JOURNALING

• The laptop computer is now considered ordinary, whereas once it was extraordinary. In what ways has this object made this transition? In what ways is *ordinary* defined by its presence in our lives? How is engaging in a virtual world now considered ordinary? What objects have we come to take for granted? How has the laptop/technology changed our daily lives?

• Compare the two perspectives brought up in the pair. Newitz's sense of "infatuation" with the identity-shaping ability of her laptop is contrasted with Pillsbury's more ominous image, which suggests obsession and loss of identity. What is gained and what is lost because of the pervasive presence of this object? How has this technology shaped our ideas about identity? How do we have a more active/passive role in shaping our identities?

• Newitz says, "It's practically a brain prosthesis." What do students make of this statement and its implication? How is the computer an extension of our brains and our thinking processes? How has this extension shaped the way we think, act, and socialize? How has it opened our eyes to more resources and voices, and how has it, at the same time, limited our ability to think?

• Pillsbury's image suggests an impact on our social relationships. In what ways has the laptop, along with its associated technology, changed our ideas and behavior in relation to social relationships? In what ways has it humanized us and dehumanized us at the same time?

• Newitz says, "Like everybody else, I was just a command line full of glowing green letters." What do students think she means by this statement? What other statements in her essay are good for analysis?

• Have students reflect on and compare the pair. Ask them to create two lists in which they pull out observations and inferences from both of the pieces. Ask them to look at the meaning and content expressed along with the treatment through the different mediums. In Newitz's essay they might pull out particular quotations or ideas expressly written. In Pillsbury's image they might also address issues of composition in images such as light and darkness, organization, and emphasis.

ADDITIONAL WRITING TOPICS AND CLASSROOM ACTIVITIES

• Have students write an essay in a similar style to Newitz's in which they explore their relationship to a particular ordinary object. Encourage them to explore, like Newitz, the presence of the object along with its impact over time for them as individuals.

• **Image/Writing Assignment:** Ask students to take six pictures of the ordinary object they wrote about in their extended writing. Have them photograph the object from different perspectives, so that the pictures consciously communicate particular ideas or opinions about the object. These various perspectives might involve placement in relation to other objects, use of light and darkness, size and scope, or arrangement within the frame. Use this assignment to emphasize the ways composition choices can communicate meaning and perspective. Follow up with a short, narrative analysis of these choices.

CONNECTIONS TO OTHER TEXTS

• Have students compare the photograph of the American family with Jesse Gordon's piece, *What Is America?*, in Looking Closer (Chapter 2, p. 220). How is America represented in each of these selections? How are the values represented similar? How are they different?

• Ask students to choose a character from a story or selection in *Seeing & Writing 4* and imagine what this person's monthly food allotment looks like. Have them write a brief description about what this person eats and explain why they believe this to be the case.

SUGGESTIONS FOR FURTHER READING, THINKING, AND WRITING

PRINT

Turkle, Sherry, ed. *Evocative Objects: Things We Think With*. Cambridge, MA: MIT Press, 2007. Print.

WEB

wired.com/gadgets/digitalcameras/news/2007/01/72595. *Wired* reviews Matthew Pillsbury's photography and his "decentering of human experience."

Larry Woiwode, *Ode to an Orange* (p. 48)

Larry Woiwode's "Ode to an Orange" is a personal narrative devoted to a childhood memory of a specific season, place, and object. The season is winter, the place is North Dakota, and the object is an orange. As the use of the word *ode* in the title suggests, Woiwode's essay is a lyrical meditation on the subject of a fruit — the orange. You might want to begin discussion by explaining that an ode is actually a formal, rhymed poem, not an informal, anecdotal essay. That Woiwode chose to call his essay an ode, then, is unusual. His use of the word also presupposes a certain literary expertise on the part of the reader: It alludes to a tradition of poetic longing. And by invoking a serious literary tradition in writing about a mundane fruit, Woiwode gives the title an almost quaint connotation. The notion that a family would seriously consider an orange to be a special treat may seem outlandish to some of your students. Remind them that Woiwode grew up in a different time and place and that the family's appreciation of and the brothers' hunger for oranges are sincere. You might direct your students to note the tone of lines like "there was no depth of degradation that we wouldn't descend to in order to get one" (para. 10).

POSSIBILITIES FOR DISCUSSION, REFLECTION, AND JOURNALING

• Once you've established that the words *ode* and *orange* in the title hint at the mix of elements to come, ask students how the serious and mundane are balanced by the end of the essay. Have they developed a new or different appreciation for the fruit? What kind of image of an orange did they have in mind before and after reading the essay? What has the orange come to represent?

• Clearly Woiwode's family was poor. Consider the modesty of the two brothers' wanting their Christmas oranges. The essay is also about what constitutes our personal visions of luxury. These are the visions that each reader brings to the essay, an example of how we also invest ordinary objects with private and public meanings. Ask students to discuss what kinds of things they hungered for when they were children: a Cabbage Patch doll? a Game Boy? a Happy Meal? From that discussion you might move on to the way parents establish power by giving and withholding what their children want, or to the magical properties we attribute to things we loved when we were young.

• A discussion of how images can be created through words could lead to a consideration of the elements of composition in a written or visual text. For example, both kinds of texts have a distinct shape and form. When we read or write an essay, we make certain assumptions about the shape the writing will take. A personal narrative presents one author's perspective, the details that are important to that person; but the reader still assumes that the essay will have a point or a thesis and that it will be organized into paragraphs. Ask students what their assumptions are about the essay form. What do they expect to see when they open their textbooks? Would it seem odd *not* to have columns of print? the title in a large bold font? the author's name below the title? How do they expect an essay to be organized? What does the image of the essay itself on the page communicate to them?

ADDITIONAL WRITING TOPICS AND CLASSROOM ACTIVITIES

• Woiwode invites readers directly into the world of a bleak Great Plains winter in the 1940s, and then he introduces a world of color summoned by the arrival of the oranges in his town. In what ways does the essay itself have a visual orientation? For one thing, orange is both fruit and color. But Woiwode also creates scenes of color as we read. Ask students to identify those scenes: begging for an orange, peeling an orange, eating an orange. Then ask them to imagine those scenes as scenes in a movie. How would they cast the film? How would they design the sets? How would they shoot each scene? What camera angles would they use?

• Woiwode is able to evoke a time and place through his memory of a simple orange. His essay evokes nostalgia for both a wholesome rural life that is disappearing from our culture and the idealized American nuclear family of our recent past. Ask students to use "Ode to an Orange" as a model in writing a description of an object that represents for them something larger and more personal about family, home, or community.

• Part of the strength of Woiwode's essay stems from his ability to play the harsh chill of winter against the warmth of the orange, as expressed in its color, its smell, and its taste. Ask students to write an analytical essay in which they explain how Woiwode contrasts the two elements, winter and orange.

CONNECTIONS WITH OTHER TEXTS

• After they read Woiwode's essay, have students look at the Sequoia Citrus Association's orange crate labels (p. 52). Ask them to consider the following questions: What is suggested by the relationship of the hand to the orange? By the shape of the orange? By the fact that the flesh of the orange is partially revealed? How is this visual presentation of an orange similar to or different from Woiwode's verbal presentation? Which one do the students find more inviting? Why?

• Woiwode's descriptions are powerful because they appeal to the senses. Ask students to consider which senses are being appealed to in the Building the Male Body advertisements in Chapter 4 (p. 354). Then separate the students into small groups, and ask each group to come up with changes for one ad that would make the ad appeal to more of the senses.

SUGGESTIONS FOR FURTHER READING, THINKING, AND WRITING

PRINT

Ackerman, Diane. *A Natural History of the Senses.* New York: Random House, 1990. Print. A beautifully written book about the senses.

Woiwode, Larry. *Beyond the Bedroom Wall: A Family Portrait.* New York: Avon, 1976. Print.

———. *The Neumiller Stories.* New York: Farrar, 1989. Print.

———. *Silent Passengers.* New York: Atheneum, 1993. Print.

WEB

fruitcratelabels.com. This site offers an online gallery of fruit crate labels from the same era as the book's reproductions, as well as an array of other product labels from the period.

ultimatecitrus.com. A web site created by the Florida Citrus Growers that offers a wonderful counterpoint to the memoir by Larry Woiwode and the old orange crate labels.

AUDIOVISUAL

King of the Hill. 103 min. NTSC, 1993. VHS, color, rated PG-13. Distributed by MCA/Universal and Gramercy Pictures. Director Steven Soderbergh's film captures the extraordinary in the ordinary and makes a wonderful and moving parallel to Woiwode's memoir; it also could be tied to Annie Dillard's "Seeing" (p. 96). The protagonist is a young boy, Aaron Kurlander, growing up alone during the Depression and struggling to survive. The film is based on A. E. Hotchner's memoir of the same title.

Mystery of the Senses. 300 min. 1995. 5 videocassettes. Distributed by NOVA. Inspired by Diane Ackerman's book *A Natural History of the Senses.* Also available individually (running time: 60 min.), by sense.

Surefire Assignment: The Value of Subtlety

Alison Russell
Xavier University

I have my students write a personal narrative of three pages or so (at least six hundred words) about a place that has had special meaning in their lives. In addition to providing specific details about the place, their essays should attempt to reveal a story the students hadn't realized was there.

Woiwode's piece and Eudora Welty's "The Little Store" (p. 147) are models of how authors use sensory description, dialogue, and reflective passages to make their writing vivid and interesting. These essays also suggest ways that students can order and pace their own narratives. (What information will they summarize? dramatize? Will they use flashbacks? flash-forwards? What tone are they aiming for? serious? comic?)

I remind students that the audience for this essay is our class, and I tell them that they should give enough context and information so that readers will be able to grasp why the place holds significance, but that they shouldn't overlook the value of subtlety. Small telling details, figurative language, and thoughtful reflection convey far more than any last-sentence announcement of the meaning of it all.

Surefire Assignment: A Cricket Hat, a Conch Shell, and an Orange

Debbie Jacob
International School of Port of Spain
(Profile, p. 13)

A cricket hat, a conch shell, and an orange. Those are the images my students use to understand how to create a visual framework for writing, beginning with the element of theme.

Because I teach in an international school, with children from Trinidad, the West Indies, and all over the world, I believe it is important to use images in music, art, and literature that relate to all students and reflect various cultural experiences, including Caribbean culture. I also try to use students' work when teaching concepts.

We begin with an examination of how objects become symbols. The cover of ca-lypsonian David Rudder's CD *Here Comes . . . the West Indies* uses nothing but a hat with a logo to symbolize the West Indian cricket team. Students discuss the impact of this image on a CD cover and then listen to the title track of the CD, which begins with a famous cricket fan—nicknamed Blue Food—blowing his conch shell, as he does at all of the cricket games. Students soon realize that Blue Food's conch shell rallies cricket fans throughout the region and creates an upbeat tone for the song.

After students identify the significance of the conch shell to cricket and West Indian culture, I show them Rachel Eckel's picture of a woman blowing a conch shell. (Eckel was a former art student in the school.) Students observe how the tone and theme shift when they see the caption of the picture: "Myrtle harmoniously plays the 'Star-Spangled Banner.'" Instantly, via the vehicle of irony, the conch shell changes from a symbol of regionalism to a symbol of colonialism.

When students understand the relationship of objects to theme and how the juxtaposition of verbal and visual images creates a mood or tone, I ask them to read Larry Woiwode's "Ode to an Orange." Then we discuss the Seeing questions at the end of the essay, and I have them write an ode to a piece of fruit as suggested in the first Writing question there.

Students then read a short story titled "Love Orange" by Jamaican writer Olive Senior. When they've finished, we talk about the contrasting tones in Woiwode's essay and Senior's story. I ask students to follow the orange through the essay and through the short story to understand how the authors use the orange to create theme and tone. They then use the orange to create a visual framework for writing a comparative essay.

By the end of this exercise, students are able to take one image and identify its significance; follow the use of that image in a picture, song, essay, or short story; demonstrate the relation of object to theme in their own ode to an object; and write a comparative essay.

Sequoia Citrus Association, *Have One* (p. 52)

POSSIBILITIES FOR DISCUSSION, REFLECTION, AND JOURNALING

• Have One's orange crate label does reflect "the accelerated pace and more sophisticated look of urban life: bolder typography, darker colors" (p. 53). Ask the students to compare this label with the earlier ones shown below it.

• You might begin discussion of the label by asking students how the label is "more sophisticated." Have them look at the details—for example, the bangle bracelet on the woman's arm and her shiny, polished nails. Is this the hand of a farmwife? If necessary, point out that the orange in the newer label has been removed from the grove and that this image seems more photographic, more like contemporary ads for food products.

• Ask students to consider the graphic design of the Have One label. Direct them to the repeated circles in the figure: the orange, the *O* in "one," the bangle bracelet, the curve of the hand. Students should also notice the similarity between the woman's fingers and the sections of the orange. All these elements constitute an image that is forceful and sensual and that ties in perfectly with the essay that precedes it.

ADDITIONAL WRITING TOPICS AND CLASSROOM ACTIVITIES

• Ask students to search their kitchens for examples of food packaging that has evocative power, and to bring one package to class. Have them write a brief reflection on what meanings the package holds for them and how the meanings are conveyed through the details and the graphic design. Be sure they attach the package itself to their work.

• Ask students to compare the different connotations of the Have One and the California Orange Growers labels. What do the design elements of the labels suggest? How are their advertising styles different? Have students answer these questions in a three-page essay, using specific details from the labels to back up their points.

• **Image/Writing Assignment:** Ask students to write an essay that compares the Have One label to a current ad for oranges or for orange juice. In their essays they should consider how corporate interests are reflected in the contemporary ad. Students might also consider if the message delivered by the current ad is as direct as the injunction to "Have One."

CONNECTIONS WITH OTHER TEXTS

• Ask students to compare and contrast the text and imagery of the Have One label with the text and imagery of Pirelli's "Power Is Nothing without Control" ad (p. 375).

• Today many businesses rely on a symbol—an icon or a logo—to build product recognition and to tie their company to a given product. By contrast, orange growers in the early twentieth century used beautiful graphic art to promote their products and distinguish their brands. Have students look at advertisements for popular brands represented by a logo or an icon (for example, Nike or Volkswagen). Then ask students to freewrite on which approach they think is more effective, and why.

SUGGESTIONS FOR FURTHER READING, THINKING, AND WRITING

PRINT

McPhee, John. *Oranges.* New York: Farrar, 1975. Print. A fascinating book about oranges, orange growers, and oranges through history.

WEB

citruslabelsociety.com. A site for collectors of citrus labels.

Surefire Assignment: From Labels to Logos

Martha Kruse
*University of
Nebraska–Kearney*

In this assignment I ask students to collect a sampling of logos from products in a single category— for example, cars, food, or fashion— and to answer a series of questions. What image are the logos trying to convey? What consumer "buttons" are the logos trying to push? Do the logos seem related to the products themselves (for example, the Chiquita banana logo for Chiquita Brands International)? Or does the power of the logo depend on the associations the viewer must form between product and logo?

Many of my students choose to analyze the logos found on athletic apparel. How do graphic artists convey the notions of speed, power, fitness, and health? How do logos combine with the name of the product to appeal to consumers? Some logos are self-explanatory—a logo made up of a designer's initials would be an example—while others require more creativity to discern their relationship to the product.

Retrospect: Phone Home (p. 54)

This Retrospect shows the progression of the phone and communication advertisements through the years. It starts in 1933 with a phone that feels primitive, old-fashioned, and comical compared to our current perspective. The following images in the series progress through the introduction of long-distance or "out of town" calls, the innovation of the cordless models, and the current interactive phones that include Internet access, texting, and cameras, among other technologically advanced functions. Students can discuss the ways things have changed through technological shifts or the ways each image reflects cultural values and beliefs. They can examine the kinds of lifestyles the advertisements promote through the images and text. They can closely read the copy, look at the images, and examine the artifacts to get a better understanding of what it means to look back, compare, and analyze.

POSSIBILITIES FOR DISCUSSION, REFLECTION, AND JOURNALING

• Students might also look at different rhetorical devices used in the ads and the relationship between images and words for effective rhetorical strategies. For example, you might introduce Aristotle's appeals that aid in persuasion: ethos (ethics and credibility), pathos (emotion), and logos (logic). Have students identify the appeals and how they work to persuade or create a feeling.

• Students can discuss the ways cultural ideologies are expressed through the photographer's choices. For example, which of the ads feature people, and which ones focus more on the technology? What do the setting, lighting, and grouping in the photos communicate? How do students interpret the artifacts included in the images? What do the images say about lifestyle, ritual, values, and beliefs?

• Today our phones are a constant presence in our lives. They have created a society in which we are always accessible. The fact that each person carries around his or her own wireless phone would have been unbelievable back in the time of the first advertisement. People talk on phones in public places, seemingly oblivious of others around. Phones now are also a convenience that we use for research, written communication, and data storage. How has this technology shaped our communication in light of immediacy, disclosure, and social relationships?

ADDITIONAL WRITING TOPICS AND CLASSROOM ACTIVITIES

• Ask students to look at each ad and try to figure out the audience demographics. What evidence can they pull from the copy and images to support their claims? How does the family in the 1958 version differ from that in the 1980 version? What is being communicated through the 1992 version, featuring an independent woman in the forefront and the statement "Don't Be Bound by Convention"?

• Another way into class discussion might be to focus on the relationships between images and words in these ads. You might photocopy the ads and white out the verbal text in each. Then separate the students into groups, and have each group write new copy for one or two of the ads. Each group could then show its ad (or ads) to the class and explain the reasons behind the new text. Did groups that worked on the same ads come up with similar text and interpretations? Finally, have students look again at the textbook and discuss the similarities and differences between their ads and the real ones.

• **Image/Writing Assignment:** Have students conduct a similar commercial analysis of both vintage and current advertisements for an ordinary object. Have them search an online image and analyze the presence and progression of their ordinary object, including lifestyle and ideologies, audience perspective, and the relationship between text and images.

CONNECTIONS WITH OTHER TEXTS

• Have students go to Annie Leonard's Story of Stuff web site and ask them to watch the entire video. Next have them write an essay in which they argue whether or not the ever-changing cell phone technology is necessary, given its negative effect on the environment.

• Have students examine ads for other products over the same periods. Do the ads from the 1940s and 1950s make use of similar techniques and express similar attitudes? Do ads from the 1970s show a shift toward irony and a greater reliance on images? Ask them to write an essay in which they analyze the similarities and differences between ads from two different decades in which significant changes occurred.

SUGGESTIONS FOR FURTHER READING, THINKING, AND WRITING

PRINT

Fischer, Claude S. *America Calling: A Social History of the Telephone to 1940.* Berkeley: U of California P, 1994. Print.

Pincas, Stéphane, and Marc Loiseau. *A History of Advertising.* Cologne, Germany: Taschen, 2008. Print.

Stern, Ellen Stock. *Once Upon a Telephone: An Illustrated Social History.* Boston: Houghton, 1994. Print.

WEB

knowledge.wharton.upenn.edu/article.cfm?articleid=1540. In an excerpt from *Idealized Design: How to Solve Tomorrow's Crisis . . . Today* (Wharton School Publishing, 2006), author Russell L. Ackoff recalls visiting Bell Telephone Labs in 1951 on the day that the vice president of the company called on his employees to completely reimagine the telephone.

corp.att.com/history/history3.html. From the AT&T web site, a history of the Bell Telephone System.

AUDIOVISUAL

History of Advertising: General, 1950–1970. 116 min. 2005. DVD. Distributed by A2zcds .com. A retrospective collection of early television ads.

Surefire Assignment: Adding to the Ad Portfolios

Charles Hood
Antelope Valley College
(Profile, p. 12)

I've been using ads in comp classes for twenty years. So to mix it up a bit term to term and to meet the strengths and weaknesses of any given batch of students, I try to have a variety of ad projects to fall back on. You would not want to try all of the following in one term, but here are five of them. I'm sure there are hundreds more, but these do work—for me and others—just about every time. I use them as fallbacks when an experimental project has flamed out or when I just can't think of something new that day.[1]

1. **Adding to the Ad Portfolio.** Solo or in teams, in the library that day or at home over a week, assign students the task of expanding the suite of ads, including some more recent than those in the book. If *Seeing & Writing* has five shoe ads, ask students to find five more from a broad historical range. This is a good chance for them to learn about microfiche, old magazines at garage sales, and used-book stores. They also may need to learn how to make good-quality color photocopies or to use a scanner properly, so there is some technological competence required in this project as well. Have the individual students or teams share their ads with the class.

2. **Adding to the Ad Portfolio, Redux.** Same project as above, but the students—again working individually or in teams—make up a new set of images, focusing on a topic not covered by the ads in *Seeing &*
Writing 4. Some suggestions: ads for diet sodas, beer, family cars, telephones, or pantyhose. This assignment works best when the topics are narrowed, at least a little bit—ads for diet sodas, then, rather than soft drinks in general. Cigarettes are a fun one to trace backward. One Camel ad used to say "More Doctors Smoke Camels Than Any Other Cigarette," which is always good for a laugh. And an ad for rotary-dial phones from the 1960s brags about one model's "un-obsolescence."

3. **Cut-and-Paste Day.** Depending on how you handle in-class work—I encourage my students to keep their journals in blank-page artists' sketchbooks, which I never, ever collect—have the class bring in back issues of magazines, along with glue sticks and scissors. In their journals or on separate pieces of construction paper, have them cut up existing ads to make a new ad that, for example, promotes a local political cause or next week's homecoming game or whatever. The point is to watch language change as it is taken from one context to another. With luck, students will juxtapose images and words in new ways, often with hilarious results. And students love the sense of "getting away with something naughty" when they are able to sneak in a suggestive phrase or to parody famous people. This kind of activity builds an esprit de corps. Bring a CD player or a laptop, and play some music. You may also want to bring in some older magazines to donate to the cause. (Friends of the Library sales are a good place to pick up old magazines.)

---

[1] I can be reached at chood@avc.edu if you have suggestions for fine-tuning these activities.

4. Selling the Seven Deadly Sins. This project's title alludes to a *Harper's* magazine bit many years ago, when the magazine solicited top ad agencies to design ads selling sin. In this exercise, done either in class with colored pencils and paper or at home with more sophisticated materials, students design ads to sell the unsellable—underage smoking, the destruction of the environment, flag burning, nuclear proliferation, or any other bête noire you can come up with. This might link well to Mark Peterson's *Image of Homelessness* (Chapter 2, p. 169); social programs do indeed lead to homelessness, so you might require students to research and promote a particularly vicious form of capitalism. The point is not to parody but to try sincerely to reach those hidden fears and desires that would cause an average consumer to be pro-X, whatever X is, even if X is inherently evil. The "Context" materials in *Seeing & Writing* lend themselves well to this activity, as does a willingness on everybody's part to let go of political correctness. This can be a frightening project. But if it makes students aware of how easy it is to sell hatred and of how close to the surface people's insecurities and misperceptions rest. . . . In other words, because this is frightening, it is a great chance to teach the hardest lessons.

5. Audience Awareness. There are several ways to use the ads in *Seeing & Writing* to teach about audience. One is the old standby, asking students to identify the target audience for a running shoe ad (for example). How did students come to that conclusion, what conventions of the genre does the ad fulfill, and so forth? Another way to approach an audience is to team up students, assign them two or three ads, and ask them to change the ad so that it finds a new audience. The key word here is *change*. You don't want them creating new ads; you want them changing only certain elements of the existing ads. For example, you might allow them to change the copy but not the image, or to change the colors and props but not the catchphrase. Their goal is to make the ad fit a new audience by making certain choices, which should help them better understand that writers, too, reach their audience by making choices.

Tracey Baran, *Mom Ironing* (p. 60)

Baran's photograph shows an older woman ironing in a small cluttered room, a few feet away from a younger woman. Ask students to examine the photograph and to point out the details that initially strike them. Do they focus on the brighter section of the photo, where the older woman is at the ironing board? or the darker section on the right, where the younger woman is sitting? What draws their attention? How does the photographer direct their attention?

POSSIBILITIES FOR DISCUSSION, REFLECTION, AND JOURNALING

• Why did Baran focus on such an ordinary activity? Can a photograph of something ordinary be art? Or is it simply reportage?

• Does the photograph seem staged? Or does it capture a slice of real life? What details in the photo support your thinking?

• What do the details in the photograph imply about the two women? What do the overflowing table and bookcase suggest about their socioeconomic status? about their interests? What about the clothes hanging above the window?

• What do the positions of the women suggest about their relationship? It seems to be comfortable but not close. With her head down, the older woman seems to be focused on ironing; the younger woman is looking away and appears to be biting her fingernails, not at all interested in what the older woman is doing.

ADDITIONAL WRITING TOPICS AND CLASSROOM ACTIVITIES

• Ask students to imagine that Baran wants to photograph them doing something ordinary in their home — cooking in the kitchen, making a bed, vacuuming the living room rug, dusting the furniture (anything but ironing). Then have them write a detailed paragraph about what the photograph would reveal. Tell students to imagine the scene as a snapshot before they write about it.

• Ask students to write an essay in which they support or oppose defining Baran's photograph as a work of art. They should provide their own definition of *art* and include examples of what they consider to be art. Tell students to write for an audience that is not familiar with Baran's picture, so they have to provide a detailed description of the photograph.

• **Image/Writing Assignment:** Ask students to create an alternate title for this photograph and then write a short essay that explains and defends their choice.

CONNECTIONS WITH OTHER TEXTS

• Pepón Osorio's *Son's Bedroom* (p. 92) displays objects without the person who owns or uses them. Still, the details allow us to make inferences about the boy. Ask students to imagine Baran's photograph without the two women. How would the photograph change? Then ask them to imagine people in Osorio's display. Who do they see?

• Ask students to locate other examples of Baran's work. How does this photograph fit in with her other works?

SUGGESTIONS FOR FURTHER READING,
THINKING, AND WRITING

PRINT

Bernhardt, Debra E., Rachel Bernstein, and
Robert F. Wagner. *Ordinary People, Extra-* *ordinary Lives: A Pictorial History of Working People in New York City.* New York: New York UP, 2000. Print.

Tillie Olsen, *I Stand Here Ironing* (p. 62)

Olsen's story is a first-person narrative in which the main character reflects on the experience of raising Emily, her oldest child. The mother's memories are triggered by a concerned statement from an unnamed person: "'She's a youngster who needs help and whom I'm deeply interested in helping'" (para. 2). Students may wonder about the identity of this person, the "you" to whom the mother speaks in her internal monologue. This person is probably a teacher or a school counselor; beyond that, the person is a device used by the author to trigger the mother's monologue.

On first reading "I Stand Here Ironing," most students will not sympathize with the mother. For one thing, she's reluctant to speak with the "you," wondering "what good it would do" (para. 3). She cites time as a factor and the possibility of guilt, concern that she "will become engulfed with all [she] did or did not do, with what should have been and what cannot be helped" (para. 4). Beyond that, of course, there are the facts of Emily's life. If students criticize the mother, ask them to imagine their own lives from their parents' perspective: How would your parents describe your childhood? your teenage years? Do you think your parents have ever felt as helpless as the mother in Olsen's story does? Direct students to the third paragraph, in which the mother states: "She has lived for nineteen years. There is all that life that has happened outside of me, beyond me."

Help students see that the mother is complicated — and therefore realistic. She cannot be characterized simply as good or bad. She encountered circumstances beyond her control, yet she feels remorse for their possible ramifications. Emily's father left when the child was eight months old because he "'could no longer endure' (he wrote in his good-bye note) 'sharing the want with us'" (para. 8). Forced to work, she had to leave Emily, "a miracle to me," with the "woman downstairs to whom she was no miracle at all" (para. 8), and then bring the child to the father's family. She desperately wanted Emily with her, but that meant saving money for the child's fare and then placing the two-year-old in a nursery school, unaware of "the lacerations of group life in the kinds of nurseries that are only parking places for children" (para. 12). Knowing would have made no difference, though: "It was the only way we could be together, the only way I could hold a job" (para. 13).

Ask students to pay careful attention to her word choice. Does she feel guilt? Does she blame herself? One moment to focus on might be when she recalls a man telling her to smile more at Emily. She wonders: "What *was* in my face when I looked at her? I loved her. There were all the acts of love" (para. 17). You might ask your students about the possible meaning of the word *acts* in this statement. Could it mean that the mother acted out of love? Or was it that she performed the necessary actions? It's not an easy question to answer because Olsen suggests the possibility only subliminally, yet it might cause students to read more carefully for what the mother mentions just briefly or does not explain at all. For instance, in paragraphs 10 and 19, the mother mentions that she had to send Emily away but does not explain why. You might ask students to find similar actions that need more explanation.

Of course the point is not to find evidence to indict the mother but to understand the complexity of her situation. As she states in the first paragraph, she is "tormented" by the request that she come talk about her daughter. Her torment is especially apparent in paragraph 24, where she recalls how she did not comfort Emily when the child had nightmares, where she admits that she put forth more effort for another daughter: "Twice, only twice, when I had to get up for Susan anyhow, I went in to sit with her."

In the end, the mother seems both hopeful and pessimistic. In the last paragraph of the story, she acknowledges that Emily will not reach her full potential: "So all that is in her will not bloom—but in how many does it?" She has hope, though, that Emily will learn that her life has not been determined by her mother's actions: "Only help her to know—help make it so there is cause for her to know—that she is more than this dress on the ironing board, helpless before the iron."

POSSIBILITIES FOR DISCUSSION, REFLECTION, AND JOURNALING

• You might ask students to imagine themselves in the role of concerned educator. How would a teacher or school counselor react to the narrator's statements? Because students tend to trust a story's narrator, this role-playing exercise might prompt them to consider the mother's claims more carefully.

• Students might notice that the iron is prominent at both the beginning and the end of the story. Ask them why Olsen might have placed the mother at the ironing board for the duration of the story. Why isn't she reading or cooking? How is the iron symbolic? How does Emily's life suggest that the young woman has been and still is "helpless before the iron"?

ADDITIONAL WRITING TOPICS AND CLASSROOM ACTIVITIES

• Ask students to write a narrative from Emily's point of view. How would she describe her life? her relationship with her mother?

• Ask students to write an essay that explains how "I Stand Here Ironing" is a feminist text. They should cite specific details from the story and explain the feminist viewpoint as though they are writing for an audience that is not familiar with feminism.

• In classroom discussion, students may have debated how much the mother is to blame for her daughter's situation. Ask them to write an essay in which they argue that parents should or should not be held responsible for their children's actions and happiness. Students should use personal examples and/or sociological research to buttress their claims.

CONNECTIONS WITH OTHER TEXTS

• Ask students to examine Tracey Baran's photograph (p. 60), which depicts a scene reminiscent of Olsen's story: An older woman stands ironing several feet away from a younger woman (possibly her daughter); yet despite their physical proximity, they seem incredibly distant. Discuss the similarities and differences between the two texts. Then ask students to compare the different techniques Baran and Olsen use to create a scene and establish a tone.

• Have students read Eudora Welty's "The Little Store" (Chapter 2, p. 147) and write an essay in which they compare how Welty and Olsen use characters of different ages and backgrounds to create different views of the world.

SUGGESTIONS FOR FURTHER READING, THINKING, AND WRITING

PRINT

Faulkner, Mara. *Protest and Possibility in the Writing of Tillie Olsen.* Charlottesville: UP of Virginia, 1993. Print.

Nelson, Kay Hoyle, and Nancy Huse, eds. *The Critical Response to Tillie Olsen.* Westport, CT: Greenwood, 1994. Print.

Olsen, Tillie. *Tell Me a Riddle.* New Brunswick, NJ: Rutgers UP, 1995. Print.

WEB

mockingbird.creighton.edu/NCW/olsen.htm. The Nebraska Center for Writers web site includes a short biography of Olsen, quotes, an interview, and critical reviews.

AUDIOVISUAL

Tillie Olsen Interview with Kay Bonetti. 77 min. 1987. Cassette. Distributed by American Audio Prose Library.

Portfolio: Pinkhassov (p. 72)

Gueorgui Pinkhassov, *Pregame Prayer; Salat-ul-Zuhr (Noon) Prayers; Day of Miracles Ceremony;* and *Satnam Waheguru Prayer*

Instructors and students often become uncomfortable when the subject of religion is brought into the classroom, and that discomfort is reflected in the general exclusion of religion from most college readers. Finding ways to talk about religion — especially inclusively — is important and can lead to enlightening discussions about personal and group identities, historical changes, and morals and values. Although these topics are addressed in depth in Chapter 5, Examining

Difference, Pinkhassov's photographs of people praying provide a safe introduction to the topic of religion.

The Seeing questions on page 80 of the textbook do an excellent job of focusing students' attention on Pinkhassov's pictures rather than the acts depicted in them. You might ask students to respond individually in writing to the questions, and then separate them into small groups to discuss their responses. Have one student in each group record significant similarities and differences in the responses. Do students feel most comfortable with *Pregame Prayer*—a function of both familiarity with the concept and the low close angle Pinkhassov chose to shoot the photograph, which makes the viewer a part of the group?

Students will probably be least comfortable with *Day of Miracles Ceremony*, which shows a woman lying facedown on the floor of a Buddhist center. Others may find themselves least comfortable with *Salat-ul-Zuhr (Noon) Prayers*, the photograph of three students kneeling and bowing in a library. If students attribute their discomfort to the fact that the men are praying in public, in a place where prayer is unexpected, ask them what makes the public aspect of this prayer different from that shown in *Pregame Prayer*?

Differences among the photographs will probably arise first in the classroom discussion, which will clear the way to talk more freely about their similarities. Students should recognize that all of the traditions Pinkhassov has photographed are "normal" to the people who practice them. By juxtaposing religious practices, Pinkhassov is disrupting the concept of normality. (The plurality of religious expressions here should also help students understand that bedtime prayers are as much a ritual as the Day of Miracles ceremony.) In looking for similarities, students might pick up the fact that most of the people in the photographs are relatively young men. Some might also be surprised by the presence of technology in photographs of what students might perceive to be ancient religious practices.

POSSIBILITIES FOR DISCUSSION, REFLECTION, AND JOURNALING

• Do any of the photographs strike students as being more or less staged than others? How does this affect their reading of the images?

• Some students might notice that, with the exception of *Day of Miracles Ceremony*, the colors red, white, and blue figure in each of the photographs: in the blue sky and the red and white logo of the ballplayers' hats, and in the students' shirts in the library. Ask students if they think Pinkhassov is making a statement here, and if so, what that statement is.

ADDITIONAL WRITING TOPICS AND CLASSROOM ACTIVITIES

• If you anticipate problems with students when it comes to discussing these photographs, you might ask them to freewrite about their views on religion first, to let them express themselves in some way before you focus on the photographs.

• Some students may be surprised by the plurality of religious practices in these photographs: What they are used to seeing in the media are expressions of Judeo-Christian practices. Ask students to research and write a short essay on religious pluralism in the United States. Is the number of different religions increasing in this country? And does an increase in the number of adherents ensure the acceptance of different religions by a society with a long religious tradition of its own? If not, what other factors might be at work?

• Put students into groups and ask them to research the religious practices displayed in these photographs. They could then write brief reports to present to the class on the day you discuss this reading.

CONNECTION WITH ANOTHER TEXT

• Ask students to examine other pictures from Pinkhassov's *Moments of Silence* series. Do students' readings of the pictures here apply to his other photographs? Does he offer other perspectives in the other images?

SUGGESTIONS FOR FURTHER READING, THINKING, AND WRITING

PRINT

Pinkhassov, Gueorgui. *Gueorgui Pinkhassov: Sightwalk*. London: Phaidon, 1998. Print.

Smith, Huston. *Why Religion Matters: The Fate of the Human Spirit in an Age of Disbelief*. San Francisco: Harper, 2002. Print.

——. *The World's Religions: Our Great Wisdom Traditions*. San Francisco: Harper, 1991. Print. Smith explores the central teachings and beliefs of the world's predominant religions.

WEB

bbc.co.uk/worldservice/people/features/world _religions/index.shtml. This BBC web site provides an overview of six major world religions.

poyi.org/61/34/02.php. Pictures of the Year International presents more photographs from Pinkhassov's *Moments of Silence* series. How do they differ from the photographs included here? How are they similar?

time.com/time/asia/features/journey2002/kor _gallery/about.html. A *Time* magazine photo-essay by Pinkhassov.

Brian Doyle, *Joyas Volardores* (p. 81)

What a gorgeous essay. Ostensibly about hummingbirds, Doyle's work becomes a meditation on the characteristics that link living creatures. As he explains in the first paragraph, the title of the essay comes from the name given to hummingbirds by "the first white explorers in the Americas," who dubbed them "flying jewels." This paragraph sets the tone for the essay: the use of detail and metaphor, the sense of wonder. Doyle uses a metaphor in the third sentence to define the size of the hummingbird's heart in familiar terms: "A hummingbird's heart is the size of a pencil eraser." His sense of wonder and knack for detail comes through in the next couple of sentences, as he describes the explorers' amazement with the birds that "came into the world only in the Americas, nowhere else in the universe," and fixes the reader's attention again on their hearts: "more than three hundred species of them whirring and zooming and nectaring in hummer time zones nine times removed from ours, their hearts hammering faster than we could clearly hear if we pressed our elephantine ears to their infinitesimal chests."

On the basis of the first three paragraphs, readers might assume that Doyle is interested only in hummingbirds. In the second paragraph he continues to note details about hummingbirds. He describes their astounding flying abilities, and he offers a long list of extinct hummingbirds—"each the most amazing thing you have never seen." Doyle uses metaphor extensively in the third paragraph, stating that hummingbirds have "race-car hearts," that the energy required to fly fries "the machine," melts "the engine."

In the fourth paragraph it becomes clear that the concept of the heart is what links the paragraphs. Here Doyle discusses the blue whale, which has the world's largest heart. Again notice the use of figurative language: "The valves are as big as the swinging doors in a saloon." In paragraph 5 Doyle links together all life-forms: "No living being is without interior liquid motion. We all churn inside." And in the final paragraph Doyle focuses on the sensitive and tender nature of the human heart.

POSSIBILITIES FOR DISCUSSION, REFLECTION, AND JOURNALING

• A good way into this reading is to ask students to discuss what they found difficult or surprising in it. Some may claim that Doyle is not focused, that he constantly switches subjects, from hummingbirds to whales to humans—even if hearts or "interior liquid motion" connects them all.

• You might ask students to look for points where Doyle hints of his final focus on humans. For instance, his description of whales seems to forecast the deep emotion inside human beings: "The animals with the largest hearts in the world generally travel in pairs, and their penetrating moaning cries, their piercing yearning tongue, can be heard underwater for miles and miles" (para. 4). Similarly, the hearts of hummingbirds almost come to a halt "if they are not soon warmed, if they do not soon find that which is sweet" (para. 2). How might these descriptions of the hearts of whales and hummingbirds apply to humans?

ADDITIONAL WRITING TOPICS AND CLASSROOM ACTIVITIES

• Imitation is a fantastic way for students to add to their writing style. Ask students to notice the rhythm of the first two paragraphs: several short sentences followed by one long sentence. Point out how the length of the longer sentence adds weight to the subject—that is, Doyle employs short and long sentences not just for variety, but for rhetorical effect. Have students rewrite one of their own paragraphs using Doyle's style of several short sentences followed by a long sentence that contains a list of some sort or that makes an almost breath-takingly long statement.

• Doyle breaks readers' expectations, not only with his ultimate point at the end of the essay but also with his playful use of language. Students might wonder how he can get away with "It is waaaaay bigger than your car" (para. 4) and his statement that hummingbirds "have incredible enormous immense ferocious metabolisms" (para. 3). Ask them to write a short reflection on Doyle's rule breaking and what it means to them as writers.

CONNECTION WITH ANOTHER TEXT

• Doyle's use of metaphor may be another way to get into the text. You might begin discussion by directing students to Visualizing Composition: Metaphor (Chapter 6, p. 558) and then asking them to circle all of the uses of metaphor in Doyle's essay. How does Doyle use metaphor? How does metaphor function in Doyle's writing? What is it good for?

SUGGESTIONS FOR FURTHER READING, THINKING, AND WRITING

PRINT

Doyle, Brian. *Credo: Essays on Grace, Altar Boys, Bees, Kneeling, Saints, the Mass, Priests, Strong Women, Epiphanies, a Wake, and the Haunting Thin Energetic Dusty Figure*. Winona, MN: Saint Mary's Press, 1999. Print.

———. *Leaping: Revelations and Epiphanies*. Chicago: Loyola Press, 2003. Print.

WEB

smokebox.net/archives/word/doyleleap202 .html. Doyle's "Leap," a moving reflection on September 11, 2001.

K. C. Cole, *A Matter of Scale* (p. 85)

K. C. Cole addresses the notion of scale in this verbal text. She discusses the biological and physical laws that apply to living creatures, and she emphasizes how size defines our capabilities in a universe ruled by gravity. Cole also suggests that our size acts as an editor of our perception. She quotes Berkeley microbiologist Norman Pace: "We're so hung up on our own scale of life that we miss most of life's diversity. . . . 'Who's in the ocean? People think of whales and seals, but 90 percent of organisms in the ocean are less than two micrometers'" (para. 26).

POSSIBILITIES FOR DISCUSSION, REFLECTION, AND JOURNALING

• This selection encourages students to consider objects at a much smaller scale than they are used to. Start class discussion by asking students which information they found interesting and which they found unbelievable. Many of the details that Cole reveals may disgust your students. How does this newfound knowledge change the way they see the ocean? insects? their faces?

• Discuss with students why Cole claims that "Superman must have been a flea" (para. 4). Why is this relevant? What point is she trying to make? Ask your students to consider this statement and to think about what other myths or legends are disproved by Cole's essay.

• Despite the many scientific details sprinkled throughout the essay, Cole is making a point about human nature. Why did she write this essay? Who is her audience? Is she arguing for a cause? Is she inciting change in her readers?

• "A Matter of Scale" offers a great opportunity to discuss evaluating sources. Does Cole make a compelling argument? Is she a trustworthy source? How do we know this?

ADDITIONAL WRITING TOPIC AND CLASSROOM ACTIVITY

• Cole addresses the difference between quality and quantity: "quantitative changes can make huge qualitative differences" (para. 2). Our society of consumers often idealizes the importance of quantity over quality. Ask students to research a marketable object — for example, a car or a cell phone — and have them argue, in essay form, in favor of a minuscule object's quality over its size or its quantity. What kind of audience do they target? Is the object cheaper or more expensive than the bigger model? (Examples of such objects are Smart cars, keychain digital cameras, and iPod Shuffles.)

CONNECTIONS WITH OTHER TEXTS

• Have students look at the detail and then the full installation of Pepón Osorio's *Badge of Honor* (p. 95). Then have them write an essay about perspective, using Cole as a source.

• Have students look at the cartoon "Wiretaps and Privacy Rights" by Clay Bennett (Chapter 7, p. 625). How does changing the scale reinforce the cartoon's message?

SUGGESTIONS FOR READING, THINKING, AND WRITING

PRINT

Bodanis, David. *The Secret House: The Extraordinary Science of an Ordinary Day.* New York: Berkley Trade, 2003. Print.

Cole, K. C. *First You Build a Cloud: And Other Reflections on Science as a Way of Life.* Fort Washington, PA: Harvest Books, 1999. Print.

———. *Mind over Matter: Conversations with the Cosmos.* Boston: Houghton, 2004. Print.

———. *The Universe and the Teacup: The Mathematics of Truth and Beauty.* Fort Washington, PA: Harvest Books, 1998. Print.

Davies, Paul. *About Time: Einstein's Unfinished Revolution.* New York: Simon & Schuster, 1996. Print.

Margulis, Lynn, and Dovion Sagan. *Microcosmos: Four Billion Years of Microbial Evolution.* Berkeley: U of California P, 1997. Print.

WEB

irl.cs.ucla.edu/papers/right-size.html. An online version of J. B. S. Haldane's 1928 essay "On Being the Right Size," from the UCLA web site.

AUDIOVISUAL

The Films of Charles & Ray Eames — The Power of Ten. 46 min. 1968. DVD. Distributed by Image Entertainment. Directed and written by Eames Demetrios, Charles Eames, and Ray Eames.

youtube.com/watch?v=wm0bIuAVmOA. 9 min. *Powers of Ten* is "a film dealing with the relative size of things in the universe." The video zooms out from a picnic on Earth to the galaxies and then zooms back in to the molecular level.

Pepón Osorio, *Badge of Honor* (p. 95)

In this work Osorio has fabricated a teenager's bedroom. You might begin discussion by asking students to compare the boy's room with their own. What is different about this room? Students will instantly note the obvious difference: the image of the boy projected onto the wall. Ask them to ignore the image for a moment and to examine the room for other details. Which objects stand out the most? What do they suggest about the boy's interests? Students might notice the bicycle, the basketballs, or the basketball posters. They also might notice a room full of masculine images — Bruce Lee and various sports figures.

This image shows only a section of Osorio's work; the other section — separated by a wall from the first — is the father's prison cell. For now, keep that information out of the discussion, and focus on the son's room. When students come to read the context of *Badge of Honor* on page 95, which shows the complete installation, you will ask them how their observations change when the son's room is put into its original and complete context.

POSSIBILITIES FOR DISCUSSION, REFLECTION, AND JOURNALING

• You might have students consider the reality of the boy's room. Does it seem exaggerated to them? Students will undoubtedly point to the video screen as evidence that the room is not real. What else makes the room seem fabricated? Talk about the sheer excess of the room: golden light gleaming on the reflective floor; hundreds of baseball cards covering the back wall; a dozen basketball posters crowding the other wall, which is lined with at least eight pairs of shoes.

• Ask students to consider why Osorio would fabricate an exaggeration of a teenager's room. Does this image say something about teenagers' preoccupation with material items? Is it attempting to counter popular media portrayals of Latinos?

ADDITIONAL WRITING TOPICS AND CLASSROOM ACTIVITIES

• Ask students to use their observations of the room to write a brief profile of its owner.

What are his interests? What is his socioeconomic background? How would they describe his personality?

• Put students into groups and ask them to brainstorm ideas about why Osorio included the video projection in the room.

• Ask students to do some research on Osorio and then to write a formal essay on how his art addresses Latino culture. They should use examples from this detail of *Badge of Honor* and from his other works. They should also consult interviews with and articles about the artist.

CONNECTIONS WITH OTHER TEXTS

• When students have taken the entire work into consideration, ask them to read the full interview with Osorio (available at bedfordstmartins.com/seeingandwriting4). You might focus on two parts in class discussion: (1) When Osorio explains the origins of the piece, you could note that trying to figure out the purposes behind other works should involve students' taking into account the social situations of the time; students need to consider not only the author's purpose but also the forces that influence the author's actions. (2) Students may want to read Joseph Jacob's essay (also available at bedfordstmartins.com/seeingandwriting4) for the "answer" to Osorio's work; in addition, you might encourage them to find their own reading by pointing them to the multiplicity of readings suggested by Osorio, particularly when he states, "Everywhere it goes, it has a different reading."

• The photograph by Mark Peterson (Chapter 2, p. 169) also makes a social statement through visual means. Ask students to consider how the visuals by Osorio and Peterson affect them. What benefits do visual texts have over verbal texts in influencing our emotions?

SUGGESTIONS FOR FURTHER READING, THINKING, AND WRITING

PRINT

Osorio, Pepón. *Con To' Los Hierros: A Retrospective of the Work of Pepón Osorio.* New York: El Museo del Barrio, 1991. Print.

Rodriguez, Clara, ed. *Latin Looks: Images of Latinas and Latinos in the U.S. Media.* Boulder, CO: Westview, 1998. Print.

WEB

feldmangallery.com/pages/artistsrffa/artoso01.html. This page on the Feldman Gallery site features some of Osorio's work.

giarts.org/conf_01/Keynote_Pepon.htm. An address by Osorio.

Surefire Class: Demystifying Prison Life for Greater Reflection

Jason Stupp
West Virginia University
(Profile, p. 20)

One of my major research interests is prison studies—a field that will continue to grow as the U.S. prison population increases. However, although prison expansion is reaching critical levels and more and more nonviolent offenders are incarcerated for longer periods of time than ever before, students tend to know very little about the realities of the U.S. carceral network. This is unfortunate since the rise of the prison has a direct impact on their education. For example, a 2009 study published by the Pew Center on the States found that, over a twenty-year period ending in 2008, state spending on corrections grew 303 percent, as opposed to a 125 percent growth in funding for higher education (14). In other words, over the past two decades, states spent almost three times as much on corrections as on higher education—a trend that is likely to continue (and perhaps worsen). This means that acknowledging and attempting to understand the profound impact of incarceration on our society is fundamentally important to our conception of the state of higher education and of the culture in which our students are being taught.

I explain all of this to my students before having them view Pepón Osorio's *Badge of Honor* (p. 95). I find that they become angry about the justificatory discourse of prison building—the promise of jobs and a boost to the local economy—when they discover that it has a direct influence on the spending resources for the state university that they attend. We discuss how tuition costs increase yearly while state support for higher education seems to decline— a dynamic that never fails to get students talking and debating. Establishing a context for discussions of incarceration is important, and it helps to get students involved early on by letting them know the stakes of the debate and how it relates to them.

After this brief introduction to the state of corrections in the United States, I place students into groups of three or four. Their first goal is to complete, as a group, the following tasks (while still not having seen Osorio's work):

1. Come up with a list of at least ten adjectives you would use to describe a typical prisoner in a state or federal penitentiary. (Interestingly, the prisoner is always male.)

2. Write a paragraph describing what you know about prisons, prisoners, and life inside. What does a typical day consist of? How do prison populations interact? What types of relationships exist between and among prisoners, guards, and other members of this population?

Students are given about fifteen minutes to complete these tasks, after which they report what they've written to the class. There are usually some awkward moments during these presentations, as well as some stifled giggling and discomfort at mentions of rape and becoming someone's "bitch." At a certain point, I'll stop the discussion and ask where students have encountered the information they are so eager to share with their classmates, and, without fail, the majority of students will reference fictional TV shows, movies, or "reality" programs that purport to depict the realities of prison life. By now, students generally begin to see where the conversation is heading, and many are ready to admit that they know little about prisons aside from sensationalized and dramatic accounts, which, besides often being fictional in nature, also undermine the very serious subject matter they deal with.

Once we come to this realization and acknowledge that there is little one can understand or "know" about prison life from the outside, it's time to turn to *Badge of Honor*. I skip right over the selective portion of Osorio's work—the bedroom by itself—and ask the groups to discuss the work as a whole. I walk around during this time and sit in with the groups, almost always as just a listener, and take note of the topics they introduce while debating the "meaning" of the piece. Generally, the topics covered are technology, separation, alienation, communication, and the idea of two different worlds or cultures. When we come together again as a class, I report what I learned while listening in on the groups. I talk about the significance of the "two different worlds" idea, as well as the possibilities (or lack thereof) for communication that they noticed in the photographs. Eventually, one or more students will connect these issues to our previous discussions and the earlier groupwork, leaving us with the notion that, as a society, we often treat the incarcerated as hostile subjects—a largely unknown, unseen, forgotten, neglected, abused, and misunderstood population.

I end with a brief description, borrowing from the words of various imprisoned and formerly imprisoned people, of the experiences of those who are incarcerated in U.S. prisons. I emphasize that no two prisons—and no two prisoners—are alike, but that they are often viewed as such. The goal is to get students to see that prisoners are more than just "criminals"—they were, and are, members of our communities, schools, churches, and, sometimes, families. Inevitably, someone will test the waters by arguing that

there is a class of "criminals" that belongs in prison, that they knew the consequences of their actions, and that they need to be locked up for reasons of public safety. I tend to let the class handle these situations because while most, if not all, students agree that prisons are necessary, many students share stories about family members or friends who have spent time in prison for some comparatively minor offense. I end class by again referencing the Pew study and informing students that one in thirty-one adults in the United States—or 7.3 million people—is under some form of criminal justice system supervision, whether it be in prison, on parole, or on probation. Students are usually shocked by these figures and leave class eager to continue the conversation at the beginning of the next class, when I ask them to freewrite for a few minutes on their experience of the previous class day.

There are many variations of this activity. For shorter classes (fifty minutes as opposed to seventy-five), it may be necessary to cut the initial discussion on the Pew study and maybe just summarize it for students. Also, I sometimes extend this activity into the next class day, asking students in the meantime to look over materials related to *Badge of Honor* online (the *Seeing & Writing* instructor's resources site has some suggested links, and the PBS web site also has many useful materials on Osorio). For a civic engagement or service learning activity, I've thought about combining this lesson with an extra credit activity in which students write letters to governors, members of Congress, or local correctional institutions advocating some kind of positive change in prison culture (whether it be better access to education/literacy programs, more recreational opportunities, and so on). At West Virginia University, the Center for Civic Engagement has contacts with many prisons and local organizations that can set up classroom visits, tours, and other related activities for students.

Overall, however, the goal of this activity is to get students thinking critically by asking them to question their expectations; to practice skills of observation, analysis, and debate; and, eventually, to reflect on the experience. I find that I can connect many of the stated goals of the course to this activity while at the same time bringing a cultural studies and social justice approach to the classroom.

WORK CITED

Pew Center on the States. *One in 31: The Long Reach of American Corrections*. Washington, D.C.: The Pew Charitable Trusts, 2009. Print.

Annie Dillard, *Seeing* (p. 96)

In this excerpt from her Pulitzer Prize–winning book, *Pilgrim at Tinker Creek*, Annie Dillard takes us on one of her walks to the creek. Drawing figurative arrows on the sidewalk, she pursues her passion to see things closely, her focus often on minutiae. Dillard's tone is childlike, personal, enthusiastic; her arrows lead the willing reader to discover the "surprise ahead" (para. 1) and the "unwrapped gifts and free surprises" (para. 2) that are like the pennies she hid for lucky passersby as a child. Dillard doesn't write about dramatic vistas like the Rocky Mountains or the Grand Canyon; instead she encourages her readers to appreciate the smaller, often fleeting spectacle of nature — a fish flashing in the water, blackbirds flying out of a tree, the green ray at sunset — what she calls "the bright coppers at the roots of trees" (para. 4).

As darkness falls, however, Dillard's enthusiasm gives way to an increasing sense of threat. She says, "Night was knitting over my face an eyeless mask" (para. 12). As her ability to see diminishes, her fright increases: "A distant airplane, a delta wing out of nightmare, made a gliding shadow on the creek's bottom that looked like a stingray cruising upstream" (para. 12). Later, safely home, Dillard begins to appreciate the vision given to her by the darkness: "I close my eyes and I see stars, deep stars giving way to deeper stars, deeper stars bowing to deepest stars at the crown of an infinite cone" (para. 14).

The essay is filled with Dillard's careful observations. That she cherishes sight, her ability to see and observe the natural world, is clear throughout the work, especially in the discussion of Marius von Senden's book *Space and Light*, which begins in paragraph 22. Of course for Dillard, seeing is a process; ultimately its value lies in the insights gleaned from observation. The very concrete world she sees around her leads her to the abstract world of inference. Dillard's passion to see and her ability to share her vision through her writing are examples of the highly productive role that being a careful observer can play in our writing lives.

POSSIBILITIES FOR DISCUSSION, REFLECTION, AND JOURNALING

• It may be interesting to ask students what kind of image they have of the writer. Is she a scientist? Or is she simply a woman who becomes frightened because she "stayed at the creek too late" (para. 10)?

• Is her story a personal narrative or a larger commentary on the relationship all of humankind has with both light and darkness? We are, Dillard writes, "still strangers to darkness, fearful aliens in an enemy camp with our arms crossed over our chests" (para. 12). Ask students what they make of that statement. Do they agree with it? Why or why not?

ADDITIONAL WRITING TOPICS AND CLASSROOM ACTIVITIES

• Ask students to write a short piece in class on a natural space that they value. They should include as many details as possible, using Dillard's work as a model.

• Have students isolate one portion of "Seeing" and write a short essay based on the author's imagery. For example, the passage that begins in paragraph 11 with "Where Tinker Creek flows under the sycamore log bridge to the tear-shaped island" and ends in paragraph 14 with "I close my eyes and I see stars, deep stars giving way to deeper stars, deeper stars bowing to deepest stars at the crown of an infinite cone" offers escalating images of fright as the darkness falls.

• Seeing question 2 asks students to consider Dillard's use of the phrases "the artificial obvious" and "the naturally obvious." Have students write a detailed description — and give a single example — of each type of seeing. (Be sure they understand the distinction: The *naturally obvious* is what we laypeople expect to see; the *artificial obvious* is evident only to experts.) As their example of the artificial obvious, students may want to choose something they consider themselves experts in — running shoes for the runners, computers for the cyber-experts, clothing for the fashionistas. Ask students to conclude by agreeing or disagreeing that experts come home with "three bags full," as Dillard suggests in paragraph 8, while to the rest of us all running shoes look alike, all computers do the same mysterious things, and all clothing serves the same function.

CONNECTIONS WITH OTHER TEXTS

• Discuss with your students the question of scale in Dillard's piece and in K. C. Cole's "A Matter of Scale" (p. 85). Both authors are interested in the natural world, and both focus on the significance of being able to see from more than one perspective. Dillard wants to take her pet amoeba outside, show it the Andromeda galaxy, and "blow its little endoplasm" (para. 20). On the other hand, Cole impresses on us how scale can be a critical factor in the physical survival of a species. Talk with your students about the significance of scale in their own lives, and then ask them to write an essay about the importance of categories in their lives and the criteria they use to select and order them.

• Ask students to read Dorothy Allison's "This Is Our World" (Chapter 3, p. 260). Although both Allison and Dillard are interested in describing the world, Allison is interested in the human-made part of it, whereas Dillard is more invested in describing the natural. Which perspective do students find more compelling? Why? Have them write a personal narrative that starts with their responses to both essays and then moves to an analysis of why one subject interests them more than the other — or why both are equally compelling.

SUGGESTIONS FOR FURTHER READING, THINKING, AND WRITING

PRINT

Dillard, Annie. *An American Childhood.* New York: Harper & Row, 1987. Print.

————. *The Living*. New York: Harper, 1992. Print.

————. *Living by Fiction*. New York: Harper Colophon Books, 1983. Print.

————. *Pilgrim at Tinker Creek*. New York: Harper Colophon Books, 1982. Print. The book from which "Seeing" comes.

————. *Teaching a Stone to Talk: Expeditions and Encounters*. New York: Harper Colophon Books, 1982. Print.

————. *Tickets for a Prayer Wheel: Poems*. Toronto: Bantam, 1975. Print.

————. *The Writing Life*. New York: Harper & Row, 1989. Print.

Sacks, Oliver. *An Anthropologist on Mars*. New York: Knopf, 1995. Print. Sacks is a well-known neurologist. His essay "The Case of the Colorblind Painter" is about an artist who can see only in black and white after he sustains a head injury.

WEB

hubcap.clemson.edu/~sparks/dillard/bio.htm. A biography of Annie Dillard.

AUDIOVISUAL

Annie Dillard Interview with Kay Bonetti. 47 min. 1989. Cassette. Distributed by American Audio Prose Library.

The Living. Performed by Laurence Luckinbill. HarperAudio, 1992. 4 cassettes (6 hrs.).

Pilgrim at Tinker Creek. Performed by Grace Cassidy. Blackstone Audio Books, 1993. 7 cassettes (90 min. each).

Surefire Assignment: Learning to See

Jon Lindsay
*Southern Polytechnic
State University*

I first conceived of this assignment as a way to get students to truly see the details and the interconnections of the details in everyday surroundings. I wanted to encourage students to examine closely things they normally take for granted or, worse, do not notice at all. By doing so, I hoped students would think about their places in the world (universe, community, physical location, etc.) and see the integral part they play in the world, as well as the influences and forces that help mold them into the people they are—their bundles of nerves, beliefs, understandings, ideas, emotions.

Besides getting students to notice their surroundings and themselves in those surroundings, I wanted them to practice close observation, to gather details to use in writing essays that are significant in terms of both personal and communal meaning. I also wanted them to explore/discover the true sense of what they have seen by putting their gathered/observed details into a meaningful order. I wanted the assignment to show students how to organize details into an essay that communicates to readers an understanding of the visual world made significant through close study. I also, simply, wanted students to synthesize the connections, feelings, thoughts, and understandings of their inner selves with the details they observe in the real world. Finally, of course, I hoped that through the writing process, students would come to know more about themselves and the world they are a part of.

I intended that successful students would use critical reading (of the place visited, themselves, and Annie Dillard's "Seeing"), analysis, exploration, and discovery through the writing process, and synthesis.

Here is the assignment:

1. Read Annie Dillard's "Seeing" (p. 96).

2. Based on your observation of a place, write a (minimum) 750-word essay discussing what you saw. Visit a place of your choosing (or that the class visits) and take notes as you observe the environment, your relationship to the environment, and your thoughts about the place. Make detailed observations, and integrate the details into your essay.

3. In your essay, use the statements below (all taken from "Seeing") to guide your thoughts and the thinking process. You may quote these statements directly or indirectly, or refer to them as concepts or as principles, but use the ideas in your essay.

    a. "It's all a matter of keeping my eyes open" (para. 5)

    b. "If I can't see these minutiae, I still try to keep my eyes open" (para. 6)

    c. "I see what I expect" (para. 7)

    d. "Sense impressions of one-celled animals are not edited for the brain: 'This is philosophically interesting in a rather mournful way, since it means that only the simplest animals perceive the universe as it is'" (para. 9)

    e. "I reel in confusion; I don't understand what I see" (para. 20)

    f. "I had been my whole life a bell, and never knew it until at that moment I was lifted and struck" (para. 38)

    g. "'Still . . . a great deal of light falls on everything'" (para. 15)

4. As you write your essay, make connections between your inner world (of thought, emotion, ideas, etc.) and the outer world. Consider such things as time, day, month, year, era, epoch, history, community (personal and public), personal awareness, sense of space, and your own self-awareness. Note and record the inferences of your considerations and understandings of their influences on you. Let your sense of understanding of time, place, and self permeate your coming to terms with the meanings you discover.

5. As a way of making connections between you and others, and the outer world, refer to at least one other essay from *Seeing & Writing 4*. Cite it in MLA style, using parenthetical documentation and a works-cited page.

6. As another way of connecting you to others and to the outer world, include in your essay the remarks of another person about what you are observing/discovering/thinking. Quote that person using MLA style, as though he or she was someone you interviewed.

Looking Closer: Unpacking Our Stuff

All the selections in this chapter ask students to look at the ways we are defined by and through our "stuff." The central question of this section is "What does our stuff say about us?" This offers opportunities to talk to students about how they might apply interpretive reading strategies across alternate mediums. You might point out that we can "read" and interpret situations, contexts, snapshots, and objects and that they all convey some sort of meaning for both authors and audiences.

Pablo Neruda, From *Ode to Things* (p. 112)

Pablo Neruda's poem "Ode to Things" explores the ways we bring meaning to the things with which we choose to surround ourselves. He suggests that meaning is not made but understood through context and experiences. He says that the "things" "conspired / to tell me the whole story" (p. 112), implying that our things become artifacts that reflect certain perceptions about our identity and lives. They often do not tell much in isolation, but when they are looked at as a collection, they reveal a larger picture. He recognizes the reciprocal relationship between defining "things" through his individual choice or need and "things" defining him through their ability to provide specific details to others. At the end of the poem he discusses the ways that we give inanimate objects life through their connection to our identity and our everyday lives.

Siri Hustvedt, *Unknown Keys* (p. 113)

Hustvedt's essay describes a time, after her father's death, when she was going through his stuff and found a collection of "unknown keys." Her father obviously marked them in this way ("unknown") because he didn't know where they fit but felt a need to hold on to them anyway. To the author of this piece they each symbolize a story that happened in the past or one that has yet to be told. As a writer, she sees the keys as a metaphorical window into "the peculiar dream spaces of fiction" (p. 113). For her they serve as "literal doubles of the imaginary keys that unlock nameless interiors." Hustvedt now keeps the keys as her own personal writing talisman to give her inspiration, thus populating them with a new, multi-layered meaning.

This essay focuses on the idea that our things often reveal unknown secrets, stories, or experiences. Hustvedt is also fascinated with the idea that her father chose to write and label the collection, thus categorizing them according to his own system or lens of interpretation. These are two ways to productively encourage class discussion as students might look at categories of things and the way their own distinctions reveal something about their personality or lifestyle. They might also reflect on hidden spaces or things long forgotten that act as both memory cues and story starters.

Akiko Busch, From *The Uncommon Life of Common Objects* (p. 114)
In this essay, Busch explores what gives objects their value. She focuses on people's desire to collect and reflect on ordinary objects. She builds a working definition of how we assign value through qualifiers such as monetary, sentimental, and narrative value. Classroom discussion might focus on how we assign value to things, supported through particular examples of these three categories. What makes something worth more on the open market—availability, connection to fame, functionality, or status? How do we attach sentiment to items such as our grandmother's quilt, a rock from a special place, or a lock of hair from our first haircut? Finally, since value is established through the narrative connected to the object, students might reflect on their own stories connected to valued objects.

Busch also talks about "symbolic value," in which there is some sort of personal and cultural value that speaks to agreed-upon meanings—like her wedding ring example. She points to the marketing trends in which businesses try to create "emotionally compelling objects" that distinguish their presence in the marketplace. Ask students to meet in small groups to discuss examples of these "emotionally compelling objects" and the ways they are marketed to create this rhetorical effectiveness.

Students might also consider the ways that the significance of items changes with their context. Point out her examples regarding the vegetable peeler that takes on new meaning when a man tries to help his wife now that she has arthritis, or the increasing need for cell phones in today's world. Have students look at how other "objects of domestic life" have shaped themselves according to changing contexts. You can also encourage them to switch their perspective and look at clusters of these common objects for the ways they reveal particular philosophies, experiences, and lifestyles. She uses the examples of the medicine cabinet, the refrigerator, and the backpack as starting points for this kind of analysis.

Busch suggests that objects act as cultural markers and that although they may be inanimate, they act as "witnesses to human experience" (p. 119). Museum artifacts and pieces of history (such as stone from the Berlin Wall or objects from the World Trade Center) give us insight into the significance and individuals behind major cultural events or historical time periods. Overall she suggests that these artifacts convey the "fragments of a story" through which we can ask students to actively fill in the gaps through theorizing, speculation, and inference making.

In conclusion, the author asserts that "we demand participation from things" and that through our connection to things we gain a "sense of measure in a physical world" (p. 120). She brings her point home through an extended metaphor about a magic box with a hidden coin. She says, "And I wonder if this is the hidden coin, the ability and inclination we have to persuade inanimate objects to be our partners in experience" (p. 120). All of these ideas are great for individual analysis, class discussion, and writing.

Trujillo-Paumier, *This is Daphne and those are her things* (p. 122)

In *This is Daphne and those are her things*, Trujillo-Paumier tries to capture the essence of an individual by photographing some of the most important things in her life. Like other selections in this section, this photograph shows the ways we connect objects and identity. Rather than some of the random, spontaneous images earlier in the chapter, this image suggests a carefully chosen collection of items. You might ask students to collect, list, and photograph a similar gathering of important everyday objects that reflect their identity or lifestyle. In this assignment, students must make particular choices and explain how meaning is communicated through those choices.

Daphne's choices are accompanied by a short biographical piece and a descriptive list that extends the meaning of the images in the photograph. Students might analyze the images first, without looking at the textual explanations, and then discuss how the textual information affects their interpretations. They might also compose a similar companion piece for their photographs of their most important stuff (This is _____ and those are her/his things). Teachers might also use this as a way for students to get to know one another by having them analyze a classmate's things and biographical descriptions.

Annie Leonard, *The Story of Stuff* (p. 124)

This selection is a screen shot from Annie Leonard's The Story of Stuff web site. Leonard explores the question "What happens to our stuff?" and approaches it from a process perspective: Extraction, Production, Distribution, Consumption, and Disposal (p. 124). The web site presentation is the result of ten years of travel and observation of what she calls the "materials economy." This selection takes a global, economic, and political look at how stuff is part of larger systems of influence and power.

Students might discuss their understanding of this process of consumerism and their roles as consumers. They might also use it to reflect on their own ideas related to politics, economic power, and civic responsibility. Have students go to the web site (storyofstuff.com) and view the twenty-minute presentation. Ask them to take notes along the way and discuss their interpretations and connections.

This interactive presentation also provides an opportunity to talk about alternate ways of presenting information. Students can analyze the visual, textual, and spoken dimensions of Leonard's site. How does Leonard use pictures, diagrams, charts, and narration to communicate her ideas? Perhaps students can draw on some of the strategies employed in Leonard's presentation and visually represent other processes.

POSSIBILITIES FOR DISCUSSION, REFLECTION, AND JOURNALING

• Many of these selections involve analysis and representation of our stuff. Generate discussion about the connection between our stuff and our identity. What do we mean when we talk about representation? Identity is a merging of how we see ourselves and how we are seen by others. What is the role of our stuff in this kind of representation? What do our individual things say about us?

• Stuff is both private and public. You might have students discuss these ideas and generate examples of each. Can stuff be both private and public at the same time? Ask students to generate examples. How do our things suggest both personal and public meaning?

• In what ways do we impart meaning to our things? How do our past experiences, connections to others, and location within a cultural context determine meaning? How do we consider inanimate items alive through their ability to move, motivate, or reflect us? How do we become our stuff?

• How does the commercialization of stuff make us want and desire certain things? Students might look at the marketing of stuff within our culture.

ADDITIONAL WRITING TOPICS AND CLASSROOM ACTIVITIES

• Students might explore in an essay the ways our stuff is commercialized. Ask them to explore what makes us want, desire, obtain, and keep certain objects. Why do we get sentimental about some things and not about others? Students can extend this knowledge through Internet research in which they retrieve particular advertisements or messages.

• You might have students "read" one another's stuff. Ask them to bring in a "grab bag" of stuff that they think says something about their lifestyle, ideas, or personality. You can give them all the same size bag so that they are limited to a consistent space. Have students switch the bags in class and make inferences about their classmates through analysis of their stuff. Once again, double-entry journals would work well here. You might follow up by asking students to write a short narrative in which they create a "portrait" of their classmates as they pull together these observations and inferences.

• This section focuses on how our stuff represents our identity. There are many opportunities for students to explore this thread and look at the concept of representation. Ask students to write on some part of their stuff. They might use the images (see below) they generate as starting points for their observations, inferences, and connections between their stuff and their identity. You can pair this thread with any of the assignments or selections below.

• You might ask students to focus on "public stuff" and explore public artifacts such as collections, artwork, landmarks, or historical artifacts. Have them go online and collect research on their public artifact.

• Ask students to read and interpret (in writing) one of their "hidden spaces" (from a list or from an image assignment), making connections between observations and inferences. What do the objects and the setting reveal about them? about the world in which they live? Encourage students to include enough detail to verbally see the space and at the same time to use it to tell a story, define a life, or expand upon a moment. Ask them to elaborate on what the objects say about their ideas, philosophies, or daily life. You might also prompt them to go into the tangential, related experiences that might be revealed through a closer look at these objects in a hidden space.

• **Image/Writing Assignment:** Ask students to take a series of pictures of common domestic objects as suggested in Busch's essay. Have them focus on places that provide insight into domestic life and, perhaps, consumer culture, such as the refrigerator or medicine cabinet. You might also modify this assignment a bit and have them take their pictures of hidden spaces, such as a junk drawer, closet, glove compartment, purse, or backpack.

CONNECTIONS WITH OTHER TEXTS

• Have students choose a family from the chapter's Opening Portfolio (or they may use Daphne from Trujillo-Paumier's photograph) and ask them to write, in Neruda's style, an ode to the family's (or Daphne's) things.

• Have students imagine that Skelcher's magic money box is their good luck charm, much like Hustvedt's "Unknown Keys." Ask them to write a short essay like Hustvedt's in which they describe why their magic money box inspires them.

SUGGESTIONS FOR FURTHER READING, THINKING, AND WRITING

PRINT

Mejivar, Mark. "Full Frontal Fridge: A Portfolio." *Orion Magazine*. September/October 2009. Text by Jennifer Sahn.

Menzel, Peter. *Material World: A Global Family Portrait*. San Francisco: Sierra Club Books, 1995. Print. An excerpt from Menzel's book *Hungry Planet* appears on page 30 of *Seeing & Writing 4*.

Postrel, Virginia. *The Substance of Style: How the Rise of Aesthetic Value Is Remaking Commerce, Culture, and Consciousness*. New York: Harper Perennial, 2004. Print.

WEB

pbs.org/wgbh/roadshow/. The online companion to *Antiques Roadshow* on PBS. The site features appraisal transcripts and slideshows of appraised objects.

AUDIOVISUAL

Hoarders. An A&E TV show takes a look into the lives and homes of people who compulsively hoard—an interesting extreme of assigning meaning to objects.

2

COMING TO TERMS WITH PLACE

How is our sense of place connected to our identities? How do we shape experience and memories through our sense of place? How can students benefit as writers through studying and writing about place? through learning the importance of memory and reflective thinking about place? through rendering portraits of place? through their connections to place and the particular naming of place? These are some of the questions and ideas presented in this chapter.

This chapter asks students to think about place. You might want to start discussion by asking students to list the terms they use for place—words like *home, school, work, town, city, chat room,* and *library,* to name a few. Have the class sort the terms by positive and negative connotations and then by whether they refer to real places or concepts. For instance, students might spend a lot of their time at a computer. Talk about virtual representations of physical places: How is a home page like a home? Ask them to think about the things they do online—research information, chat with friends, shop. In a sense the Internet has become a series of new places: a library, a coffee shop, a mall. You may also want to introduce the notion of virtual community. Students could look at sites like Facebook, MySpace, or Ning, sites that use language associated with community and communal space.

Discuss the distinction former Oakland mayor Jerry Brown makes between place and space: "People don't live in place, they live in space" (p. 130). Do we live in space? And if we do, is that good or bad? Do students agree with Brown that living in space is "an alienated way for human beings to live"? How has the concept of space been redefined in light of our participation in virtual spaces?

The introduction to Chapter 2 is illustrated with Joel Sternfeld's photos of ordinary places that were also the site of some tragic event: such as Mount Rushmore, the grocery store in which Emmett Till was killed, the site where plutonium for the atomic bomb was manufactured, and a bus stop at which a homeless person froze to death. As students look over Sternfeld's work, you might discuss how place is rarely a static thing. Ask students to think about places they know that have changed over time through external factors, perhaps an event or a renovation. Then ask them to think of a place that has changed because of a shift in their perceptions. There is a saying that you can't go back to your childhood home. How do maturity, experience, and distance affect our understanding of and connection to place? Talk about the ways we assign cultural meanings to particular places and the ways our places are both personal and communal. What do students see today, for instance, when they drive by their elementary school? Before talking about these questions in class, have students write down their responses so that they can return to them over the course of the chapter.

Another way to introduce the topic of place is to hand out postcards of a particular city, attraction, or landmark. Give one postcard to each student and then put the students into groups. What does each postcard say about the place? How does it say it? With point of view? lighting? typeface? How do we, as a culture, capture our sense of place through images?

The study of place helps us in our teaching of writing as we encourage students to concentrate on what it means to specifically and particularly render experiences through descriptive narrative. However, it is in connecting these places to memory and meaning in writing that is more significant. Although we want to re-create through words a sense of place to others, we also want students to use these connections to say something interesting, significant, and purposeful. When students reflect on their own connections to place, they will discover more about the nature and order of their experiences and, thus, their identities. The readings in this chapter help students mine this wide range of experiences through this single lens.

POSSIBILITIES FOR DISCUSSION, REFLECTION, AND JOURNALING

- Where are you from? This is a common question that we use to get and give information about our identity. Talk about how this makes us distinctive and, at the same time, part of a larger group. We look for similarities in relation to connections to place, whether it is our hometown or common places we have visited.

- There are cultural assumptions associated with place that leave a mark on our character. Students might discuss how living in their hometown shaped their thinking, actions, and behavior — or what the authors call our sense of "public identity."

- In order to describe place, we must rely on specific details. This subject provides a way for us to talk to writing students about how to render portraits of place through the selection of purposeful details. Students can explore the language and strategies that create effective representation of space and work to incorporate that into their own writing.

- Our relationship with place has changed over the years as we are a more mobile culture. In the past, people stayed in one place for long periods of time. Now a large percentage of Americans change their residence on a more frequent basis. How has this disconnection or fragmentation of space changed our thinking, behavior, and cultural identity?

- How has consumer culture reshaped our notions of space? Students might explore architectural trends that create neighborhoods and lifestyles within suburbia. How are lifestyles such as urban and country living marketed? Ask students to think about how communities are formed through consumer culture icons such as fast food restaurants and department stores.

- How has the Internet and virtual places affected our understanding of place? In these contexts, place is less about physical locality and more about identity construction in visual worlds. How do virtual places like Facebook and MySpace create new language environments?

- Is place really about location, or is it defined through layers of experience? As the authors say, "It can mean the smell of chicken roasting in the oven, the sound of traffic, or a certain song, the sight of a familiar stretch of land." They also recognize that place is about "relationships . . . and our associations with a particular time and space." Encourage students to recognize the ways these layers or spheres of experience exist separately and work together to create a cohesive sense of place.

- Expand on students' sense of place through additional research. They might focus on a particular place and explore folklore, history, politics, land, people, and ideas related to that place. Ask them to incorporate these details (including proper documentation) into an essay in which they describe a particular place.

- Ask students to come up with a brochure for a place of their choosing. Have them isolate what they think is most important to communicate to others through this brochure. They might make this a persuasive document ("Come visit . . .") or a reflective document in which they look at historical or cultural influences. Ask them to think about the rhetorical situation of the brochure as they make choices about purpose, audience, and context. Have students include images, captions, and graphics as they consider document design and visual rhetoric.

- Have students create a community portrait project and conduct a mini-ethnography in which they immerse themselves in a community through fieldwork observation. This project can be completed individually or in small groups. Students should choose a community to which they have strong, personal connections. You might encourage them to consider actual, virtual, or conceptual communities. Have students observe and interview people within that community in terms of their impressions and stories. Ask them to collect and analyze artifacts and historical documents from that community. Have them complete field notes along the way and practice interviewing strategies. You can give them the option of presenting the project in different forms, such as an individual photoessay or a PowerPoint presentation. Ask them to pay particular attention to audience and purpose as they decide on their presentation format.

Surefire Class: Coming to Terms with Place

Kirk Lee Davis
*University of
Michigan–Ann Arbor*
(Profile, p. 10)

Comparison is a writing technique that virtually every college student recognizes as valuable, and most will use it with some frequency in their writing. Not uncommonly, however, when faced with the host of other issues that accompanies the writing process, students fail to sufficiently examine the logic behind their basis of comparison, or set up a comparison so that it yields troublesome either/or arguments.

Scott Russell Sanders's essay "Home-place" (p. 172) can serve as an excellent model for students seeking to use comparison effectively in their writing. But before addressing Sanders's work in the classroom, I open discussion by asking the students to consider Edward Hirsch's poem "Edward Hopper and the House by the Railroad (1925)" (p. 142) in relation to the painting on which it is based. I ask students how their understanding of each piece affects the way they see the other, how they might come to understand the one in terms of the other.

A little grounding in the ideas of color theorist Josef Albers can be useful at this point. I bring to class reproductions of paintings from his *Homage to the Square* series to illustrate a point regarding relationship. Each of his paintings depicts nothing more than a series of two or three colored squares nested within one another. These paintings point to a critical distinction between pigment and hue: When a painter applies paint from a particular tube to backgrounds of various colors, that paint looks different in each instance, a result of its relationship to the background color. Context, then, can change the very color of a color. Similarly, a writer can place two subjects alongside each other to recolor the way their audience sees each subject—in a sense, making each thing into something entirely new.

As they continue to compare Hopper's painting and Hirsch's poem, the students often catch themselves making qualitative judgments, saying that the painting is better in some ways or that the poem is more original. And then, often, someone throws up his or her hands and says it doesn't matter, that they're just different, that one can't expect a painting to "mean" in the same way that a poem does, or vice versa.

That student can then be commended for recognizing that good critical thinkers guard against the temptation to oversimplify, that it's often incorrect to reduce the world to terms of this or that. But I'm quick to point out to my students that in expository writing an author may set up a simple opposition as a kind of dummy, as a way of entering a subject, only to complicate and ultimately renounce the fallacious premise from which he or she begins.

For example, "Psychologists tell us," Scott Russell Sanders writes, "that we answer trouble with one of two impulses, either fight or flight." But he continues, "I believe that the Millers exhibited a third instinct, that of staying put" (para. 4). I highlight this sentence for my students, and we proceed to discuss the many other ways that Sanders treats binary ways of thinking. In the end, then, students learn not only about the either/or rhetorical fallacy but also about how a skilled writer can exploit it as a writing tool.

You can use this discussion to lead into a variety of writing assignments. One I commonly employ asks students to define an abstract noun. Through this kind of exercise your students should come to understand that they will likely have to think more in comparing, say, *kindness* to *compassion* than in comparing *love* to *hate*. It's a fine distinction that separates the first pair: They seem almost to be indistinguishable shades of the same color. The student who attempts to distinguish between two words that seem to be synonyms must address the problem at the heart of all good expository writing—the comparison of what seems to be and what is.

Portfolio: Sternfeld (p. 132)

Joel Sternfeld, *Mount Rushmore National Monument, Black Hills National Forest, South Dakota, August 1994; The Former Bryant's Grocery, Money, Mississippi, June 1994; Hanford Reservation, Hanford, Washington, August 1994;* and *Metro Bus Shelter, 7th Street at E Street, Southwest, Washington, D.C., April 1995*

At first glance there is nothing indicating trauma in these four photographs; only after reading Joel Sternfeld's notes do we begin to find the images disturbing. One could say that the photographs act as a kind of memorial. Of course Mount Rushmore *is* a national memorial. The carved faces of Presidents Washington, Jefferson, Lincoln, and Theodore Roosevelt send a message of a country that is solid, lasting, and powerful. But Sternfeld's photograph (p. 132) is not about "purple mountain majesties." Unlike most pictures of Mount Rushmore, this one does not focus on the faces. The dark frame of trees on the edge suggests a dark history. In the foreground Sternfeld has exposed artifice, the lights that add majesty to the mountain. (The environmentalists among your students may point out that, for the lights to do their work effectively, someone had to cut down the trees in front of them.) Before we read Sternfeld's text describing how the federal government wronged the Sioux Nation, we can tell that Sternfeld is not presenting the typical view of Mount Rushmore.

The story of the second photograph — *The Former Bryant's Grocery* (p. 134) — may be familiar to students. They might know that Emmett Till's murder galvanized the civil rights movement and inspired Bob Dylan to write "The Death of Emmett Till" (if you can find this rare song, play it in class). They might have heard about the recent exhumation of Till's body to conduct a proper autopsy and to potentially find anyone alive who might have been connected with his death (the two men who were charged and found not guilty eventually confessed to killing him). Students also might have heard a different story from the one Sternfeld is telling: Some report that Till whistled at the woman as well. Sternfeld's text is especially effective in its serious and spare documentary tone: "Millam and Bryant were found not guilty by an all-male, all-white jury. The deliberations lasted a little over an hour."

In *Hanford Reservation* (p. 136) we see what looks to be a construction site. Even without the verbal text, something seems awry here: The lifeless area of dirt in the foreground and the machinery in the background contrast sharply, and even amusingly, with the gentle scene of nature depicted on the billboard — a scene right out of *Little House on the Prairie*—and the claim "It's the Nature of Our Business." Sternfeld's text reveals that this was the site of a nuclear reactor and that the U.S. Army purposefully poisoned nearby residents with radiation and poured billions of gallons of chemical and radioactive waste into the ground. The last line of Sternfeld's text—"A massive cleanup effort is underway"—nicely plays off the dirt mound in the picture. The implication: A cover-up, not a cleanup, is in progress.

One unifying feature in the first three photographs is the white sky. In each image the colorless sky makes for a surprisingly stark frame. In *Metro Bus Shelter* (p. 138), the grayish-white building in the background serves the same purpose. According to Sternfeld's text, a forty-three-year-old woman froze to death in this bus shelter across the street from the Department of Housing and Urban Development. By filling the background with the building, Sternfeld makes the bus shelter seem that much smaller. And all of those windows (they continue beyond the frame) suggest that the people inside the building could not have been blind to the conditions outside.

POSSIBILITIES FOR DISCUSSION, REFLECTION, AND JOURNALING

• Ask students to freewrite about what they think memorials do: What is the purpose of a memorial? Then ask them if Sternfeld's photographs do what they think memorials should do. Do his images meet or complicate students' expectations?

• Ask students to look at the photograph on page 134. How would students describe the store? Does it look like just another old market in rural America, quaint and harmless?

• After reading Sternfeld's account of the murder of Emmett Till, ask students to consider the tone of his statement. Is it effective? How do they think viewers would respond to a more emotional account of the murder and trial?

ADDITIONAL WRITING TOPICS AND CLASSROOM ACTIVITIES

• As an in-class assignment to spur more discussion on the tone of Sternfeld's work, have students rewrite the text so that it is more emo-

tional, more judgmental. Then separate students into small groups and ask them to exchange their writings and study Sternfeld's images again with the new text. What happens to their readings of the pictures?

• Ask students to freewrite about the Sternfeld photograph that affects them the most. How do Sternfeld's words play into this? Beyond the emotional impact of his words, how does the composition of the photograph affect them? Ask them to imagine different angles and different lighting. How would those alterations change the power of the photograph?

CONNECTIONS WITH OTHER TEXTS

• Looking Closer: Shaping Memory (Chapter 3, p. 308) presents various representations of the iconic photograph *Marines Raising the Flag on Mount Suribachi, Iwo Jima*. Compare Sternfeld's photograph of Mount Rushmore with the various portrayals of the flag raising. What can students learn about the effectiveness of iconic symbols? What do these landmarks stand for? What are their messages?

• While Sternfeld's photographs allude to lamentable moments, Chris Jordan's capture the direct aftermath of the devastating catastrophe of Hurricane Katrina (Chapter 3, p. 290). Ask students to compare Sternfeld's and Jordan's images. Sternfeld uses his captions to describe the disturbing happenings that occurred, while Jordan uses images alone. Which method is more effective and why?

SUGGESTIONS FOR FURTHER READING, THINKING, AND WRITING

PRINT

Borglum, Lincoln. *Mount Rushmore: The Story behind the Scenery.* Las Vegas: KC, 1977. Print.

Hudson-Weems, Clenora. *Emmett Till: The Sacrificial Lamb of the Civil Rights Movement.* Troy, MI: Bedford, 1994. Print.

Metress, Christopher, ed. *The Lynching of Emmett Till: A Documentary Narrative.* Charlottesville: U of Virginia P, 2002. Print.

Smith, Rex Alan. *The Carving of Mount Rushmore.* New York: Abbeville, 1985. Print.

Sternfeld, Joel. *On This Site: Landscape in Memoriam.* San Francisco: Chronicle Books, 1996. Print.

WEB

citypaper.net/articles/032097/article016.shtml. *Philadelphia City Paper*'s online article about Sternfeld's *On This Site.*

nps.gov/moru/. The National Park Service offers a different view of Mount Rushmore.

pbs.org/wgbh/amex/rushmore/. PBS's companion site to the film *Mount Rushmore,* which originally aired on *American Experience.*

pbs.org/wgbh/amex/till/. PBS's companion site to the film *The Murder of Emmett Till,* which originally aired on *American Experience.*

AUDIOVISUAL

Mount Rushmore. American Experience Series. 60 min. 2001. VHS/DVD. Distributed by PBS Home Video.

The Murder of Emmett Till. American Experience Series. 60 min. 2003. VHS/DVD. Distributed by PBS Home Video.

Pair: Hopper & Hirsch (p. 142)

Edward Hopper, *House by the Railroad*
Edward Hirsch, *Edward Hopper and the House by the Railroad (1925)*

This pair of verbal and visual texts is organically related: Hirsch wrote his poem about Hopper's painting. You might start by giving students this information and then asking them what reflections of the painting they see in the poem. Hopper centers the house in the frame of the painting, "in the exact middle" (line 1). As Hirsch notes, it is a solitary object, "so desperately empty" (l. 13). There are no signs of life anywhere in the painting: The sky "is utterly vacant / . . . There are no / Trees or shrubs anywhere" (ll. 15–17); even the train tracks are empty. For Hirsch there is nothing welcoming about the house by the railroad.

In the first two stanzas of the poem, Hirsch personifies the house: It is "gawky" (l. 2) and "ashamed of itself" (l. 5). In the third, he introduces the painter as a personality. And in the sixth, he assigns to the painter the same emptiness and shame the house "feels": "The house begins to suspect / That the man, too, is desolate, desolate / and even ashamed." You might want to work through the poem line by line with the class and track the way in which Hirsch shifts between the house and the painter. The poem eventually becomes, at least in part, a meditation on how an artist's inner self, an emotional space, becomes the source of his or her art.

Hirsch's poem contains the lines "the house / Must have done something against the earth" (ll. 17–18). But the house, in fact, is not "against the earth"; it seems to have no foundation.

POSSIBILITIES FOR DISCUSSION, REFLECTION, AND JOURNALING

• Ask students if it was Hopper's intention to make the house look abandoned, alone. Are there other aspects of the painting, aspects that Hirsch doesn't mention in the poem, that add to the sense of desolation? If necessary, point out the windows, which are curtained, shaded, or black. The gray house could be seen as growing out of the similarly gray sky or as a stark silhouette superimposed on its environment.

• Ask students to identify the story of this poem. Is it about a man creating a place? Or is the place "writing" the man?

• The two works raise the question of how artists create and define a space, how they delimit one space from another. Hirsch mentions the architectural elements of this painting (the rooftop, the porch). Ask students to study the picture. Has Hopper succeeded in using those elements to build a three-dimensional space out of flat canvas?

• Ask students to study the final lines of Hirsch's poem: "someone American and gawky, / Someone who is about to be left alone / Again, and can no longer stand it" (ll. 38–40). Is there something singularly American about being alone, both in the sense of being an individual and in the sense of not being secured to a place?

ADDITIONAL WRITING TOPICS AND CLASSROOM ACTIVITIES

• Before they read Hirsch's poem, ask students to study Hopper's painting and write their own short description of it. Then have them read the poem. How does their descriptive language differ from the language Hirsch uses? How do they explain the points of convergence and divergence?

• Hirsch writes: "the man behind the easel is relentless; / He is as brutal as sunlight" (ll. 9–10). Ask students to write an essay in which they explore how Hopper uses sunlight, and the shadows it creates, in his painting. How do light and dark in the painting combine to create meaning?

CONNECTIONS WITH OTHER TEXTS

• Hirsch's poem colors how we read Hopper's painting, much like Joel Sternfeld's words alter our reading of his photographs. Have students turn to the Sternfeld Portfolio, which begins on page 132, and look only at the photographs.

(They can cover the verbal text with a sheet of paper; or you might photocopy the photographs, whiting out the text.) Ask them to record their impressions. Then have them look at the images again, this time reading Sternfeld's words, and record their impressions again. How have the verbal texts changed their readings of the visual texts?

• Refer students to James Nachtwey's photograph *Crushed Car* (Chapter 3, p. 284), which presents a desolate image of New York City on September 11, 2001. Ask students to list five adjectives that describe Nachtwey's photograph and five adjectives that describe Hopper's painting. Do the works evoke similar feelings? If students agree that they do, ask them why. How does each artist set the tone of his work?

SUGGESTIONS FOR FURTHER READING, THINKING, AND WRITING

PRINT

Berkow, Ita. *Edward Hopper: An American Master*. New York: Smithmark, 1996. Print.

Hirsch, Edward. *Earthly Measures: Poems*. New York: Knopf, 1994. Print.

————. *For the Sleepwalkers: Poems*. New York: Knopf, 1981. Print.

————. *How to Read a Poem and Fall in Love with Poetry*. New York: Harcourt Brace, 1999. Print.

Hirsch, Edward, ed. *Transforming Vision: Writers on Art*. Boston: Little, Brown, 1994. Print. Famous writers' thoughts on works of art, selected and introduced by Edward Hirsch.

Levin, Gail. *Edward Hopper: The Art and the Artist*. New York: Norton, 1991. Print.

Strand, Mark. *Hopper*. Hopewell, NJ: Ecco, 1993. Print.

WEB

artcyclopedia.com/artists/hopper_edward.html. The Artcyclopedia guide to online sites on Edward Hopper.

AUDIOVISUAL

Edward Hopper: The Silent Witness. 43 min. 1995. VHS. Distributed by Kultur. A docudrama tour of Cape Cod in conjunction with paintings by Hopper. "Chiefly criticism of his work."

Surefire Assignment: Haunted Houses

Martha Kruse
*University of
Nebraska–Kearney*

Of *House by the Railroad*, Edward Hirsch writes, "The house must have done something horrible / To the people who once lived here" (ll. 11–12). Popular culture offers many examples of haunted houses. In this assignment I ask students to describe how memories or ghosts can haunt a place, or why the haunted house, this cultural icon, has such a claim on our imagination. Many students write about the haunted houses they have seen in films, but others describe haunted houses in their own neighborhoods, houses whose occupants have suffered tragic or untimely deaths. One particularly memorable essay began with the scene in *Forrest Gump* in which Jenny throws rocks at the house where she had suffered her father's abuse. The student went on to describe a similar situation in her hometown; after the family suddenly left town, the house remained vacant and was finally torn down. I have inferred that even in the smallest towns, there is usually a house that harbors sad secrets.

Eudora Welty, *The Little Store* (p. 147)

"The Little Store" is a poignant remembrance of what a child sees (and doesn't see) as she grows up, as well as a study of the way in which place can be at once incredibly expansive and narrow when viewed through the eyes of a child. Welty centers her memoir on a specific place, the neighborhood grocery. You can help students understand how Welty uses that place to organize the structure of the narrative by walking through the narrative with them. First comes her trip to the store, related through the sights and sounds she encounters (paras. 3–11). She remembers the trip by people as well as places.

Welty's trip to the store is marked by sights and sounds; once there, though, she responds first to the smells—of "licorice" and "dill-pickle brine" and "ammonia-loaded ice" and "perhaps the smell of still-untrapped mice" (para. 13). Then she proceeds to catalog the store's items. Point out to students that her descriptions situate readers at "child's eye level" (para. 17): The cheese is "as big as a doll's house" (para. 16), and "a child's hand" reaches in for the candy (para. 17). But remind them that the narrative combines both the child's voice and the adult's, as toys and candies are balanced against influenza and violent death.

Talking about "The Little Store" is a good springboard for a more general discussion about how an author creates a sense of place. Welty does this by appealing to all the senses, not just sight. She also evokes a realm beyond sense, what we cannot really see about places and people. When she writes of seeing things "at a child's eye level," she is reminding us not just of what she could see but also of what she could not. In fact, Welty tells us almost as much about what she couldn't see as about what she could: She had never seen the Monkey Man at the store or sitting down (para. 25); she "seldom saw" Mr. Sessions and the woman who worked at the back of the store—his wife? his sister?—"close together, or having anything to say to each other" (para 28); she had never seen the family "sitting down together around their own table" (para. 28). She had never even thought about the family "living . . . in the upstairs rooms behind . . . the shaded windows" (para. 28).

POSSIBILITIES FOR DISCUSSION, REFLECTION, AND JOURNALING

• Ask students to consider whether the insular world of a small town encourages associations such as those Welty makes to the sidewalk and the principal's house. Do all familiar places carry associations? To what degree do those associations determine our identities and memories?

• Welty writes, "Setting out in this world, a child feels so indelible. He only comes to find out later that it's all the others along his way who are making themselves indelible to him" (para. 11). Make sure students understand the word *indelible*. Do they agree with Welty's observation?

- Ask students to look at *Storekeeper, 1935* (p. 146), a photograph taken by Welty. Point out that she allows the viewer to see only half of the storekeeper clearly: Half of his face and a little more than half of his body are in shadow. How does what we cannot see of a person or a place help to define our sense of that person or place?

ADDITIONAL WRITING TOPICS AND CLASSROOM ACTIVITIES

- Ask students to list the ways in which they experience their favorite place with all five senses and then to use their lists to build a short paper, focusing on one sense in each paragraph. This exercise can help students understand the devices that give structure to paragraphs and essays.

- The last paragraph of Welty's piece begins with a dramatic statement: "We weren't being sent to the neighborhood grocery for facts of life, or death. But of course those are what we were on the track of, anyway" (para. 31). Ask students to write an analysis of "The Little Store" using this statement as a point of departure. How does the trip to the neighborhood store offer the young Welty "facts of life, or death"?

- Welty writes, "But I didn't know there'd ever been a story at the Little Store, one that was going on while I was there" (para. 28). It is only in retrospect that she comes to understand the importance of this place and story. Ask students to write a short memoir of a place, with the goal of revealing the story they hadn't realized was there.

CONNECTIONS WITH OTHER TEXTS

- Ask students to compare the descriptive language used by Welty with that used by David Guterson in "No Place Like Home" (p. 158). What kind of language does each writer use to draw the reader into a specific place?

- Have students compare the narrative points of view in Welty's memoir and Larry Woiwode's "Ode to an Orange" (Chapter 1, p. 48). How does each author use a child's point of view to convey a sense of wonder in relating an everyday experience?

SUGGESTIONS FOR FURTHER READING, THINKING, AND WRITING

PRINT

Welty, Eudora. *Collected Stories*. New York: Harcourt Brace Jovanovich, 1980. Print.

———. *Eudora Welty: Photographs*. Jackson: U of Mississippi P, 1989. Print. With a foreword by Reynolds Price.

———. *The Eye of the Story: Selected Essays and Reviews*. New York: Random House, 1978. Print.

———. *One Time, One Place: Mississippi in the Depression*. New York: Random House, 1971. Print. A collection of Welty's black and white photographs, including *Storekeeper, 1935*.

WEB

olemiss.edu/depts/english/ms-writers/dir/welty_eudora/. A directory of Welty's photographs and a long article placing her works in the context of the South. The site is maintained by the University of Mississippi.

AUDIOVISUAL

Eudora Welty Reads. HarperCollins, Caedmon, 1992. 2 cassettes (98 min.). Includes "Why I Live at the P.O.," "A Memory," "A Worn Path," "Powerhouse," and "Petrified Man."

Retrospect: 65 East 125th St., Harlem (p. 156)

This Retrospect offers twelve photographs by Camilo José Vergara of the same address in Harlem over a thirty-one-year span, from 1977 to 2008. The first image (*December 1977*) shows a funky yet clean establishment painted in bright colors. In January 1980 the building is painted black but is still clean, and decorated tiles lead to the front of the store. By December 1983 the store has been split in two—there seem to be two owners now—and the neighborhood clearly has changed: Safety is an issue (notice the security door on the right), and deterioration has set in (notice the condition of the decorative tile). In November 1988 the stores have new owners again. Point out that just one of the tenants, the small, dark grocery/candy/smoke shop, remains at the address over several years. Ask students to consider why and how the store is able to stay in business while the store on the left has trouble maintaining a tenant. What does the grocery store offer to area residents? By November 1988 the decorative elements of both stores have disappeared.

In September 1992 the first graffiti appear on the storefront on the left; by August 2001 the problem has spread to the grocery store too. The sidewalk is cleaner in August 2001, but the building has lost all of the charm and character it had in 1977: The decorative tile is gone, the paint is dull, and the empty store is battered. The 2001 Top Gear store, which hoped to appeal to a younger market with clothing and CDs, is already empty by April 2003. In 2004 Sleepy's ("The Mattress Professionals") enters the scene.

POSSIBILITIES FOR DISCUSSION, REFLECTION, AND JOURNALING

• Ask students to compare the tenants who have shared this location. How is the latest tenant different? Does the fact that Sleepy's looks as though it is part of a chain signal hope? What do students make of the two people looking at the store?

• In the discussion you may want to ask why Vergara chose to photograph this particular place, an address in Harlem. Was he anticipating change here? Was he expecting the obvious decline over the years in the neighborhood?

Certainly the deterioration reveals social, cultural, and economic changes that affect inner cities far more harshly than they do suburbs, and inner cities in the Northeast—areas that often relied on industry—the hardest.

ADDITIONAL WRITING TOPICS AND CLASSROOM ACTIVITIES

• You might ask students to list the details that they immediately notice about Vergara's photographs. What stands out? Why? Which photo draws their attention first? Ask them to write a short piece in class on how one particular photograph captures their eye.

• Ask students whether these pictures reveal the transience of our society—our sense of space rather than place. Or do they think the photographs capture an urban landscape that actually changes little? Have students write a brief essay in which they support one or the other of these theses using the photographs as evidence.

• Despite the street's decay, the grocery/candy/ smoke shop manages to stay in business for close to a decade. You might direct students to investigate the issue of smoking and African Americans, a controversial topic within African American medical and social-activist communities.

CONNECTIONS WITH OTHER TEXTS

• Ask students to compare the later photographs in this series with Mark Peterson's *Image of Homelessness* (p. 169). What similarities do they notice in the framing? in the objects included? In an essay ask students to examine the ways in which photographers guide their viewers to form opinions about a subject.

• Have students look at Retrospect: Phone Home (Chapter 1, p. 54). Ask them to write a narrative from the perspective of an immigrant who moved to the United States in the 1980s. Based on the products shown in the Retrospect from Chapter 1 and the storefronts shown in Chapter 2, what would the immigrant think of consumer culture in America in the 1980s?

SUGGESTIONS FOR FURTHER READING, THINKING, AND WRITING

PRINT

Vergara, Camilo J. *The New American Ghetto.* New Brunswick, NJ: Rutgers UP, 1995. Print.

WEB

harlemlive.org/main.html. An online publication about Harlem by Harlem youth that includes valuable links and offers a solid counterpoint to this chapter's Retrospect.

Surefire Assignment: "The Building Said It"

Joyce Stoffers
Southwestern Oklahoma State University
(Profile, p. 18)

For a journal writing assignment of at least 250 words, I ask students to write a first-person narrative adopting the persona of the building in Vergara's photographs. Because the pictures cover a twenty-seven-year span and because most of my students are only about seven years shy of having spent that much time on this planet, they have a starting point for their identification. I encourage them to draw parallels with events from their own lives and to refer to those events in some way. For example: "When Krista Hall was just starting school, I was also starting something new—a new business. I was so excited!" This is one of the few times when just about all of the students are willing to read their work to the class without much coaxing. I think the mask of writing in an adopted persona helps protect them. If what they write is a bit edgy or experimental, it's okay because they have the rare opportunity to disavow responsibility by looking innocent and saying (much like Flip Wilson used to blame the devil), "The building said it." In the tense first weeks of classes, the exercise is an effective icebreaker. And it's an effective writing tool. In addition to learning about description, point of view, voice, tense, tone, and historical context, students also learn to make organizational decisions: Should they write the piece in chronological order, following the sequence of the images? Should they write it in retrospect? Should some years be grouped together thematically? During the revision phase we inevitably wind up discussing ways to make the writing more interesting. For example, we usually address ways to avoid starting each sentence with a date or a year, which gets students practicing coordination, subordination, and transitions. And because the exercise is a touchstone for so many concepts, we refer to its lessons throughout the year.

David Guterson, *No Place Like Home: On the Manicured Streets of a Master-Planned Community* (p. 158)

Guterson's essay describes his trip to and encounters with residents of Green Valley, Nevada. He uses several rhetorical strategies to indicate that this place is really "no place like home." For example, Guterson uses comparison to play the sterility of the community against the wildness of the desert. He encourages the reader to identify with the rebellious children, especially with Jim Collins, and to pity the frightened adults, like the Andersons. He even compares the failures of Green Valley with the failures of Eden: "Even Eden—planned by God—had serpents, and so, apparently, does Green Valley" (para. 27). The reader is led to believe that those who have come to this place have found not utopia but an empty promise.

Guterson argues that residents of the town become part of the place, that it shapes them by "Green Valley-ing" them. The process involves rigid standardization, so that one house looks like the next and the community becomes a "seamless facade of interminable, well-manicured developments" (para. 2). The city is one of a growing number of planned communities in the United States, and the proliferation of these developments is clearly troublesome to Guterson.

Authors often deploy information to make their own points, with varying degrees of subterfuge about that purpose. Guterson presents himself as "a journalist" (para. 25), which would lead readers to think that his presentation is neutral, objective. However, although Guterson never comes out and says, "Green Valley is insidiously evil," that is essentially his message. If students don't see this, you should alert them to Guterson's use of connotation. When he writes, "I'd come to Green Valley because I was curious to meet the citizens of a community in which everything is designed, orchestrated, and executed by a corporation" (para. 3), he starts with an innocent term, *curious*, but ends with *executed*—a wonderful turn of phrase. Guterson also paints the citizens of Green Valley in unflattering terms. In the end Guterson's judgment of the citizens of Green Valley is harsh: They are fools who have traded "personal freedoms" for "false security" (para. 38).

POSSIBILITIES FOR DISCUSSION, REFLECTION, AND JOURNALING

• Green Valley is a planned community that "is as much a verb as a noun, a place in the process of becoming what it purports to be" (para. 2). You might ask students to consider how a city can be a verb, how its name can connote an action as well as a place.

- You may want to discuss Guterson's bias. What is his agenda? Did he go to Green Valley on a fact-finding mission? Or did he start out with a conclusion and then gather facts to support it?

- Do we need to know that Phil Anderson, the accountant, is "overweight" (para. 14)? Should we take at face value Guterson's characterization of the residents' responses to his queries as "almost never entirely forthcoming" (para. 25)?

ADDITIONAL WRITING TOPICS AND CLASSROOM ACTIVITIES

- Ask students to consider how closely their neighborhood resembles Green Valley. Have them write a short essay in which they argue for or against planned communities on the basis of their own experience.

- Guterson presents his research on Green Valley not just to inform his readers but also to persuade them to agree with his point of view about planned communities. Ask students to write an analysis of Guterson's persuasive language, paying special attention to how he characterizes both the community and the people he interviews. If you feel comfortable with the terms, explain the basic argumentative appeals *ethos*, *pathos*, and *logos* to students, and have them identify the ways in which Guterson appeals to authority, emotion, and logic.

- Guterson notes that no one seems to use the Green Valley civic center plaza, describing it as "deserted, useless, and irrelevant" (para. 4). Ask students to identify a broad open area on campus or in a nearby town. They should do a brief field study of the area, sketching its layout, charting its use at different times of day, interviewing visitors, and so on. From this information, have them construct a persuasive essay that identifies two or three key reasons for the success or failure of this public space.

CONNECTIONS WITH OTHER TEXTS

- Based on what students have learned from *Image of Homelessness* (p. 169), how do they think Mark Peterson, the photographer, might read Guterson's essay? How do they think the homeless person might read the essay?

- At the end of *The Wizard of Oz*, Dorothy returns from Oz by clicking her ruby slippers together and repeating, "There's no place like home." Guterson borrows his title from Dorothy's invocation. Have students draft an essay in which they consider the implications of Guterson's title and compare the description of the master-planned community with the wonderful world of Oz.

SUGGESTIONS FOR FURTHER READING, THINKING, AND WRITING

PRINT

Frantz, Douglas, and Catherine Collins. *Celebration U.S.A.: Living in Disney's Brave New Town*. New York: Henry Holt, 1999. Print. The authors and their children lived in Disney's planned community for two years.

Guterson, David. *The Country ahead of Us, the Country Behind*. New York: Harper & Row, 1989. Print.

———. *East of the Mountains*. New York: Harcourt Brace, 1999. Print.

———. *Snow Falling on Cedars*. San Diego: Harcourt Brace, 1994. Print.

Sternfeld, Joel. *American Prospects: Photographs*. New York: Times Books, 1987. Print.

AUDIOVISUAL

The Wizard of Oz. 110 min. 1939. VHS/DVD. Distributed by Warner Studios. The film is alluded to in the title of Guterson's essay. It is an excellent primer on how an artist uses color and tone to establish place.

Surefire Assignment: You Are Where You Live—or Are You?

Maureen Ellen O'Leary
Diablo Valley College
(Profile, p. 16)

I begin my freshman composition course with a unit on place. I use place as the prompt for the writing sample I like to get from students during the first week of class. Taking my cue from the introduction to Chapter 2 of *Seeing & Writing*, I ask students to respond to the saying "You can take the kid out of Brooklyn, but you can't take Brooklyn out of the kid." Their task is to replace *Brooklyn* with their own town or city, one they have spent a significant amount of time in or one that has had a significant impact on them. Not surprisingly, some students respond eagerly to the prompt, writing pages upon pages, while others struggle mightily to eke out even one page, unable to identify particular characteristics of the place they live or lived in, never mind identify how those characteristics are reflected in themselves.

This writing exercise not only breeds a lively postwriting discussion but effectively introduces the issue we will explore together in the following few weeks: What connection is there between place and identity, between where we live and who we are? In discussions, students notice very different answers from those who live, for example, in Berkeley and San Francisco and those who live in suburban communities like Walnut Creek, Danville, and Pleasant Hill (where our college is). We have rich and often passionate discussions about whether a kid raised in the suburbs is different (And how and why and does it matter?) from a kid raised in, to introduce a personality-heavy city,

Oakland. Some students cling to the idea (desperately?) that *where* you are really makes little difference in *who* you are or might become. Others argue the opposite with equal tenacity. We end up gravitating toward one large place/identity question with two prongs: Can we find specific qualities, traits, and values reflected in particular places? And what shaping effect—if any—do these places have on their inhabitants? We explore these and related questions through a series of interconnected readings, visuals, focused freewrites (at home and in class), and small-group and whole-class discussions. All of this work on place culminates in a formal essay with a number of topic choices.

One topic is based on Guterson's "No Place Like Home: On the Manicured Streets of a Master-Planned Community." This essay provokes strong responses from the students, in class and on paper. A number of my students live or have lived in gated communities exactly like the one Guterson describes. Some—recognizing that it is not cool to approve of these communities and, perhaps, exaggerating their responses—condemn them, lamenting how sterile and rule-bound they are, how superficial and materialistic the residents are. They talk dismissively about the look-alike houses and the perfect lawns and the life-empty streets. Others defend their gated communities; they feel fortunate, they say, and talk about the "family values," safety, and easy, healthy living enjoyed in these carefully regulated settings. Many students make a clear distinction between the kind of place it is okay to live in when one is young and the kind of place appropriate for raising a family. They argue that a suburban setting, not unlike Green Valley, is the ideal place to raise children—and that they intend to do just that. I urge students to consider what is lost and what is gained in this kind of environment, what we must sacrifice and what we get in return. Green Valley claims to be "all that a community can be" (para. 11). What, I ask them, is that? What should a community be? Often we invoke Scott Russell Sanders's essay "Homeplace" (p. 172)—the first text students read—in our discussion of Green Valley. I ask them if Sanders could have written his lovely essay if he had grown up in Green Valley, and if not why not.

For their formal essay, I give students this prompt: *Guterson paints a pretty grim portrait of planned and, by extension, suburban communities as yet untouched by the "undesirable aspects of the city." Using material from "No Place Like Home" and your own experiences with such communities—both direct and indirect (from films, say, or other readings)—write an essay exploring who or what we become as a consequence of living in a controlled environment. You can challenge or confirm Guterson's views—or do both.*

This prompt has generally produced interesting, thoughtful essays. Although most students share the concerns Guterson reflects in his essay, a few do not; and they argue passionately and persuasively that planned communities offer families a good, safe, happy life. And who doesn't want that?

Mark Peterson, *Image of Homelessness* (p. 169)

Mark Peterson's photograph may be jarring to students. If homelessness has not come up in class discussion as you've moved through the chapter, this would be a good time to talk about the growing population of people who don't have a home, whether by choice or otherwise. Many of the selections in this chapter focus on rural or small-town spaces, and many of the selections in the textbook have been produced by people who have been educationally and economically privileged. *Image of Homelessness* reminds us that some people don't have the freedom to choose the kind of place they inhabit.

POSSIBILITIES FOR DISCUSSION, REFLECTION, AND JOURNALING

• Ask students how this image — a cardboard box with a pillow and blanket visible within — says something different about homelessness than a photograph of a person sleeping on a park bench would.

• How has this homeless person created a sense of place? What details in the photograph suggest a larger space?

• Do students think Peterson is trying to make a specific social statement? If so, what is it?

ADDITIONAL WRITING TOPICS AND CLASSROOM ACTIVITIES

• Ask students to write a personal response to Peterson's photograph. How does it make them feel to look at this image? What aspect of the image causes a particular response? Would they respond in the same way to other images of homelessness?

• Ask students whether they think homeless people have the same sense of home, place, and community as do those who pay rent for an apartment or have a mortgage on a house. Have students write an essay that considers the effects of a person's economic circumstances on his or her attitude toward an issue like place.

• Have students spend some time researching homelessness in their community. How extensive a problem is it? What is the community doing to address it? Students should also obtain statistics about the number of homeless people in their state and in the country so that they have a context within which to evaluate their own community. Ask them to write a paper that sums up their findings and draws conclusions about homelessness as a local, state, and national problem.

CONNECTIONS WITH OTHER TEXTS

• Both Mark Peterson's *Image of Homelessness* and Camilo José Vergara's images of an address in Harlem (p. 156) document urban settings. Have students write informally about the statement they think this group of photographs makes about urban environments.

• Have students watch *My Own Private Idaho*, a movie that seems to glorify the lives of homeless youth. Assign a paper in which students define *homelessness* as the movie presents it and then compare that definition with the definition suggested by Peterson's *Image of Homelessness.*

SUGGESTIONS FOR FURTHER READING, THINKING, AND WRITING

PRINT

Kozol, Jonathan. "Are the Homeless Crazy?" *Harper's* 277 (September 1988): 17–19. Print.

WEB

poormagazine.org. An online magazine that focuses on poverty-related issues.

AUDIOVISUAL

My Own Private Idaho. 102 min. 1991. VHS/DVD. Distributed by New Line Cinema (VHS)/ Criterion Collection (DVD). The story of two male hustlers living on the streets.

Surefire Assignment: Narrative Newsletters ———————

Rich Lane
Clarion University
(Profile, p. 15)

One of the classes I teach early on in the semester is closely linked with the reading and visuals in *Seeing & Writing*. It comes within a unit in which students are developing narrative newsletters. The students have read the narratives and viewed the visual compositions in two chapters of *Seeing & Writing*, have studied the content and narrative structures of the readings, and have produced drafts of their own narratives.[1] This class comes in the middle of the unit and begins to address focus, detail, and reflection. In this particular class, students confront stories of homelessness through both Mark Peterson's *Image of Homelessness* and a song by Nanci Griffith titled "Down 'n' Outer."

We begin with a brief review of the students' narratives and the elements of an "effective" narrative concerning place. Then we listen to Griffith's song and discuss the details that drive the plot of the song and story. We concentrate on the level of detail Griffith produces in the narrative and the ways that focused detail acts as metaphor, creating connotations beyond the literal plot. We also discuss the content of the song, the myths about homelessness that students share with the general public. We quickly move on to write about Peterson's photograph, depicting a homeless man in a box that, it implies, he calls home. The writing produced from this short exercise helps students further discuss the myths of homelessness. More important, the discussion and their written responses lead students to think about the level of reflection in their narratives—moving from a simple telling of a place to the act of reflecting on this "event." The sensitive issue of homelessness acts as a catalyst for connections that students begin to make between themselves and their stories, and the larger world. It is often an emotional class, in which students begin to see that a sense of consciousness about their writing of narratives is crucial to both the telling of stories and the work of academic writing. The photograph also helps students think about the influence of the visual in their newsletter: They learn that in this composition, the visual and verbal texts must work together to have the wanted impact on readers.

---

[1] Ed. note: Lane often uses this exercise after students complete both this chapter and Chapter 3 of the textbook, *Capturing Memorable Moments*, in a consideration of both place and moment.

Scott Russell Sanders, *Homeplace* (p. 172)

Sanders's essay initially seems to be a celebration of commitment to place, but it evolves into something more: a celebration of our connection to the land, of that tangible, physical tie. The structure of the essay mirrors the progression of his thoughts, evolving into a singular conception of self and space: "If you stay put, your place may become a holy center" (para. 15). He then asks us to consider what it means "to be alive in an era when the Earth is being devoured, and in a country that has set the pattern for that devouring" (para. 20). By the end of the essay, Sanders firmly asserts that "there is only one world, and we participate in it here and now, in our flesh and our place" (para. 22).

POSSIBILITIES FOR DISCUSSION, REFLECTION, AND JOURNALING

• Ask students to chart how Sanders moves from a general discussion of "staying put" (para. 4) to a tightly focused examination of each individual's responsibility for the fate of the planet.

ADDITIONAL WRITING TOPICS AND CLASSROOM ACTIVITIES

• Ask students to write an essay that argues the exact opposite of Sanders's point: that movement is good and stasis is bad. They should collect their examples from the same types of sources that Sanders uses, modeling his structure.

• **Image/Writing Assignment:** Ask students to bring in two advertising images: one that represents staying put and one that represents moving. Their task is to write a short essay analyzing how the elements of each ad combine to convey its message and explaining which ad seems more convincing and why.

• In large part Sanders attributes our need to keep moving to the cultural belief that there is always something better out there. Restlessness has become a touchstone of the American character. You might ask students to write about their own experiences with moving. If students have moved a lot in their lives, they could write about how such experiences have shaped them. If they have not, they could even write about their experience of moving to college.

CONNECTIONS WITH OTHER TEXTS

• The people pictured in Katharine Harmon's "The Road to Success" (p. 179) are in constant movement. What would Harmon say about Sanders's argument that "wholesale displacement" does not occur "without disastrous consequences for the Earth and for ourselves" (para. 10)? Ask students if they agree with Sanders, with Harmon, or with both. Can we seek success while "staying put"?

• Sanders cites a number of scientists, writers, and philosophers in his essay. Ask students to read a work by one of these sources — Salman Rushdie, Gary Snyder, or Thich Nhat Hanh, for example — and to analyze Sanders's essay in light of that reading.

SUGGESTIONS FOR FURTHER READING, THINKING, AND WRITING

PRINT

Larson, Gary. *The Far Side*. Kansas City: Andrews McMeel, 1982. Print. Cartoons from Larson's syndicated strip.

———. *The Prehistory of the Far Side: A Tenth Anniversary Exhibit*. Kansas City: Andrews McMeel, 1989. Print.

Sanders, Scott Russell. *Secrets of the Universe: Scenes from the Journey Home*. Boston: Beacon Press, 1991. Print.

———. *Staying Put: Making a Home in a Restless World*. Boston: Beacon Press, 1993. Print.

———. *Wilderness Plots: Tales about the Settlement of the American Land*. New York: Morrow, 1983. Print.

WEB

aao.gov.au/images.html. On this web site run by the Anglo-Australian Observatory are some thirty pictures of galaxies and nebulae that could be used in teaching Sanders's "Homeplace" or Cole's "A Matter of Scale" (Chapter 1, p. 85).

Surefire Class: The Places We See

Keri DuLaney
Diablo Valley College

At the end of our second unit, the students have discussed the concept of place in light of Sanders, Guterson, the movie *American Beauty*, and several images from the textbook. They have encountered ideas about suburbia (walls, sameness, security, etc.), home, freedom versus isolation, being rooted in ideas versus being rooted in a place, food as it pertains to place, and point of view, among others. We've talked about our place in life, in relationships, in image and perceptions. We've thrown around the notion of authentic places versus inauthentic places (think Kevin Spacey in *American Beauty*). The list could certainly go on.

At this point, I ask them to synthesize the ideas of others as expressed in essays, film, poetry, and photography into a work all their own about place. In an essay of 750 to 1,250 words they choose one of the following statements from Pico Iyer's essay "Why We Travel" and use it as a thesis:

1. We invent the places we see.

2. We carry our sense of home inside of us.

3. All of the significant movement we ever take is internal.

Support for the essay must come from "Homeplace" and may also draw on Peterson's *Image of Homelessness* (p. 169), Guterson's "No Place Like Home" (p. 158), *American Beauty*, and personal experience.

Katharine Harmon, *The Road to Success* (p. 179)

The map presented in the text is a sample from Katharine Harmon's book *You Are Here: Personal Geographies and Other Maps of the Imagination* (2004), which contains more than 150 maps. Although some of these are traditional maps that attempt to objectively define place, most of the maps in her book are what she calls "Maps of the Imagination." They use word and image in a combination to explore psychological and social landscapes. All of the maps included in the book "transcend the norm because of the mapmaker's personal viewpoint, or sense of humor, ingenuity, or all of the above" (p. 181). Harmon suggests that people have a *mapping instinct*—a fascination with maps as a way to help locate themselves and to understand their relation to other people.

Some of the maps in Harmon's book show perspective, such as in the "New Yorker's Idea of the United States of America," in which the city is shown as larger than all the other states including California. This is a good opportunity to discuss the idea that our sense of place is more than location and that we connect our own meaning to it because of our experiences and unique position. Other maps, such as the 1960s heart-shaped map from *McCall's* magazine entitled "Geographical Guide to a Man's Heart," address psychological and social rituals, while some are completely of the imagination, such as "A Dog's Idea of the Ideal Country Estate." Still others provide a more personal perspective, such as the map that labels physical and emotional scars on a body.

The map in this selection, "The Road to Success," is a subject that always provides great classroom discussion because most students feel as if they want to be or already are on this road. Many of them, quite naturally, see their current experience in college as an important stop on their road to success. This is a good opportunity to get them to reflect on their own road so far and how they see it playing out in the future. This subject asks them to take a concept and speculate through visuals and language.

POSSIBILITIES FOR DISCUSSION, REFLECTION, AND JOURNALING

• Ask students to look closely at the map. Have them discuss the ways that the artist/author chose to communicate meaning along the way. Discuss the ways that the visuals and the text work together.

• Ask students what they think about the road to success. Have them write individually and then share in small groups what they think they will encounter along the way. Explore the ways our culture markets success to us and how that version might be an idealistic representation of reality. Where do we get our ideas about success? Have students compare these messages with their own sense of success.

• This map uses the overall metaphor of the mountain. What other metaphors might we use to map out success? Have students discuss and generate metaphors for this or other subjects. Use this as an opportunity to discuss metaphors in general and the ways we use them in writing.

ADDITIONAL WRITING TOPICS AND CLASSROOM ACTIVITIES

• Students can analyze, in writing, the ways that the visuals and the text work together in "The Road to Success." Have them explore the overall metaphor and the parts (or evidence) that make it successful. Talk about the structures, shapes, and people along the road. Have them illustrate and label their own "Road to Success" and share their ideas in small groups.

• Have students look up an actual map of their city, town, or neighborhood. Ask them to identify places that they feel are familiar or hold memories and then to print the map and add labels and visuals to the places of importance. Have them think carefully about emphasis, size, image, and language choice as they label their maps.

• **Image/Writing Assignment:** Ask students to draw and label a "Map of the Imagination" of their own. They might focus on a particular location, such as their hometown or the neighborhood in which they grew up, or address a psychological or social map, such as the ones described through Harmon's work. They can incorporate humor, personal perspective, and cultural critique. Ask them to include both textual and visual cues as part of their map. As part of this assignment, you might include a process statement in which they explain their choices, metaphors, and meanings.

CONNECTIONS WITH OTHER TEXTS

• Have students read "The Americano Dream" (p. 222) and ask them to draw a map of Balcita's journey from immigrant to American.

• Have students take a look at the selections in Chapter 4, Projecting Gender. Then ask them to write an essay in which they argue whether they think women's map of the road to success today would look different from men's.

SUGGESTIONS FOR FURTHER READING, THINKING, AND WRITING

PRINT

Harmon, Katharine. *The Map as Art: Contemporary Artists Explore Cartography.* New York: Princeton Architectural Press, 2009. Print.

———. *You Are Here: Personal Geographies and Other Maps of the Imagination.* New York: Princeton Architectural Press, 2004. Print.

Jacobs, Frank. *Strange Maps: An Atlas of Cartographic Curiosities.* New York: Penguin, 2009. Print.

WEB

mcwetboy.net/maproom/. *The Map Room,* a blog hosted by Jonathan Crowe, is a great resource for exploring different types of maps with categories that range from "historical maps" and "geotagging" to "art" and "fun."

Richard Ford, *At Home. For Now* (p. 182)

Richard Ford's essay "At Home. For Now" explores the definitions of the concept of home. Much of his writing examines this concept in relation to place as he explores the connections between identifying oneself with a particular landscape. Once again, this essay provides an opportunity for students to discover the ways we bring meaning to words through substantiation. He points out that home is a "variable concept" that relies on perspective and experiences.

Ford consults the dictionary as well as his own experiences with relocating (which he did quite a bit) to try to get at the sense of this concept. He relays experiences from places where he lived and uses examples to support ideas such as personal positioning, home as place, home as familiarity, home as a pattern, and others.

POSSIBILITIES FOR DISCUSSION, REFLECTION, AND JOURNALING

• At one point, Ford looks up the definition of *home* in the *Oxford English Dictionary*. Students often turn to the dictionary or similar online sources for their first attempts at definition. He is not satisfied with this definition and expands on it through trying out different theories or speculating in writing. Ask students to look through the essay and discuss the ways that Ford builds his definition through these multiple perspectives.

• Ford distinguishes between home the feeling and home the place. He says that "moving's not unusual, but still home's a notion that we routinely put into play" (para. 4). Ask students to talk about the differences between home the feeling and home the place.

ADDITIONAL WRITING TOPICS AND CLASSROOM ACTIVITIES

• Before students read this selection, you might ask them to write their own definition of home, using examples and experiences to support their claims. They can either read them aloud to the full class or in small groups or save them until after the reading for further reflection.

• Ask students to choose a couple of short passages that stand out to them in the text. They can choose a couple of sentences or a full paragraph. First have them identify (perhaps in groups) why they think it is effective. Then ask them to write a couple of imitation sentences that draw on Ford's style.

• Ford uses a lot of metaphors in the piece. Near the end he finds a single phrase from the poet Czeslaw Milosz that most sums up his ideas: "concise, as if hammered in metal." Discuss what he means by this and how this metaphor works. You might have students construct a similar sentence or short essay in which they develop a metaphor and support it through their writing. First ask them to generate metaphors for their concept of home (or some other concept) and then build up to the metaphor throughout the essay.

• **Image/Writing Assignment:** Ask students to find images on the Internet and/or take pictures that represent their concept of home—both home the feeling and home the place. Ask them to discuss their findings in a short essay in which they include the images.

CONNECTIONS WITH OTHER TEXTS

• Have students read the essay "The Streets Change, But Memories Endure" by Kenji Jasper (p. 189) and ask them to write an essay in which they compare and contrast Ford's definition of home with Jasper's.

• Ford's statement "I've settled on the idea of home as a place I choose, rather than a place where I was simply, will-lessly born" sums up his essay. Have students read "Imagining Home-lands" by Bharati Mukherjee (p. 204) and con-sider how home is (or is not) a choice in the context of each of Mukherjee's "narratives . . . of expatriation, exile, immigration, and repa-triation." Ask students to write an essay explor-ing how Ford's experience of home in America differs for someone who was born outside of the country.

SUGGESTIONS FOR FURTHER READING, THINKING, AND WRITING

PRINT

Allard, William Albert. *Portraits of America*. Washington, D.C.: National Geographic, 2001. Print.

Ford, Richard. *The Bascombe Novels*. New York: Everyman's Library, 2009. Print.

———. *Women with Men*. New York: Vintage, 1998. Print.

WEB

writing.upenn.edu/wh/people/fellows/ford .html. The Kelly Writers House at UPenn posts streaming audio of a reading and dis-cussion with Richard Ford in February 2006, as well as a written biography and introduc-tion to Ford's work by John Carroll.

Kenji Jasper, *The Streets Change, But Memories Endure* (p. 189)

In this short essay, Jasper reflects back to the neighborhood in which he grew up—Fairfax Village in Washington, D.C. When he goes back to the neighborhood, he compares his memories with his new sense of place upon his return. The place of his childhood is apparently one where "class lines were blurred" (para. 1). He comments on the gentrification of the neighborhood that was once one of crime and violence that "deterred middle-class Washingtonians from planting stakes in the area" (para. 4). When he revisits it, he notices clean paint, new buildings, and missing landmarks, such as "old tennis and basketball courts" (para. 5). He explores the notions of "shifting demographics" and the effects of gentrification.

Jasper runs through different kinds of memories that involve personal ex-periences, such as learning to ride his bike or dueling with "bamboo swords" with his best friend. All of these experiences and memories are intricately con-nected to Jasper's sense of place as he remembers them in relation to places such as the wide ditch, the sewer pipe, and the forest behind a building.

As stated in the context for this piece, Jasper focuses on the influence of place in childhood and identity development. He says, "Your neighborhood, growing up in the city, is pretty much the boundaries by which you define your life, and that's your frame of reference." He concludes his essay with the thought that, although his neighborhood has changed, he keeps it alive in his mind through his memories, and then his children's memories. He says, "I left my 'hood more than a decade ago. But I'm making sure that it will never leave me" (para. 16).

POSSIBILITIES FOR DISCUSSION, REFLECTION, AND JOURNALING

• Jasper alludes to the issue of boundaries. He says, "Your neighborhood, growing up in the city, is pretty much the boundaries by which you define your life, and that's your frame of reference." Ask students to discuss the significance of this statement. How do we merge this sense of self and community?

• Jasper focuses on the issue of gentrification, during which neighborhoods experience "shifting demographics." In class have students discuss positive and negative changes produced by, as well as the cost of, gentrification and urban renewal. They can look up case studies of gentrification online that show this phenomenon of moving more affluence into economically depressed areas.

• This essay provides a good place to talk about connecting place and experience. Ask students to review Jasper's essay and identify the kinds of experiences he discusses. Read the examples aloud and categorize them (family, individual, social, historical, etc.). Notice the ways he connects these experiences to his larger purposes. What makes these *purposeful* experiences worthy of inclusion?

ADDITIONAL WRITING TOPICS AND CLASSROOM ACTIVITIES

• **Double-Entry Journal:** Have students think about the neighborhood in which they grew up. Ask them to describe their experiences and memories in connection to their sense of place. In a double-entry journal, have them list particular places they remember in one column and associative experiences in the other (as Jasper does in his essay). Have them extend their ideas in an essay in which they bring together the concept of place and experience.

• Ask students to research their old neighborhood, town, or community. They can do this on the Internet or at the library. What can they learn by looking at city or neighborhood maps, businesses, and other images or documents? In a short essay, have them document the changes they notice through these observations. You might also modify this assignment to have students look at the changes on their campus community as they explore archival information and interview community members.

• Have students experiment with voice and point of view as they write about a certain place from the past, present, and future perspectives. They might start with the point of view of a child living in the present and then move to the perspective of an adult looking back through reflective experiences; or they might use a fictionalized first-person perspective of looking back to the present from a time when they are older.

CONNECTION WITH ANOTHER TEXT

• The narrator's voice in this selection is both nostalgic and matter-of-fact. Do you sense any sentimentality in the author's tone? Ask your students to compare Jasper's imagery with the frames in the Retrospect (p. 156). How do the frames correspond to Jasper's memories?

SUGGESTIONS FOR FURTHER READING, THINKING, AND WRITING

PRINT

Williams, Brett. "'There Goes the Neighborhood': Gentrification, Displacement, and Homelessness in Washington, D.C." *There's* *No Place like Home: Anthropological Perspectives on Housing and Homelessness in the United States.* Ed. Anna Lou Dehavenon. Westport, CT: Bergin and Garvey, 1999. 145–164. Print.

WEB

metropolismag.com/story/20051121/in-praise-of-gentrification/. This article asks readers to look at gentrification from an economic viewpoint; for example, financial investment is better than no investment at all.

Zacks, Stephen. "In Praise of Gentrification." *MetropolisMag.Com.* Metropolis Magazine, 21 Nov. 2005. Web. 14 Dec. 2009.

Portfolio: Flickr Student Spaces (p. 192)

This Portfolio includes four photographs representing students' personal spaces. The photos, which range in style and content, are from Flickr, the online photo-sharing site. Like the more familiar YouTube (in which users share video), Flickr allows for posting, commenting, and cross-referencing of images through keyword tags. The site offers many interesting ways to search for and explore images and is an excellent resource that students can use for many assignments in this book.

For this Portfolio students can explore the four images in relation to the subject of personal space. They might discuss how people define their spaces and how things such as frame of reference, lighting, and positioning affect meaning in the compositions. This exercise is especially interesting for college students who have recently remade their personal spaces when they transitioned from their family homes to their campus homes (dorms, apartments, etc.).

POSSIBILITIES FOR DISCUSSION, REFLECTION, AND JOURNALING

• What do we mean by personal space? How do we define our own sense of personal space? Are there certain objects that define personal space?

• What boundaries mark out personal space, and how are they set? How do we understand other people's boundaries? How do people compose these spaces so that we know about these boundaries? When and how do we blur these lines?

• What kinds of modifications do we make when transitioning between places or when sharing a place with others? How is cohabiting an exercise in compromise and collaboration?

ADDITIONAL WRITING TOPICS AND CLASSROOM ACTIVITIES

• Send students to the Flickr web site (flickr .com). Ask them to experiment with different keywords and search strategies to get into different categories. Once students are familiar with the site, have them work with the photographs that they find. You can try several activities:

  • Ask students to look closely at the composition of the images. Have them conduct a rhetorical analysis in which they examine purpose, audience, and meaning along with rhetorical choices of light, positioning, inclusion of particular objects, color, expression, and so forth. Ask them to apply concepts such as specificity, tone, and arrangement to the photographs. This is a great opportunity to demonstrate the ways we engage in "acts of composition" across different mediums.

  • Work with the photos in small groups or as a whole class. Copy or project some of the images and discuss the ways they communicate meaning and make us think. Many of the photos include comments from the photographers that explain how they fit in with the larger subject.

• **Writing/Image Assignment:** Ask students to take six digital images of their personal spaces. Have them write a reflective essay in which they analyze this collection (or an individual photograph) through observations and inferences. Ask them to compare their own definitions and assumptions about personal space with the images presented in the textbook or on Flickr.

CONNECTIONS WITH OTHER TEXTS

• Ask students to choose one photograph in this Portfolio and have them compare it to *This is Daphne and those are her things* (Chapter 1, p. 122). Do they think a person's personal space or possessions present a clearer sense of identity? Why or why not?

• Have students take another look at Pepón Osorio's photograph *Badge of Honor* (Chapter 1, p. 95). Ask them to imagine the boy from this room taking pictures of his space for Flickr. What do they imagine his photographs would look like? Why?

SUGGESTIONS FOR FURTHER READING, THINKING, AND WRITING

PRINT

Marien, Mary Warner. *Photography: A Cultural History*. 2nd ed. London: Laurence King Publishing, 2006. Print.

AUDIOVISUAL

pbs.org/wgbh/pages/frontline/kidsonline/. "Growing Up Online." *Frontline*. PBS. *Frontline* explores the new realities of childhood in the Internet age. Public versus private selves and spaces are examined.

Julia Alvarez, *Neighbors* (p. 199)

Julia Alvarez often writes about the places where cultures come into contact. She considers herself a Dominican–hyphen–American, and as we learn from the context statement, she finds that "the most exciting things happen in the realm of that hyphen—the place where two worlds collide or blend together" (p. 201).

This theme is at the center of "Neighbors." Alvarez tells the story, through dialogue, of a white couple who attempts to approach a little Haitian girl as their neighbor. The wife is anxious and curious to meet the girl, whereas the husband is skeptical and resistant to the introduction. The wife does eventually approach her and tells her that they are neighbors who "live up the road on that hill" (para. 14). Although the woman returns several other times, she remains on the outside of the Haitian girl's world and feels that the mother of the little girl "decided the white woman cannot be trusted" (para. 16). The piece ends with the husband asking his disappointed wife, "What do you expect? What on earth do you expect?" This essay offers a good opportunity to talk about social class, race, and expectations.

POSSIBILITIES FOR DISCUSSION, REFLECTION, AND JOURNALING

• How is this piece about the idea of territory and how is it defined? Territory is commonly defined as the desire to claim space or domain over a particular area. You might discuss how we are defined by our territories and what we do to protect them. It might also be interesting to look at the different kinds of territory (physical, intellectual, social) and the ways we mark it—both literally and figuratively.

• Alvarez brings up the issue of cross-cultural trust. What is the difference between being an insider and being an outsider? Are there certain cultural boundaries that are impossible to cross?

• Ask students to visit a place that is unfamiliar to them—to take a *cultural journey*. Before the visit, have them write down their expectations of the place. During the visit, have them record observations and inferences, paying special attention to the difference between their expectations and the reality. You might have them conduct an interview to deepen their perspectives.

• Alvarez's piece is written in a style that relies heavily on dialogue. Ask students to take one of their writings (or generate a new writing) and rewrite it to include dialogue. You might even use the cultural journey assignment described above and recast it by creating characters and dialogue based on their observations.

ADDITIONAL WRITING TOPICS AND CLASSROOM ACTIVITIES

• Alvarez writes about a situation in which "worlds collide." Ask students to think and write about a time when this happened to them. What were the two worlds? How were they defined through territorial clues? Have students write about the experience and how they dealt with it, as well as what they learned from it.

CONNECTIONS WITH OTHER TEXTS

• Ask students to look closely at the different characters' perspectives in the story. How does each person—the wife, the husband, the little girl, and her mother—see the situation and why? Have students read Paul Fussell's essay "A Touchy Subject" (Chapter 6, p. 505) and then have them use this character division to discuss larger issues such as territory, expectations, and cultural and class differences.

• Have students reread the story imagining that the husband and wife are black and the little girl in the photograph is white. Much like in Tibor Kalman's photographs (Chapter 5, p. 436), how does the story change when the races are reversed?

SUGGESTIONS FOR FURTHER READING, THINKING, AND WRITING

PRINT

Erickson, Leslie Goss. *Re-Visioning of the Heroic Journey in Postmodern Literature: Toni Morrison, Julia Alvarez, Arthur Miller, and American Beauty.* Lewiston, NY: Edwin Mellen, 2006. Print.

Johnson, Kelli Lyon. *Julia Alvarez: Writing a New Place on the Map.* Albuquerque: U of New Mexico P, 2005. Print.

Sirias, Silvio. *Julia Alvarez: A Critical Companion.* Westport, CT: Greenwood, 2001. Print.

WEB

juliaalvarez.com. The author's official web site. Includes a brief autobiography, descriptions of Alvarez's publications, interviews with the author, and images from her books.

Looking Closer: Envisioning America

This section focuses on what it means to see America and how it creates a sense of place through the lens of immigrant experiences. It explores the questions of what we mean by the American Dream and the immigrant experience in the United States.

All of these writers and photographers reveal the conflicts of blending cultures and making decisions based on this sense of connection or exclusion. These texts might get students to question what makes up America for them and how they process the icons and images that are distinctly American. How has America's sense of place shaped our individual and cultural identities? These selections all address different perspectives and bring up both social and personal questions related to this subject.

Bharati Mukherjee, *Imagining Homelands* (p. 204)

Mukherjee notes that immigration is "the stage, and the battleground, for the most exciting dramas of our time" (para. 4). The reason for the drama is the complicated nature of immigration, which she defines as "the act of adopting new citizenship, of going the full nine yards of transformation" (para. 5). Other possibilities are expatriation and exile. Expatriation is "self-removal from one's native culture, balanced by a conscious resistance to total inclusion in the new host society" (para. 6). The expatriate can "exercise to the fullest the dual vision of the detached outsider" (para. 8). The exile does not possess this detachment because he or she does not make the choice to immigrate: "Self-removal is replaced by harsh compulsion" (para. 10). Mukherjee moves to an analysis of the outcomes. Her position as an integrationist leads her to this key statement: "Because I am here, I am changed totally by you and by my commitment to this country and its problems, but so are you. . . . I'm just as mainstream as anyone else. I am also a proud India-born, Bengali-speaking Hindu. These positions need not be antithetical" (para. 18). For all of the immigrants coming into the country, Mukherjee is concerned not about their status as "undocumented aliens" but that "we may never encounter one another," and that, she says, "is an immigration tragedy" (para. 26).

Samantha Appleton, *A Mexican American Family Celebrates a Quinciniera* (p. 214)

This photograph shows a family celebrating a *quinceañera*—a Latin American coming-of-age ceremony for fifteen-year-old girls. These celebrations involve ritual, religion, and values along with social introduction. Appleton, who is a photographer for Noor Photography, an agency "whose collective mission is to tell the truth through photography," believes that this kind of communication makes us stop and think and critically examine the world in which we live, no matter how painful. In this particular image, however, she shows a more personal side of this coming-of-age ritual that provides room to discuss the importance of rituals and how they are reinterpreted within an American context.

Monica Almeida, *A Mother Walks Home with Her Children after School in Dearborn, Michigan* (p. 215)

Almeida's photo shows a family dressed in the traditional clothing of their homeland. Her image addresses the conflict between assimilation and identity, and questions what we consider normal within our culture. You might use this image to bring up ideas of how we balance these identities or the ways that stereotypes contribute to our impressions and expectations. You can also discuss the ways that we make assumptions based on what we observe in others, such as their clothing.

Jon Lowenstein, *Protest in Humboldt Park against Bomb Testing on the Island of Vieques, Puerto Rico* (p. 216)

Jon Lowenstein, also part of the Noor collective, specializes in "hard hitting documentary photography." This photograph of a Puerto Rican protester is part of his collection *Shadow Lives*, in which he presents a series on the experiences of undocumented Latino immigrants. He works to show the connection through place and people, along with the conflict of living in adopted homelands.

Alex Webb, *Little India* (p. 217)

Little India demonstrates the repatriation of immigrant experiences through immigrant communities. This photo addresses the ways that people re-create their experiences in a new land through marketable goods and ethnic identity.

Amy Tan, *Fish Cheeks* (p. 218)

The story takes place around a dinner table in which the narrator's mother is entertaining an American family for Christmas dinner. Amy, the narrator, feels particularly confused because she has a crush on the minister's son and wants to impress him. Her mother serves items that are traditional to her culture, but Amy knows the Americans will view them as "appalling mounds of raw food" and describes them as "slimy," "rubbery," and "resembling bike tires." Although the rest of her family enjoys these delicacies, she can only see them as repulsive as she tries to see them through their guests' eyes. She is most embarrassed when her father plucks out the fish cheek—just below the eye—and says, "Amy, your favorite."

After the dinner is over, Amy's mother gives her an early gift of a miniskirt—something she considers distinctly American. She says, "You want be same like American girls on the outside. . . . But inside, you must always be Chinese. You must be proud you different. You only shame is be ashame" (para. 7). Years later, Amy comes to understand her mother's words and actions through the realization that "she had chosen all my favorite foods" (para. 8).

Jesse Gordon, *What Is America?* (p. 220)

The twenty-four photos featured are part of a larger collection that appeared in the *New York Times* on July 3, 2000. Gordon posed this question to the participants: "What is America?" The series shows the participants all holding an American flag. The text below each image includes a single word or short phrase from their answers along with their place of origin. Gordon also chose to include a bit of context in the background of each image. Students might discuss how all these variables connect to the answers to the question. How do issues such as age, race, and place of origin shape the ideas?

Students might discuss the meanings of America for themselves. They can look at the collection as a whole and analyze the patterns, overlaps, and disparity between the images and ideas. They might also look at the individual images to get a sense of perspectives and context. You might have students answer this same question before they read the piece and compare their own ideas to those in the photoessay. It would be interesting to note how answers and images change over the course of time. How do the answers from the year 2000 differ from the ones we might see today?

Angela M. Balcita, *The Americano Dream* (p. 222)

Balcita's essay focuses on the American Dream and takes us through a process of cultural expectations. This creative, nonfiction essay is written in a unique style in which the author works with blocks of compact text that provide snapshots. For her, the American Dream starts out full of promise, when you dream of "green lawns, big cars, and a house with many rooms" (para. 1), and then, through a series of disappointments, you realize that things are not exactly the way they were first imagined. Balcita also questions many of the cultural assumptions and practices that become part of the Dream. Students might look for examples of these practices, such as the love of baseball or a suburban backyard.

She asks questions regarding cultural allegiance and choice of identity: "Do I cheer for the place I'm from or the place I'm going?" (para. 12). Although the progression is one of questioned assimilation, the author does end up settling into her idea of the American Dream as she reinvents it based on her own experiences. The character "accidentally" becomes a gardener and returns to her "roots," suggesting a comfortable blending of cultures.

Students might discuss the ways they envision the American Dream and the ways we reinvent it through time and experience.

Pat Mora, *Immigrants* (p. 225)

Pat Mora is an essayist, memoirist, and poet who writes about Mexican American experiences and the ways they are influenced through borders. In this poem she addresses the issue of "internal borders" as people form their identities through more than one culture. This poem expresses the desire of immigrating families to gain acceptance in a new country. Throughout the poem Mora gives examples that speak to the ways that the members of this family try to make themselves more "American," such as "feed[ing] them mashed hot dogs and apple pie" (line 2) or "buy[ing] them blond dolls that blink blue / eyes or a football and tiny cleats / before the baby can even walk" (ll. 4–6). The poem ends with a question regarding this desire for acceptance: "Will they like / our boy, our girl, our fine american / boy, our fine american girl?" (ll. 12–14).

The poem is told from the point of view of the parents, who are concerned about assimilating their children in the new culture. Although the parents seem to be willing to do whatever it takes to have their children fit in, they still hope that a part of their cultural background will remain. They "whisper in Spanish or Polish / when the babies sleep" (ll. 9–10), indicating that this is something they must hide or utter in hushed voices. Issues of language and tradition are a big part of this conflict.

• Much in this section concentrates on the concept of the American Dream. What stereotypes or myths are popular about America? *Land of milk and honey. Streets paved with gold.* How do these myths match up with reality? What are students' own interpretations of the American Dream?

• How is America promoted and commercialized? You might discuss some of the early promotional materials for America along with modern-day depictions. For example, students might enjoy looking at propaganda in political or military campaigns, or at dramatic, fictional representations through television sitcoms. There are many sources to consider through this perspective.

• What is the difference between first- and second-generation immigrants? How do people negotiate the ideas about and connections to their native culture and their immigrant culture? How does this new dynamic shape relationships and ideas between generations?

ADDITIONAL WRITING TOPICS AND CLASSROOM ACTIVITIES

• **Image/Writing Assignment:** You might have students explore questions such as "What is the American Dream?" or "What is America?" through conducting an interview/image project similar to Jesse Gordon's photoessay. Place students in small groups and have them interview people by asking the same question or another question of their choosing. Have them take pictures and imitate the style of Gordon's photoessay or have them interpret their findings in another, original way. Ask each group to write a short, accompanying paper in which

they explore the meaning of their findings and interpret the photos. They can present this to the class through a PowerPoint presentation or in the form of a paper that accompanies their photoessay.

• This section provides an opportunity to discuss ideologies in general and, specifically, American ideologies. You might address this by having students conduct an analysis of an American magazine to identify ideologies and artifacts. First ask them to generate two lists: one of ideologies and the other of artifacts. Next have them read across the whole text and construct an overall reading of the publication. In writing, they might analyze the patterns, themes, audience, and overall assumptions demonstrated. Consider the ways that the individual artifacts work together to influence their thinking about America. This assignment can also work with a single advertisement or several ads, images, or language artifacts that speak to the same ideological assumption.

CONNECTIONS WITH OTHER TEXTS

• There are many films that explore immigrant experiences. Have students analyze a film in relation to this subject. You can show a film in class and work as a group or have students view films independently and turn in reviews. A quick online search or a visit to the Internet Movie Database (imdb.com) pulls up many titles that involve immigration experiences, such as *The Kite Runner* (2007), *The Namesake* (2006), and *The Joy Luck Club* (1993), all of which take on serious topics of assimilation and balance between cultures. Other films, such as *My Big, Fat Greek Wedding* (2002) and

Coming to America (1988), are humorous depictions or present America in stereotypical terms. You will also find many documentaries on immigration experiences that focus on real-life situations and conflicts.

• Have students visit the Noor agency web site (noorimages.com) and look through the collections and categories. They can analyze the collections and discuss them in small groups. How do these images tell a truth? What truths do they tell? How do the categories isolate meaning for intense reflection? What do students understand through the individual selections? Ask students to write down the ways the authors have isolated the truths they wish to tell. Some truths are told through tragic events and circumstances; others focus on place and people (inhabitants), a cultural phenomenon, or personal experiences.

SUGGESTIONS FOR FURTHER READING, THINKING, AND WRITING

PRINT

Daniels, Roger. *Coming to America: A History of Immigration and Ethnicity in American Life.* 2nd ed. New York: Harper Perennial, 2002. Print.

Fountas, Angela Jane, ed. *Waking Up American: Coming of Age Biculturally.* Berkeley: Seal Press, 2005. Print. Includes Angela M. Balcita's "Raising the Mango."

Mora, Pat. *Nepantla: Essays from the Land in the Middle.* Albuquerque: U of New Mexico P, 2008. Print.

Roberts, Sam. *Who We Are Now: The Changing Face of America in the 21st Century.* New York: Times Books, 2004. Print. Roberts, a *New York Times* editor, interprets demographics reflected in the 2000 U.S. Census.

WEB

america.gov. Includes news articles and images pertaining to American life, its economy, global challenges, and its relationships with other countries.

americanheritage.com/immigration/. Immigration page of the American Heritage web site. Features slideshows of immigrant images, their stories, and links to blogs that debate the issue itself.

pbs.org/destinationamerica/usim.html. Companion site for *Destination America* (featured below). Features in-depth interviews with the immigrants.

AUDIOVISUAL

Coming to America. 2007. NTSC. Distributed by American Life TV Networks. Part of the PBS American Family series, this volume follows immigrants, as they leave their homelands and begin anew in America.

Destination America: The People and Cultures That Created a Nation. 60 min. 2006. DVD, NTSC. Distributed by PBS Paramount. Uses the personal experiences of individual immigrants to more closely explore mass migration to America.

3

CAPTURING MEMORABLE MOMENTS

What does it mean to capture a moment? How do all our moments make up a life, a culture, a generation? How do images create and recall memories? How do they shape our cultural identity as they become part of our communal narratives? How do we, as writers and thinkers, interact with and capture our own moments through language and pictures?

This chapter asks students to consider moments that are of both personal and national interest. And many of the texts within it question how the act of capturing those moments affects how we remember them. Susan Sontag once said, "In America, the photographer is not simply the person who records the past, but the one who invents it." This is a good statement to return to over the course of the chapter.

In addition to shared cultural moments, many of the selections in this chapter guide us toward personal experiences that shape us as individuals. These might include rites of passage, monumental "firsts," or other events that might seem insignificant but that actually change the way we think about and experience the world. The selections in this chapter show how writers and artists capture different kinds of memorable moments—both public and personal. They also demonstrate the ways in which we are agents creating these moments through our participation and contribution, through language and visuals. In this chapter students have the opportunity to mine a rich range of ideas through which their experiences connect to larger understandings.

POSSIBILITIES FOR DISCUSSION, REFLECTION, AND JOURNALING

- Begin discussion by asking students to talk about shared memorable moments from their generation. As suggested in the chapter introduction, they might recall the catastrophe of Hurricane Katrina, the mass killing on the Virginia Tech campus, or the historic election of Barack Obama as the first African American president.

- The authors argue that the terrorist attacks on the World Trade Center, which "altered the American political and cultural landscape in profound ways," became a defining moment for this generation. Ask students to discuss their memories of September 11, 2001. Some may say that the first thing they did that morning was turn on the television, only to see the nightmare being played and replayed on the screen; others may say that they heard about the terrorist attacks from some other source — the radio, the Internet, a friend — and then turned on the television.

- Ask students whose first experience of the events of September 11, 2001, was not visual to comment on how the experience of *seeing* what had happened was different from that of hearing about it. Some have observed that they did not comprehend the events of that day or even feel an emotional response to them until they witnessed the television footage of the planes crashing into the towers and of the towers crumbling to the ground. If students are too young to remember this incident, they still might have heard about it from others through pictures or stories. You might have them concentrate on the differences between primary and secondary accounts in these situations or focus on a defining moment that happened within the course of their lifetime.

ADDITIONAL WRITING TOPICS AND CLASSROOM ACTIVITIES

- To raise the topic of how we attempt to capture most of our memorable moments by visual means, ask students to consider the snapshots they've saved over time. How many of their most memorable experiences — birthdays, proms, graduations, weddings — have been captured on film or in digital images? Is the reality of those experiences ever overshadowed by the recording of them? How do these images stay in our minds and become touchstones for our own memories and identities?

- Consider the ways that historical, cultural, or political moments are captured for us by the media. How do these public images shape our understanding of and emotions about the events and people? How do new visual mediums like Facebook and other photo-sharing technologies capture experience? You might have students look at the voyeuristic moments generated by celebrities or memorable "viral videos" from YouTube. What makes a moment memorable? How does this medium shape how we see our defining images?

Surefire Class: Capturing Memorable Moments

Lisa Albers
Pierce College,
Fort Steilacoom

I originally devised this assignment when using the first edition of *Seeing & Writing*, which of course predated one of the most memorable events in American history, the 9/11 terrorist attacks. It was very surprising for me to discover that many of my students disagreed with Brian Gnatt's observation that before September 11, 2001, "[his] generation [had] no single event of the same caliber." The nature of their disagreements reflects, I suppose, the "diverse and idiosyncratic personal experiences" that the McQuades speak of in the chapter introduction. For example, my college is sandwiched between two military bases; consequently students are much more likely to cite wars—from Korea to Vietnam to the first and current Iraq wars—as their most memorable moments because they themselves served in those conflicts, or they have family members who served or were lost or injured. Other students have described a certain level of trauma and emotional proximity to the Columbine school shootings, citing lockdowns and new codes of discipline in their own schools as administrators there reacted to the tragedy.

What I enjoy most about this assignment, and why I think it continues to work even though the McQuades have since revised the chapter, is the way students gleefully accept the task of putting themselves on an equal footing with the editors of the textbook. It's an exciting occasion to have students work both with and against the grain of those experts, and they come away with an understanding of what it takes to create a college textbook. Here is the assignment:

The first edition of *Seeing & Writing*, published in 2000, was already out of date the following year because of the 9/11 terrorist attacks. Imagine a chapter titled Capturing Memorable Moments that doesn't mention 9/11! The editors knew immediately that they would have to revise Chapter 3. (Actually this is not rare; many textbooks are revised every few years to update information and references.)

Your task is to play the role of editors, to update the chapter again. Together, you will decide what material stays in and what comes out. Then you'll choose your own material to include in the new chapter. This is material written or created by other people and published in a variety of sources. The only part that you yourselves will write this time is a new introduction to the chapter.

You may choose from a wide range of images (photographs, video stills, drawings, paintings) and writings (poems, stories, interviews, essays, articles). Keep in mind that the material you select should inspire students to write college-level papers. Please proceed with this in a way that recognizes the comfort level of everyone in your group. If you feel you're too close to the war in Iraq right now, or that it's too early to decide what material best captures it, focus on something else. And you don't have to limit yourself to covering recent events: If you believe other events or issues should have been presented in the chapter, here's your chance to get them in.

Things to do and think about:

1. **Trade contact information with your group members.** Make sure you can get hold of one another if you need to.

2. **Schedule a few group meetings next week.** You'll need at least a session to plan, another to look at your materials, and maybe a third to pull everything together. One idea is to meet in the library each day during the time we would normally have class (and when you're not scheduled for your conference with me).

3. **Examine the photographs and pictures in Chapter 3 of the textbook.** What hits you the hardest? Which images call to you? Identify images that you think are so strong, they should not be cut from the chapter. Why are these visual texts important to you?

4. **Do the same for the essays.** We've already read many of them, but read the remaining material in the chapter and talk about which ones to keep and which ones to replace.

5. **Don't forget the Looking Closer section at the end of the chapter.** The chapter doesn't end until page 315.

6. **Have fun with your research.** Use the checklist to make sure you have everything.

7. **Look for writing of high quality that discusses an issue in a complex way.** Newspaper articles are okay every once in a while for effect, but you can't always get a good essay out of them.

8. **Note your sources.** You don't have to prepare a formal bibliography, but do write down the name of the publication where your material first appeared (magazine, newspaper, web site) and the author's (photographer's, artist's) name. Then attach the sheet to the end of your manuscript.

9. **Write the new introductory essay after you've culled the material for the chapter.** Use the original introduction (pp. 231–235) as a model. What do you have to say about the ability of images and words to successfully capture memorable moments? What can you tell readers that will prepare them for the material in your new chapter?

10. **How long does the chapter have to be?** Roughly the same length as the chapter in the book.

Portfolio: Parr (p. 236)

Martin Parr, *Paris, 18th District; Greece, Athens, Acropolis; Latvia Beaches;* and *Italy, Pisa, Leaning Tower*

Martin Parr's photography presents people capturing memorable moments at various places. These tourists seem almost indifferent to what is around them: They seem to be gathering evidence of their experience at the expense of the experience itself.

POSSIBILITIES FOR DISCUSSION, REFLECTION, AND JOURNALING

• Ask students to consider these photographs as an argument: Together, what are they saying? How do the placement and the posture of the people in these images support Parr's argument?

• If students have trouble examining the photographs in this way, ask them to imagine the photographs taken from different angles or at different moments. For instance, what might be lost from *Greece, Athens, Acropolis* (p. 237) if the other group of tourists wasn't in the photograph facing the Parthenon? Similarly, in *Paris, 18th District* (p. 236), what if Parr had framed just the man with the video camera, leaving the yellow binoculars out of the picture?

ADDITIONAL WRITING TOPICS AND CLASSROOM ACTIVITIES

• Ask students to examine three other photographs by Parr from either his books or his website. Then ask them to write a brief essay describing Parr's style as a photographer based on his work here and in the other photographs. What are his interests? How does he want to portray his subjects? Tell them to use examples from the photographs to support their points.

• Ask students to freewrite about a time when the recording of an experience interfered with the experience itself.

• Tourists seem to have a bad rep, and Parr captures some of that in his photographs. Ask students to freewrite about tourists as a cultural stereotype. Why is that stereotype a negative one? What behaviors do people expect from tourists? What behaviors do your students expect from tourists? Have they ever behaved badly as tourists? been treated badly as tourists? How might the notion of the tourist be constructed in a positive way?

CONNECTIONS WITH OTHER TEXTS

• In his images, Parr seems to be arguing that the camera is an obstacle between our eyes and the world. Ask students not to defend or refute Parr's argument but to write about how looking through a lens can both increase and restrict our vision.

• In "On Photography" (p. 304), Susan Sontag notes how photographs no longer merely capture moments. According to Sontag, photography can "interfere with" or "invade" the moment to the point of becoming "an event in itself" (para. 8). How do Parr's photographs support her assertion?

SUGGESTIONS FOR FURTHER READING, THINKING, AND WRITING

PRINT

Parr, Martin. *Boring Postcards USA*. London: Phaidon, 2000. Print.

WEB

martinparr.com. Martin Parr's official site contains sample galleries and information on his books and his latest work.

Pair: Canin

Ethan Canin, *Vivian, Fort Barnwell* (p. 242)

Canin's brief piece demonstrates a different way in which a photograph can be an icon of family life. In this case the feeling elicited by the photograph is genuine, but the image itself does not correspond to the memory Canin associates with it. For years he thinks the photo is a snapshot of his mother on a day he remembers clearly: The family had had a picnic, and he and his brother, splashing in their truck-tire pool, had soaked some movers' blankets. In the picture, his mother has hung the blankets on the line to dry. She is smiling: "My father was mad but she wasn't. She was never mad at us" (para. 1). He later discovers that those are not blankets in the photograph; they are leaves. And the smiling woman in the photograph is not his mother but his grandmother.

POSSIBILITIES FOR DISCUSSION, REFLECTION, AND JOURNALING

• What does this selection suggest about our memories? about the possibilities for misreading photographs?

• How might Canin's loss of this piece of photographic evidence affect his perception of that memory?

ADDITIONAL WRITING TOPICS AND CLASSROOM ACTIVITIES

• Ask students to choose one of their own photographs and to write a personal essay describing the moment and emotions it captured.

For a more thorough analysis, it might be interesting to have them ask their parents or siblings what they remember about the moment that the picture depicts. What are some of the differences in memories? What accounts for the differences in memories?

• For an in-class writing assignment, ask students to bring an old photo to class. Then have them pair up, exchange images, and write a narrative about their partner's photograph. Finally (and perhaps during the next class), have the pairs describe the difficulties in narrating a moment they didn't partake in and the similarities and differences between the real photograph's story and their partner's narrative.

CONNECTIONS WITH OTHER TEXTS

• Have students choose and examine an image from *Seeing & Writing 4*. Then have them put the image aside and write about what they remember about the image and what feeling it evoked. Next have them write an essay about what they remembered and why they think that memory was tied to their emotional reaction.

• Have students read "Ethics in the Age of Digital Photography" by John Long (Chapter 7, p. 669) and then have them write an essay on how they believe digital photography will ultimately affect our culture's collective memory.

SUGGESTIONS FOR FURTHER READING, THINKING, AND WRITING

PRINT

Canin, Ethan. *America, America*. New York: Random House, 2008. Print.

———. *The Palace Thief*. New York: Picador, 1994. Print.

WEB

archive.org/details/EthanCaninsamBurch Reading/. Streaming audio of Ethan Canin reading from his book *America, America*.

ethancanin.com. Ethan Canin's official web site.

AUDIOVISUAL

The Emperor's Club. Universal, 2002. DVD. Directed by Michael Hoffman. With Kevin Kline and Emile Hirsch. Film adaptation of Ethan Canin's short story "The Palace Thief."

Sarah Vowell, *The First Thanksgiving* (p. 245)

Sarah Vowell's description of her first experience hosting Thanksgiving paints an amusing and touching portrait of her relationship with her family. Vowell's deft wit is everywhere in the essay, and because we come to expect humor in her words, it's surprising when a bittersweet moment arrives.

Teaching humorous works can be difficult, at least at first. Perhaps because students are not accustomed to reading humorous pieces in the classroom, they often miss the humor, or there's a long pause between the joke and the laughter — as though a joke grenade has been detonated. I've found that discussing the uses of humor is a good way to prepare students for reading it. Students seem to think — through no fault of their own — that humor has no business in writing or in serious thought. You may find it helpful to screen an episode of *The Daily Show* in class. Most students are familiar with the program: It's where most college students get their news. And even though the show is heavy on humor, it's not empty humor; its political satire is pervasive and sharp.

The first example of hyperbole comes at the end of the first paragraph: "I've always had these fantasies about being in a normal family in which the parents come to town and their adult daughter spends their entire visit daydreaming of suicide. I'm here to tell you that dreams really do come true." The humor here works not just because of the exaggerated comment about suicide but also because of the overturned expectation in the sentence. Students should also notice Vowell's metaphorical references to the Pilgrims and other immigrants as she tells her story. As she notes the many firsts of this Thanksgiving—her parents' visiting her house, their having none of the usual distractions from each other—she likens her situation to that of the Pilgrims: "We are heading into uncharted and possibly hostile waters, pioneers in a New World. It is Thanksgiving. The pilgrims had the *Mayflower*. I buy a gravy boat" (para. 3). These references, which appear throughout the essay, provide humor and cohesion.

Yet despite all the humor in the piece, there are some genuinely touching moments. As Vowell, her parents, and her sister look at the display cases at Ellis Island, Vowell thinks about the family's move from Oklahoma to Montana: "I think of my grandfather, how we just drove off, leaving him behind, waving to us in the rearview mirror" (para. 11). And then there's the bittersweet ending, which comes from simple repetition and Vowell's unexpected insight into how her family works: "And there we stand, side by side, sharing a thought like the family we are. My sister wishes she were home. My mom and dad wish they were home. I wish they were home too" (para. 23).

POSSIBILITIES FOR DISCUSSION, REFLECTION, AND JOURNALING

• You might begin discussion by having students name authors they find humorous. They are likely to list Dave Barry, David Sedaris, Douglas Adams, P. J. O'Rourke, Hunter Thompson, and Jon Stewart—all writers with a unique way of crafting humor. Ask students if they can characterize the humor of the writers they've named.

• Point out that Vowell uses irony throughout the essay, mainly through understatement and hyperbole. Lead the class through the essay, asking students to identify instances of irony.

ADDITIONAL WRITING TOPICS AND CLASSROOM ACTIVITIES

• One of the major subjects in Vowell's essay is how this new experience—her family's coming to New York to spend Thanksgiving with her—made her recognize their changing relationships. Ask students to write about a time when they noticed a change in their relationship with their family. Ask them to write the narrative in a humorous tone.

• Again ask students to write about a time when they noticed a change in their relationship with their family, but this time ask them to write the narrative in a serious tone. If you assign both humorous and serious essays, point out to students how a writer's choice of tone changes the presentation and inclusion of information.

CONNECTIONS WITH OTHER TEXTS

• As an introduction to how humor can be used to talk about serious issues, you might take students to the *Onion* web site, one of the most successful purveyors of irony and satire.

- Despite the humor in this essay, Vowell is addressing serious topics. Ask students to examine Art Spiegelman's "Nature vs. Nurture" (Chapter 4, p. 380) for another example of how this is done.

SUGGESTIONS FOR FURTHER READING, THINKING, AND WRITING

PRINT

Vowell, Sarah. *Assassination Vacation*. New York: Simon & Schuster, 2005. Print.

————. *The Partly Cloudy Patriot*. New York: Simon & Schuster, 2003. Print.

————. *Radio On: A Listener's Diary*. New York: St. Martin's, 1998. Print.

————. *Take the Cannoli*. New York: Simon & Schuster, 2000. Print.

WEB

dir.salon.com/topics/sarah_vowell/index.html. Includes more than seventy articles Vowell has written for her column at *Salon.com*.

hearingvoices.com/sv/. RealAudio clips of Sarah Vowell reading her work on *This American Life*.

theonion.com. A great web site for satire.

Retrospect: Yearbook Photos (p. 250)

Thankfully, looking at other people's yearbook photos is easier than looking at our own. However, you might gather your own yearbook photos and ask students to bring theirs and those belonging to older siblings and parents, which will add to the selection here. Don't worry about representing every decade; one main purpose in bringing additional photos is for the added personal element, which could help students get more involved and help them see that the ordinary events and objects in their lives can be observed in this way.

In the 1950s through the 1970s, we see an important difference: black faces alongside white faces, an effect of the Supreme Court's landmark decision in *Brown v. Board of Education* (1954). By the 1970s we can see a major shift in clothing: The man seems to be wearing a tuxedo (notice that humongous bow tie); and the woman is wearing a white dress—gone are the dark top and pearls of the 1950s and 1960s. This change in clothing continues beyond the 1970s: Clothing becomes a means of personal expression in these pictures. Although the man in the 1990s wears a suit, it doesn't have the look of a typical business suit. And the women's clothing in the last two decades does not suggest "business world" either.

Another major difference in the last few decades is in background. The photos from the 1980s, like the other pictures, have a generic blank background; yet those from the 1990s have backdrops: a fake woodland setting in the man's and possibly a real one in the woman's.

• Ask students about the significance of these pictures. As students glance over them, you might direct them to freewrite about the changes in our society that have occurred between 1920 and 2000. These writings may come in use as you look at particular decades. Then ask students to consider these questions: What values do these pictures express about our culture? What makes senior-year pictures so special? What "memorable moment" do they capture? And how do these photographs reveal or represent that moment? How do the photographs, and hence the representation, change over time?

• Looking at the photographs through the decades, do students see any noticeable differences? In the early pictures, all the men are wearing suits, a practice that continued into the 1960s but is much less common today. Do their suits suggest that these men are going into business? What about the women? By the 1940s, the woman's clothing does not look very different from the man's. What might this suggest about the status of women at the time? What do students make of the shift in clothing over time?

• If the early photos show people ready to go into the business world, what do the pictures from the 1970s on show? If these are more about personal expression, what might account for this shift in purpose? How do students' pictures further add to these changes?

ADDITIONAL WRITING TOPICS AND CLASSROOM ACTIVITIES

• A recent controversy centers on what is acceptable in yearbook photos. For instance, several high schools do not allow students to pose with guns. Ask the class to consider the personal rights of the students versus the high school's right to project a particular image of its students.

Students should imagine different scenarios or investigate real ones. Should students be able to wear what they want, even if it's offensive or revealing? Should they be able to pose with a gun or a baby?

• Have students choose two people from different decades and write brief narratives about their lives after senior year. What do students know about these decades that might inform their narratives?

CONNECTIONS WITH OTHER TEXTS

• Ask students to examine photographs of themselves taken under different conditions: their high school yearbook picture, their driver's license picture, pictures taken by friends and family. What moment does each of these photographs capture? Do students feel the photographs are accurate representations of those moments? How do the settings, the purposes, and the people involved affect the representations?

• Grade school yearbooks might also be interesting to look at. You might ask students to borrow yearbooks from siblings, friends, and parents that cover some time span, even if it's only a decade or two. Ask them to photocopy a page from each yearbook and to bring those pages to class. What changes over time are illustrated in the yearbooks? Are children represented differently from high school students? How?

SUGGESTION FOR FURTHER READING, THINKING, AND WRITING

WEB

thedailystar.com/news/stories/2000/02/05/yearbook.html. Just one of many news stories about controversies over high school yearbook photos.

N. Scott Momaday, *The Photograph* (p. 252)

In his narrative, Momaday cautions us about relying too much on photographic images. He describes the disillusionment of "an old Navajo crone" who asked Momaday's father to take her picture. But when she saw the photograph — a "true likeness," says Momaday — "she was deeply disturbed, and she would have nothing to do with it" (para. 8). Momaday theorizes that she probably had never seen her image before and that the photograph "was a far cry from what she imagined herself to be" (para. 8). Or perhaps she realized that the camera "in its dim, mechanical eye . . . had failed to see into her real being" (para. 8).

POSSIBILITIES FOR DISCUSSION, REFLECTION, AND JOURNALING

• Ask your students why they think the older woman didn't like the photograph of herself. Is there more to it than what Momaday assumes at the end of his essay?

• Why did Momaday title this piece "The Photograph," even though he talks about the photo only in the last paragraph? What is the purpose of the paragraphs preceding it?

ADDITIONAL WRITING TOPIC AND CLASSROOM ACTIVITY

• Ask students to research the history of photography. How was photography initially used? How did people react to the technology? to the picture-taking process? to the product? How has photography changed over time? Then ask students to use their research to write an essay that compares and contrasts early and modern perceptions of photography. They can use Momaday's essay or others in Chapter 3 to support their argument.

CONNECTIONS WITH OTHER TEXTS

• Have students compare Momaday's essay with Canin's short prose in "Vivian, Fort Barnwell" (p. 242). Do they agree with Momaday that we as a culture shouldn't rely too heavily on photographs? Have them think about this in the context of the fact that Canin's memory is completely different from the actual photograph.

• In his essay, Momaday theorizes that the Navajo woman had probably never seen a photograph of herself before. Ask students to turn to the Peter Menzel and Faith D'Aluisio Portfolio (Chapter 1, p. 30). Have them research the prevalence of photography in the African community from which the Aboubakar family originates, and then ask them to theorize on whether this family would have felt that their photograph was an honest depiction of the way they look.

SUGGESTIONS FOR FURTHER READING, THINKING, AND WRITING

PRINT

Alexie, Sherman. *The Lone Ranger and Tonto Fistfight in Heaven*. New York: HarperPerennial, 1994. Print.

———. *War Dances*. New York: Grove, 2009. Print.

Charles, Jim. *Reading, Learning, Teaching N. Scott Momaday*. New York: Peter Lang, 2007. Print.

Steve McCurry, *Sharbat Gula, Pakistan, 1985* (p. 256) and *Sharbat Gula, Pakistan, 2002* (p. 257)

McCurry's first photograph of Sharbat Gula abounds in both print and electronic forms, so finding the original image should be easy. You might present the picture to students and ask what, if anything, they know about it. Most students are likely to have seen the image but may not know the particulars; and a few may know that a more recent photograph was taken — but nothing more than that.

POSSIBILITIES FOR DISCUSSION, REFLECTION, AND JOURNALING

• Ask what students can piece together about the girl from the way she looks and from her clothing. What do they read in her face? in her haunting green eyes? Do they see hope for this girl?

• How do students explain the prevalence of the image in the media? Why do they think she is important?

• Direct students to the side-by-side pictures from 1985 and 2002 and to the Seeing questions in the textbook. Expand the discussion of the purpose of these photographs to the role of purpose in students' writing and to how purpose can have different meanings for you as a teacher, for them as students, and for all of you within the bounds of your particular department and institution.

ADDITIONAL WRITING TOPICS AND CLASSROOM ACTIVITIES

• Ask students to freewrite about what makes these pictures so effective. Would the 2002 image of Gula alone be enough to make people care about her situation? Does the 1985 photograph work primarily because she was a photogenic child?

• At first Gula resisted having her picture taken for the 2002 article, but she changed her mind when she was told how she could once again bring attention to the plight of her people. Critics of *National Geographic* say that the magazine tends to "exoticize" foreign lands and people. Ask students to freewrite about the positive aspects of this picture as well as the potential for romanticizing the "other."

CONNECTIONS WITH OTHER TEXTS

• Gula's face set the tone for the original *National Geographic* story and has become a symbol for the Afghan people. Look at other covers of *National Geographic* or another newsmagazine — *Time, Newsweek, U.S. News & World Report* — and examine how the publication uses faces to tell stories. Without reading the stories inside, what do the faces tell you?

• In his essay "Ground Zero" (p. 285), James Nachtwey states: "There is power in the still image that doesn't exist in other forms" (para. 17). How do these pictures of Gula demonstrate Nachtwey's claim? You might ask students to re-create a sense of the Gula pictures through descriptive writing. Ask them to use dramatic fragments and vivid words. What problems do they run into?

SUGGESTIONS FOR FURTHER THINKING, READING, AND WRITING

PRINT

Bendavid-val, Leah. *National Geographic: The Photographs*. Washington, D.C.: National Geographic, 2002. Print.

Ellis, Deborah. *Women of the Afghan War*. Westport, CT: Praeger, 2000. Print.

Lutz, Catherine, and Jane Collins. *Reading National Geographic*. Chicago: Chicago UP, 1993. Print.

WEB

nationalgeographic.com/ngm/100best/storyA _story.html. The original story and photograph of Sharbat Gula.

news.nationalgeographic.com/news/2002/03/ 0311_020312_sharbat.html. The full story with pictures of how *National Geographic* found Sharbat Gula in 2002.

stevemccurry.com. Steve McCurry's home page, with more of his photography.

Dorothy Allison, *This Is Our World* (p. 260)

Allison's work is structured around the rhetorical device of the fragment, which opens up the essay in thought-provoking ways. This structure encourages active participation from the reader, who is forced to draw connections between the sections of the essay. However, it may also confuse students who are more comfortable with a linear structure.

The narrative elements in Allison's essay share a common thread: They force us to look at life as an ongoing testament to the power of art. Allison writes of being seven years old and fascinated with the overly beautiful image of Jesus and its ability to calm her with "genuine sympathy" (para. 15). It is that sympathy she offers readers in her work, the ability through her writing to comfort readers with her truth (paras. 37–38). Her friend Jackie, the painter, holds the same "'bit of magic'" (para. 27) that Allison accords to the painter of Jesus. What defines art—and what makes even a simple ad a form of art—is the power to lay bare "our emotional and intellectual lives" (para. 39). The power of art is to sustain and reveal our lives or—in the language of this chapter—to capture our most memorable moments.

POSSIBILITIES FOR DISCUSSION, REFLECTION, AND JOURNALING

• To engage students initially, you may want to break up the class into groups and assign each group a fragment of the essay. Ask them to answer several basic questions: What is Allison's point in this selection? How does she support it? What figurative language does she use? Then bring the class back together to discuss the work as a whole. Ask students to identify recurring themes, paying close attention to those that have appeared in more than one group's analysis of its fragments.

• Midway through the essay Allison writes, "I think that using art to provoke uncertainty is what great writing and inspired images do most brilliantly. Art should provoke more questions than answers and, most of all, should make us think about what we rarely want to think about at all" (para. 35). Ask students to discuss how the very structure of this essay forces a reader to think, to ask questions, and to feel less than certain about his or her conclusions.

• In leading students through the essay, you might ask them to focus on Allison's vocabulary. They could construct a glossary of the terms she uses to discuss art and draw from those terms a working definition for art as Allison sees it. Be sure to point out the imagery she uses throughout the piece to link art with religion ("In art, . . . revelation [is] a sacrament") and with truth ("In art, . . . pursuing one's personal truth [is] the only sure validation"). Then ask students to consider their own definition of art in relation to Allison's.

ADDITIONAL WRITING TOPICS AND CLASSROOM ACTIVITIES

• Ask students to write a short piece in which they respond to Allison's contention that art holds a "'bit of magic.'"

• Have students write an essay in which they delineate Allison's definition of art and then apply it to a nontraditional type of art. They might

select an art form that Allison mentions — murals, ads, folk art — or choose one of their own, but they should not choose a traditional, "high" art form.

• Allison writes: "Sometimes, I imagine my own life as a series of snapshots taken by some omniscient artist who is just keeping track — not interfering or saying anything, just capturing the moment for me to look back at it again later" (para. 16). Ask students to document their lives for one day, taking at least ten pictures, one for each hour of the day. Then have them construct a visual essay of that day on the basis of their photos, writing a fragment for each one and modeling the fragments on Allison's shared-theme structure.

• Ask students to consider why Allison so often links art with children. What cultural association is she making use of here? How does that association bolster her definition of art?

CONNECTIONS WITH OTHER TEXTS

• You might ask students to consider the images and texts in this chapter and how they apply to Allison's criteria: "Art should provoke more questions than answers and, most of all, should make us think about what we rarely want to think about at all" (para. 35).

• Allison writes that she believes in "the nobility of the despised, the dignity of the outcast, the intrinsic honor among misfits" (para. 37). Ask students to look back at Pepón Osorio's *Badge of Honor* (Chapter 1, p. 92) in relation to this observation and to her contention that artists have a special perspective that is not shared by "the sheltered and indifferent population" (para. 37).

SUGGESTIONS FOR FURTHER READING, THINKING, AND WRITING

PRINT

Allison, Dorothy. *Bastard Out of Carolina.* New York: Dutton, 1992. Print.

———. *Cavedweller.* New York: Dutton, 1998. Print.

———. *Skin: Talking about Sex, Class & Literature.* New York: Firebrand, 1994. Print.

———. *Two or Three Things I Know for Sure.* New York: Dutton, 1995. Print.

WEB

tulane.edu/~wc/zale/allison/allison.html. A 1995 interview with Dorothy Allison.

AUDIOVISUAL

Bastard Out of Carolina. 97 min. 1996. DVD, rated R. Distributed by Fox Lorber.

Surefire Assignment: Personal Photo Analysis

Martha Kruse
*University of
Nebraska–Kearney*

I ask my students to select a photograph or series of related photographs that they find personally significant. These can be photographs of people they don't know or of people they know quite well. The photograph(s) may even be of the student. In an essay (I have students attach a photocopy of the photo to the paper), they address the following topics:

A. What situation was occurring at the time?

B. Who decided to take a photograph and why?

C. Why is this particular photograph significant?

D. Does this photograph meet Dorothy Allison's criteria for art? Why or why not?

Clive Thompson, *This Just In: I'm Twittering* (p. 270)

In this short essay, Thompson looks at the phenomenon of Twittering. The word comes from a social media tool that lets people communicate through short (limited to 140 characters) updates about their "everyday thoughts and activities to the Web via browser, cell phone, or IM" (para. 1). He gives examples that define the tool and how people are using it.

Through the rest of the essay he discusses the value and the drawbacks of the tool and the ways that it affects communication. Although he critiques some aspects of it, he generally feels that it is positive in its ability to aid in community building among people as it "makes the group more than the sum of its parts" (para. 11).

POSSIBILITIES FOR DISCUSSION, REFLECTION, AND JOURNALING

• Thompson suggests that using Twitter might be seen as the "banal extreme" (para. 2) in that many of the postings seem pointless. You might have students talk about the nature of the messages they see and post on Twitter. What is their purpose? their language and content?

• Thompson posits that the true value of this tool lies in the "surprising effects that come from receiving thousands of pings from your posse" (para. 3). Ask students what they think he means by this statement. He suggests that receiving tweets is affirming in terms of popularity and a sense of belonging, but he takes the idea further and talks about the power of constant-contact media to create what he calls "social proprioception." In other words, Twitter gives a group a "sense of itself" through an awareness of factoids about people.

• We live in a culture of disclosure where we all know more about one another than ever before. How does Twitter function in light of this culture of disclosure? How does it change the nature of experience to know information about people before (or instead of) interacting face-to-face? How much are we now communicating aloud (or in writing) that we used to keep in our heads? How are relationships changed because of this voyeuristic perspective? How much information is too much information (TMI—a common acronym/emoticon used by students)? How does this medium create a sense of curiosity and entitlement (to information) in our culture?

• Thompson says, "Twitter substitutes for the glances and conversations we had before we became a nation of satellite employees" (para. 8). How has our changing culture and workforce created an environment in which Twitter is necessary or desirable?

ADDITIONAL WRITING TOPICS AND CLASSROOM ACTIVITIES

• Ask students to explore and analyze the ways that social media are used for marketing, commercial communication, and "viral marketing." Send students toward primary research to collect particular examples, by visiting particular sites such as Facebook or Twitter. They can also extend to secondary research to learn about strategies and theory regarding social media and marketing. Ask them to write about their observations across this topic or to do a close analysis of a particular marketing campaign.

• Flash fiction (also called micro-fiction, sudden fiction, nanofiction, or instant fiction, among other terms) is a form of fiction that is defined by its brevity. Students can start by researching these terms to find out more about the forms and by looking at particular examples through online e-zines such as the *Vestal Review*, *Flashquake*, and *Smokelong Quarterly*. Many social media sites have created their own places for experimental, flash, sudden, and micro-fiction. Twitter, in particular, lends itself to the format because of the 140-character limit imposed by the technology. Once students have researched the genre and its forms, ask them to experiment through composing one or more pieces of flash fiction of their own. You might limit their word allowance or have them follow submission guidelines from one of the many micro-fiction sites and actually submit their work online. Have them share them in class or online and respond and revise as they would a longer piece of writing. Talk about the rhetorical differences of this form and the strategies required as a writer of short fiction.

CONNECTIONS WITH OTHER TEXTS

• Have students read "The First Thanksgiving" by Sarah Vowell (p. 245). Next ask them to pretend to be Vowell, and, using the essay as a guideline, ask them to create several tweets about the visit. Then ask them to write an essay about how the prose description of the holiday differed from the description in the tweets.

• Ask students to look at Retrospect: Phone Home (Chapter 1, p. 54) and have them create a Twitter viral marketing campaign designed to sell one of the phones.

SUGGESTIONS FOR FURTHER READING, THINKING, AND WRITING

PRINT

Fitton, Laura, Michael Gruen, and Leslie Poston. *Twitter for Dummies*. Hoboken, NJ: Wiley, 2009. Print.

Thomas, James, and Robert Shapard. *Flash Fiction Forward: 801 Very Short Stories*. New York: Norton, 2006. Print.

Thompson, Clive, ed. *The Best of Technology Writing 2008*. Ann Arbor: U of Michigan P, 2008. Print.

WEB

collisiondetection.net. Clive Thompson's blog about science, technology, and culture.

twitter.com/Pomeranian99. Clive Thompson's Twitter page.

Front Pages of *USA Today, Anchorage Daily News, The Commercial Appeal,* and *The Oregonian* (p. 273)

These four images show newspaper front pages from a single day, all focusing on the same story—the historic election of Barack Obama in 2008. We are often led to believe that print news is objective and speaks a deeper "truth" than other mediums. This sequence displays the ways that the news is subjective and dependent on perspective and rhetorical choices. Each publication has its own agenda and way of presenting the information.

POSSIBILITIES FOR DISCUSSION, REFLECTION, AND JOURNALING

• How do we get and process information in our culture? We are inundated with information sources on a daily basis: television, radio, newspaper, the Internet. What kinds of choices do we make when we choose one medium over another? How does this affect our ideas about truth, knowledge, and facts?

• All of the pages address the issue that Barack Obama made history because he crossed a racial barrier as the first African American president. Discuss the significance of this idea and the ways it is portrayed in the different newspapers.

• Ask students to focus on the images on the front pages. How does the selection of images suggest one thing or another? For example, how does the picture depicting Obama and his family on *USA Today* compare with the waving, smiling Obama in Washington on *The Oregonian*?

ADDITIONAL WRITING TOPICS AND CLASSROOM ACTIVITIES

• Students might compare the front pages and discuss how the editorial decisions affect what is included in each. Have them look at headlines, subheads, graphics, and images as they record their impressions. Ask them to try to analyze the audience for each publication. You might have students go to the sites for the publications listed — *USA Today, Anchorage Daily News, The Commercial Appeal*, and *The Oregonian* — to see what they can learn about their rhetorical situations. They might compare these to current front pages to determine patterns and trends in content, layout, and other consistent biases.

CONNECTIONS WITH OTHER TEXTS

• The book authors recommend the site newseum.org for comparing and contrasting media portrayals of events. On this site students can see the same-day front pages of different newspapers across the country. You can send them to the site to explore the way in which the news of the day is reported or ask them to look at some of the archival collection in the online museum. Ask them to write an analysis of three of the front pages and include particular examples from the texts along with their own connections and ideas.

• A modification of the previous assignment involves placing students in small groups and having them analyze the four front pages and then report back to the class for a larger comparison. They can also do the same thing with "Today's front pages" on the Newseum site.

SUGGESTIONS FOR FURTHER READING, THINKING, AND WRITING

WEB

konigi.com/design/obama-election-news-us -sources/. U.S. newspaper and online front pages from the day after the 2008 presidential election.

newseum.org/todaysfrontpages/archive.asp. "The Newseum keeps an archive of national and international front pages that chronicle events of historical significance."

poynterextra.org/gallery/frontpages.html. Front pages considered for inclusion in the Poynter Institute's book on the 2008 presidential election.

Surefire Assignment: *Time* Magazine: News or Fluff? ———

Charles Hood
Antelope Valley College
(Profile, p. 12)

For this assignment, I call students' attention to the fact that styles of news presentation evolve. In the past, the *Los Angeles Times* was considerably lurid. Of the old days at the paper, Iris Schneider (in *Images of Our Times: Sixty Years of Photography from the Los Angeles Times*) writes:

> In the early 30s and 40s, photojournalism was pretty cut and dried. Photographers covered society balls, and celebrity benefits, and now and then shot human interest, or "feature" art—such as the little old lady who had sewn 10,000 buttons on her dress. But the bread and butter work was at crime scenes, accidents, and in the courts. They shot divorcées (if they were pretty), car crashes and train wrecks (if they were big), and court proceedings or trials (if they were scandalous). And they often were.
>
> Sensationalism ruled the front page.

Schneider's use of the past tense implies that this is no longer so, and perhaps for the *Los Angeles Times* it no longer is. But what about the newspaper's sober uncle, the weekly news magazine? Have publications like *Newsweek*, *U.S. News & World Report*, and *Time* gone through a similar metamorphosis, only in reverse? As the dailies become less like tabloids, does sensationalism now rule the weeklies' front pages?

I ask the students to decide if *Time* magazine has less significant content now than it used to have, and, once they decide, to present their findings in a persuasive typed or computer-printed essay. I require that they look at at least four back issues of *Time*, with each issue dated at least twenty years earlier than the one before.[1] They might pick the same date for each, such as a birthday or Bastille Day. Implied in this assignment is a consistent definition of what we mean by *significant content*; each essay should define *significance* at some point. After all, what to one person may be news lite to somebody else may be an essential update on Madonna's marital status. As *Seeing & Writing* shows, students should consider not just the words and topics but also font, layout, and the ratio of color to black and white and of text to illustration. Further questions to ask include these: Has vocabulary become dumbed down? On what subjects do special essays and theme issues focus? How many movie stars are there per issue versus civic leaders or novelists or revolutionaries? What in an issue (if anything) is controversial? What is the average length of an article? What has been cropped out of photographs? How many ads are there, and where are they placed? How has the cover evolved? Which other magazine (e.g., *People*, *Playboy*, *Foreign Policy*, *The Economist*) most resembles the issue of *Time* you are looking at?

---

[1] Ed. note: The magazine was first published in 1923.

Portfolio: Savulich (p. 278)

Andrew Savulich, *People Watching Jumper on Hotel Roof; Man Complaining That He Was Attacked after He Gave His Money to Robbers; Taxi Driver Explaining How an Argument with His Passenger Caused Him to Drive into the Restaurant;* and *Woman Laughing after Car Wreck*

The headnote tells us that this series of photographs presents "spot news — spontaneous photographs of the violence and accidents, the humorous and odd events of everyday life, especially in urban areas" (p. 282). None of the photos here relate to political figures or to political situations. Each photo seems to be about the private plight of an individual in an extraordinary situation. The events depicted are violent, and the photos have a grimy, urban feel and were shot at night. Moreover, they look like newspaper photos, so they would seem to promise truth and objectivity.

POSSIBILITIES FOR DISCUSSION, REFLECTION, AND JOURNALING

• You might ask students to begin by discussing what constitutes news in our culture. When they read these images as news, what kinds of inferences can they draw about the nature of the news that is being presented? For example, each of these photographs is concerned with some kind of violent or life-threatening event. Is that what makes the photographs a type of news?

• Ask students if they recognize the people in the photos. Does celebrity have anything to do with news in these kinds of photographs?

• When students have made a series of observations, ask them to write a short essay about the composition of these photos and what is — and what is not — newslike about them. For example, you might point out that these are black and white images and that we generally think of black and white photography as "documentary."

By shooting his work in black and white, is Savulich suggesting that the images are real? Also, the apparent spontaneity of the photographs seems to support the idea that they are unposed. How does that spontaneity support the sense that what they depict, in Savulich's words, is "really *happening*"? Are there other aspects of these images in addition to their color (or absence of it) and seeming spontaneity that lead us to accept them as truth before we even analyze their content?

• Would these images be news today? Or would students argue that the photographs, although they look like news shots, are art? To give them practice at making concrete observations and writing concrete details, ask students to write a paragraph in class that depicts a black and white snapshot of a moment in their own lives.

• To continue developing your students' awareness of the relationship between seeing and writing, ask them to write a short piece in which they discuss the visual elements that construct meaning for each of Savulich's photographs. Which of the pictures would work without a caption? Why?

• **Image/Writing Assignment:** Ask students to write an essay that compares and contrasts two of Savulich's photographs with two color photographs from the Internet that also depict spot news. Students should consider the importance of captions in their essay.

CONNECTIONS WITH OTHER TEXTS

• Students' readings of these pictures are influenced by the photographer's captions. Refer students to other news photographs in the chapter — Joe Rosenthal's *Marines Raising the Flag on Mount Suribachi, Iwo Jima* (p. 308) and James Nachtwey's *Crushed Car* (p. 284), for example — and ask them to generate a number of captions for each picture. How do the captions change their perceptions of the events depicted in the photographs?

• People collect memorable moments by capturing images of those moments. Ask students to classify the kinds of memorable moments that are regarded as significant in the many images in this chapter and to define each photograph's characteristics — private versus public, celebrity versus anonymous, political versus apolitical, historical versus ahistorical, and so on. What is the importance of Savulich's photographs in comparison to these other images? What makes a photograph newsworthy? What makes it art?

SUGGESTION FOR FURTHER READING, THINKING, AND WRITING

AUDIOVISUAL

The Killing Screens: Media and the Culture of Violence. 41 min. 1994. VHS. Distributed by Media Education Foundation.

James Nachtwey, *Crushed Car* (p. 284) and *Ground Zero* (p. 285)

In his essay, Nachtwey relates his experiences of seeing the Twin Towers burn and crumble, of looking for shelter from the falling debris of the second tower, and of taking pictures of the aftermath at Ground Zero. A good point of discussion here involves the subject of visible versus invisible suffering. You might begin by asking students to examine Nachtwey's photograph and the thoughts and emotions it elicits.

What do students make of Nachtwey's descriptions? Nachtwey compares the site where the first tower fell to "a movie set from a science-fiction film" (para. 4). Point out to students that although that description is not unusual, Nachtwey's perspective is. Many people who watched the televised images of the planes striking the towers and the horrible aftermath compared them to scenes from a movie. But Nachtwey was there — he was living the experience — and still he compares the scene to something made in Hollywood.

Nachtwey's unaffected tone—particularly in the first few paragraphs—might surprise some students. As he recounts his first reaction to the tragedy, he does not describe feelings of dread or loss; instead, he matter-of-factly states: "When I saw the towers burning, my first reaction was to take a camera, to load it with film, go up on my roof, where I had a clear view, and photograph the first tower burning" (para. 2). Point out that his lack of emotion here is not due to a lack of empathy. As he explains, in a situation like this, his actions are based on instinct: "Documenting a crisis situation that's clearly out of control is always very instinctual. There's no road map. No ground rules. It's all improvisations" (para. 4). Later in the essay he attributes his survival on 9/11 and his continuing to work to his long experience documenting combat: "I don't fold up in these situations. I've been in them enough times to somehow have developed the capacity to continue to do my job" (para. 7).

Throughout the essay Nachtwey draws on his experience photographing war in his descriptions of events at the World Trade Center. The attack on the Twin Towers was different from war, he writes, because the falling towers were the only danger: "It wasn't as if people were shooting at us or we were being shelled or there were land mines there" (para. 12). Another element that made this experience different was that the "frontline troops . . . were firemen, and they put themselves in jeopardy. . . . They . . . didn't kill anyone; they were there to save people" (para. 13).

For Nachtwey probably the most important difference between this event and his wartime experience is the visibility of the suffering. He writes that he hasn't been able to fully process the attacks on the Twin Towers because "I didn't see the dead. . . . I didn't witness people suffering, . . . they were invisible. I didn't feel it as strongly as when I witnessed people starving to death or when I've seen innocent people cut down by sniper fire" (para. 15). Students might argue that to see two skyscrapers burn and crumble is to witness visible suffering, but few of them are likely to have had Nachtwey's experience of seeing death up close.

Cameras captured the actual destruction of the Twin Towers; they made us witnesses to the horror in New York City that day. What we saw of the attack in Washington, D.C., and the crash in Pennsylvania was the aftermath, still horrible but somehow less so—and so, less televised—than the attacks on the towers.

POSSIBILITIES FOR DISCUSSION, REFLECTING, AND JOURNALING

• Ask students to look at Nachtwey's photograph *Crushed Car* and to compare it with his description of the area: "Very apocalyptic—sunlight filtering through the dust and the destroyed wreckage of the buildings lying in the street" (para. 4). Do students see any resemblance in the picture to the set of a science fiction movie?

• Ask students to recall their own first experience with the events of September 11, 2001. Was it visual or aural? If some students first heard about the event and later saw images, ask them which had a stronger effect. Most students probably will say that the images had greater impact. Ask why they think this is so. Are the things we see innately more powerful than the things we hear or smell or taste or touch? Or have we been conditioned by a culture that has become increasingly visual? If students doubt the power of visual images, ask how often they think about the Pentagon or Flight 93 (the plane that crashed in Pennsylvania) when they think of September 11, 2001.

• If this discussion is hampered by students' being understandably too close to the subject, you might redirect the discussion to other horrible events in the past. Ask them to think about the most tragic events in history—don't name a specific branch of history (American, European, or world)—and then to list the first few events that come to mind. Most likely the Holocaust will be near the top of the list. Some students might focus on American history: the bombing of Pearl Harbor, the assassinations of John F. Kennedy and Martin Luther King Jr., the Vietnam War, the explosion of the space shuttle *Challenger*, and the recent spate of school shootings. Of course they will also list other events, but most—if not all—will have connections with visual images. As students list the events, think about possible visual connections, particularly those made through film (*Pearl Harbor, Schindler's List, Platoon, Saving Private Ryan, JFK*). Although these events are certainly tragic, many others are often overlooked because they do not have strong visual ties. For example, many students will think of the Holocaust because of *Schindler's List*. Fewer students will think of slavery in America, and even fewer will think of the treatment of Native Americans.

ADDITIONAL WRITING TOPICS AND CLASSROOM ACTIVITIES

• This essay raises an interesting issue regarding the importance of vision in how we process events intellectually and emotionally. As Nachtwey states, "I didn't witness people suffering, because they were invisible. I didn't feel it as strongly as when I witnessed people starving to death or when I've seen innocent people cut down by sniper fire" (para. 15). Ask students to write an essay in which they argue a position on whether visible suffering has more of an emotional impact than invisible suffering.

• Again referring to Nachtwey's words in paragraph 15, ask students to write an expository essay on why vision is—or has become—vital in the mental and emotional processing of events. You might suggest that students research deaf and blind cultures for more insight.

• In his essay Nachtwey states: "There is power in the still image that doesn't exist in other forms" (para. 17). Ask students to write an essay that compares and contrasts still images (photographs) with moving images (film). Do they agree or disagree with Nachtwey's assertion?

CONNECTIONS WITH OTHER TEXTS

• Nachtwey states that photographers need to document tragedies with "compassion and in a compelling way" (para. 19). Ask students to look again at the Sternfeld Portfolio in Chapter 2 (p. 132), photographs of sites linked to oppression or tragedy. To what extent do your students think that Sternfeld's photographs fit Nachtwey's criteria?

• Nachtwey writes that "there is power in the still image that doesn't exist in other forms." An essayist might write that "there is power in the written word that doesn't exist in other forms." Ask students to write a brief essay that compares one photograph and one essay from this chapter, with these statements as guides. What is the power of each? Advise students that this essay should be more exploratory than definitive, that they do not have to defend one form over the other.

SUGGESTIONS FOR FURTHER READING, THINKING, AND WRITING

PRINT

Nachtwey, James. *Inferno*. London: Phaidon, 2000. Print.

WEB

dirckhalstead.org/issue0110/seeing_intro.htm. The Digital Journalist web site features video interviews with several September 11 photographers, including Nachtwey.

johnpaulcaponigro.com/lib/artists/nachtwey .php. An interview with Nachtwey regarding his views on journalistic and collective responsibility.

pbs.org/newshour/gergen/jan-june00/nachtwey _5-16.html. An interview with Nachtwey on his book *Inferno*.

september11news.com/AttackImages.htm. A comprehensive resource on September 11, 2001, which includes timelines, international and U.S. news web archives, international and U.S. magazine covers, and images of the attack and the aftermath (four pictures by Nachtwey appear on the site).

time.com/time/photoessays/shattered/. *Time*'s exclusive collection of Nachtwey's September 11 photographs.

AUDIOVISUAL

Ground Zero America: First Response. 50 min. 2002. VHS. Distributed by the History Channel.

Bill McKibben, *Year One of the Next Earth* (p. 291), and Chris Jordan, *In Katrina's Wake* (pp. 290, 299, 300)

This reading selection and these photographs focus on the devastating effects of global warming demonstrated through the example of Hurricane Katrina. The essay opens by asking readers to look at the pictures and to contemplate the question, "Is this a crime scene?" Although we consider hurricanes to be natural disasters, McKibben extends his questions to consider blame: "If there's a crime, is there a criminal?" (para. 12).

Throughout the essay McKibben shows the history and facts associated with global warming, and its connection to hurricane strength and frequency. He also implies that this trend is intricately connected to our addiction to oil and our unwillingness to modify our behavior to control this addiction.

This pairing points out the ways that a defining moment—like a natural disaster—can change our thinking both before and after the event. It suggests that although the knowledge of global warming was evident before Katrina, it took something of this magnitude to get us to reflect on our choices.

• McKibben states that hurricanes destroy "huge swaths of what we've taken for granted" (para. 3). What are other events and happenings that have helped us realize what we are taking for granted once it is lost or forever changed? In what ways have other events had this effect?

• McKibben presents a series of facts and statistics that act as evidence in the piece. Students might talk about how he constructs his argument and what makes it convincing. What different kinds of evidence are presented?

• McKibben also suggests that although we have building knowledge of global warming, "it's human to resist change until you're sure you have to shift" (para. 15). How do we as human beings deal with change? Why do we resist it? What are the kinds of experiences that force us into change? Which experiences do we conveniently ignore in order to avoid change?

• McKibben ends his essay with a call to action. He says, "This is year one of the next earth. This is where we start" (para. 34). Discuss what he means by this statement and ask students to reflect on the personal choices they are willing to make at this point.

ADDITIONAL WRITING TOPICS AND CLASSROOM ACTIVITIES

• Have students work in small groups to discuss events of magnitude that caused them to change their thinking or their behavior. They can list the events individually, share them with one another, and then look for patterns, trends, and connections among them. Have them report back to the class on their findings.

• Ask students to write a research paper on Katrina or some other major event that gave a face to a scientific or political issue. Ask them to review images and articles and construct a persuasive argument explaining the connections between the event and ideological shifts.

• In the essay, McKibben suggests that we resist change. Ask students to write an essay in which they talk about a time when they resisted change. Why did they resist? What were the arguments in favor of change?

CONNECTION TO ANOTHER TEXT

• Both McKibben and Jordan suggest that it was the images from Katrina that "put a face on global warming" (para. 20). They talk about the particulars such as the wreckage, the evacuation lines, the wrecked lives wiped out in a moment. Ask students to look at images from *Seeing & Writing 4* along with other, online images of this disaster and to discuss the ways these particular images shaped our reactions, emotions, and actions. When does scientific knowledge become personal? How do the images engage our imagination?

SUGGESTIONS FOR FURTHER READING, THINKING, AND WRITING

PRINT

Flannery, Tim. *The Weather Makers: How Man Is Changing the Climate and What It Means for Life on Earth*. New York: Atlantic Monthly, 2005. Print.

Jordan, Chris, Bill McKibben, and Susan Zakin. *In Katrina's Wake: Portraits of Loss from an Unnatural Disaster*. New York: Princeton Architectural Press, 2006. Print.

McKibben, Bill. *Earth: Making a Life on a Tough New Planet*. New York: Times Books, 2010. Print.

——. *Fight Global Warming Now: The Handbook for Taking Action in Your Community.* New York: Holt, 2007. Print.

WEB

billmckibben.com. The author's official web site includes an autobiography, descriptions and testimonials of McKibben's publications, suggestions for reading, and contact information.

chrisjordan.com. Photographer Chris Jordan's web site, with images of his work, a list of events, and contact information.

AUDIOVISUAL

An Inconvenient Truth. 96 min. 2006. DVD. Distributed by Paramount.

Looking Closer:
Shaping Memory

Through photography we create artifacts that become part of our identities through their ability to capture the past and construct us through images — or as Sontag calls it, "certifying experience" (para. 5). These selections invite students to examine not only how Rosenthal's photograph of the flag raising on Iwo Jima has been used in different contexts but also how it echoes in other images.

Susan Sontag, *On Photography* (p. 304)

Sontag's selection brings to light just how pervasive photography is in our culture and in our lives. She describes it as "a social rite, a defense against anxiety, and a tool of power" (para. 1). It is increasingly present in our daily lives, especially with the popularity of social networking sites such as Facebook and with the convenience of the camera phone. Students are taking, tagging, and sharing photographs as they compose in these online settings. Students analyze and produce photographs at an alarming rate with these technologies. This selection offers a good opportunity to discuss the ways we represent ourselves as a culture through this medium.

Joe Rosenthal, *Marines Raising the Flag on Mount Suribachi, Iwo Jima* (p. 308) and *Flag Raising on Iwo Jima, February 23, 1945* (p. 309)

Rosenthal's photograph is one of the most famous images of World War II; it is also one of the most recognizable images in American history. This was not the only photograph Rosenthal took that day; he also took a picture of a large group of soldiers posed around the flag. But that picture remains largely unknown, while this candid shot has worldwide recognition. What is it about this image that makes it so affecting? so lasting? Although Rosenthal's essay does not touch on these questions, you might begin discussion with them. Students will probably note that *Marines Raising the Flag* represents America's pride in its victory. You might tell them that the image became famous only after it was cropped so that the flag runs diagonally throughout the entire frame. How does knowing about this change influence students' perception of the image? Ask students to imagine differences in the picture so that they can see the importance of details. Would an image of a flag already raised be as moving? What if different timing had enabled Rosenthal to capture the faces of the soldiers? What if the shrapnel had been cleared from the ground?

You could also begin discussion by having students examine the photograph before they read the essay. Ask whether they know the circumstances surrounding the photograph. If they have not heard or read much about the battle or the photograph, ask them to infer the circumstances from the details in the image. Then you could direct students to read the essay and note the parts that affect how they view the photograph.

Mark Zingarelli, *Memorial Day* (p. 311)

Mark Zingarelli's cover of the June 1994 *New Yorker* magazine is part of a series of images in the book that draw from Joe Rosenthal's iconic photograph of a group of soldiers raising the flag at Iwo Jima. This image has been recast as a military statue, a postage stamp, and other popular culture images such as the one represented here. Zingarelli's version shows a crowded beach scene in which a couple is raising an umbrella through a pose similar to the one in the Iwo Jima photograph. He details the consumer culture of tourism graphically juxtaposed with the original, classic image.

Students can look at other illustrations and cartoons by Zingarelli on his web site, House of Zing (houseofzing.com), to get a sense of his style and approach. His illustrations, which often parody different cultural phenomena and historical events, have appeared on many magazine covers. You might ask students to directly compare Zingarelli's image with the original Rosenthal image (also included in the text) to analyze what they think he is trying to communicate. Students might discuss what it means to parody and the ways that particular images become iconic through capturing moments.

Thomas E. Franklin, *Flag Raising, World Trade Center* (p. 312)
David J. Phillip, *Superbowl XXXVI* (p. 313)

Ask students to examine the different contexts in which Rosenthal's photo appears. How does each one change its meaning? Do other stamps or Super Bowl pregame shows come to mind as students look at the images here? By now students should know that an image's meaning depends on its context. But can the original meaning of an image be changed by being "the most widely reproduced photograph of all time"? In the case of *Marines Raising the Flag*, many people have probably seen the original photo only after seeing one or more of its countless imitations.

POSSIBILITIES FOR DISCUSSION, REFLECTION, AND JOURNALING

• Ask students to freewrite about a personal photograph that has had a lasting effect on them. Why has this photograph, out of the countless number of photos they have seen, stayed with them for so long?

• Rosenthal's photograph captures an image of one victory, "an incident in the turn of the battle" (p. 310). Ask students to imagine that the United States lost the war. Then have them write a short description of Rosenthal's picture with this imaginary history in mind. How would a different outcome in the war affect their reading of the photograph? (If the imaginary-history assignment prompts interesting responses, you might have students use it as the basis for an essay that analyzes how historical context plays into our readings of photographs.)

ADDITIONAL WRITING TOPICS AND CLASSROOM ACTIVITIES

• Ask students to write about how the feelings evoked by Franklin's photograph compare to those inspired by Rosenthal's picture.

• Have students analyze the contexts here to determine how they create meaning and change the meaning of Rosenthal's photograph. Encourage students to search online for other contexts in which Rosenthal's photograph has been used. How do the different contexts affect the meaning of the original?

• Have students compare and contrast Rosenthal's photograph with Franklin's *Flag Raising, World Trade Center*. Do they agree or disagree with the assertion that the success of Franklin's photograph rests on Rosenthal's picture? Why or why not?

CONNECTIONS WITH OTHER TEXTS

• In "On Photography" (p. 304) Susan Sontag writes: "A way of certifying experience, taking photographs is also a way of refusing it—by limiting experience to a search for the photogenic, by converting experience into an image, a souvenir" (para. 5). The image in Rosenthal's photograph has been reproduced many, many times. Ask students whether the popularity of the image—the possibility of its being a souvenir—lessens the importance of the experience it captures.

• Patriotism is a theme that runs through several of the most famous American images. For example, consider the photograph of astronauts Neil Armstrong and Buzz Aldrin planting an American flag on the moon in July 1969. Ask students to research famous images from other countries. Do they share a common theme of national pride?

• Ask students to research the history of an iconic image. How has it changed over the years? How has it been used? Have them examine several of its many contexts and explain how the icon takes on different meanings in those contexts.

• Rosenthal's other picture of the soldiers posed around the flag has largely gone unnoticed. Is it the sense of motion in *Marines Raising the Flag* that has made it an icon? Does that photograph suggest a narrative about the United States that resonates with its citizens? What might that narrative be? Encourage students to examine other pictures of flags being raised or of people posing with flags. What kinds of narratives do they suggest?

SUGGESTIONS FOR FURTHER READING, THINKING, AND WRITING

PRINT

Bradley, James. *Flags of Our Fathers.* New York: Bantam, 2001. Print.

Kreitler, Peter Gwillim. *United We Stand: Flying the American Flag.* San Francisco: Chronicle Books, 2001. Print. A collection of more than one hundred magazine covers that focused on the American flag in the summer after Pearl Harbor.

Ross, Bill D. *Iwo Jima: Legacy of Valor.* New York: Random House, 1986. Print.

Thomey, Tedd. *Immortal Images: A Personal History of Two Photographers and the Flag Raising on Iwo Jima.* Annapolis, MD: Naval Institute Press, 1996. Print.

WEB

iwojima.com. This comprehensive web site about Iwo Jima includes a description of the battle, as well as photographs and film clips of the flag raising.

nps.gov/gwmp/usmc.htm. The National Park Service's picture and description of the Marine Corps War Memorial, a statue based on Rosenthal's photograph.

AUDIOVISUAL

Heroes of Iwo Jima. 100 min. 2001. VHS. Distributed by A&E. Presents the battle of Iwo Jima through photographers' viewpoints and interviews with nearly fifty people. Rosenthal's famous photo is discussed in the interviews.

4

PROJECTING GENDER

Where do gender definitions stem from? What do media representations of gender convey? How do gender assumptions change across the globe? What makes someone masculine or feminine? In some instances, is it better to be one rather than the other?

You might want to begin by asking whether students agree with the definition of *gender* given in the introduction to the chapter: "a cultural category, . . . the behavioral or psychological standards for masculine or feminine behavior" (p. 317). That gender — maleness or femaleness — is based on cultural assumptions about and prescriptions for behavior is critical to understanding the materials here.

To open the discussion, you might ask students to answer the questions about the male and female icons presented in the introduction. Reiterate that the key feature that distinguishes one icon from the other is the dress or skirt on the icon that represents "woman." You might mention the historical styles of clothing for women and men and how they have changed over the years, even though the tendency to associate women with dresses has not changed.

POSSIBILITIES FOR DISCUSSION, REFLECTION, AND JOURNALING

- How exactly do these icons communicate gender difference?
- What cultural assumptions are embedded in them?

- Why are differences in clothing such a clear indicator of gender identity and sex?

- How do different cultures train children to identify with — and project — gender from an early age?

- How do these representations of difference relate to larger issues of the equality of the sexes and the social construction of gender?

- Have students look around the classroom to see how many female students are wearing dresses or skirts. Chances are, very few. Why, then, are dresses and skirts so emblematic of "female"?

ADDITIONAL WRITING TOPICS AND CLASSROOM ACTIVITIES

- **Image/Writing Assignment:** For fun, and to show students that alternatives do exist, ask them to think about the characteristics they associate with maleness and femaleness and then to design their own icons to replace those presented here.

- Another topic for discussion is whether gender lines are breaking down. By asking students to give examples from popular culture of how men and women are represented, you are preparing them for the work they'll be doing as they read the selections in the chapter. Which texts make clear, even polarizing, distinctions between the genders? In which texts are gender differences blurred? Depending on the students' perspectives, they may have widely varying responses to these questions as they read each selection. You might ask students to consider the cultural assumptions about gender they bring to this chapter; then ask them to chart, in a journal, the ways in which those assumptions affect their response to each selection.

Surefire Class: Projecting Gender

Rebecca Burns
*St. Louis Community
College, Meramec*
(Profile, p. 7)

My surefire strategy for helping students write a highly critical and reflective cause-and-effect paper involves three steps:

1. Introduce the specifics of the causal analysis paper.

2. Have students read Susan Bordo's "Never Just Pictures" (p. 367) and study the pictures in Retrospect: Building the Male Body (p. 354) and Lauren Greenfield's *Ashleigh, 13, with Her Friend and Parents, Santa Monica* (p. 378).

3. Discuss the essay and images in conjunction with an exploration of digital images.

Beginning with Susan Bordo's essay is an excellent way to initiate a discussion of a very serious subject: the media's effect on body image. As Bordo points out in "Never Just Pictures," thanks to television, films, magazines, and tabloids, "children in this culture grow up knowing that you can never be thin enough and that being fat is one of the worst things one can be" (para. 1). After reading this quotation, we turn to Figure 2 ("Advertising anorexia?") and study this image. I ask students if they feel that being exposed to pictures like this one contributes to eating disorders. Then I like to explore some web sites, beginning with Calvin Klein advertisements, and it should be noted that the images are risqué. However, looking at these ads and pointing out how all of the models—both male and female—are unnaturally lean and buff are important. Furthermore, this segment corresponds wonderfully with Bordo's mention

of Calvin Klein models. She points out that while Klein has "begun to use rather plain, ordinary-looking, unmadeup faces in [his] ad campaigns . . . looks—a lean body—still matter enormously in these ads" (paras. 11–12). She adds that these advertisements are actually "reasserting the importance of body over face as the 'site' of our fantasies" (para. 12).

Next we discuss the pictures in Retrospect: Building the Male Body because it is important to point out that women are not the sole victims of eating disorders, that men are plagued by them also. As shown in this series of images, men have been targeted by the media for at least a century. They have been told that weakness is "a crime" (p. 354), that it brings "shame" (p. 355), and that women cling to your body when your waistline is trim (p. 356). I point out to students that men are still victims of this type of advertisement. In beer commercials in particular, men— lean and muscular men—are always surrounded by beautiful women. Never do we see pictures of the average male—one with smaller pectorals and tiny love handles. Then I like to show students the hilary .com/fashion/bikini.html site. It contains excerpts from magazine interviews with various models and celebrities who admit that their photographs have been air-brushed: The images of perfect bodies that we are bombarded with are not true representations of the body.

Finally we discuss Lauren Greenfield's *Ashleigh, 13, with Her Friend and Parents, Santa Monica*. As we look at the image of Ashleigh and discuss her apparent obsession with weight, we discuss how tragic it is that a child this young could be suffering from an eating disorder. We talk about the images that we have analyzed and how they influence adults, and I point out that, unlike adults, who may actually realize that photographs are airbrushed, children believe what they see. Then we explore two web sites that contain statistical information on anorexia and bulimia: abouteatingdisorders.org and annecollins.com/eating-disorders/statistics.htm. The data on these sites helps solidify for students the seriousness of eating disorders in our country and around the world. After discussing the alarming statistics on these sites, I like to end the visual discussion with images from the following web site: museumofhoaxes.com/skinny.html. The images of anorexic models here are startling, even shocking.[1]

I close this particular class discussion by asking students, working in groups, to list the part the media play in defining body image. At the close of this class, in addition to being prepared to write an interesting cause-and-effect paper, students are left feeling shocked by the prevalence of eating disorders and feeling somewhat angry with the world of advertising and the media. They also are left with a different view of society and their role in it. In addition, the next time they see an advertisement featuring beautiful bodies, they are likely not only to question the authenticity of the image, but also to wonder how other people are being influenced by it.

---

[1] Editor's note: Be sure students understand that these images may have been manipulated. The site, after all, is devoted to hoaxes.

SUREFIRE CLASS

Portfolio: Mapplethorpe (p. 320)

Robert Mapplethorpe, *Self-Portraits*

In the first photograph, Mapplethorpe's clothes, hair, and cigarette, even his facial expression, all indicate a character (in literary terms, we might even call it a stereotype): the street tough. But notice that Mapplethorpe is making a comment on gender here. He has feminized this masculine stereotype: His hair is carefully and excessively styled; his clothes are specifically chosen; his skin is pristine.

The other portrait here ostensibly offers an image of naked honesty: the bared chest; the squared shoulders; the open, direct gaze. But those elements stand in contrast to the heavily made-up face. (Even for the 1980s, a time of overstated makeup for women, Mapplethorpe's face is excessively adorned.) So in this portrait too, despite his lack of clothing, Mapplethorpe seems to be in costume. Ask students to look at how his face is lit in the photograph: It is half in shadow, perhaps hinting at secrecy, and the light itself is not especially flattering. In the first portrait, the light flattens and smooths out Mapplethorpe's features. In the second, it reveals all his facial flaws: the grease shining through the makeup, the bags beneath the eyes, his pores. The message seems to be that we cannot hide everything about ourselves, no matter how hard we try.

POSSIBILITIES FOR DISCUSSION, REFLECTION, AND JOURNALING

•   In the second Seeing question on Mapplethorpe's works (p. 322), the authors cite Jennifer Blessing's comment that Mapplethorpe's portraits "are more frequently consciously contrived studio portraits." Using this comment as a starting point, ask students to consider how in both self-portraits Mapplethorpe seems to be in costume.

•   Ask students to think about how all the choices they make about their appearance and their clothing amount to choices about their character in the dramatic sense—about how they want to be perceived by others.

ADDITIONAL WRITING TOPICS AND CLASSROOM ACTIVITIES

•   Ask students to ignore the subject matter of the photographs for a moment and to look at the lighting and its effect on the composition. Which self-portrait is more appealing? Why?

•   In the introduction to the chapter, the authors mention "codes for gender behavior" (p. 318). Ask students to write an essay in which they identify these codes within Mapplethorpe's two self-portraits.

•   The most striking element of the second self-portrait is Mapplethorpe's use of dramatic makeup. Ask students to consider how and why many women and some men use makeup. What are they trying to hide? What are they trying to highlight? Then have students write a short essay in which they respond to these questions, considering them both literally and figuratively.

CONNECTIONS WITH OTHER TEXTS

• Ask students to consider both of Mapplethorpe's self-portraits in conjunction with the Pirelli ad featuring Carl Lewis (p. 375). What do these images suggest about how masculinity is constructed?

• Ask students to compare the pose of masculinity adopted by Mapplethorpe in the first self-portrait with the bodybuilding poses adopted by the men in the images in this chapter's Retrospect (p. 354). How do these images reveal our cultural definition of masculinity? What defines a man?

SUGGESTIONS FOR FURTHER READING, THINKING, AND WRITING

PRINT

Danto, Arthur C. *Playing with the Edge: The Photographic Achievement of Robert Mapplethorpe.* Berkeley: U of California P, 1996. Print.

Hughes, Robert. "Art, Morals, and Politics: Effects of Robert Mapplethorpe's Photography on American Art and Culture." *New York Review of Books*, April 23, 1992: 21+. Print. The esteemed art critic Robert Hughes discusses Mapplethorpe in an extensive (seven-page) article.

WEB

ocaiw.com/mapple.htm. Photographs by Mapplethorpe are available for viewing at this site, and there is a list of Mapplethorpe-related books.

Pair: Cardona & Martínez (p. 324)

Jacinto Jesús Cardona, *Bato con Khakis*
César A. Martínez, *Bato con Khakis*

Martínez's painting is based on Cardona's poem. You might keep this information from students until after they've examined the painting.

Martínez's painting is made of indefinite outlines and scribbles of color. The jagged lines and scribbles reflect the studied carelessness of the poem's character: "looking limber in a blue vest, / laid-back in my dark shades" (lines 6–7). Notice how the artist uses the figure's posture—the slouch, his hands in his pockets—to emphasize the young man's nonchalance. The indefinite outlines show a young man too cool to be concerned with how he is represented, but the lack of definition also reflects the insecurity revealed in the third stanza of the poem: "Alas! I'm the bifocals kid; / cool bato I am not" (ll. 8–9).

POSSIBILITIES FOR DISCUSSION, REFLECTION, AND JOURNALING

• While students are studying Martínez's painting, ask them to comment on how the artist uses shape and color to create a personality. What does the figure's posture suggest about his character? Have students make a list of the character traits they see in the painting.

• Then turn to Cardona's poem. Before discussing the meaning of *bato*, ask students to read the poem and write a brief description of the character depicted in it. Then have them read and discuss the Seeing questions on page 327. Use the definition of *bato* in the first question there to lead the discussion back to Martínez's painting. If students cannot guess the meaning of *Spanglish*, you can tell them that it is what the word suggests: Spanish mixed with English (often with faulty English).

• As students compare the painting with the poem, ask them to look at the lists they made earlier. Do the character traits they saw in the painting match those they find in the poem? Have students discuss and possibly argue their interpretations of each piece.

ADDITIONAL WRITING TOPICS AND CLASSROOM ACTIVITIES

• Ask students to write an expository paper about the strategies Martínez used to translate Cardona's verbal text into a visual one.

• Reverse the second Writing question on page 327 of *Seeing & Writing 4*. Ask students to write an essay in which they support or challenge the claim that Martínez's painting would not be effective in the absence of Cardona's poem.

• Ask students to write a short essay explaining which piece appeals to them more: the painting or the poem. Tell them to be specific about why the other piece is less appealing.

CONNECTIONS WITH OTHER TEXTS

• Ask students to compare the representations of gender in Martínez's painting and in William H. Johnson's *Li'L Sis* (p. 328). What are the effects of the colors in each painting? What does the posture of the figure in each painting suggest?

• Ask students to examine Robert Mapplethorpe's *Self-Portrait, 1980* (p. 320) and then to write a poem from Mapplethorpe's perspective (in the first person) that describes the painting.

SUGGESTIONS FOR FURTHER READING, THINKING, AND WRITING

PRINT

Cardona, Jacinto Jesús. *Pan Dulce.* San Antonio: Chili Verde, 1998. Print.

Quirarte, Jacinto. *Mexican and Mexican American Art in the United States, 1920–1970.* Austin: U of Texas P, 1973. Print.

WEB

aaa.si.edu/collections/oralhistories/transcripts/martin97.htm. Smithsonian Art Archives Institute interview with Martínez.

Jamaica Kincaid, *Girl* (p. 329)
William H. Johnson, *Li'L Sis* (p. 328)

Kincaid's story takes the form of a long speech by a mother to her daughter. This is not a conversation: The girl interjects just twice — notice the italic type — but neither time does she slow her mother's diatribe. The mother's tone is harsh and unloving. Several times she refers to her daughter as a slut, and her directions are unceasingly demanding. Neither character is ever named, but the title of the piece, "Girl," highlights not only the gender inscription that is part of the mother's message but also the distance between mother and daughter: The daughter is just another girl to her mother.

Kincaid grew up in Antigua in the 1950s and 1960s, and the lessons imparted by the mother give shape to a specific cultural definition of what women were expected to do in that place at that time: clean, cook, shop, sew, go to church, iron, garden, show modesty, set a table, keep themselves clean, act as nurses, and budget money. Women were essentially inscribed as servants, with no interests beyond those necessary for keeping a home. A second strand in the mother's lessons involves sexuality, which she clearly presents as a danger. The mother warns her daughter about acting "like the slut you are so bent on becoming" (p. 329) and repeats that phrasing two more times. She worries about her daughter's modesty: "you are not a boy, you know" (p. 329). She tells the girl that she should not expect to enjoy sex with her husband: "this is how to love a man, and if this doesn't work there are other ways, and if they don't work don't feel too bad about giving up" (p. 330). And she lets her daughter know "how to make a good medicine to throw away a child before it even becomes a child" (p. 330).

William H. Johnson's *Li'L Sis* offers the image of a girl with a slightly sad expression. You might direct students to the child's face, to her downturned eyes and flat mouth. Her stance seems almost defensive, her raised arm fending off the viewer. You could ask students to think about how Li'L Sis is connected to the images around her. The color red ties the hair comb to the swatter to the baby carriage. In the carriage, the red seems slightly threatening, especially in the red dots on the carriage cover. The bright white of the dress collar is repeated in Li'L Sis's eyes and nails, and — importantly — the doll's gown. In the tradition of folk art, the child is one-dimensional, flattened against the dull mustard background, and she seems almost imprisoned by the tight frame of the painting.

• Have students make a list of all the tasks the mother mentions and then consider the type of life they describe.

• You might ask students to consider how the very structure of the story underscores the mother's message. It is one long sentence broken only with commas and semicolons. There are no stops here, no room for the girl to assert herself. Have students refer back to the chapter introduction to think about cultural assumptions of gender and how they are communicated to members of the culture.

• Ask students to note the elements in the painting that indicate gender expectations. For example, the girl has a comb in her hair, a brightly colored dress on her slight figure. Point to the objects in the picture: the doll-baby in the buggy and what looks like a rug-swatter — all indications of domesticity. This young girl's realm is the home.

ADDITIONAL WRITING TOPICS AND CLASSROOM ACTIVITIES

• In reading "Girl," most students identify with the daughter, not the mother. In a short piece, ask students to describe what the mother's motivations might be for telling her daughter these things. How is the mother, however misguidedly, attempting to help her daughter fit into their culture?

• Ask students to write an essay in which they analyze the connotations of the colors Johnson uses in *Li'L Sis*. How do the colors contribute to the tone he has taken toward his subject? (Johnson's palette is limited to just a few colors, so this is a manageable assignment.)

• Johnson's painting is small — just 21¼ inches by 26 inches. Like Kincaid's story, it is compact, limited. How do the size and structure of each work underscore what it is saying about the role of women in society?

CONNECTIONS WITH OTHER TEXTS

• Ask students to compare what Kincaid and Johnson are saying about women's place in society with the message Lauren Greenfield conveys in *Ashleigh, 13, with Her Friend and Parents, Santa Monica* (p. 378). They should pay close attention to the emphasis on appearance in all three works.

• Although Kincaid's story is almost entirely in the mother's words, we respond to those words as the daughter would. In this sense, Kincaid has written the story from the daughter's perspective. Tillie Olsen, in her classic story "I Stand Here Ironing" (Chapter 1, p. 62), is writing from the mother's perspective. Ask students to compare the mother–daughter relationships in these two works.

SUGGESTIONS FOR FURTHER READING, THINKING, AND WRITING

PRINT

Friday, Nancy. *My Mother, My Self: A Daughter's Search for Identity*. New York: Delacorte, 1977. Print.

Kincaid, Jamaica. *The Autobiography of My Mother*. New York: Plume, 1997. Print.

Powell, Richard J. *Homecoming: The Art and Life of William H. Johnson*. New York: Rizzoli for the Smithsonian American Art Museum, 1991. Print.

WEB

emory.edu/ENGLISH/Bahri/Kincaid.html. This site includes a biography of Kincaid and links to several interviews.

AUDIOVISUAL

Jamaica Kincaid. 60 min. American Audio Prose Library, 1991. Cassette.

Judith Ortiz Cofer, *The Story of My Body* (p. 332)

Cofer's memoir begins with a quote from Victor Hernández Cruz ("Migration is the story of my body") that sets the tone for the piece. Her story describes her ethnic heritage and the way in which her ethnicity is read differently as she moves from place to place. She writes: "I spent the first years of my life [in Puerto Rico] hearing people refer to me as *blanca*, white" (para. 3). But in a supermarket in Paterson, New Jersey, the butcher yells at her: "'You always look dirty. But maybe dirty brown is your natural color'" (para. 6). It is the culture that assigns positive and negative values to Cofer's color and body. In the United States the ideal body is symbolized by "Susie, the talking schoolteacher doll" (para. 5), with its pure white skin and "fine gold hair" (para. 7). Cofer cannot possibly measure up to this ideal, no matter how much she scrubs. Her skin will never be "pink like [her] friend Charlene . . . who had blue eyes and light brown hair" (para. 6). Nor can she measure up in the looks category: In elementary school she finds that "the hierarchy for popularity was . . . pretty white girl, pretty Jewish girl, pretty Puerto Rican girl, pretty black girl" (para. 15). And later, in high school, she loses her date for the dance because his father "had seen how the spics lived. Like rats" (para. 17).

The Latino standard for beauty is exemplified by Cofer's mother: "long, curly black hair, and round curves in a compact frame" (para. 13). As a child, Cofer is rewarded for being "*bonita*, pretty" (para. 13). She describes herself as being dressed up "like a doll" (para. 14), but as she grows older, she fits neither the Latino nor the American definition of beauty. She is judged too skinny by the Puerto Rican boys and is not white enough for the Americans.

Cofer's reaction in sixth grade is to drop out of the beauty game: "That is when I decided I was a 'brain'" (para. 15). Ask students to consider that reaction. Clearly Cofer has thrived as an intellectual and an academic. She ends her essay on a positive note, stressing that her "sense of self-worth" now comes from her "studies" and "writing" (para. 18). However, the tone of her essay and her ability to recall with such precise detail the definitions of beauty that excluded her suggest that there is some lingering pain attached to her memories.

- To open discussion, you might direct students to consider how and why Cofer's skin color "changes" when she moves from Puerto Rico to the United States.

- You might ask students to examine Cofer's essay for a sense of how the definition of beauty changes from culture to culture.

- Ask students to think about the structure of Cofer's essay, specifically its division by headings ("Skin," "Color," "Size," "Looks"). Why does she use these headings? How does each heading comment on or reflect the information that follows? How do the sections of the piece connect to one another and to Cofer's purpose for writing the essay?

- Ask students, working in groups, to examine one heading and its relationship to the essay as a whole. Each group could discuss the literal and figurative relationships between the heading and its section. You could ask the groups to select one sentence within the section that exemplifies the head and/or connects it to the other sections. For example, in the first section, "Skin," Cofer tells us that she was scarred by chicken pox: "This was when I learned to be invisible" (para. 2), she writes. In the "Looks" section, she repeats the theme of invisibility, hiding "behind my long black hair and my books" (para. 15). Such examples could lead into discussions of how students can create coherence in similar ways in their essays.

ADDITIONAL WRITING TOPICS AND CLASSROOM ACTIVITIES

- Cofer ends with the statement "My studies, later my writing, the respect of people who saw me as an individual person they cared about, these were the criteria for my sense of self-worth that I would concentrate on in my adult life" (para. 18). Ask students to write a short statement that explains their own criteria for establishing a sense of self-worth.

- In paragraph 15, Cofer speaks about "presentability" as a quality by which students at her school were judged. Ask your class to flesh out the definition of *presentability* in the essay. What is Cofer's attitude toward this quality?

- Early in the essay Cofer writes, "I started out life as a pretty baby and learned to be a pretty girl from a pretty mother" (para. 2). Later she refers to her mother as "a stunning young woman by Latino standards" (para. 13) and remembers, "My mother was proud of my looks, although I was a bit too thin. She could dress me up like a doll" (para. 14). Ask students to write an essay that analyzes how physical beauty and its consequences figure into Cofer's relationship with her mother.

CONNECTIONS WITH OTHER TEXTS

- Cofer discusses how the concept of beauty varies among cultures. Point to the Nikki S. Lee Portfolio in Chapter 5 (p. 397) for visual examples when discussing this part of Cofer's essay.

- Both Cofer and Amy Tan, in "Fish Cheeks" (Chapter 2, p. 218), recount the difficulties of growing up as "other" in the United States. Ask students to write an essay in which they compare and contrast these writers' autobiographical works, paying close attention to the details in and the tone of each.

SUGGESTIONS FOR FURTHER READING, THINKING, AND WRITING

PRINT

Cofer, Judith Ortiz. *An Island like You: Stories of the Barrio.* New York: Orchard, 1995. Print.

WEB

mclibrary.nhmccd.edu/lit/cofer.html. A Judith Ortiz Cofer page established as part of an authors' series by Montgomery College in Texas.

Surefire Class: Our Bodies, Our Selves

Maureen Ellen O'Leary
Diablo Valley College
(Profile, p. 16)

For each of the units in my freshman writing class, I try to define a core question. For our unit on "The Body" (Chapter 4, Projecting Gender), the question is a rather obvious but extremely critical one: What is the relationship between body and self-identity, between *who we are* and *how we appear physically* to the world?

At the beginning of the unit, students speak rather glibly about the gap between our physical selves and "who we *really* are"; it doesn't matter how you look, they say, because it's what you are on the inside that counts. Although this is true in so many important respects, I encourage students not to ignore the complications of our body/soul duality: Although the content of our hearts and minds and souls matters most, we meet the world and the world meets us through and with our bodies. I ask students to consider all the situations in which what is on the inside does not count as it should and the consequences of that. How can we negotiate that land-mined terrain between how others see us with their eyes and how they see us as people—that is, how they make judgments about who we are?

Whether we speak about it or not, all of us are aware that we are judged by our appearance. And we are often our own harshest critics when it comes to our looks. This is trebly true for college students, who, even in a community college like ours, fall primarily between the ages of eighteen and twenty-five. Although some students are reluctant to speak directly about specific

insecurities they may have regarding their appearance, they address their particular concerns through discussions of the rich variety of written and visual texts we explore together. Even if silent in class, many give voice to powerful, often deeply painful body-related experiences in the reading responses, freewrites, and formal essays that they submit to me.

Throughout the unit, I call students' attention to the distinction between the stories that our bodies overtly tell about us—for example, our age, gender, race, and so forth—and the stories that we ourselves choose to tell through our bodies—through clothing and hairstyle, body piercings, tattoos, cosmetic surgery, and the like. Then there are the stories we "half-tell" about ourselves through our bodies, the physical manifestations of mental or emotional distress (for example, signs of alcohol and drug addiction, or being excessively under- or overweight) and of physical illness. We try to pin down together what others *do know*, what they *think they know*, and what they *can never know* about us through our bodies. We make distinctions between justifiable assumptions and unjustifiable, or false, assumptions about us based on our appearance.

Clearly, our nonphysical identity is to some extent shaped by our physical identity because other people's reactions to our appearance have emotional, psychological, and mental effects on us. Part of our sense of who we are, part of who we end up being, is determined by the judgment on our looks that is reflected back to us from the world. And this judgment often fluctuates throughout our lives.

Judith Ortiz Cofer addresses some of these issues head-on in her rich essay, "The Story of My Body." She divides her essay into separate categories or "chapters": "Skin," "Color," "Size," "Looks." Cofer's essay wonderfully illustrates the fluctuations in the valuing—by others and ourselves—of physical aspects of ourselves. In Puerto Rico she was "a white girl"; in the United States she "became a brown girl." She considered herself "a pretty girl" until she discovered that according to the hierarchy of her elementary school, Puerto Rican girls were low on the beauty list. I ask my students to consider what categories or chapters they would come up with in writing their own body autobiographies. We put some of them on the board: separate parts of their bodies, different ages, and so forth. At home, all students write one "chapter" of their body story and share it in groups.

I include "The Story of My Body" as a topic choice for the formal essay that completes the unit: *Using Judith Ortiz Cofer's essay "The Story of My Body" as a model as well as for support, write a carefully constructed story of your own body. Avoid over-generalizing; include specific examples; and bring genuine reflection and analysis into your account. You do not have to use Cofer's categories; feel free to develop your own depending on what story about your body you want to tell.* This topic produces rich, often moving, often funny essays. Students are very creative in the ways they structure their material. One student wrote a lively essay about clothing her body from adolescence through young womanhood (from "Padded Bras" to "Jeans, ChapStick, and Ponytail"). Another tracked his own and others' responses to his height at different periods. One student talked about how she was seen—and saw herself—as she moved with her family from one country to another. All of the bodies we had seen together in the unit helped the students to be brave and bold in telling their own stories. However, I am always careful to include topic choices that allow students to avoid sensitive or painful material. Students are never coerced into sharing any stories that they are not yet ready to tell.

Marjane Satrapi, *The Veil* (p. 343)

In "The Veil," an excerpt from the graphic novel *Persepolis: The Story of a Childhood*, Satrapi presents her ten-year-old self as the narrator of events surrounding the Islamic revolution of 1979 in Iran and the institution of the veil in 1980.

Satrapi shows the introduction of the veil in the fourth panel on page 343: A woman, veiled herself, hands the girls their veils as they walk into school. There is no explanation; she simply tells them, "Wear this!" Ask students to describe Satrapi's tone in this panel. Does that tone change when they consider the young girl peering over the school wall? Then have them look at the fifth panel on the page, which shows the girls playing around with their veils. Point to the background, to the girl — wearing the veil — who is choking another child and saying, "Execution in the name of freedom." How does this interaction affect the tone of the panel?

Because the selection ends on a note of uncertainty about how to read Satrapi, you might direct students to look back at the pages in which she declares her intentions of becoming a prophet. Do the additional rules and the discussion with her grandmother (see page 347) point to the difficulty of implementing Zarathustra's original rules?

POSSIBILITIES FOR DISCUSSION, REFLECTION, AND JOURNALING

• You might ask students to discuss the choice of the girl as narrator. What does this choice grant Satrapi in her telling of the story? How does the narrator's youth, her innocence, shape the story? Then ask them to imagine how the story would be different if Satrapi had chosen an older narrator.

• Ask students to consider the adults' reactions — "Bravo!" and "What wisdom!" (p. 344) — to the command to close down bilingual schools. How does the medium of the comic strip make this kind of irony work?

• What seems to be the attitude of the adult Satrapi toward the child Satrapi's wanting to be a prophet?

ADDITIONAL WRITING TOPICS AND CLASSROOM ACTIVITIES

• Ask students to research the current status of women in Iran. How is that information likely to influence Satrapi's sequels to *Persepolis: The Story of a Childhood*? Given that information — what Satrapi has to portray in the sequels — how might she use her young narrator to her best advantage?

• Ask students to freewrite about Satrapi's choice of her young self as narrator. How does this point of view achieve certain effects? How does it help her readers? Does it restrict her readers in any way? Ask students to explain their answers.

CONNECTIONS WITH OTHER TEXTS

• Ask students to compare the narrators' tones in Satrapi's "The Veil" and Spiegelman's "Nature vs. Nurture" (p. 380). Each author offers a different perspective, in part based on the narrator's age—Satrapi's is innocent, Spiegelman's is cynical—yet they both are sharply critical. How does each author achieve that effect?

• Ask students to describe the picture Satrapi presents of gender, to think of the placement of this selection in the chapter on gender. How does this view of women in a specific place affect their reading of other works by women in this chapter?

SUGGESTIONS FOR FURTHER READING, THINKING, AND WRITING

PRINT

Kahn, Shahnaz. *Muslim Women: Crafting a North American Identity*. Gainesville: UP of Florida, 2002. Print.

Nafisi, Azar. *Reading Lolita in Tehran: A Memoir in Books*. New York: Random House, 2003. Print.

Neshat, Shirin. *Women of Allah*. Turin, Italy: Marco Noire Contemporary Art, 1997. Print.

Satrapi, Marjane. *Persepolis: The Story of a Childhood*. New York: Pantheon, 2003. Print.

WEB

alpertawards.org/archive/winner00/neshat.html. Includes a brief profile of Shirin Neshat; lists of exhibitions, awards, and publications; and Neshat's comments on her own work.

bookslut.com/features/2004_10_003261.php. An interview with Satrapi.

iranian.com/Arts/Dec97/Neshat/index.html. This Iranian web site, published by Jahanshah Javid, features images from Neshat's *Women of Allah*.

Context: Satrapi (p. 352)

Marjane Satrapi, Introduction to *Persepolis: The Story of a Childhood*

If you've discussed the tone of the young narrator with your students, you could turn to Satrapi's introduction to *Persepolis* for an example of how the adult Satrapi "sounds." In this piece Satrapi provides a quick history of Iran, from its settling in the second millennium B.C., the establishment of the first Iranian nation in the seventh century B.C., and the conquest that made it Persia until 1935, to the more recent conquests and invasions. She observes that its "wealth" and "geographic location" often made Iran "subject to foreign domination" (para. 2). Given the ironic, critical tone of "The Veil," students may be surprised by Satrapi's tone here, especially when she first celebrates Iran's heritage: "Yet the Persian language and culture withstood these invasions. The invaders assimilated into this strong culture, and in some ways they became Iranians themselves" (para. 2). In paragraph 5, Satrapi explains why she wrote *Persepolis*: "Since [1979], this old and great civilization has been discussed mostly in connection with fundamentalism, fanaticism, and terrorism. As an Iranian who has lived more than half of my life in Iran, I know that this image is far from the truth."

POSSIBILITIES FOR DISCUSSION, REFLECTION, AND JOURNALING

• Ask students to look back at "The Veil." Do they see Satrapi's intentions more clearly now? Can they point to the panels that illustrate "the wrongdoings of a few extremists" (para. 5)?

ADDITIONAL WRITING TOPICS AND CLASSROOM ACTIVITIES

• Before students read Satrapi's introduction to *Persepolis*, ask them to write a brief paragraph about Satrapi's feelings toward Iran based on "The Veil." They should point to specific panels to support their claims. And then you might discuss how the introduction changes their perception of "The Veil."

• Before students read the Context selection, ask them to freewrite about the image they have of Iran. What are the sources of their information? their perspective?

CONNECTIONS WITH OTHER TEXTS

• Put students in pairs and ask them to turn this introduction into a one-page comic strip. They don't have to draw the images; they can pick them up from the web. But they should use Satrapi's style in "The Veil" for their text, limiting themselves to just a few sentences per panel as she does. When they've finished, ask them how the tone of the essay influenced their choices of both visual and verbal texts. Then ask them to compare their comic strip with "The Veil."

• Ask students to research one or two web sites that feature Iranian history. In a brief, informal paper, they could discuss how the histories presented by the web sites are similar to and different from the history presented by Satrapi. How do they reconcile the differences? How do they judge the reliability of the authors? What still puzzles them?

SUGGESTIONS FOR FURTHER READING, THINKING, AND WRITING

PRINT

Elton, Daniel. *The History of Iran*. Westport, CT: Greenwood, 2000. Print.

Keddie, Nikki. *Modern Iran: Roots and Results of Revolution*. New Haven: Yale UP, 2003. Print.

WEB

tehran.stanford.edu. Stanford University's site on Iranian culture.

Retrospect: Building the Male Body (p. 354)

This Retrospect invites students to look at stereotypes of the male body throughout the twentieth century. Each image—magazine cover and ads—focuses on the male body, revealing flesh and emphasizing muscle. The implication is that physical fitness isn't enough; men must be muscular to be manly, to defend themselves, and to be sexually attractive.

The first image suggests a relationship between physical health and moral health. "Weakness A Crime; Don't Be A Criminal" declares *Physical Culture* magazine on its cover. The image shows the male body in a "before and after" context. The "normal condition" is presumably weak, or at least weaker than the chiseled body presented after a seven-day fast.

The message of the ad on page 355 is also explicit. The words tell us "How Joe's Body Brought Him FAME Instead of SHAME." In this case, a drama unfolds in the comic strip: The weakling, after being humiliated at the beach by a muscular bully, goes home and reshapes his body by building his muscles (particularly his upper body, which is visible in the last frame of the comic strip). He then becomes the "Hero of the Beach" and draws admiring glances from one and all, most importantly from the woman who sees that he is "a real man after all." The ad lets us know that it is up to the individual man (in this case, the man reading the ad) to achieve the ideal masculine body shape—to be a "New Man . . . in Only 15 Minutes a Day"—by using the Charles Atlas body-building method.

The ad on page 356 for the paradoxically named Relax-A-cizor uses a semi-nude man to send its message about what makes men attractive. The effect of the ad depends on several assumptions about what is attractive in and to a man. Ask your students to notice where their eyes go when they first look at the ad. They will probably say that their eyes first go to the photograph of the man standing at the left of the ad. This image suggests that an attractive man is trim and strong, with a tight waistline and muscled arms and legs. (Students who didn't grow up watching beach-blanket movies might laugh at the notion of this guy being the poster boy for manliness.) In case we doubt this man's attractions, the woman clinging to his leg and gazing up at him is proof. And where do students' eyes go next? Probably to the text above the man. Here we take in the odd product name, which implies another assumption—that men would like to look good without working for it.

The last ad catches the male subject in a dilemma regarding his pursuit of fitness. He is between the light and the dark of the laundry closet and the darkened hallway—perhaps on his way to a predawn run. The ad's question is, "Does it matter to you that if you skip a day of running, only one person in the world will ever know? Or is that one person too many?" The furrowed brow in the top third of the frame of the advertisement signifies that this is an important issue. Again, the message is explicit: The man has a responsibility to work toward maintaining himself as athletic, muscular, and fit—in sum, to not be criminal, to not be shamed, and to not lie to himself about the level of his commitment to bodily excellence.

POSSIBILITIES FOR DISCUSSION, REFLECTION, AND JOURNALING

• Have students look at the ad from *Physical Culture* magazine and ask them how the black background works in this picture. Does the left-to-right orientation of the figures suggest evolution, progress? You might also ask students to think about any current presentations (in magazines, in movies, etc.) that relate physical health to moral health.

• The ad for Relax-A-cizor implies that men would like to look good without working for it. Ask your students what this implies about cultural attitudes toward exercise in the late 1960s. Are those attitudes toward fitness different from the ones we hold now? How do modern ads portray exercise? Students are likely to point to television commercials that show athletes working out, glistening with sweat. If they fail to mention the ads that still appear in Sunday supplements and on late-night infomercials, ads that offer quick weight loss and easy exercises for tightening the body, be sure to mention them. The products these ads are promoting, like the Relax-A-cizor, are meant to be seen as offering a solution: effortless fitness.

ADDITIONAL WRITING TOPICS AND CLASSROOM ACTIVITIES

• Ask students to write a personal narrative in which they recount their first awareness of the ideal body shape for their gender. Who is the person they first admired as a physical ideal for themselves? Was it a person they knew? a celebrity of some sort? a fictional character? Ask them to describe this person or image and to discuss why they felt it was ideal.

• Ask students to write an analysis of the progression of male body shapes presented in this series of images. What do their observations about these physical ideals suggest about the social construction of masculinity?

CONNECTION WITH ANOTHER TEXT

• Ask students to compare and contrast the male body ideal with the female body ideal as represented in advertisements that are not selling physical fitness. Ask students to include images or screen shots to support their arguments.

SUGGESTIONS FOR READING, THINKING, AND WRITING

PRINT

Andersen, Arnold, Leigh Cohn, and Tom Holbrook. *Making Weight: Healing Men's Conflicts with Food, Weight, and Shape.* Carlsbad, CA: Gurze Books, 2000. Print.

Bordo, Susan. *The Male Body: A New Look at Men in Public and in Private.* New York: Farrar, 2000. Print.

Gaines, Charles. *Yours in Perfect Manhood, Charles Atlas: The Most Effective Fitness Program Ever Devised.* New York: Simon & Schuster, 1982. Print. With photographs by George Butler.

Pope Jr., Harrison, Katharine Phillips, and Roberto Olivardia. *The Adonis Complex.* New York: Free Press, 2000. Print.

WEB

cagle.com/hogan/features/atlas.asp. Daryl Cagle, *Slate* magazine's resident cartoonist, maintains an index of cartoonists. Also here is an interesting article about the evolution of Charles Atlas ads and their parodies.

Portfolio: Burson (p. 360)

Nancy Burson, *Untitled Images from the* He/She *Series*

This group of photographs calls our attention to the human face and challenges our perception of gender as one of the first evaluations we make about an individual. In the case of these six images, all face shots, there are barely any indications of gender — no clothing, posture, makeup, or hairstyle to announce the maleness or femaleness of the subjects. There is also no context in which to place the faces, no social clues — occupation, for example — that might hint at gender. Finally, there are no verbal clues, no captions. These are simply untitled images from a series called *He/She*.

What is presented in this selection is a group of androgynous faces, partially in shadow and all lit with a rose-colored light. The faces are all approximately the same size in the frame, and the expression on each face is neutral. The hair is only slightly visible in all of the images but one; and what's visible of the hair is not gender specific. In effect Burson is issuing us an invitation to guess: he or she? We are left with only the faintest of clues, which may tell more about our own expectations and assumptions than about the gender of the people in these photographs. How do we decide? The information in these six cases is limited to skin, eyebrows, lips, teeth, hair, and gaze. In each case, our decision could go either way.

POSSIBILITIES FOR DISCUSSION, REFLECTION, AND JOURNALING

• You might ask students working individually to guess the gender of Burson's subjects. Have them write down their guesses and the reasons for them. Then go through each photo as a class. Does everyone agree? How did students make their determinations?

ADDITIONAL WRITING TOPICS AND CLASSROOM ACTIVITIES

• Still photographs deny us one of our primary ways of determining gender — seeing how a person moves. Have students write a catalog of motions that they would consider either masculine or feminine.

• Ask students to research visual indicators of gender in another culture, outside the United States. Have them write an essay in which they report on the customs that denote masculinity or femininity in that culture.

CONNECTIONS WITH OTHER TEXTS

• Ask students to gather examples of other face shots and to analyze each photograph for the way in which it does or does not indicate the gender of the subject.

• Ask students to look at Mapplethorpe's self-portraits (p. 320) for examples of how easily the face can be transformed in terms of gender.

What are some characteristics of gender that could be considered fluid? What characteristics might students consider to be more solid?

SUGGESTIONS FOR FURTHER READING, THINKING, AND WRITING

PRINT

Burson, Nancy. *Faces.* Santa Fe: Twin Palms, 1993. Print.

Kaplan, Michael, and Evelyn Roth. "Altered States." *American Photographer*, July 1985: 68+. Print. An article subtitled "Nancy Burson's Witty Visual Comments Question the Foundations of Our Most Basic Notions."

WEB

songweaver.com/gender/gendergallery.html. Images of many androgynous icons, among them k.d. lang, Annie Lennox, RuPaul, and Andy Warhol.

AUDIOVISUAL

Boys Don't Cry. 114 min. 1999. DVD, rated R. Distributed by 20th Century Fox Home Entertainment. Based on the true story of Teena Brandon, a young woman who "passed" as a man—she used the name "Brandon Teena"—in a small town. When she was found out, tragedy ensued.

Susan Bordo, *Never Just Pictures* (p. 367)

In this essay, Bordo primarily addresses cultural images of the body—both male and female—and the destructive effect that media images have on self-image and psychological health. The subheading "Bodies and Fantasies" alerts us to her viewpoint.

In the first paragraph Bordo asserts, "Our idolatry of the trim, tight body shows no signs of relinquishing its grip on our conceptions of beauty and normality." She compares that idolatry to an "obsession" that "seems to have gathered momentum, like a spreading mass hysteria" (para. 1). Her tone is one of alarm. She is warning us of what she sees as a dangerous trend "pummeling and purging our bodies, attempting to make them into something other than flesh" (para. 1). Moreover, this cultural malaise is not limited to adults. Bordo states: "Children in this culture grow up knowing that you can never be thin enough and that being fat is one of the worst things one can be" (para. 1), even worse than being physically handicapped.

Bordo traces the beginning of this obsession to the end of World War II. She demonstrates the shift in preferred body type with an advertisement for CitraLean, a diet product (p. 373). The "Before" label tells us that "a perfectly healthy, nonobese body" is "unsightly" (para. 2); it also suggests—and the bathing cap and bathing suit confirm—that that body type is old-fashioned. The fault for the current trend toward skinniness, according to Bordo, lies with fashion designers and models and their "blatant glamorization of the cadaverous, starved look" (para. 2).

As if emaciation was not enough, Bordo's analysis of current advertisements indicates that it is now fashionable for models to "appear dislocated and withdrawn, with chipped black nail polish and greasy hair, staring out at the viewer in a deathlike trance" (para. 7). "Why has death become glamorous?" she asks in paragraph 8. Bordo does admit that eating disorders do not result from such images; she recognizes that eating disorders are a "complex, multi-layered cultural 'symptom'" (para. 5). Although she acknowledges that other factors are also at work here, she refuses to absolve the fashion industry and its profit motive of responsibility: "Cultural images . . . reflect the designers' cultural savvy, their ability to sense and give form to flutters and quakes in the cultural psyche. . . . They want their images and the products associated with them to sell" (para. 10).

In conclusion Bordo notes that the latest strategy seems to involve the unadorned face, perhaps the irregular face—but always paired with a flawless, rail-thin body. Although on the surface these more individual faces might signal a welcome variety in body types, in reality they do not. They simply reflect an economic fact of life, that "encouraging [young people] to spend all their money fixing up their faces rather than buying clothes is not in [the fashion industry's] best interests" (para. 12). The result, Bordo writes, is that clothing manufacturers "are reasserting the importance of body over face as the 'site' of our fantasies" (para. 12).

POSSIBILITIES FOR DISCUSSION, REFLECTION, AND JOURNALING

• One way to begin discussion of this essay is to ask students to consider the possible significance of the title. This might be a good time to restate the case for the predominance of images in American cultural life and the importance of training ourselves to read these images with critical awareness. After all, as Bordo states, they are "Never Just Pictures."

ADDITIONAL WRITING TOPIC AND CLASSROOM ACTIVITY

• Before students read Bordo's essay, ask them to freewrite about the pressures they encounter with body image and how they deal with those pressures.

CONNECTIONS WITH OTHER TEXTS

• Ask students to find photographs of famous athletes on the Internet and to analyze those body images. Do your students consider them to be "healthy" images? (You might refer them to Bordo's discussion of the Olympics in paragraph 3.)

• Have students examine the photographs of models in a women's fashion magazine and in a men's fashion magazine. Ask them to discuss the bodies and expressions presented in each context. How well do they mirror what Bordo is saying in "Never Just Pictures"?

SUGGESTIONS FOR FURTHER READING, THINKING, AND WRITING

PRINT

Bordo, Susan. *The Male Body: A New Look at Men in Public and in Private*. New York: Farrar, 1999. Print.

Shute, Jenefer. *Life-size*. Boston: Houghton, 1992. Print. This novel follows the battle of the narrator, Josie, as she struggles with anorexia. The writing is darkly humorous and terribly poignant, and the book ties in well with Bordo's essay.

WEB

cddc.vt.edu/feminism/Bordo.html. This site includes biographical information and lists books and articles by Susan Bordo.

Surefire Assignment: Gender Ad Analysis

Martha Kruse
*University of
Nebraska–Kearney*

For this assignment I ask students to find at least three images of female or male body shapes from current advertising media and to analyze the images they find, considering the following factors:

- The size of the body in the frame (For example, do women take up as much space as men?)
- The part of the body that is dominant (Do images of women focus on their "feminine" attributes or their physical prowess? Do images of men connote strength or sensitivity?)

- The context in which the body is pictured (Is the figure shown interacting with others, or in solitary achievement of an ideal?)
- The lack of or the type of clothing the figure is wearing (Does the subject's apparel emphasize sexual characteristics? Does the clothing imply an intimate or professional setting?)
- The product being advertised (Does either a male or female subject necessarily seem more appropriate in the given context?)

I ask them to write their analysis and draw conclusions from their observations in an essay, attaching a copy of the images to their paper.

Pirelli, *Power Is Nothing without Control* (p. 375)

Carl Lewis is advertising Pirelli tires by showing that he is able to maintain the control and strength necessary to win races even when wearing high-heel shoes. By using a world-renowned runner and putting him in high heels, Pirelli is able to capitalize on all of our associations with competitive running — endurance, strength, control, determination, power — and associate those traits with the Pirelli product, tires. The tag line "Power Is Nothing without Control" reinforces this message and distinguishes Pirelli's tires from those made by other tire companies — that is, other brands of tires might be strong, but strength is nothing without control. The ad also subverts our traditional notions of masculine/feminine by showing Carl Lewis wearing high heels in a pose usually associated with an athlete on a track wearing sneakers.

POSSIBILITIES FOR DISCUSSION, REFLECTION, AND JOURNALING

• Have students think about the framing of this advertisement. How would it be different if Carl Lewis were not looking directly at the viewer?

• How does the choice of color help drive home the point of the ad? Does the monochromatic background serve to emphasize the red of the high heels?

ADDITIONAL WRITING TOPICS AND CLASSROOM ACTIVITIES

• **Image/Writing Assignment:** Have students choose a Virginia Slims ad or some other advertisement that plays with our assumptions about femininity in the same way that this Pirelli ad plays with our assumptions about masculinity. Ask them to draft a paper that examines the feminine and masculine qualities in both ads.

• Have students form groups of four and collaborate in creating lists of ten characteristics they associate with men and ten characteristics they associate with women. (You might divide the groups by gender to make this assignment more interesting.) Then have each group present its lists on the board and go through them as a class. Which characteristics are natural? Which are cultural?

CONNECTIONS WITH OTHER TEXTS

• Ask students to compare the Pirelli ad with the advertisements in Retrospect: Building the Male Body (p. 354). Ask them to analyze how advertising directed at men has changed over the decades.

• Ask students to compare Carl Lewis's face in the image here with the faces in Nancy Burson's photographs, which begin on page 360. Then ask them to freewrite about how this image might fit in with Burson's work.

SUGGESTIONS FOR FURTHER READING, THINKING, AND WRITING

PRINT

Lewis, Carl. *Inside Track: The Autobiography of Carl Lewis.* New York: Simon & Schuster, 1990. Print.

WEB

pirelli.com. The official web site for the Pirelli tire company.

Looking Closer: Engendering Identity

The texts in this section offer different views on the fluidity of gender identity and show how cultural shifts influence our ideas of who we are and who we can be.

Lauren Greenfield, *Ashleigh, 13, with Her Friend and Parents, Santa Monica* (p. 378)

Greenfield's photograph invites us right into the bathroom of a contemporary nuclear family in California. Ashleigh is a thirteen-year-old girl who seems to be dressed up for a date or some formal event. Ask students to comment on the central figure in the frame. What do we know about her? How do we know it? You might point out the tight black clothing and the pearls, for example, as visual clues that this thirteen-year-old is trying to look grown up. But Ashleigh's clothing isn't the focus of the photograph. The fact that she is standing on a scale, looking down at the record of her weight, dominates other impressions we might have of her. We understand that she is checking her image. But notice that she is not doing so in the mirror; instead she is measuring herself against some abstract standard to see if her weight is acceptable.

Art Spiegelman, *Nature vs. Nurture* (p. 380)

Spiegelman's comic strip explicitly illustrates and makes fun of the idea that if parents simply give their children different toys, they can alter the myriad ways in which even young children are already firmly ensconced in their gender roles. Furthermore, in the father's enthusiasm for the truck—its speed, its noise, its power—we see the lack of awareness about themselves as gender models that parents often exhibit.

Katha Pollitt, *Why Boys Don't Play with Dolls* (p. 381)

Pollitt's essay discusses one of the major influences supporting sex-role stereotypes—the props with which parents train their young. Pollitt guides us away from the facile idea that if parents just give "boy" toys to girls and "girl" toys to boys that they can circumvent or reinvent their children's learning about gender. She asks us to stop "looking at kids to 'prove' that differences in behavior by sex are innate" and to instead "look at the ways we raise our kids as an index to how unfinished the feminist revolution really is" (para. 4).

Brian Finke, *Untitled (Cheerleading #81)* and *Untitled (Football #75)* (p. 384)

How do these pictures of buff male cheerleaders and the discrepancy in size between the two football players subvert expectations? Students might recall Will Ferrell's *Saturday Night Live* portrayal of an effeminate male cheerleader. That's certainly not what comes across with the men in Finke's *Untitled (Cheerleading #81)*. They could be football players.

U.S. Military, *Today's Military* (p. 386)

This is one advertisement in a campaign that tried to present different views of the military to the present-day young audience it was trying to target. The series presents Americans who served in the military along with images representing other life skills they acquired during their service. For example, the woman in this advertisement, Valerie Vigoda, is a musician and founder of the band GrooveLily.

This particular image is important to the campaign because it was one of the few that featured and targeted women and attempted to persuade its audience to see women as a regular part of military personnel. The campaign not only normalizes her participation but also presents Vigoda as having a well-rounded life — something it is presumed that many women want. The advertisement shows her playing the violin in her army gear, emphasizing the connection between these skills — particularly character skills such as "perseverance," "follow through," and "the ability to play the hand you're dealt."

POSSIBILITIES FOR DISCUSSION, REFLECTION, AND JOURNALING

• Ask students to write brief reflections on what they've learned about gender identity from the chapter so far. What impact do the texts in this section, with their alternative viewpoints, have on students' thinking about the issues raised in the chapter?

• Use the selections in this chapter to discuss and write about issues of gender and the media, audience analysis, or our definitions of identity as they relate to the roles we take on.

• Have students research and review other military advertisements or look at the whole campaign "Today's Military." You might also have students review other advertising campaigns to recognize the ways that gender is communicated through this medium.

ADDITIONAL WRITING TOPICS AND CLASSROOM ACTIVITIES

• Women aren't just joining the armed services; they are also fighting fires and driving trucks and running businesses, all professions that at one time were considered the purview of men. And many professions that were once considered "feminine"—nursing and secretarial work, for example—are now open to men. Ask students to explore contemporary ads for images of men and women that reinforce and/or subvert traditional gender roles. For instance, do ads for household cleansers still suggest that women are in charge of cleaning the house? And do ads for power tools always show a man using those tools?

• Ask students to write a research essay that documents the ideal female image in each decade of the twentieth century. In their report ask them to note the parallels between the ideal and the cultural status of women at the time.

• Ask students, working in groups, to create a list of admirable human qualities. Then have each student write a journal entry in which he or she categorizes those qualities according to assumptions about the appropriate gender for each. Conclude by asking students to read their journal entries aloud to the class.

• Suggest that students read Greenfield's photograph of Ashleigh in terms of the role of the female teenager in our culture.

CONNECTIONS WITH OTHER TEXTS

• Have students read Dorothy Allison's "This Is Our World" (Chapter 3, p. 260) and take notes on the statements Allison makes about class. What do they think Allison would say about Lauren Greenfield's photograph? Would it meet her criteria for art?

• Ask students to consider the people depicted in this chapter. How have their identities been fashioned? How much do personal changes depend on social changes?

SUGGESTIONS FOR FURTHER READING, THINKING, AND WRITING

PRINT

Greenfield, Lauren. *Fast Forward: Growing Up in the Shadow of Hollywood.* New York: Knopf/Melcher Media, 1997. Print. With an introduction by Carrie Fisher.

Hoffman, Katherine. *Concepts of Identity: Historical and Contemporary Images and Portraits of Self and Family.* New York: Harper, 1996. Print.

Kimmel, Michael S. *The Gendered Society.* New York: Oxford UP, 2000. Print. A wonderful resource for instructors and students alike.

Pollitt, Katha. *Subject to Debate: Sense and Dissents on Women, Politics, and Culture.* New York: Random House, 2001. Print.

WEB

brianfinke.com. Brian Finke's web site.

Surefire Assignment: Being All You Can Be

Charles Hood
Antelope Valley College
(Profile, p. 12)

For a good in-class essay prompt, I ask if the army ad "Today's Military" perpetuates stereotypes or breaks them. (This assignment works even better if you can place the army ad in the context of other ads, some more stereotypical and some less so.) Students seem able to argue convincingly for both sides. Whatever happened to "Be all you can be" as a slogan? It always seemed like a good motto for teaching in general. Use the ad to start students on a research project, which should include gathering statistics about women in the military today and an analysis of America's changing perceptions of gender roles.

5

EXAMINING DIFFERENCE

How do we define difference? How do we determine its value? What do issues of race and ethnicity mean to Americans in the twenty-first century? to people in other countries? How have the ways people identify with racial or ethnic groups changed?

Barack Obama's successful campaign for the White House in 2008 raised many questions about the state of race in our country, particularly the question of whether America has entered a post-race era. Some scholars and politicians argue that race is no longer as important a category as it once was and that we are slowly moving toward a time when racial difference seems like no difference at all.

As the introduction to the chapter reminds students, race has often been treated in an essentializing manner—that is, it has been considered a fixed set of traits, a view that easily leads to stereotyping. In earlier decades, race was tied to biological determinants and pseudo-scientific theories of difference. Now many people see race as a matter of identification as much as genetics. For example, we might say that someone is African American because he or she identifies as such, not because of any particular physical or genetic features. Does this view of race as self-identification solve the problems of racial classification? In what ways could this way of classifying fail?

Because students may not take the time to unpack its meaning, you may also pause on this important statement from the textbook: "Racism is a structural problem, a form of discrimination based on group identity that is grounded in institutional processes of exclusion. As such, racism is a social construct, more a cause than a product of race" (p. 393). That is, racism is a systemic problem, not necessarily a personal one. Of course, racism does exist at a very personal level, but many of us probably hold views that come from the system in which we were raised. Talking about racism at the personal level—saying things like "I'm not racist, but . . ." and "I have friends who are _____"—does little to reduce systemic racism.

Several of the works in this chapter, especially the Looking Closer section on double consciousness, encourage students to go beyond binary thinking about identity. The reminder they offer—that a more nuanced thinking is necessary for accurate understanding of the world—is also an opportunity to bring up binary opposition in writing. Often, opposing two entities is useful, as in a paper that compares texts or concepts. However, students will benefit by learning from writers like Ta-Nehisi Coates that their subjects rarely fall so neatly into either-or propositions. Coates sets out to determine whether Bill Cosby's message of black self-sufficiency is prophetic or insane. His careful analysis of the roots of this message in African American political life reveals that it is much more complicated than either of those possibilities.

POSSIBILITIES FOR DISCUSSION, REFLECTION, AND JOURNALING

- You might begin by speaking about group identities. Nikki S. Lee's photographs offer a good opportunity to talk about groups. How are ideas about these groups formed? Do these pictures really capture the essence of these groups? For instance, does the selection from *The Hispanic Project* (p. 399) actually reflect young Hispanic men at the time and place where the photograph was taken? How would this picture be different if it had been photographed in Illinois? Suppose Lee had composed *The Caucasian Project* and *The African American Project*. How would those two projects differ by place? How is being a white male teenager in Iowa different from being a white male teenager in California?

- You might ask students whether they think race and ethnicity are still contentious issues for their generation. If so, on what grounds are racial battles still being fought? Where and when do tensions still arise? If not, then what other factors have taken precedence in our understanding of difference? Do class and sexual orientations make important dividing lines?

- Ask students to think of responses to race that might be systemic rather than inherently personal. One example might be the idea of upward mobility with which many of us have been raised. How do we truly know that "you can achieve anything if you simply try hard enough"? Ask students to think back to the first time someone spoke these words to them. Or was the myth of upward mobility always there, as the theme of the stories they were told as toddlers, the ethos that pervades American history books, the foundation of media reports on self-made millionaires? Is it a coincidence that Americans believe in upward mobility and that the United States is one of the few (possibly the only) industrialized nations without a Labor Party? You might point to the Declaration of Independence and the Constitution for examples of other systemic beliefs that have little basis in reality—the belief that "all men are created equal," for instance.

- Several of the readings in this chapter challenge the notion of fixed racial identity. But can identities change over time? What is fixed about our identities? What depends on circumstances or context?

ADDITIONAL WRITING TOPICS AND CLASSROOM ACTIVITIES

- Ask students to examine Obama's famous campaign speech on race. What does it say about the state of race in America today? What rhetorical strategies does Obama use to convey his point?

- Consciously or unconsciously, students may assume that there is a norm against which "difference" is defined. Have them write about their own definition of what is different and what is normal or mainstream. Where did they get these definitions? Are they accurate?

- Ask students to think about a time when they felt most different. Maybe it was during a study abroad program or a trip to a part of the United States far from home. Maybe this feeling arose in a more mundane setting, like the first day they moved into a dorm. Have them freewrite about what caused the feeling of difference.

Surefire Class: Deep ReVision

Kim Haimes-Korn
*Southern Polytechnic
State University*
(Profile, p. 11)

The use of visuals in the writing classroom asks students to engage in acts of composition as they translate what they know about words, texts, and ideas into images. Visual assignments have the potential to draw students into traditional acts of composition, such as invention, arrangement, style, and delivery. They get them to think deeply about their rhetorical situation—their purposes, audiences, and subjects. Although many recent classroom methods concentrate on the analysis of visual images, I like to extend that to include the production of visuals in conjunction with the written word.

For each of the subjects students take on in writing, they complete an accompanying image assignment that encourages them to question the ways they see the world around them, through visual and textual analysis of their personal, social, and cultural experiences. The sequence involves them in photo assignments in which they are either composing their own pictures or working with artifacts and found images on the Internet.

This type of assignment does not require sophisticated photographic equipment. I have students take their pictures with disposable digital cameras (available everywhere) and have them developed onto a CD-ROM so they can print and reuse them at different times during the course.

The following assignment on ethnic identity is one example from this sequence. I have found that college writers often struggle with issues of identity.

Several chapters in *Seeing & Writing*—in particular Chapters 4 and 5—deal with the ways our identity is constructed through image and self-reflection. I try to get students to understand that identity is a function of both how we see ourselves and how we are seen by others. This is particularly true when students look specifically at ethnic identity. Some students are immediately able to identify with a particular ethnic group, but many others, because they are not from a minority group or a country outside of the United States, feel they have no ethnicity. This assignment asks them to broaden their definitions, to recognize that ethnicity is influenced by factors like language, family background, region, artifacts, stereotypes, and media depictions.

Reading and Invention. I start by asking students to read, annotate, and review the introduction to Examining Difference, three readings of their own choosing, and all of the images in the chapter. Once they have completed their reading they respond in writing to the following definition of *ethnicity*:

> A word used to describe human difference in terms of shared values, beliefs, culture, tradition, language, and social behavior. *Ethnicity*, like *race*, is a social construct rather than a biological attribute, and both terms are the product of historical processes. (p. 395)

Using this definition from the book, have students list the ways their ethnic identity is formed. They should list as many examples as possible under the categories described in the quotation (values, beliefs, culture, tradition, language, social behavior). They can use this exercise to identify and explore their sense of ethnic identity and the ways it is shaped through cultural artifacts, icons, and media depictions.

Images and Artifacts. Ethnic identity is represented through a multitude of images. Students might associate their ethnicity with food, rituals, clothing, appearance, or family heirlooms. On closer observation they can recognize that their surroundings are full of images and artifacts that somehow represent their ethnicity.

For this image assignment I ask them to take ten digital pictures and/or to find ten images on the Internet that somehow represent their ethnic identity. (They can also collect and present tangible artifacts to the class.) The goal here is to get them to understand the concept of representation through images, artifacts, and objects.

Writing Assignment. Once they have completed the invention portions of the assignment, students can move to more-extended writing in which they explore their ethnic identity. Have them refer back to or incorporate items from their lists and images/artifacts. Encourage them to comment on the ways that identity is constructed through both internal and external factors as evidenced in their invention work.

Portfolio: Lee (p. 397)

Nikki S. Lee, *The Ohio Project (7), The Punk Project (6), The Hispanic Project (27), The Yuppie Project (19),* and *The Seniors Project (12)*

Lee's photographs capture the identity of punks, Hispanics, yuppies, and other groups. Remarkably, Lee appears in each image, altering her own identity to fit in with the subjects of the photograph. Because Lee appears in each photo, her photographs also point to the fluidity of identity, to the fact that it can be changed by context.

POSSIBILITIES FOR DISCUSSION, REFLECTION, AND JOURNALING

• Ask students to describe the groups presented here. Which details in each photograph indicate the group's identity? If Lee had photographed her subjects against a white background, would students still be able to identify their group identity?

• Ask students what we can learn about identity from these pictures. And what is missing from these pictures? What do these photographs fail to show about the group identity of their subjects?

ADDITIONAL WRITING TOPICS AND CLASSROOM ACTIVITIES

• Lee's insertion of herself into her photographs demonstrates the flexibility of identity. Ask students to write a narrative about a time in which they adopted the appearance and behaviors of others to fit in. In their conclusion, they should consider how that experience has had a lasting effect on who they are.

• Split students into small groups and ask them to talk about how their personalities change in different situations. Based on these discussions, ask students to brainstorm a list of five other groups and then to write about how Lee might photograph each of them.

• **Image/Writing Assignment:** Ask students to walk around the campus or their community, taking pictures of and talking to different groups of people. Then have them write a brief account of both the photographs and the conversations. What surprised them about the groups? What did they learn in their conversations that couldn't come across in the picture? What did they learn about these groups of people?

CONNECTIONS WITH OTHER TEXTS

• To generate more discussion in class, have students go online to examine more of Lee's Project photographs—for example, images from The Hip Hop Project and The Skateboarders Project. Be sure students know that Lee does not come to these groups with preconceived notions or judgments about them. She does her best to understand them so that she can become a part of them. Then ask students what group of people they would like to understand better.

- Ask students to imagine Lee's pictures as selections in Chapter 4, Projecting Gender. How does Lee characterize gender in each group?

SUGGESTIONS FOR FURTHER READING, THINKING, AND WRITING

PRINT

Lee, Nikki S. *Projects*. Ostfildern, Germany: Hatje Cantz Publishers/New York: D.A.P., 2001. Print.

WEB

tonkonow.com/lee.html. This site includes galleries of Lee's various projects.

Pair: Giovannoni & Hsu (p. 404)

Stefano Giovannoni and Michael Hsu, *The Squint and the Wail*

Hsu states very clearly the central question of this essay: "How can an object that makes so many Americans squirm be so palatable to the rest of the world?" (para. 10). In other words, why would people from other countries not sense the same racial prejudice in the Chin Family that Hsu and his friends do? Hsu's initial reaction is shock and disgust so strong that he feels compelled to ask others for their opinions on the objects. The different responses he hears, from total outrage to a whimsical desire to play with the salt shakers like toys, lead to the closer analysis of the figures that this essay performs.

One of the features of the Chin Family that Hsu's initial reaction did not account for is their basis in classical Chinese art. The museum curators who chose Giovannoni's designs for display found the issue of racial insensitivity a "very small matter" because they were primarily assessing their artistic value. The approach the museum takes is similar to what Hsu finds Taiwanese people saying about the exhibit: The visual motifs are familiar, even a kind of homage to Chinese culture. The features that Hsu finds overstated and offensive, these viewers recognize as historically accurate in their stylization.

In the end, Hsu considers whether what makes the objects questionable also makes them more democratic. The potentially offensive nature of the images interferes with the "feelings of superiority derived from highfalutin design preferences" (para. 17). While more neutral designs might allow people to feel self-congratulatory about their taste, the Chin Family forces them to think about the meaning of everyday objects.

• Have students discuss the different responses of Hsu's friends. Why does Kathy, a first-generation Chinese American, feel differently than the others? Why does Hsu point out that all of his friends are "left-leaning"?

• Hsu says that the Chin Family products are "East-West mash-ups." Ask students to restate what is "East" about them. Then have them discuss in what ways they are Western, a subject Hsu addresses less directly.

• Have students make a list of other products—physical objects, books, movies—that have been found objectionable. Do any of them deserve a reassessment? You might ask them to do some research to support their decisions.

ADDITIONAL WRITING TOPICS AND CLASSROOM ACTIVITIES

• Spending time with the Chin Family products helped Hsu revise his opinion of their meaning. Ask students to think about household objects they have lived with for a long time, things they or their parents own. Then have them choose an object or two to write about. How would these objects look different to an outsider than to those who have seen them many times?

• Based on statements by the museum directors, have students imagine how the Chin Family was presented to visitors. Working together, they might write introductory text that would introduce museum guests to the objects they would see in the exhibit.

• **Image/Writing Assignment:** Look at an online collection of photographs, or even better, take students to a museum exhibition of artifacts from a particular place and time. Using existing photos, photos students take, or sketches, each person or group should make a small collection of colors, shapes, and design motifs from the artifacts that they find interesting. How would they incorporate these features into a new line of consumer products?

• **Image/Writing Assignment:** Ask students to collect photos of other examples of design in contemporary household goods. Then have them think about what the designs signify or what they offer to people who buy them. Do they support Hsu's feeling that design can give consumers a sense of superiority?

CONNECTIONS WITH OTHER TEXTS

• Have students review the photo spread *This is Daphne and those are her things* (Chapter 1, p. 122). Ask them to create a similar profile of a fictional person and a collection of his or her belongings. They should include the Chin Family salt and pepper shakers as part of the collection. Have students write a description of this person, including an explanation of why the Chin Family salt and pepper shakers are important to this person.

• Point students to the essay and image *Unknown Keys* by Siri Hustvedt (Chapter 1, p. 113). Have students imagine a published writer suffering from writer's block who looks to the Chin Family salt and pepper shakers for inspiration. Have students write a short story about this fictional writer that includes an explanation of why the Chin Family salt and pepper shakers are able to cure him or her of writer's block.

Luc Sante, *Be Different! (Like Everyone Else!)* (p. 409)

Individualism has long been one of the features that people associate with the American character, but according to "Be Different! (Like Everyone Else!)" it may be growing increasingly elusive. Sante argues that by putting us into contact with so many other people, technologies like the Internet have the opposite effect of making us feel more unique. Rather, they divide us by our small idiosyncrasies into "micropersuasions" (para. 3), cultural subdivisions that turn any attempt to distinguish oneself into just another focus group. It is much easier now, Sante argues, to become invisible than to stand out. This leads to a situation in which, rather than changing styles, we live with a number of styles "present all at once" (para. 8). That is, at any given time, any particular style will be in vogue with some particular group. Sante argues that following general fashions is a thing of the past; only those who are initiated into a group could notice the small and rapid changes that determine what is up-to-date.

Sante gives his argument historical support by surveying previous generations' attempts to be different. For example, French bohemians of the nineteenth century found ample ways to stand apart from the mainstream. They "drank wine from human skulls, assumed bizarre names, dyed or perfumed or sculptured their beards in strange shapes, slept in tents pitched on the floors of their garrets and so on" (para. 4). Sante claims, however, that in earlier decades the need to express one's originality was felt primarily by the rich, "the only people who had the means or the time to pay attention to style" (para. 4). As popular culture arose, fashion became the province of a larger number of people. Sante tracks counterculture through the beats and the hippies but arrives at the conclusion that culture is now so scattered and multiple that a coherent counterculture can't exist.

POSSIBILITIES FOR DISCUSSION, REFLECTION, AND JOURNALING

• Challenge your class to examine how all of their "appurtenances are gang signs" (para. 8). Each student might make a list of the things he or she is wearing or carrying to class that day. How would Sante explain those items in "I am" statements like "I am an architect" or "I am a

Deadhead"? Do students find that their lists are self-contradictory?

• One of Sante's primary concerns in this essay is the relationship between individuality and commodity. Have students find instances in the essay of acts of rebellion that turned into acts of marketing. How does this happen? Is it a problem?

• Ask students to discuss Sante's claim that it is easier to make yourself invisible than to be an individual. What does he mean when he talks about invisibility? How can people become invisible in our culture?

ADDITIONAL WRITING TOPICS AND CLASSROOM ACTIVITIES

• The tone Sante takes in this essay is often humorous or even sarcastic. Ask students to point out specific places where he uses humor in the essay and then have them think about the purpose of the humor. How does humor help him make his points? What does he really think is laughable?

• Sante claims that "everyone everywhere speaks in some kind of a code." Have students write about the codes they use with their own friends or coworkers. How would they explain these codes to an outsider? You might remind students that Sante includes visual as well as verbal signs as part of the code.

• **Image/Writing Assignment:** Sante suggests that the United States "has always had an equivocal attitude toward individualism" (para. 5). Ask students to find a few advertisements that use ideas about what it means to be an American in order to sell a product. Do the ads have anything to say about individualism? Ask students to choose one and to write an analysis of the ad's stance toward the individual. Does it

confirm Sante's notion that Americans are uneasy with individualism?

• Have students assemble a portfolio of counterculture "looks," including those Sante describes and others they can think of. Since the images are likely to differ widely, you might ask them to reflect on whether there are any commonalities to the styles they have found. What motivates each style, or how does it express difference?

CONNECTIONS WITH OTHER TEXTS

• Encourage students to take another look at the photographs by Nikki Lee that open the chapter (p. 397). Have students write an essay in which they argue whether or not Lee would agree with Sante's claim that it is easier now to be invisible than to stand out.

• Have students look at Matthew Pillsbury's photograph *Penelope Umbrico (with Her Daughters), Monday, February 3, 2003, 7–7:30 p.m.* (Chapter 1, p. 45). Then have them write an essay in which they use the photograph to support Sante's opinion that new technology has the opposite effect of making us feel more unique.

SUGGESTIONS FOR FURTHER READING, THINKING, AND WRITING

PRINT

Sante, Luc. *The Factory of Facts*. New York: Vintage, 1999. Print.

———. *Low Life: Lures and Snares of Old New York*. New York: Vintage, 1992. Print.

WEB

believermag.com/exclusives/?read=interview_sante. An interview with Luc Sante.

pbs.org/wnet/newyork/series/interview/sante.html. A PBS interview with Luc Sante.

Donnell Alexander, *Cool Like Me* (p. 415)

This essay takes the reader across the slippery slope of cool as a style and an attitude. Donnell Alexander opens his piece with a raplike list of the ways he is cool, but his introduction ends with a caveat: "Know this while understanding that I am in essence a humble guy" (para. 10). Evidently modesty is cool too.

Alexander maintains that "the question of whether black people are cooler than white people is a dumb one, and one that I imagine a lot of people will find offensive" (para. 14). Nonetheless, he asserts, "But, cool? That's a black thang, baby" (para. 15). The origins of cool, according to Alexander, are in black slavery. He says that the impulse "to make animal innards—massa's garbage, hog maws, and chitlins—taste good enough to eat" (para. 16) gave rise to cool.

As Alexander catalogs the essence of what's cool and what's not, he acknowledges that "white folks began to try to make the primary point of cool— recognition of the need to go with the flow—a part of their lives" (para. 19) and asserts that Elvis brought cool to the white majority (para. 18). Alexander warns, however, that there are strains of cool and that big business has sensed that cool is a marketable commodity. He wants us to beware of tainted cool: "an evil ersatz-cool . . . that fights real cool at every turn," the cool of "advertising agencies, record-company artist-development departments, and over-art-directed bars" (para. 23).

In the end he wants even the black originators of cool to be careful of the business of cool. He says, "blacks remain woefully wedded to the bowed head and blinders. Instead of bowing to massa, they slavishly bow to trend and marketplace" (para. 29). He warns us not to be taken in by "clone cool" but to recognize that "the real secret weapon of cool is that it's about synthesis" (para. 29).

POSSIBILITIES FOR DISCUSSION, REFLECTION, AND JOURNALING

• Some students may find Alexander's essay difficult to understand, and some may even accuse him of being racist or just an angry black man (as several of my students suggested in their written responses). Some may look to the end of the essay for a nice, neat moral about unity, ignoring their uneasiness with earlier sections. Before students read the essay, let them know that they may find it difficult and ask them to keep a journal nearby. As they read, they should record their responses to the selection, which will help with the class discussion. You might ask them to consider these questions as they read: What do they find troubling, and why? What do they agree with, and why? Can they think of other evidence to back up Alexander's claims? How do they see modern race relations?

• You might ask students to freewrite about the portions of the essay that they found easy to read and those that they found difficult. As a class you could then locate and discuss those portions of Alexander's work first in isolation and then connected into a whole.

ADDITIONAL WRITING TOPICS AND CLASSROOM ACTIVITIES

• Ask students to choose an example of a slang expression that is currently used in their peer group and to define that expression in the language of the group—with that group as their intended audience. In a revision exercise, you could ask students to rewrite their definition for someone outside their peer group.

• Have students examine the essay for the shifts in diction that Alexander uses when he is being cool. Then have them write a description of how he uses language as an indicator of cool.

CONNECTIONS WITH OTHER TEXTS

• Ask students to imagine Alexander's essay in Chapter 4, Projecting Gender. Alexander focuses primarily on men. How would students extend his examples of cool to women?

• Students may not be aware of the recent emergence of privilege and whiteness as courses of study. Ask them to research books about and web sites on whiteness studies and then to write brief responses to what they find in their research. You might start them out with some prewriting about their perceptions of socio-economic privilege. Then give them some questions to direct their reading: How do they react to these areas of study? What do they find that surprises them? Have any of their perceptions changed?

SUGGESTIONS FOR FURTHER READING, THINKING, AND WRITING

PRINT

Delgado, Richard, and Jean Stefancic, eds. *Critical White Studies: Looking behind the Mirror.* Philadelphia: Temple UP, 1997. Print.

Majors, Richard. *Cool Pose: The Dilemmas of Black Manhood in America.* New York: Simon & Schuster, 1993. Print.

Tate, Greg. *Everything but the Burden: What White People Are Taking from Black Culture.* New York: Random House, 2003. Print.

WEB

euroamerican.org. A multiracial organization that studies whiteness and white American culture.

AUDIOVISUAL

Get on the Bus. 121 min. 1996. VHS, rated R. Distributed by Columbia Pictures. A Spike Lee movie that follows four men as they head to the Million Man March in Washington, D.C., from Los Angeles.

Roger Shimomura, *24 People for Whom I Have Been Mistaken* (p. 422)

What Shimomura is saying here is that despite the differences among these people, they are lumped together by their race. Shimomura himself may not have been mistaken for the man beneath the title, but someone of Asian descent probably has been.

• Students may wonder how Shimomura was mistaken for some of these people. They certainly don't look alike. After letting students discuss the variety of faces here, you might direct them to the title of the work: *24 People for Whom I Have Been Mistaken*. Does "I" necessarily mean Shimomura, a particular man with particular facial features? Could "I" refer not to Roger Shimomura but to anyone of Asian descent?

• After directing students through the Seeing questions in the textbook, you might ask them to consider the larger social ramifications of this piece. As stated in the headnote, Shimomura's work is a comment "on his internment experience [during World War II] and on the xenophobia and racism he still encounters in America." Can students think of similar modern experiences his work touches on— racial profiling in police and antiterrorism strategies, perhaps?

ADDITIONAL WRITING TOPICS AND CLASSROOM ACTIVITIES

• Students may not be aware of the studies that reveal the difficulty people have distinguishing among individuals from other races. This is not a problem in the abstract: It has real consequences for the people identified in police lineups and in eyewitness testimony, for instance. Ask students to research this topic and to write a brief essay responding to the social consequences of the problem.

• Ask students to collect ten to twenty photographs of people from either their own race or another race and to use them as examples for the second Seeing question on page 424.

CONNECTIONS WITH OTHER TEXTS

• Ask students to write an essay comparing Shimomura's photographs with Carlton Davis's portraits of black men (p. 440). What do Davis's photographs say about commonalities and differences among people of the same race?

• Ask students to locate more of Shimomura's work online and to write a brief essay explaining how those works further elucidate Shimomura's purpose and style as an artist.

SUGGESTIONS FOR FURTHER READING, THINKING, AND WRITING

PRINT

Daniels, Roger. *Asian America: Chinese and Japanese in the United States since 1850.* Seattle: U of Washington P, 1988. Print.

WEB

gregkucera.com/shimomura.htm. The Greg Kucera Gallery features a great deal of Shimomura's work and includes a statement by the artist.

ljworld.com/section/shimomura/story/169060/. *The Lawrence Journal-World* contains a wealth of material on Shimomura: a feature story, galleries, audio, and video.

rshim.com. The artist's own web site.

AUDIOVISUAL

kera.org. The public radio and television site for North Texas features a video interview with Shimomura.

Yang Liu, *Party* and *Ich* (p. 426)

As the biographical note in the textbook points out, Yang Liu's designs for the East Meets West series reflect her German and Chinese backgrounds. The images are provocative for the questions they raise about the relation between the two sides of the image. Are East and West opposed to each other? Are they conflicting? Or do the images bring the East and West into conversation?

Ich (the German word for "I") makes a statement about the difference between notions of the self in the two cultures. The much larger human figure on the blue ground suggests that Westerners put more emphasis on the individual. The red side suggests that Eastern cultures see the individual as a relatively small concern. By simplifying the graphics, Liu not only makes the images accessible to both cultures but also deals with large issues in a concise way that heightens their impact. Although her designs can't account for the nuances of individual identity in the two cultures, they convey a basic idea efficiently.

Party is a more intricate graphic and makes a slightly more complex, though related, statement. On the left side, the dots representing partygoers in groups of one and two indicate the dynamic of a party in which people move around frequently and interact with others one-on-one. On the right, Liu represents a different kind of party with a circle of dots spaced equidistant from one another. In this party, all of the people present are participating together in the experience. You might ask students to think about how this image builds on the argument Liu sets up in *Ich*. That is, do the two different conceptions of the "I" help students interpret these two pictures of social relations?

POSSIBILITIES FOR DISCUSSION, REFLECTION, AND JOURNALING

• How do these images capitalize on the spare graphics used in public signage? How is this choice part of Liu's message?

• These are only a few images from the East Meets West project. Students might be interested in searching online for more images from the project. Why did Liu make so many images for the series? What do several of these posters accomplish that just one wouldn't?

ADDITIONAL WRITING TOPICS AND CLASSROOM ACTIVITIES

• In an interview for trendburo.de, Yang Liu said that East Meets West is a "personal diary of my life, 13 years in China and 13 years in Germany. Since I'm a designer, my diary happens to be in a visual language instead of words. It shouldn't be generalized just as a book about cultural habits." Ask students to consider what their own visual diaries might look like. What observations would they make, and what form would those observations take?

•   While many writers and thinkers have talked about a clash of cultures between the East and the West, many more have argued that this vision of the world is reductive. Ask students to consider where Liu falls: Does she seem to think that the two cultures clash? Would they argue that she separates the two sides too starkly?

•   **Image/Writing Assignment:** Have students research signs from various countries and make their own pairings. For example, they might put an image of a restroom sign from the United States next to one from India. Do the signs tell a similar story to Liu's carefully planned images? What do they leave out?

CONNECTIONS WITH OTHER TEXTS

•   How could Liu's method of comparison be used to represent the "Chin Family" figures

Michael Hsu discusses in his essay "The Squint and the Wail" (p. 405)?

•   Have students review the photograph *A Mexican American Family Celebrates a Quinciniera* by Samantha Appleton (Chapter 2, p. 214). Mimicking Liu's style, have students draw a comparison between a bat mitzvah and a *quinceañera*.

SUGGESTIONS FOR FURTHER READING, THINKING, AND WRITING

WEB

blog.nationmultimedia.com/print.php?id=1748. *The Nation*'s blog presents more images from Liu's exhibit, East Meets West.

notcot.com/archives/2007/11/_jean_posted_ab .php. This popular design site features an interview with Liu.

yangliudesign.com. The artist's web site.

Retrospect: Reel Native Americans (p. 428)

The seven images in this Retrospect—three movie posters and four stills—convey some of the stereotypes of Native Americans in our movie culture. *The Life of Buffalo Bill* poster explicitly shows the relationship between the native population and the European culture that became dominant as Europeans moved across the continent. Ask students to consider the vertical axis of the image: The white man rides a white horse, has blond hair and light skin, and occupies the entire upper half of the poster. Furthermore, he is named as Buffalo Bill, and the movie claims that his life story is worth three reels of film. The Native Americans take up the lower half of the poster. They are huddled around the rock pedestal on which the white man, astride his horse, towers dramatically. These people have no names; they have no horses; they sit submissively below the white man.

The vertical axis clearly identifies the man on the horse as the most powerful figure in the image. Point out the man sitting alone on the left side of the poster. You might ask students to discuss their observations about the two distinct groups of Native Americans in the poster. Why do they think the figure on the left is alone?

The next poster, for the movie *Redskin*, also shows contrasting European and Native American cultures, but here we see the same man dressed both in a Western suit with a short haircut and in Indian clothing with a headdress. The image suggests that people can cross between the two cultures, living as a Native American or "passing" as white. However, students might note that the face of the man in Native American gear is turned away and that we see the Westernized version in fuller profile, perhaps suggesting that he is moving away from his past to present a new assimilated image.

The next poster, for *The Indians Are Coming*, is the most kinetic of all the images in this Retrospect, depicting the height of a battle between Native Americans with bows and arrows and a white man with a pistol. As in the poster for *The Life of Buffalo Bill*, the arrangement of the figures helps to tell the story — again here, the white man occupies the topmost position in the poster. He shoots down from atop his horse at a man on the ground. The poster's complicated perspective also shows, in the background, two Indians fleeing on horseback and, in the foreground, several Indian faces. The subtitle of the film, "Flaming Frontiers," reinforces the sense of heated struggle that the poster is designed to convey.

The first of the four stills, taken from the TV show *The Lone Ranger*, pairs the white man and the Native American as a team rather than pitting them against each other. The positioning of the two men, side by side and both on horseback, is an important sign of their equality — though Tonto remains the Lone Ranger's sidekick and not the other way around. The actor playing the Lone Ranger is still outfitted with the white hat and white horse that mark the hero in classic westerns.

The cartoon still from Disney's *Peter Pan* shows Native Americans and European Americans drawn in very different styles. The children at the center of the picture, tied together as if they are about to be burned, are drawn with rounded features, button noses, and large eyes. While these cartoon boys are not exactly realistic, the Native Americans who surround them are drawn in an even more stylized way. They feature prominent, beaklike noses, slits for eyes, and straight lines for mouths. These drawings reinforce stereotypes of Native Americans as harsh and even savage by contrasting them so starkly with the cutely drawn children they have captured.

The next still is the only one in this Retrospect to prominently feature a woman. Accordingly, this still shows that the conflict has shifted in this particular western, so that the contact between cultures becomes a romantic battle.

Also, in this image the Native American is in control while the white man is constrained. The two figures look right into each other's eyes, suggesting an attempt at individual interaction, not just an example of relations between races.

The image from the movie *Smoke Signals*, directed by Chris Eyre and based on a book by Sherman Alexie, shows a laughing young man in the center of the frame and a serious young man in the background. The movie places these two in a narrative that is not about war, romance, or a particular historical incident; instead it is about friendship, father-son relationships, community, and two friends' journey into adulthood. Thomas, the reservation nerd, is always telling stories that people don't want to listen to; nonetheless, he is a cheerful and optimistic narrator, as is evident from his smiling face. His friend, Victor, who is pictured with a serious expression, is dealing with the death of his absentee father. The friends travel together to bring back the body of Victor's father for burial. The two young men are participants in a narrative that could take place in the context of many ethnic groups. Both the image here and the movie are more about individuals than about races.

POSSIBILITIES FOR DISCUSSION, REFLECTION, AND JOURNALING

• Have students discuss the difference between the drawings and illustrations in the posters and cartoon stills versus the photographic images from the films. How do they characterize Native Americans differently? Which of the drawings are most realistic? most artificial?

• Students will be immediately drawn to talking about the people in each image, so you might want to direct them to other elements, such as the typography in the three posters. How do graphic choices about text and borders contribute to the meaning of the image? For example, why does the poster for *Redskin* use two different fonts?

ADDITIONAL WRITING TOPICS AND CLASSROOM ACTIVITIES

• Ask students to write a research paper about the legend of Pocahontas, using as their sources history textbooks from different decades. If they find any images of Pocahontas or John Smith, ask them to compare and contrast those images with the still that depicts Pocahontas.

• Assign an essay in which students reflect on the portrayal of skin color in several of these images. How do the relative shades of the people in the image — which in the stills may be emphasized by makeup or lighting — contribute to the meaning of the image?

• **Image/Writing Assignment:** Ask students to search the web for posters from other movies that portray the colonization of the western United States. Then have them analyze the posters' depiction of Native Americans.

• Have students re-create these images in a way that critiques their original intent. How would they reframe the images, and what text would they include to accomplish this critique? Would they make it funny or serious? You might have them just discuss these choices, or you might ask them to actually scan or copy the images and create new posters.

CONNECTIONS WITH OTHER TEXTS

• Ask students to consider how the historical image of the Native American changes from the first image in the Retrospect (1910) to the last (1998). In what ways has the visual image changed?

• Ask students to read Sherman Alexie's book *Smoke Signals* and to view Chris Eyre's movie. Then ask them to write about the differences in the literary and cinematic versions of the story. Suggest that students begin their essay with the stereotype suggested by the words *smoke signals* and then explore the complex kinds of communication that the book and movie address.

SUGGESTIONS FOR FURTHER READING, THINKING, AND WRITING

PRINT

Alexie, Sherman. *The Lone Ranger and Tonto Fistfight in Heaven.* New York: Atlantic Monthly, 1993. Print.

Custer, George Armstrong. *My Life on the Plains—or, Personal Experiences with Indians.* Norman: U of Oklahoma P, 1962. Print.

Erdrich, Louise. *The Antelope Wife.* New York: HarperCollins, 1999. Print. This short novel covers a century of myth and loss in Native American culture. The tale is told through the visions of a contemporary woman interwoven with the story of her family history.

Heard, Norman J. *White into Red: A Study of the Assimilation of White Persons Captured by Indians.* Metuchen, NJ: Scarecrow Press, 1973. Print.

Hilger, Michael. *From Savage to Nobleman: Images of Native Americans in Film.* Metuchen, NJ: Scarecrow Press, 1995. Print.

Rothenberg, Randall. "A Native-American Ad Agency Bids to Change Tired Images." *Advertising Age*, August 2, 1999: 24. Print.

WEB

eiteljorg.org. The web site of the Eiteljorg Museum, a museum devoted to Native American art.

heard.org. The site of the Heard Museum of Native American Art.

AUDIOVISUAL

American Indians: Yesterday and Today. 20 min. 1993. VHS. Distributed by Film Fair Communications. People from three tribes in different areas of the country (California, Montana, and New York) talk about past and present lifestyles.

The Indian Fighter. 88 min. 1955. VHS. Distributed by United Artists. A movie that demonstrates many classic stereotypes of the western genre. In the story, a wagon train scout becomes involved with a Native American chief's daughter.

Smoke Signals. 89 min. 1998. VHS, rated PG-13. Distributed by Miramax. Sherman Alexie wrote the screenplay.

Surefire Assignment: Writing Fences

Susan Al-Jarrah
*Southwestern Oklahoma
State University*
(Profile, p. 7)

Most of my students have grown up in a conservative rural area of Oklahoma, where children are still taught to be seen and not heard. Consequently we sometimes have difficulty getting our students to talk, let alone write. I have found *Seeing & Writing* a wonderful textbook for teaching students how to make connections, not only between visual images and the written word, but also between the media and the culture surrounding them. One particularly effective example happened when I asked my students to look quickly at Retrospect: Reel Native Americans and take no more than three minutes to write a response to the photographs. Weatherford is located in the heart of Southern Cheyenne Arapaho territory, yet many students feel little connection to our Native American population. Invited to share their responses, students began to examine some of their own stereotypes about Indians. Their responses ranged from the politically correct to passionate argument over past injustices. Next they read Sherman Alexie's short essay "The Joy of Reading and Writing: Superman and Me"[1] and were asked to respond to Alexie's statement that "a smart Indian is a dangerous person, widely feared and ridiculed by Indians and non-Indians alike." This led to more questions and a growing awareness that most of us weren't sure about whether or not we agreed with Alexie's statement.

A few of us decided to visit the Cheyenne Cultural Center in Clinton, about fifteen miles down the road. Although the cultural center is located on a main road, no one in the group had ever visited the site. Lawrence Hart, a peace chief for the Cheyenne people, graciously received us and spoke about the Cheyenne heritage. From there we traveled to the recently dedicated national historic site of the Battle of Washita, known to some as the site of the "Washita massacre." There we met history teacher and park ranger Steve Black, who gave a balanced historical account—from both the U.S. Army's and the Cheyenne people's perspectives—of the loss of life that occurred there on November 27, 1868, under the direction of General George Custer. We walked and talked with Ranger Black, and later shared a picnic and writing session at the site. When we shared our writing, many of us compared and contrasted the drama and bloodshed that had taken place on what was now such a peaceful spot of prairie. At the end of the visit, each student voiced a marked change in appreciation for our local history. Later each created his or her own "fences" (Alexie's term for paragraphs) to describe the conflict. In this way we moved from viewing images, to writing short responses, reading essays, performing primary research, and, finally, writing well-thought-out essays that incorporated creativity, higher-order cognition, and an ability to connect media with real life.

---

[1] From *Seeing & Writing 2*, pp. 251–52.

Tibor Kalman, *"Arnold Schwarzenegger"* (p. 436) and *"Queen Elizabeth II"* (p. 437)

Kalman's photographs are recolorings, literally, of celebrity portraits. According to the headnote on page 438, "to counteract both the dishonesty and the superficiality of corporate advertising, Kalman created an offbeat, often humorous design vocabulary." That vocabulary is operating here, in Kalman's critique of our fascination with both celebrity and race. Viewers' reactions to the photos show that race, which some claim is a "superficial" quality, is actually often a determining factor in their attitudes toward others.

POSSIBILITIES FOR DISCUSSION, REFLECTION, AND JOURNALING

• Schwarzenegger starred in a number of action films in the 1980s and 1990s, a period that saw few inroads for African Americans in Hollywood. You might ask students to consider what his chances for success would have been if he had been African American.

• The portrait of the queen is complicated by the fact that for hundreds of years the English monarchy held slaves of many ethnic backgrounds in colonies around the globe. Ask students to analyze the image in that context.

• You might ask students if a black woman could ever be the queen of England. Because the crown passes through generations within the same family, the answer is almost certainly no; and for the most part, the upper echelon of Britain's Parliament is white as well. Students might discuss the ways in which the message a monarchy sends to ethnic populations differs from the one a democracy sends.

ADDITIONAL WRITING TOPICS AND CLASSROOM ACTIVITIES

• Ask students to write a short reaction to the recoloring of these portraits. How has the re-coloring process changed their thinking about the person depicted?

• Ask students to imagine Superman and Wonder Woman recolored by Kalman. Many black superheroes — Blade, Luke Cage, Black Panther, Storm, Spawn — play supporting roles and/or have their faces covered; they are rarely given the prominence of Superman and Wonder Woman. How would their being black change our perception of Superman and Wonder Woman?

CONNECTION WITH ANOTHER TEXT

• Gordon Parks's *American Gothic* photograph (Chapter 6, p. 525) plays on Grant Wood's painting (Chapter 6, p. 516) in a number of ways, perhaps the most prominent being the race of the person pictured. Ask students to write an essay that compares the strategies used by Kalman and Parks and that explains the effects of those strategies.

SUGGESTIONS FOR FURTHER READING, THINKING, AND WRITING

PRINT

Kalman, Tibor. *Perverse Optimist*. New York: Princeton Architectural Press, 1998. Print.

Published on the occasion of the San Francisco Museum of Modern Art's exhibit of Kalman's works.

WEB

salon.com/people/obit/1999/05/19/kalman/. An article written about Kalman after his death in 1999.

AUDIOVISUAL

White Man's Burden. 89 min. 1995. VHS, rated R. Distributed by 20th Century Fox. Much of this film — which stars John Travolta and Harry Belafonte — is an interesting attempt at imagining an alternative United States in which the socioeconomic situations of blacks and whites are reversed. Some of the opening scenes may be worth watching in class.

Surefire Assignment: In-Situ Art Object Writing Assignment

James M. Wilson
Flagler College
(Profile, p. 20)

I find that an out-of-classroom exercise about three-quarters into the semester helps to reenergize my classes. Also, by the time students reach Chapter 6, Confronting Class—especially the essay on the details of *American Gothic*—I believe they are ready to be tested by artistic pieces outside of the book.

The purpose of this assignment is to use the Seeing skills discussed in *Seeing & Writing 4*. My students tend to use vague descriptions in their writing, so I push them to use concrete descriptions. In this assignment, I attempt to show students that all artistic work can be analyzed. I ask them to speculate about what the meaning of an artwork is, including, if possible, what they think the argument of the piece is. Some students are quickly dismissive of any piece of art. The assignment is designed to help them move away from merely "liking" or "disliking" a piece and toward a more articulated position. These skills will allow them to be better editors of their own and others' work.

1. I make arrangements to visit a local museum with a variety of art objects. I require that my students write about human-made objects rather than natural objects. I take my students only to museums that offer us free entrance and that are just a few minutes' walk from the classroom.

2. I meet my students in the classroom. My syllabus calendar states cryptically that I plan to have "in-class writing" for that day. I explain that we're going on a field trip. I wait a few minutes for stragglers, and we leave. Students must bring their bags and books along.

3. At the entrance of the museum, I give students a handout (below). I ensure that each of them brings paper and pen. Most museums will require that students leave their packs at the desk.

4. After making sure that all of my students have entered the museum, I enter the museum myself.

5. I wander around the museum and chat with students about what they are writing about. Once I finish, I sit at the entrance waiting for them to exit.

6. As they leave the museum, I collect their writing. Some of my students stay to write. That is okay, as long as I receive their writing.

7. Later, I read their pieces and comment on them. However, I do not grade the pieces. I give a predetermined number of points, unless someone turns in a less than adequate piece.

The handout reads as follows:

Pick an art object and write a complete description of it (four to six pages—it doesn't need to be perfect!) in the time we have. Start out by using the Listing method to generate descriptions, and then write some short paragraphs of ideas about the piece using Burke's Pentad to help you. This section should be about two pages (of the four to six).

Once you work through the description, speculate about the meaning of the piece, including, if possible, the argument of the piece. Consider the chapters of *Seeing & Writing* that we've discussed recently. What is the artist saying through the piece? Let the meaning/argument rise out of what you described.

You may be sitting on the floor to write this assignment. Leave room for people to move by you!

Please turn it in to me before you leave—you'll receive credit for all this work! If you leave the museum after I do, please drop off your piece at my office as soon as possible.

Portfolio: Davis (p. 440)

Carlton Davis, *Gevonni Davis, Witchita; Andrew "Twin" Jones, New York; Imam Taalib Mahdee, Boston; Stanley Nelson, New York; and James Anthony, Natchez*

The ideal of portraiture is to capture the subject's essence—not a fleeting moment, but an enduring likeness of a person's character as well as his or her looks. For Davis, the subject's head-on gaze is important because it gives the viewer the feeling of direct eye contact with the man in the picture. While other aspects of the photos—hairstyles, clothing and accessories, placement of the face in the frame—help to characterize the subject, the facial expression is perhaps the most important element. The only one of the five men who does not look directly into the camera, Stanley Nelson, conveys a great deal in his spontaneous-seeming smile.

Though all of Davis's subjects are black men, the diversity he finds among them is apparent from these selections. Without any further information about the men, viewers know that they are of widely divergent ages. They display very different styles of dress. Davis finds that these differences contribute to his goal for the series. He hopes that the photos will encourage Americans to rethink the simplistic ways they portray black men. The title of the series, Hue Man, may play on the idea of being a "race man," someone who is guided largely by loyalty to his racial identity. However, it also guides our attention to the many "hues"— both of skin color and of personality—that make up African American communities. Finally, Davis's clever title puns on "human," emphasizing commonalities among different races.

POSSIBILITIES FOR DISCUSSION, REFLECTION, AND JOURNALING

• What does it mean, as Davis puts it, to "minimize the viewer's awareness of the photograph as a photograph"? Why does he want to do that? In what cases might such an effect not be desirable? You might ask students to find other photos in the book that maximize awareness of the photograph as photograph.

• All of Carlton's subjects willingly responded to his advertisement for African American males. Ask students to think about how this might affect the photos he takes. Do the men in these photos seem interested in communicating something to the viewer?

• Have students choose one of the photos and examine it more closely. Then ask them to write down as many observations as they can about the details of the photo, no matter how small or how obvious they seem. At the end of the exercise, ask them to reflect on what this extremely close observation helped them see.

ADDITIONAL WRITING TOPICS AND CLASSROOM ACTIVITIES

• Have students propose their own photography project, one in which they would identify a group and then photograph members of the group. How would they gather subjects? What choices would they make in framing them? For example, would they choose spare backgrounds and full-face portraits, as Davis does? or some other arrangement? It might help them to imagine an audience for their proposal—perhaps a museum or publication that would display the images.

• Many of the images on Davis's web site are still lifes, and in his biographical note on the site he says that still life offers "creative freedom and the ability to experiment." Ask students to write about why still life might offer these qualities to the artist. Do the photographs in Hue Man have any characteristics in common with still lifes?

• **Image/Writing Assignment:** Help students search for images from movies, television, magazines, or other mediums that portray black men as "either super heroes or super villains." Then have them write an essay in which they compare the stereotyped images with one or several of Davis's portraits.

• **Image/Writing Assignment:** Ask students to take portrait photographs of several family members or friends, keeping in mind the difference between a quick snapshot and a portrait that conveys character. How successful do they think they were at accomplishing the latter?

CONNECTIONS WITH OTHER TEXTS

• The photograph of Gevonni Davis is reminiscent of Nancy Burson's *He/She* photographs (Chapter 4, p. 360). Have students write an essay in which they compare and contrast this portrait by Davis with one of Burson's.

• Have students write an essay in which they compare Davis's portraits of Gevonni Davis and Andrew "Twin" Jones with those of Robert Mapplethorpe (Chapter 4, p. 320). What about Gevonni's and Andrew's poses are typically feminine and typically masculine?

SUGGESTION FOR FURTHER READING, THINKING, AND WRITING

WEB

carltondavis.net. The artist's web site features biographical information and examples of his consumer photography.

Ta-Nehisi Coates, *"This Is How We Lost to the White Man"* (p. 447)

In this essay from *The Atlantic*, Coates examines Bill Cosby as a figurehead for a transitional time. He provides a history of Cosby's career alongside broader observations of this time in which "the civil-rights generation is exiting the American stage" (para. 11). Coates notes that key figures from 1960s-era activism have passed away and that organizations founded during that movement, like the NAACP, have been losing relevance (para. 17). From the beginning of his career as an entertainer, Cosby "proffered the idea of an America that transcended race" (para. 13), but, in spite of this seemingly benign message, he has also been very controversial. However, even as he provokes outrage in liberal thinkers such as Michael Eric Dyson, Cosby's ideas are appealing to a conservative set of African Americans that Coates says can be found "in black barbershops, churches, and backyard barbecues" (para. 23).

Coates claims that the debate between Cosby and Dyson is a new incarnation of a long-standing division in black intellectual life, one that dates to Booker T. Washington's Atlanta Compromise and the outrage it caused among integrationists like W. E. B. Du Bois. Even black conservatism, though, can be read two ways. Washington's Compromise, which accepted segregation as a temporary solution, was adopted and adapted by radicals who called for a Black Nationalism wholly separate from the default American culture. Segregation became "not an olive branch to whites" but a "statement of black supremacy" (para. 26). Thus black conservatives have an uneasy relationship with the conservative Republican Party. While they "favor hard work and moral reform over protests and government intervention," their "black-nationalist leanings make them anathema to the Heritage Foundation and Rush Limbaugh" (para. 31).

Cosby offers both positive and negative values as solutions for African Americans today. He calls for strong family values, but much of his vision depends on embarrassment. Part of the problem now, he claims, is that young people are not embarrassed to have children young and out of wedlock. Ultimately, Coates sees what is uplifting in Cosby's calls for black self-sufficiency, but he also rejects the notion that most problems African Americans face can be attributed to failings in African American culture.

POSSIBILITIES FOR DISCUSSION, REFLECTION, AND JOURNALING

• Coates compares Cosby to a preacher, spreading the word of "black self-reliance." Ask students to discuss what is preacherly about Cosby's methods or his message. Why does he bill his appearances as "call-outs"?

• Have students examine the connections Coates makes between Cosby's talks and the state of politics in African American communities. What has changed in the new generation of African American leaders? Are they moving toward or away from Cosby's vision of racial progress?

• Near the end of the essay, Coates makes a personal connection with the arguments at hand: "I'd take my son to see Bill Cosby, to hear his message, to revel in its promise and optimism. But afterward, he and I would have a very long talk." Ask students to discuss this turn as a rhetorical strategy. How did it affect them as readers? And what do they think Coates's talk with his son would be about?

ADDITIONAL WRITING TOPICS AND CLASSROOM ACTIVITIES

• Ask students to summarize Coates's assessment of Cosby's position. What does Coates find valuable in it? With what parts of the message does he take issue? Then have them write a response. What would Cosby say to Coates's objections?

• Cosby expresses disgust for many cultural trends, from hip-hop and styles of dress to how people name their children. Ask students to choose one aspect of contemporary culture they think Cosby dismisses too readily and to write a defense.

• Cosby is known for being a comedic actor, but he seems to use comedy very little when he talks about political matters. Ask students to look at statements by Cosby within this essay or perhaps comments they find elsewhere. When and how does he use comedy as a rhetorical tool? How would they characterize this kind of comedy?

• **Image/Writing Assignment:** In paragraphs 33 and 34, Coates includes some startling statistics about income levels for African Americans. Ask students to make graphic representations of these statistics to illustrate reports. Groups of students might want to work together to find the clearest way of conveying the information.

CONNECTIONS WITH OTHER TEXTS

• Coates claims that the current debate between conservative Bill Cosby and liberal Michael Eric Dyson is similar to the intellectual division between Booker T. Washington and W. E. B. Du Bois. Have students read Du Bois's essay (p. 464) and write an essay in which they compare Cosby's sensibilities with those of Du Bois.

• Susan Bordo claims that contemporary images of skinny female models negatively affect women's body images. Have students examine contemporary images of black men in popular culture, whether on television, in music, or in ads. Point students to Alexander's essay "Cool Like Me" (p. 415), especially the lines "I'm a cop-show menace and a shoe commercial demi-god—one of the rough boys from our 'hood and the living, breathing embodiment of hip-hop flava" (para. 11). Ask students to think about how popular culture affects the new generation of African American leaders. Have students write an essay in which they analyze popular culture's effect on Cosby's vision of racial progress.

SUGGESTIONS FOR FURTHER READING, THINKING, AND WRITING

PRINT

Cosby, Bill, and Alvin F. Poussaint. *Come On People: On the Path from Victim to Victor.* Nashville, TN: Thomas Nelson, 2007. Print.

WEB

ta-nehisicoates.theatlantic.com. Coates's page on *The Atlantic*'s web site features his blog and links to his other articles.

ta-nehisi.com. Coates's web site and blog.

AUDIOVISUAL

americanrhetoric.com/speeches/billcosbypound cakespeech.htm. A recording of Bill Cosby's address at the National Association for the Advancement of Colored People (NAACP) on the fiftieth anniversary of *Brown vs. Board of Education.*

Looking Closer:
Doubling Consciousness

The title of this section plays on W. E. B. Du Bois's famous term *double conscious-ness*. The selections gathered here examine racial identities that are not singular or easily defined. At the end of a chapter on the complexities of contemporary race relations, they serve as an important reminder that race itself is a complex concept. As we move toward what many have called a post-racial America, people of mixed race or multiple identities are emblematic of a broader move away from a simplistic understanding of race. However, as Naomi Schaefer Riley suggests, we are still far from reaching a point at which teasing out the constituent parts of a mixed-race identity no longer seems important.

W. E. B. Du Bois, *Double Consciousness* (p. 464)

Du Bois's claim that the "problem of the twentieth century is the problem of the colorline" has been repeated many times in many contexts. Students may be surprised to see that in the twenty-first century many of his observations still ring true. Du Bois argues that being African American means having two iden-tities, black and American, and that these two identities are self-contradictory and constantly at war. His "American Negro" desires to retain both parts of the self without allowing them to cancel each other out: "He would not Africanize America, for America has too much to teach the world and Africa. He would not bleach his Negro soul in a flood of white Americanism, for he knows that Negro blood has a message for the world" (para. 3). Ultimately, Du Bois claims, there is no America without the black and Native American people who were subjugated in its founding and ascent to power.

Guillermo Gómez-Peña, *Authentic Cuban Santera* (p. 465)

Authentic Cuban Santera is part of an early series, Norte/Sur, which made ironic commentary on moments of contact between cultures. In this photo, Gómez-Peña questions the idea of authentic ethnicity by staging a mock-authentic photo of practitioners of the Caribbean religion Santeria, which combines Christian beliefs with elements from African religion. The two figures pose be-fore a background of ornate leaves and flowers in the style of Mexican art. The woman, with her turban and white clothes, is dressed as a Santeria priestess, and the man wears a headdress, breastplate, and loincloth of Aztec design. How-ever, the woman has American dollars pinned to her clothes, and both figures display products of American culture: a Coke bottle and a very un-authentic taco pizza.

James McBride, *What Color Is Jesus?* (p. 466)

McBride begins this memoir in a specific moment of remembrance: driving to see his stepfather's grave. This act leads him into discussing his childhood in a mixed-race family. Often he felt as though he was presented with a difficult choice: "I vacillated between being the black part of me that I accept and the white part of me that I could not accept" (para. 5). This feeling of having to be one thing or the other leaves the narrator constantly on edge: "Being mixed feels like that tingly feeling you have in your nose when you have to sneeze" (para. 9).

As he recounts in this memoir, McBride's own father died when he was a small child. He was raised by his mother's second husband, a man whom he characterizes as "solitary, gruff, busy" (para. 3). His stepfather was a man who valued work and commitment more than lofty ideas about identity or equality. Though the narrator fears that his stepfather would not approve of his artsy choice of career, which blends writing with playing music, his memory of the man provides McBride with a model for how to teach his children about their identity. Thinking of his stepfather, McBride decides, "I was not put on this earth to become a leader of mixed-race people, wielding my race like a baseball bat" (para. 90). Instead, he wants to model for his children that what you do is more important than being able to say exactly what you are.

Kip Fulbeck, *Part Asian, 100% Hapa* (p. 476)

In pairing portraits with handwriting, Fulbeck allows his subjects to speak both through their expression and through their own descriptions of their identity. Many of the statements that accompany the pictures address how others want to put labels on race—from the kind of survey questions that ask whether an individual is white, Asian, or "other" to a romantic partner's desire to exoticize mixed race. As in Carlton Davis's photos, Fulbeck uses minimal backgrounds and photographs his subjects looking directly into the camera so that viewers can focus on their expressions. Fulbeck even takes the further step of removing all clothing and accessories so that all we see are the subjects' bare shoulders.

Naomi Schaefer Riley, *The Risks of Multiracial Identification* (p. 484)

The change in the way college admissions officers ask students about their race signals a larger change in the way we understand racial identity. Riley notes that more and more, students entering college come from mixed-race backgrounds, and, now that much of the stigma has been removed from interracial marriages, their numbers will continue to rise. But rather than creating an atmosphere in which pinning down one's race no longer matters, young people "seem more focused than ever on figuring out and defining themselves by each individual part of their racial identity" (para. 6). Riley takes Fulbeck's Hapa project as evidence of this trend: "It seems inevitable that one day no one will bother asking Fulbeck's question because no one will find multiracial faces worthy of notice" (para. 12), but for now finding a way to describe one's identity still seems crucial.

POSSIBILITIES FOR DISCUSSION, REFLECTION, AND JOURNALING

• Gómez-Peña uses parody to comment on the contact of different racial identities along the southern border of the United States. Ask students to discuss what exactly he is saying about Hispanic and European identities in his photo. Would it convey different ideas to different audiences?

• The statements that Fulbeck's subjects make have some sentiments in common with James McBride's reflections on racial identity. Have students choose some sentences from McBride's memoir to set next to Fulbeck's captions. What ideas do they share about being of mixed race?

ADDITIONAL WRITING TOPICS AND CLASSROOM ACTIVITIES

• Ask students to write memoirs about their parents, using McBride's memoir as a model for style and structure. What did they learn about identity from their parents? And how do parents convey such messages to their children?

• Kip Fulbeck is also the author of a novel, *Paper Bullets*, which he describes as a "fictional autobiography." Ask students to read some sections from the novel and then write an analysis of how Fulbeck's novel and photographs treat Hapa identity.

• **Image/Writing Assignment:** One of Fulbeck's photographic subjects creates a kind of mock survey to comment on identity, and Riley's essay begins by discussing changes to the way colleges collect data about students' ethnic identity. Ask students to work together to create their own survey forms. They might make these realistic or fantastic, but they should comment on the way students think their peers identify themselves.

CONNECTION WITH ANOTHER TEXT

• Ask student to compare Du Bois's more metaphorical concept of "double consciousness" with the literal doubling of identity of the subjects in Kip Fulbeck's photographs. How does Du Bois's term provide a way of talking about their experience?

SUGGESTIONS FOR FURTHER READING, THINKING, AND WRITING

PRINT

D'Souza, Dinesh. *The End of Racism: Principles for a Multicultural Society*. New York: Free Press Paperbacks, A Division of Simon & Schuster, 1995. Print.

Obama, Barack. *Dreams from My Father: A Story of Race and Inheritance*. New York: Three Rivers, 2004. Print.

O'Hearn, Claudine. *Half and Half: Writers on Growing Up Biracial and Bicultural*. New York: Pantheon, 1998. Print.

AUDIOVISUAL

nytimes.com/interactive/2008/03/18/us/politics/20080318_OBAMA_GRAPHIC.html. President Obama's speech on race.

6 CONFRONTING CLASS

What factors determine a person's class? Where and how do we learn about class distinctions? How is class changing in the twenty-first century?

In the introduction to this chapter, the McQuades write, "What you wear, what you say and how you say it, what you eat and how you eat, where you work and what you do there, as well as what you watch on television and whether you watch TV are significant expressions of your class standing." That is, class is tied to behavior, to the personal expression of taste. Some students may resist this idea, insisting, for example, that all types of people eat at McDonald's, so you might start by having students freewrite in response to the McQuades' statement about class. Can they think of how it is true for them? If students have trouble discussing or writing about this statement, you might have them read the selections here with an eye toward identifying social indicators.

An alternative way to get students talking about class is to listen to songs from rock, country, and rap. How do these songs illustrate class? How do these genres regard class types? How are some genres constrained by class? As a fun exercise, you might ask students to create song titles that would be typical or atypical of rock, country, and rap music when it comes to the issue of class.

The chapter begins with several selections that consider what is perhaps the least visible class in America: the working class. Brooks Jensen's photos focus on working-class men and the tools of their trades, while the paired Renoir painting and Billy Collins poem consider a waitress. Later in the chapter, William

Deresiewicz's essay returns to questions about the working class in an attempt to understand why most middle-class Americans know so little about it. The chapter also contains works that model a canny reading of class markers. The essay, poem, and many artistic reinterpretations inspired by Grant Wood's *American Gothic* show what careful attention to details can reveal about the class of the characters it pictures.

By focusing on how they understand class, maybe even in ways that are subconscious, students will practice interrogating their assumptions. This practice should be useful not only in the way they reason about class but also in the way they write about it. You might remind them that a good way of understanding where a writer is coming from is to try to articulate the assumptions that underlie his or her work. The more students consider the grounds on which their own ideas and the ideas of others stand, the better they will become at making and responding to arguments.

POSSIBILITIES FOR DISCUSSION, REFLECTION, AND JOURNALING

- Discuss how the advertising and marketing worlds understand class. Do students notice particular stores or products being marketed to specific classes? What means do advertisers use to target people according to class?

- How do class issues affect the students' local community? Ask them to think about the class makeup of the town in which they go to school. Do they think it is changing?

- Have students reflect on what class they expect to enter when they leave college and begin their working lives. Will they be in the same class they grew up in? If not, how or why will they change?

ADDITIONAL WRITING TOPICS AND CLASSROOM ACTIVITIES

- Assign an essay in which students argue how class exists online. Can they observe usual markers of class on social networking sites like Facebook or Twitter? How are class cues written into these media? Or would students argue that the Internet offers an escape from class? Have them cite specific examples from one popular social networking site.

- Education is one of the factors most closely tied to class. Ask students to reflect on their own education so far. What was the status of their high school? What meaning does their choice of college have for future class position? More broadly, what are the class differences between public and private high schools? among different colleges? What determines a "good" school, and does going to one affect one's class?

- Ask students to watch and analyze two television shows that offer different perspectives on class. How do these shows re-create class settings in clothing, on the set, or in the apparent values of the characters? What does each show's attitude seem to be toward the class it is representing? What do viewers gain from seeing the class represented this way?

Portfolio: Jensen (p. 493)

Brooks Jensen, *Standing Drill Bits, Ellensburg, Washington; Three Drills, Hockinson, Washington; Felix Muñoz, Cuero, Texas; Vernon Barrow and Grandson, Denison, Kansas; and Joe Sasak, Leroy, Wisconsin*

In the first two of the photos featured here, Jensen enlarges the tools of labor to give them a monumental presence. In *Standing Drill Bits* he focuses on the sculptural form of the tools, with their spiral threads. Their arrangement could also be read as referring to a group of standing people. In *Three Drills* Jensen's focus is not quite as tight, but the way he frames the tools still focuses our attention on their forms. The light picks up the sheen on the metal surfaces, and the way the drills are arranged is almost like a still life. As in *Standing Drill Bits*, we can see both sameness and difference, as the tools bear a family resemblance but may be distinguished as different from one another.

The other three pictures are more traditional portraits, but they focus on nontraditional subjects. Portraiture, especially before the invention of the camera when all portraits had to be painted, has largely been the province of the wealthy and powerful. Jensen turns his camera on people who might otherwise be overlooked. The picture of Felix Muñoz connects Jensen's portrait work to his photos of tools by positioning the subject in front of a wall of hubcaps. Lined up in rows, they form a pleasing geometric pattern that also refers to the working-class position of the subject. In contrast to the shiny metal and the crisp fabric of his work pants and shirt, Muñoz's skin is deeply wrinkled and veined, a sign of the years of work he has put in during his life.

In the picture of Vernon Barrow and his grandson, Jensen gives us a glimpse of how mechanical skills are passed to new generations. In this photo, the background is less carefully composed, but behind the two subjects we can see the tools and materials of a metal shop. Like Felix Muñoz, Barrow and his grandson wear the baseball hats that become an important marker of class. Joe Sasak, too, has a baseball cap. His overalls are another example of dress that originated among the working class. He poses standing for his photo, and Jensen frames him in the door to his workshop. In his setting, we can see both the equipment for his work — the large gas tanks and hoses — and some decoration in the form of old metal signs.

POSSIBILITIES FOR DISCUSSION, REFLECTION, AND JOURNALING

• Ask students to think about the perspective from which Jensen photographs the tools. Is it similar to the perspective of the men who work with them? Why or why not? How would a photograph by one of Jensen's subjects in *Made of Steel* be different from the ones Jensen takes?

- The captions that accompany the portrait photos relate brief moments that help to characterize the subjects. Have students discuss what these captions add. What is Jensen's purpose in including them?

ADDITIONAL WRITING TOPICS AND CLASSROOM ACTIVITIES

- **Image/Writing Assignment:** Assign students a photoessay on work. They should focus on a specific job or occupation and then choose whether their series will examine the tools of the trade, like *Standing Drill Bits* and *Three Drills*, or whether they would rather create portraits. The pictures they take, along with any captions they choose to include, should work together to tell a story about the occupation they have chosen.

- Many of Jensen's other photographs can be found online. Ask students to look up some of his nature photos. Have them think about the way close-ups of natural elements relate to the close-ups *Standing Drill Bits* and *Three Drills*. How do they use similar arrangements or reveal similar textures? Have students choose images from nature to pair with the two pictures of tools reprinted here and then explain their choices.

- What do photographs of the men in *Made of Steel* convey that written accounts of their lives could not? What additional details could a narrative provide? Ask students to write about the choice of photography as a medium for Jensen's project. What are its relative benefits and drawbacks?

- Jensen's series is interested specifically in men. What would a series of photographs that focus on working-class women look like? Have students consider what locations, implements, or types of women would appear in the series.

- Ask students to rewrite the captions from the perspective of the men in the photographs. How would they describe themselves, or their encounter with the photographer, differently?

CONNECTION WITH ANOTHER TEXT

- Jensen's methods fall solidly in the tradition of documentary photography, which was especially prevalent during the Great Depression years. Ask students to compare one of these three portraits to Dorothea Lange's *Migrant Mother* (p. 560). What techniques might Jensen have learned from earlier documentary photographers? How does his approach to his subjects differ from Lange's?

SUGGESTION FOR FURTHER READING, THINKING, AND WRITING

WEB

brooksjensenarts.com. The artist's own web site, which includes examples of his nature photography.

Pair: Renoir & Collins

Pierre-Auguste Renoir, *A Waitress at Duval's Restaurant* (p. 500)
Billy Collins, *The Waitress* (p. 501)

The waitress in Renoir's painting looks out at the viewer with her head tilted to the side and her hand on her hip. While many of Renoir's works re-create elaborate scenes, with many figures interacting with one another, this painting is composed simply, with the single woman centered against an unobtrusive background of wallpaper and curtains—apparently the decor of the restaurant where she works. As a way into talking about the painting, students might want to discuss what is captivating about the waitress, both as an individual woman and as a representative of her profession. What might have drawn Renoir to compose this scene?

Like the painting, Collins's poem presents the waitress in a straightforward manner. He simply states her actions: bringing the restaurant patron a drink and a menu, asking how his dinner is. However, in the sixth stanza she is transformed in the speaker's mind into "every waitress / who has ever served me, / and every waiter, too" (lines 16–18). In this transformation, she becomes emblematic of the very act of serving others, a task that is often taken for granted by those being served. The poem ends with an autumnal image—the colored leaves of fall form the room in which all of those waiters and waitresses of memory dance—and with the speaker alone on the "nearly empty streets" (l. 45). You might have students discuss how the meditation on the waitress's work turns the speaker to this lonely or even elegiac mood. What change does his thinking undergo in the course of the poem?

POSSIBILITIES FOR DISCUSSION, REFLECTION, AND JOURNALING

• Ask students to interpret the expression of the waitress in Renoir's painting. What emotions do they read in her face?

• The speaker of "The Waitress" leaves a tip he describes as "sentimental" (l. 33). Have students discuss what this means. What kind of tip is it? What does it say about the speaker's emotional response to this particular waitress?

• Have students identify several turning points in Collins's poem. What do they notice about how he transitions from one idea or mood to another? If this were a piece of music, where do the "movements" fall, and how could each one be characterized?

ADDITIONAL WRITING TOPICS AND CLASSROOM ACTIVITIES

• **Image/Writing Assignment:** Though the works are quite familiar now, in its time Impressionist painting was a radical departure from the prevailing aesthetic—both in its technique and in its subjects. Ask students to find a few more Impressionist portraits that they could include in a portfolio of paintings about work. Once they have compiled their images, they should write an explanatory note on each painting's treatment of its subject and of the theme of work.

• Have students consider how they would visually represent the ending of Collins's poem. Would the pictures he creates with words be best suited to photography, painting, or film? How would students set the scene or choose people to appear in it?

• Do Renoir and Collins romanticize the job of being a waitress? Or do they present it in fairly realistic terms? Ask students to write an argument about the degree to which the waitresses are romanticized. Does it matter that the writer and the painter are men while the subjects are both women? You might point out to students that Renoir's waitress seems to be wearing a wedding ring. Is this a significant detail?

• **Image/Writing Assignment:** Ask students to find a depiction of a waitress in yet another medium — perhaps a movie or a song. Then have them write an essay comparing this new example with one of those found in the book. How does it treat the job or the individual? What does each work emphasize about waitresses?

CONNECTION WITH ANOTHER TEXT

• Ask students to compare this poem to Collins's "Traveling Alone," which also considers the relationship of the speaker to people in service positions. How do the two poems complement each other, and what do they have to say about the service sector of the workforce and about how we view the individuals in it?

SUGGESTIONS FOR FURTHER READING, THINKING, AND WRITING

PRINT

Collins, Billy. *Sailing Alone around the Room: New and Selected Poems.* New York: Random House, 2001. Print.

———. *The Trouble with Poetry: And Other Poems.* New York: Random House, 2005. Print.

Renoir, Jean. *Renoir, My Father.* New York: New York Review of Books, 1962. Print.

Rose, Mike. *The Mind at Work: Valuing the Intelligence of the American Worker.* New York: Viking, a Division of Penguin, 2004. Print. This book features a chapter entitled "The Working Life of a Waitress," which provides insight into the mind and work of today's waitresses.

WEB

akoot.com/billycollins5.html. A web site that features the text of the poem "Traveling Alone."

biography.com/articles/Pierre-Auguste-Renoir-9455662/. Biographical information for the famous painter.

mootnotes.com/art/renoir/. An extensive online gallery of Renoir's paintings.

AUDIOVISUAL

billy-collins.com. A source for Collins's poems and books that also features several free recordings.

Paul Fussell, *A Touchy Subject* (p. 505)

In Fussell's witty, perceptive essay, he notes that "it is the middle class that is highly class-sensitive and sometimes class-scared to death" (para. 3). You might start by asking students why this might be. Why would people in the lower and upper classes be more comfortable thinking and talking about their socioeconomic status? Does the middle class's tenuous position alter its perception of class? For example, a sudden misfortune could propel a middle-class family into poverty, while a smart investment or a winning lottery ticket might raise a family into the ranks of the wealthy. According to Fussell, each class defines class differently: To the lower class, it's about money; to the middle class, it's about money combined with education and profession; and to the upper class, it has to do with behavior and values (para. 4).

POSSIBILITIES FOR DISCUSSION, REFLECTION, AND JOURNALING

• Ask students to think about the title of Fussell's essay. Why do they think class is "a touchy subject"?

• Do students believe they are in the same class as their parents? Why or why not?

ADDITIONAL WRITING TOPICS AND CLASSROOM ACTIVITIES

• Have students refer back to Visualizing Composition: Metaphor (p. 558). Ask them to think about and list the different "metaphors of mobility — the ability to move from one class to another," that, according to the McQuades in the chapter's introduction, have "surfaced more frequently in American public discourse."

• This piece by Fussell works because he treats a sensitive topic with humor. The text deflates the seriousness of the issue while making valid points. Ask students to draft an essay in which they attempt to desensitize readers to a touchy subject through humor (one suggestion: advising parents how to approach their teenagers on the issue of sex). As they consider topics and strategies, remind students that the humorous pieces here manage to be funny without being offensive. Going too far with the humor may turn readers away.

• The McQuades briefly touch on the history of the term *class* in the introduction to this chapter. Ask students to complete a more detailed research paper exploring the early associations of class with social and economic position.

CONNECTION WITH ANOTHER TEXT

• Ask students to think about what other pieces in this chapter support Fussell's thinking. Have them choose one and write an essay about how this selection either reinforces or complicates his thesis.

SUGGESTIONS FOR FURTHER READING, THINKING, AND WRITING

PRINT

DeMott, Benjamin. *Created Equal: Reading and Writing about Class in America*. New York: Harper, 1996. Print.

———. *The Imperial Middle: Why Americans Can't Think Straight about Class*. New Haven: Yale UP, 1992. Print.

Fussell, Paul. *Class: A Guide through the American Status System*. Carmichael, CA: Touchstone, 1992. Print.

Graham, Lawrence Otis. *Our Kind of People: Inside America's Black Upper Class*. New York: Harper, 1999. Print.

hooks, bell. *Where We Stand: Class Matters*. New York: Routledge, 2000. Print.

Lareau, Annette. *Unequal Childhoods: Class, Race and Family Life*. Berkeley: U of California P, 2003. Print.

Moss, Kirby. *The Color of Class: Poor Whites and the Paradox of Privilege*. Philadelphia: U of Pennsylvania P, 2003. Print.

WEB

pbs.org/peoplelikeus/. The site for PBS's documentary *People Like Us: Social Class in America*.

AUDIOVISUAL

O'Riley, Christopher. *Three Love Waits.* Sony, 2003. CD. O'Riley's piano instrumentals, which Sony distributes under its "Classical" label, are covers of songs by the alternative band Radiohead. Since many students will be familiar with Radiohead, O'Riley's "upper-class" versions could be the springboard for a discussion about how music reflects one's tastes and possibly one's class.

People Like Us: Social Class in America. 120 min. 2001. DVD. Distributed by PBS. Or-

dering information is available at the PBS web site.

Springsteen, Bruce. "Mansion on the Hill." *Nebraska.* Sony, 1982. CD. A subtle, brilliant song with a narrator who observes the upper class.

———. "Working on the Highway." *Born in the U.S.A.* Sony, 1984. CD. Just about any song from this album will do for representing the working class.

Wilson, Gretchen. "Redneck Woman." *Here for the Party.* Sony, 2004. CD.

Margaret Bourke-White, *The Louisville Flood* (p. 513)

The irony should be clear: In the background is a billboard that proclaims "world's highest standard of living" and shows a happy white family (with a happy dog) out for a drive in the family car; and in the foreground stands a row of poor black people waiting in a breadline. The smiling people on the billboard clearly aren't thinking about the plight of the others. Some students might realize that the breadline was a response to the flood, that perhaps these people were just unlucky. That suggestion raises another issue: geography and class. Do social conditions place people who are poor in areas where they are at greater risk of floods? Obviously, this image will bring to mind the recent images students saw after Hurricane Katrina. Ask them to discuss the changes in class and geography since 1937. Do they believe much has changed? Why or why not?

POSSIBILITIES FOR DISCUSSION, REFLECTION, AND JOURNALING

• Ask students to think again about class and geography. Have them discuss whether they believe it is easier or harder, or no different, than it was in 1937 to change social class.

ADDITIONAL WRITING TOPICS AND CLASSROOM ACTIVITIES

• Ask students to go out and photograph an ironic situation as Bourke-White has done. An alternative would be to have them describe an ironic situation.

• Ask students to find photographs of the people living in New Orleans right after Hurricane Katrina hit and have them compare and contrast these images with Bourke-White's.

• Have students freewrite about their first impressions of the photographer. Based on this photograph, would they assume that Bourke-White is white or black? Why? After they have made their initial assumptions, have them do some research on Bourke-White and write a brief research paper on her life that includes at least two different outside sources. Have students also write about how their reaction to the photograph changed once they knew more about the photographer. If their reaction didn't change, have them explain why not.

CONNECTIONS WITH OTHER TEXTS

• Have students refer back to the images by Tibor Kalman (Chapter 5, p. 436) and also have them reread the essay by Ta-Nehisi Coates (p. 447). Ask them to use both in an argument paper arguing whether they believe that socioeconomic factors are still correlated with race.

• Direct students back to Chris Jordan's photographs of the damage done by Hurricane Katrina (Chapter 3, pp. 290, 299, 300). Ask them to look closely at these photographs and pick out some possessions in the wreckage. Is there anything to indicate what class the people belonged to who used to live in the house, based on their possessions?

SUGGESTIONS FOR FURTHER READING, THINKING, AND WRITING

PRINT

Bourke-White, Margaret. *Portrait of Myself.* New York: Simon & Schuster, 1963. Print.

Bourke-White, Margaret, and Erskine Caldwell. *You Have Seen Their Faces.* Athens, GA: U of Georgia P, 1995. Print.

WEB

smartwomeninvest/peoplepics.htm. A brief article on Margaret Bourke-White, with more of her photographs.

AUDIOVISUAL

Schiller, Lawrence, prod. *Double Exposure: The Story of Margaret Bourke-White.* TNT, 1989. Film. Unfortunately, the filmmakers focus more on Bourke-White's stormy relationship with her husband than on her extraordinary career. It still may be worth showing some of the few scenes of Bourke-White, well played by Farrah Fawcett, at work.

Grant Wood, *American Gothic* (p. 516)

Wood's painting should be familiar to most students. Even if they've never seen a reproduction of the original, they will probably recognize it from the numerous parodies of it that have been created for, among other things, cartoon characters and film posters.

POSSIBILITIES FOR DISCUSSION, REFLECTION, AND JOURNALING

• You might start class discussion by asking students why this 1930 painting has endured as an American icon. Does the stoic farmer represent the hardworking America, the backbone of the country, or is the painting outdated? Does it still represent America? Why or why not?

- Ask students to freewrite about the lives of the figures in the painting. How do they see the people in the painting? How do they read their expressions? What is the relationship between the man and the woman? Why is the woman looking away?

ADDITIONAL WRITING TOPICS AND CLASSROOM ACTIVITIES

- Have students think about how they would create their own reproduction of the famous painting. Would they create a parody? Have students present their idea as well as the thinking behind it.

- When *American Gothic* was first exhibited, art critics were offended by the possibility that Wood was mocking rural Americans. Ask students to research the painting's critical background and to write a short research paper that details their findings.

CONNECTIONS WITH OTHER TEXTS

- Ask students to take another look at Joe Rosenthal's picture of the flag raising on Iwo Jima (Chapter 3, p. 308). Rosenthal and Wood have created two of the most popular American images. Ask students to write a paper that compares and contrasts the American values represented by each work.

- Many icons have struggled with their "genuine" personas. Have students take another look at Tibor Kalman's portraits of Arnold Schwarzenegger and Queen Elizabeth (Chapter 5, pp. 436–437). How has each struggled with his or her popular image? What does this struggle mean for how we read icons? How do the alterations Kalman makes in his photographs further complicate our readings of icons?

SUGGESTIONS FOR FURTHER READING, THINKING, AND WRITING

PRINT

Biel, Steven. *American Gothic: A Life of America's Most Famous Painting*. New York: Norton, 2005. Print.

WEB

artcyclopedia.com/artists/wood_grant.html. Artcyclopedia's online archive offers paintings by and information on Grant Wood. The site includes links to articles on the artist.

Guy Davenport, *The Geography of the Imagination* (p. 518)

Davenport states that Wood's sister and dentist posed for the painting in 1929 and that the dentist held a rake, not a pitchfork (para. 2). In the rest of the essay he examines elements of the painting—from the architecture of the house to the clothing of the figures—and supplies the historical and cultural derivation of each, providing readers with a different way to look at "this painting to which we are blinded by familiarity and parody" (para. 3). In paragraph 5, for example, Davenport notes that the bamboo sunscreen curtain is a Chinese invention and the sash windows are a European one, while the screen door is "distinctly American." In paragraph 6, he offers a brief look at the lineage of the wife's cameo brooch: "an heirloom passed down the generations, an eighteenth-century or Victorian copy of a design that goes back to the sixth century B.C." But it is the figures' pose that predates everything: "The pose is . . . that of the Egyptian prince Rahotep, holding the flail of Osiris, beside his wife Nufrit—strict with pious rectitude, poised in absolute dignity, mediators between heaven and earth, givers of grain, obedient to the Gods" (para. 11).

Davenport does discuss the painting's formal organization, but only briefly in regard to the pitchfork, "whose triune shape is repeated throughout the painting, in the bib of the overalls, the windows, the faces, the siding of the house, to give it a formal organization of impeccable harmony" (para. 21). Davenport acknowledges the possibility that the painting is "a statement about Protestant diligence on the American frontier," but he observes another theme: "a tension between the growing and the ungrowing, between vegetable and mineral, organic and inorganic, wheat and iron" (para. 22).

POSSIBILITIES FOR DISCUSSION, REFLECTION, AND JOURNALING

• Ask students to freewrite about their reaction to Grant Wood's painting *American Gothic* (p. 516) now that they have read Davenport's essay. Are they able to see the painting from a fresh perspective? Or have they been "blinded by familiarity and parody"?

ADDITIONAL WRITING TOPICS AND CLASSROOM ACTIVITIES

• Have students discuss whether or not they feel Grant Wood's painting *American Gothic* (p. 516) has become too familiar and why. Ask them to analyze the tools Davenport uses in "The Geography of the Imagination" to present the familiar in a different way.

• Have students research an iconic work from another culture and write an essay that offers a fresh perspective on it.

CONNECTIONS WITH OTHER TEXTS

• Have students take another look at Pobilio Diaz's photograph *Camino a Manabao* (Chapter 2, p. 198). Then ask students to write an essay about the photograph in which they research and explain the significance of each object in the photograph's background.

• Like Davenport's piece, Joel Sternfeld's photographs in Chapter 2 (pp. 132–139) force viewers to see the familiar with fresh eyes. Ask students to compare the impact of familiarity on their experience of viewing Sternfeld's photographs.

SUGGESTIONS FOR FURTHER READING, THINKING, AND WRITING

WEB

geocities.com/chuck_ralston/07_dav.htm. This web site provides some background on Davenport as well as examples of his work.

nytimes.com/2005/01/07/books/07davenport.html. Davenport's obituary, published in the *New York Times*, provides biography information.

Surefire Assignment: Reading Personality

Jean Petrolle
Columbia College Chicago
(Profile, p. 17)

I ask students to bring a family photograph or a photograph of a friend to class (do *not* have students read Davenport's essay before class). Ideally the photograph should be posed rather than candid, but it need not be professionally made: Any snapshot will do.

We read Davenport's essay aloud in class, and I ask students to make a list of Davenport's claims about what can be inferred from the painting about the couple and their material environment. Here is a prompt for getting them to do this:

> In his "reading" of Grant Wood's painting *American Gothic*, Guy Davenport draws a number of conclusions about the couple and their environment. In paragraph 3, for instance, he describes the couple's "Protestant sobriety and industry." He observes a bit later, in paragraph 8, that the woman is "a step behind her husband," a position he attributes to Protestant tradition. In paragraph 12, by referencing the "Netherlandish tradition of painting middle-class folk with honor and precision," he implies that the farmer and his wife are middle class. He confirms that "reading" from the material trappings that surround the couple. Please read the essay again carefully and make a list of these and other types of claims Davenport makes about the couple, their social class, and their environment.

After they have made their lists, I ask the students to look again at the painting and see if they agree with Davenport's conclusions.

Next I have them look at the photograph they have brought with them and make a list of statements detailing what they can conclude about the subject(s) based on the material trappings surrounding the subject(s) as well as the body language, pose, expression, and overall self-presentation of the subject(s). Then, I pair the students up and have each pair exchange photographs, so that someone who does not know the subject(s) can try to "read" the personality and class position of the subject(s) from the photo. The "outside" reader also makes a list of observations. The paired students can then compare their lists of observations. The class ends with a full-group discussion about how we "read" images.

Context: Gordon Parks, *American Gothic* (p. 525)

Gordon Parks's photograph *American Gothic* plays on Grant Wood's famous painting of the same name. Taken in 1942 (twelve years after Wood finished the painting), the photograph shows a black cleaning woman holding a broom and standing next to a mop in front of the American flag.

POSSIBILITIES FOR DISCUSSION, REFLECTION, AND JOURNALING

• Direct students to examine the compositional elements in the photograph and in Grant Wood's painting *American Gothic*. Students will quickly note that Parks presents the cleaning woman in much the same way that Wood presents the farmer: the stare, the glasses, the serious expression. Of course the pitchfork — the center of Wood's painting, what ties it together — has been replaced with a broom. Parks positions the cleaning woman between the broom and a mop. What does this suggest about her status?

• Remind students that Wood uses the shape of the pitchfork throughout the painting to give it unity. Parks also repeats certain images to tie his work together. Students might observe that the white dots on the woman's uniform resemble the blurred stars in the flag. Less obvious is the repetition of the flag's vertical stripes in the vertical bristles of the broom.

• You might also ask students about the position of the flag. Would they react differently to this picture if the flag were horizontal instead of vertical? Do they see oppression in the way the stripes fall on the woman?

ADDITIONAL WRITING TOPICS AND CLASSROOM ACTIVITIES

• At this point in the course, students have come across a number of images that rely on other images for their power. You might ask students to examine a television show or movie that relies on previous television shows or movies for its effectiveness. Have students trace the similarities and differences between one particular example and its predecessors. How is the TV show/movie relying on these predecessors? How is it breaking away from them? What does this reliance on previous examples suggest about originality and creativity?

• Poverty and racism are often the subjects of Parks's photography. Ask students to research Parks's work as well as the status of African Americans in the 1940s. Then have them write an essay that explores how this information affects their reading of Parks's photograph and its reference to Wood's painting.

CONNECTIONS WITH OTHER TEXTS

• Ask students to examine Gordon Parks's photograph and freewrite about the feelings it evokes. Then ask students to compare the photograph to Grant Wood's *American Gothic* (p. 516). Have them compare their reactions to the works. Do they feel that Wood's painting celebrates America, whereas Parks's photograph indicts it? Do they see stoicism in the farmer's face? in the cleaning woman's face? Is Parks's photograph just a parody of Wood's work or something more?

- Ask students to examine Retrospect: An American Classic Revisited (p. 526) and to find other takes on Wood's painting that are clearly parodies. Have them write an expository paper about how these parodies tap into our understanding of the original to create new meanings. On the surface many parodies seem to be merely selling something, not creating new cultural meaning. However, urge students to examine how the goals of the parodies are meanings in themselves. For variety, you could also suggest that students research Leonardo da Vinci's *Mona Lisa*, Edvard Munch's *The Scream*, James McNeill Whistler's *Whistler's Mother*, and Michelangelo's *Creation of Man*—all of which have been parodied as well.

- Ask students to read Jane Yolen's poem on Wood's painting (p. 523) and to follow the form of the poem as they write their own poem about Parks's photograph. If students have a difficult time comparing the photograph and the painting in class discussion, you can use this exercise as another way to deal with the comparison.

SUGGESTION FOR FURTHER READING, THINKING, AND WRITING

WEB

pdngallery.com/legends/parks/mainframeset
   .shtml. Provides some background on Parks's
   photograph.

Retrospect: An American Classic Revisited (p. 526)

The four images in this Retrospect show a few ways in which the iconic image by Grant Wood has been used in American culture. Whether it is used for political comment and satire or mass marketing, the familiarity of the painting and the surprising twists people put on it make for powerful and memorable images.

Image from 1960 (p. 526)

The earliest of the four images, from 1960, recasts the two figures as hippies. While the composition of the painting and the faces of the people remain largely the same, subtle changes associate them with the growing protest movement. The print on the woman's dress has been changed to a peace sign motif, and the cameo at her neck becomes an iron cross symbol, which was appropriated by the surfer culture after World War II. The man sports a flower power pin, and his pitchfork has been replaced with a message representative of the peace movement's distrust of the government. By characterizing these classic American figures as activists, the illustrator makes a claim that the emerging counterculture had deep roots in the American character, particularly the spirit of individualism that this lone farmer may represent.

Image from 2001 (p. 526)

This image, which dates to the year of the September 11 attacks on the World Trade Center, shows the two figures in iconic New York T-shirts. As in the previous image, the composition is largely the same, with the same Gothic window between the two heads, but the line drawing here is a much simplified, and even stylized, version of the original painting. By linking these two figures of Middle America with New York, this illustration expresses the solidarity that the entire country felt with the victims of the attack.

Image of Paris Hilton and Nicole Richie, 2003–2007 (p. 527)

This take on *American Gothic*, a promotional image for the reality TV show *The Simple Life*, casts the two stars of the show as farmers. To appreciate the irony of this image, viewers have to understand the public personae of the two women pictured, Paris Hilton and Nicole Richie. The two are famous for nothing in particular, or rather they are famous for being wealthy and out of touch with the lives most Americans live. The premise of the show was that, if put in situations with average Americans, the two women will behave in outrageous and entertaining ways. Of the four images, this one is furthest from the original, and it is also the only one that uses photography. However, by retaining key elements — two people side by side, the house and window behind them, and perhaps most importantly the pitchfork — the creators of this image can invoke Wood's painting for humorous effect.

Image of Portia de Rossi and Ellen DeGeneres, 2008 (p. 527)

Finally, the *Advocate* cover from 2008 employs *American Gothic* to comment on gay marriage. In place of the couple in the original painting, this artist includes the Hollywood couple Ellen DeGeneres and Portia de Rossi. Their marriage in 2008, after the California ban on same-sex marriage was lifted, was widely publicized. Associating them with Wood's painting underscores the desire on the part of gay marriage advocates to make same-sex unions part of the status quo — something not exotic or strange, but entirely familiar.

POSSIBILITIES FOR DISCUSSION, REFLECTION, AND JOURNALING

- Ask students to discuss the spirit in which each of these images adapts the original. Do they revere Wood's painting, and, if so, what about it is so exemplary? If they are satirizing the painting, what qualities make it susceptible to humor?

- How does each of the images use color differently? Have students discuss how they would characterize the color palette in each. How does color draw their eyes to different parts of the image?

ADDITIONAL WRITING TOPICS AND CLASSROOM ACTIVITIES

• Assign students to create their own takes on *American Gothic*. Ask them to consider what interests them about the original and how they might update it to say something about contemporary life. They might use Photoshop or even a collage to reinterpret the iconic image.

• Have students put together a portfolio on parodies of another iconic painting. They should use captions to explain the context of each new version and how it alters the original.

• Have students write a letter or an editorial on one of the images. What would they say to the creator about his or her interpretation? How does it preserve the spirit of the original or depart from it?

• Which of the images do students find most timely or important? Ask them to write about which image they think has the most impact. They could also search the Internet for more *American Gothic* parodies. Using Davenport's essay as inspiration, have students write a close analysis of the various cultural signs in one of these parodies. For example, what do the clothes in the *Simple Life* picture indicate? What about Hilton's dog? What other details are meaningful?

CONNECTION WITH ANOTHER TEXT

• Ask students to think about other paintings that have been frequently reused and reinterpreted — for example, the *Mona Lisa*. Do these paintings share any features with *American Gothic*? What turns a work of art into a cultural icon?

SUGGESTIONS FOR FURTHER READING, THINKING, AND WRITING

PRINT

Parr, Ann, and Gordon Parks. *Gordon Parks: No Excuses*. Gretna, LA: Pelican, 2006. Print.

WEB

loubeach.com/work.html. This contemporary artist's web site provides another parody of *American Gothic* that comments on American affluence.

memory.loc.gov/ammem/fsahtml/fachap07.html. This web site, from the Library of Congress, provides biographical information as well as a gallery of some of Parks's photographs.

nytimes.com/2006/03/08/arts/design/08parks.html. Parks's obituary from the *New York Times* provides biographical information.

AUDIOVISUAL

pbs.org/newshour/bb/entertainment/jan-june98/gordon_1-6.html. Listen to an interview with Gordon Parks.

Surefire Class: Mash-Up Art

Brian Oliu
University of Alabama

One of the papers that I assign for this class is a comparison-and-contrast essay in which students take one of their favorite musical artists and analyze how his or her music, style, and popularity have changed over the years or from album to album. As a result, the general theme for the two weeks we spend on this comparison-and-contrast project is music. In my syllabus this unit comes after our discussions about photography, so I like to use concepts from the section we just completed to bridge the gap between old material and new material.

After reading the Retrospect in Chapter 6, I have students create a piece of original work from another person's work. We then listen to a song that samples other artists' material to create an entirely new song. We discuss the differences between our exercise and the song we listened to and how the selections in the text fit in with our ideas of creating art out of other people's work. This assignment also works well with found art, as well as showing photos of Marcel Duchamp's *Fountain* (a urinal) or *L.H.O.O.Q.* (Mona Lisa with a mustache and a goatee).

For an in-class writing assignment, when my students first arrive, I go around the room and ask them what their favorite song is, or whatever song they are enjoying at the moment or heard on the way to class. I write each song title on the board and write one of mine down for good measure. After we have accumulated a list of song titles, I have them create a poem or story using as many of the song titles as possible. I have a few students share their poems/stories aloud (most are ridiculous, highly entertaining, and good for waking up students, especially if you teach at 8 a.m.!), and then I play them a song by a deejay called Girl Talk that uses more than twenty-five samples of other people's music in a three-minute song (you can use any other song that samples another piece of art). I explain to them that in this deejay's particular case, he did not clear any of the samples or pay royalties to use these songs. Although he did offer the album for free download and therefore isn't earning any money on record sales, he has been able to make a name for himself and is making money through his live performances. I then ask students what the difference is between what they did on the board and what Girl Talk has done with his music. This starts a discussion about copyright as well as the definition of public domain. As visual evidence, I have them look at Andy Warhol's artwork and have them compare what he has done with Campbell's soup cans and Coca-Cola bottles to the music we listened to as well as our writing assignment earlier. From here, I put students in groups and have them write an explanation of the differences and similarities among all the different types of "mash-up art" that we have examined.

William Deresiewicz, *The Dispossessed* (p. 529)

In "The Dispossessed," Deresiewicz points out how little attention the working class receives in American culture—to the point that the author finds himself "abysmally ignorant" about "working-class career expectations, working-class family structures" (para. 2). Deresiewicz's lack of knowledge about the working class is no coincidence: "such knowledge had been withheld from me by my culture" (para. 2). He notes a few exceptions, including the television show *Roseanne*. However, for the most part, even people with working-class jobs appear on television and in movies to be living middle-class lives. Our culture creates the illusion that we're all part of a single class, "the great middle" (para. 5). Deresiewicz points out that the South is the last true bastion of working-class culture and that even in places as far-flung as Portland, Oregon, working-class people have adopted aspects of southern culture as their own.

One of the problems, ultimately, is that the middle class is regarded as "normal and normative" (para. 5). What little commentary we do have on the working class is seen from middle-class perspectives, like that of Barbara Ehrenreich. The decreasing power of unions has played a large role in the disappearance of the working class from our political and cultural consciousness. In fact, class has almost been eliminated as a category. Toni Morrison noticed Bill Clinton's working-class traits and proclaimed him our "first black President," substituting race for the disappearing category of class. Deresiewicz also argues that we have a less nuanced appreciation of class, so that middle-class people often can't tell the difference between working-class people and poor people.

To make up for his ignorance, Deresiewicz offers some hard definitions. For example, he suggests that "a member of the working class is someone who receives an hourly wage" (para. 8). He laments the fact that the term *working class* is disappearing from political discourse in favor of *working poor* and *working families*. The former, he argues, is useful because it points out that some wage earners still don't make enough to cross the poverty line. The latter, he suggests, is simply a euphemism, one that blurs any line between the working and middle classes, and another example of how we turn away from real discussion of class issues.

POSSIBILITIES FOR DISCUSSION, REFLECTION, AND JOURNALING

• Deresiewicz paraphrases Roseanne Barr, saying, "Only middle-class women care about feminism" (para. 1). Ask students to discuss why he thinks this is true. Do they agree with his reasoning?

• Have students think about whether they could update the examples Deresiewicz gives of TV shows that deal with class. Can they think of any recent programs that address the issue of class or prominently feature working-class characters?

- By Deresiewicz's definition, which is based on hourly wage versus salaried workers, many high school and college students would be deemed working class. Ask your students to consider whether this is true. Does it complicate the definition? How would they refine Deresiewicz's terms?

ADDITIONAL WRITING TOPICS AND CLASSROOM ACTIVITIES

- Ask students to collect images from television, movies, or print media of people with working-class jobs. Once they have assembled a portfolio of images, they might attempt to categorize them. Which seem to represent the working class accurately? Which promote stereotypes? Which images show, as Deresiewicz points out, people with working-class jobs living middle-class lives?

- **Image/Writing Assignment:** Deresiewicz takes photographs of New Orleans after Hurricane Katrina as an opportunity to discuss how middle-class observers read class. Ask students to look at the photograph reprinted in the text, or other photos they can find, and to analyze the class of the people pictured in the post-hurricane city. What clues help viewers determine the socioeconomic status of the people in the pictures?

- Ask students to write an essay about some aspect of what Deresiewicz calls working-class culture. Does it have roots in the South? Does it follow the pattern he identifies of spreading outside of the South to other working-class areas in the country?

- Have students write an account of one moment in which they became aware of class differences. Like Deresiewicz, they might use personal observation to expand into broader reflections on class in their communities or in American culture.

CONNECTION WITH ANOTHER TEXT

- In a related essay for the *American Scholar* called "The Disadvantages of an Elite Education," Deresiewicz speaks from his own highly educated experience to discuss the things his Ivy League degrees didn't prepare him for. Ask students to read this essay (available at theamericanscholar.org/the-disadvantages-of-an-elite-education/) and write an essay comparing the perspective in the two pieces.

SUGGESTIONS FOR FURTHER READING, THINKING, AND WRITING

WEB

thenation.com/directory/bios/william _deresiewicz/. A profile of Deresiewicz that includes articles he has written for *The Nation.*

AUDIOVISUAL

bloggingheads.tv/diavlogs/14561/. A video discussion between Deresiewicz and Mark Edmundson, of the University of Virginia, regarding teaching and evaluating in the university.

Portfolio: How Class Works (p. 540)

The graphics in this Portfolio illustrate the results of a battery of survey questions that the *New York Times* asked people nationwide. They display an interesting mix of optimism and cynicism about class and upward mobility. For example, graphs show that while people believe that upward mobility is possible, relatively few believe that they will become rich. Though they believe hard work pays off, most of the poll respondents supported programs that assist those who come from low-income backgrounds.

These figures also reveal how people define wealth and the elusive American Dream. The answers for how much money a family must make to be considered rich range from less than $100,000 to more than $1 million. As might be expected, people with higher income levels report increasingly good health. However, students may be surprised to see that there is a negative correlation between income levels and the importance of religious faith among the respondents. One common denominator at all income levels, though, is the belief that education is an important factor in determining success, and just over half of the people surveyed thought a college degree was the level a person would need to achieve.

POSSIBILITIES FOR DISCUSSION, REFLECTION, AND JOURNALING

• Ask students to think about how they would answer the questions posed in this Portfolio. You might even consider polling the class and then calculating the statistics on a few of the questions. How do the students' responses compare to the results in the *New York Times*?

• Have students reflect on which of the results in the *New York Times* poll surprise them the most. Which are the least surprising? Do they see any contradictions in the results?

• This poll was designed more to test attitudes about class and income than to determine actual figures. Ask students to find some statistics on income levels from the federal government's Bureau of Labor Statistics. How are income levels measured differently than the *New York Times* poll measured them? Do the statistics tell a different story than the *New York Times* poll does?

ADDITIONAL WRITING TOPICS AND CLASSROOM ACTIVITIES

• **Image/Writing Assignment:** Ask students to create a visual spectrum of their answers to the question "How much does an American family need to make to be considered rich?"

Each student should find a picture that answers the question. It may be of a house or car, of some kind of consumer good, or even of an individual or a family that represents wealth. When you add all the pictures together, what do they say about the class's definition of wealth?

• What other questions do your students think would be interesting to ask these poll respondents? Ask them to think about what kinds of answers they would get and what kind of chart or graph would represent those answers.

• The charts reprinted here (pp. 540–547) offer a wealth of information in visual form. Assign students an essay in which they translate this information into a narrative. Ask them to summarize the statistics that the charts convey and to draw some conclusions.

CONNECTION WITH ANOTHER TEXT

• The results of this poll were reprinted in a book called *Class Matters* along with essays from several *New York Times* journalists and first-person accounts of "encounters with class." Ask students to survey the poll results and to read one of the journalistic pieces and one of the personal essays. Then have them write an essay in which they compare these different forms and their approach to questions of class.

SUGGESTIONS FOR FURTHER READING, THINKING, AND WRITING

PRINT

New York Times Correspondents. *Class Matters.* New York: Times Books, 2005. Print.

WEB

nytimes.com/packages/html/national/20050515 _CLASS_GRAPHIC/index_04.html. A link to the original study published in the *New York Times*.

Barbara Ehrenreich, *This Land Is Their Land* (p. 549)
Woody Guthrie, *This Land Is Your Land* (p. 554)

Ehrenreich's essay is motivated by the disturbing observation that "if a place is truly beautiful you can't afford to be there" (para. 2). She argues that in places like Jackson Hole, Key West, and the Hamptons, the wealthy have squeezed out the original residents who gave those places character. In the title and again at the end of this piece, she refers to Woody Guthrie's "This Land Is Your Land" to contrast the song's inclusive message with the unavailability of those beautiful landscapes to anyone but the very rich. In this she updates what was originally a protest song; "This Land Is Your Land" already questions whether the promises of America really extend to all of its citizens, even those who rely on the "relief office."

Ehrenreich finds the acquisition of sites of natural beauty by the wealthy emblematic of a larger problem in American society: the widening gap between the rich and the poor. Indeed, she cites statistics suggesting that more equalized income levels would lead to greater happiness for all citizens. She finds that "some of the most equal nations — Iceland and Norway" (para. 8) have the highest levels of happiness. While we are apt to think of poverty as a social problem to be solved, we rarely consider that "extreme wealth is also a social problem" (para. 8). In "This Land Is Their Land," Ehrenreich asks readers to consider what great wealth takes away from the general population.

POSSIBILITIES FOR DISCUSSION, REFLECTION, AND JOURNALING

• Ask students whether they can think of other examples that support Ehrenreich's point that "extreme wealth" is a problem. Besides real estate, are there other areas in which the rich establish a kind of monopoly? Or can students think of examples to the contrary — ways that wealth solves rather than creates problems?

• The anecdote Ehrenreich relates about shopping in Sun Valley dramatizes a moment in which she realizes she is outside of her class's usual sphere. Have students think about whether they have had similar moments. Ask them to discuss or to freewrite about how particular places contain class markers.

ADDITIONAL WRITING TOPICS AND CLASSROOM ACTIVITIES

• **Image/Writing Assignment:** Have students choose one of the locations Ehrenreich discusses or a different resort town. Then ask them to do some photo research to find recent images of the place and images from twenty or thirty years ago. Do their findings support Ehrenreich's argument? What changes do they notice in the pictures?

• **Image/Writing Assignment:** Ask students to choose images from fine art that support the notion of "biophilia," which Ehrenreich picks up from Edward O. Wilson. Judging by the way artists treat nature, what does it provide to humans? What emotions or ideas do the works of art link with natural beauty?

• In class, play a recording of Guthrie singing "This Land Is Your Land" and have students listen to some versions by other artists (for example, Bruce Springsteen, Sharon Jones, or Tom Morello of Rage Against the Machine). Have them write an essay about a few versions of the song and how it has meant different things to different artists.

• Ehrenreich writes, "Of all the crimes of the rich, the aesthetic deprivation of the rest of us may seem to be the merest misdemeanor" (para. 7). Have students write an argumentative essay, either supporting the notion that wealth brings far greater problems than depriving people of beauty or arguing that access to beauty is far more important than some might believe.

CONNECTIONS WITH OTHER TEXTS

• Ask students to think about this essay in terms of William Deresiewicz's claim that our knowledge of the working class comes from middle-class commentators like Ehrenreich. Where do her sympathies lie in this essay? What parts of it provide clues to the writer's class identity?

• Ask students to write an imagined history of the neighborhood featured in Camilo José Vergara's photographs (Chapter 2, p. 156) the way Ehrenreich writes about the changing character of Key West.

SUGGESTIONS FOR FURTHER READING, THINKING, AND WRITING

PRINT

Ehrenreich, Barbara. *Nickel and Dimed: On (Not) Getting By in America.* New York: Holt, 2001. Print.

———. *This Land Is Their Land: Reports from a Divided Nation.* New York: Metropolitan, 2008. Print.

WEB

barbaraehrenreich.com. The writer's web site features biographical information, a listing of her written works, and her blog.

AUDIOVISUAL

youtube.com/watch?v=gDgFiW2xtf0/. Ehrenreich herself stars in this video about the working class, based on her book *Nickel and Dimed.*

youtube.com/watch?v=WBAlv2vNmWk/. Ehrenreich joins a discussion on the relevance of socialism to the current economic crisis at the Meltdown Forum hosted by *The Nation* magazine and The Nation Institute on March 6, 2009.

Tina Barney, *The Reunion* (p. 555)

Tina Barney creates portraits of her family and friends, many of whom are upper-class New Englanders. She once said, "The human gesture is one of the great loves of my life," and her intimate portraits often reveal plenty about their subjects just in the subtle gestures caught on film.

POSSIBILITIES FOR DISCUSSION, REFLECTION, AND JOURNALING

• In addition to their clothing, what signals that the people in Barney's photograph are upper class? Is it the artwork in the background? the man in the back who might be a servant? the apparent fascination the people have with the statue on the table?

ADDITIONAL WRITING TOPICS AND CLASSROOM ACTIVITIES

• Ask students to stage a photograph of a middle-class family reunion. Who would be there? What would they be wearing? Where would the reunion take place? What objects would be in the background? Have them describe why they chose these people, clothes, and setting.

• Have students discuss how they believe each person in the photograph relates to the others. Ask them to explain their choices.

• Ask students to write a fictional narrative of a scene from a reunion of family or friends that brings together people of different classes.

• Have students examine the people in Tina Barney's photograph closely and, for each person, write about what their gestures reveal about their personality and about their class.

CONNECTIONS WITH OTHER TEXTS

• Have students reread "I Stand Here Ironing" by Tillie Olsen (Chapter 1, p. 62) and "Girl" by Jamaica Kincaid (Chapter 4, p. 329). Next have them choose a voice, either Olsen's mother's or Kincaid's daughter's, and in that voice tell the story of one of the women in Barney's photograph.

• Have students reread Visualizing Composition: Tone (Chapter 2, p. 188) and write an essay in which they describe the tone of Barney's photograph. Make sure they remember to back up their argument with specific examples from the photo.

SUGGESTIONS FOR FURTHER READING, THINKING, AND WRITING

PRINT

Barney, Tina. *Friends and Relations.* New York: Smithsonian, 1991. Print.

Barney, Tina, and Andy Grundberg. *Theater of Manners.* New York: Scalo, 1997. Print.

WEB

janetbordeninc.com/artists/index.php?page= Barney. This agency, which represents Barney, has several of her photographs on its web site.

mocp.org/collections/permanent/barney_tina .php. The Museum of Contemporary Photography's web site features more photos by Barney as well as some biographical information.

Surefire Assignment: Playing with Metaphor

Dan Keller
University of Louisville
(Profile, p. 14)

I'm a sucker for a good metaphor. When one student wrote an essay about how becoming friends with certain people in high school (e.g., jocks, brains) was like having mob connections (jocks to watch your back, brains to help with accounting homework), something inside me got all warm and fuzzy. I try to encourage moments like these as much as possible in class; I particularly want students to think about how metaphor can be used to "resee" for hypothetical and practical purposes, and several sections in *Seeing & Writing* help me do that.

After discussing Visualizing Composition: Metaphor, we turn briefly to the photographs by Tibor Kalman (Chapter 5, p. 436) to talk about how the reversal of race in these images helps us see the familiar in a new way: Because these images present a different take on what is real, they provide a playful launching point for ways to resee. I point out that metaphors can do the same.

Continuing with the idea of how metaphor can be used to resee the familiar, I incorporate a practical exercise involving punctuation. I know students are usually bored beyond belief with grammar and punctuation exercises, but this one is almost always fun, and I'm constantly surprised by how involved students get.

After handing out some brief examples and rules for punctuation marks, I ask students to consider metaphors for them. Naming all of the punctuation marks on the board, I start them off with the period as a stop sign or a red light. Students quickly get in on the game, suggesting other traffic markers —"Yield" or "Slow, Children at Play" for the semicolon; a highway information sign for the colon; "Detour" for parentheses; "Duck Crossing" for the dash (elegantly defended by one student). We usually have three or four traffic markers for each punctuation mark, and students readily demonstrate their knowledge by playfully debating the accuracy of the metaphors. It's also fantastic to have these traffic markers as references throughout the semester. I can't describe the joy I felt in one class when I overheard one student remark to another in peer review, "Dude, you should use a 'Duck Crossing' here."

Looking Closer:
Rereading an Icon

Like Grant Wood's *American Gothic*, the photograph *Migrant Mother* has been viewed and interpreted in many different contexts. The essays and images grouped here show the continued importance of the image, but they also help students excavate its meanings.

Dorothea Lange, *Migrant Mother, Nipomo, California* (p. 560)

Students will probably be familiar with this photograph, which was taken in 1936 in Nipomo, California, and came to symbolize the Great Depression. They might not know that the woman is named Florence Owens Thompson or that this photograph is one of many that Lange took for the Resettlement Administration (later the Farm Security Administration) while on a month-long trip photographing migratory farm labor in California. In 1960, Lange recounted her experience in an interview in *Popular Photography* magazine and said of the photograph:

> I saw and approached the hungry and desperate mother, as if drawn by a magnet. I do not remember how I explained my presence or my camera to her, but I do remember she asked me no questions. I made five exposures, working closer and closer from the same direction. I did not ask her name or her history. She told me her age, that she was thirty-two. She said that they had been living on frozen vegetables from the surrounding fields, and birds that the children killed. She had just sold the tires from her car to buy food. There she sat in that lean-to tent with her children huddled around her, and seemed to know that my pictures might help her, and so she helped me. There was a sort of equality about it. (From *Popular Photography*, Feb. 1960)

Sally Stein, *Passing Likeness: Dorothea Lange's* Migrant Mother *and the Paradox of Iconicity* (p. 561)

Stein's essay is long and makes a complicated argument. So before you assign it, consider telling your students to keep in mind that Stein makes a nuanced argument, not a simple claim of good or bad. Students might not readily understand the concept of passing, which Stein explains in paragraphs 19 and 20. To help illustrate the concept, you could ask students to turn to Tibor Kalman's images (Chapter 5, p. 436). In these images, Kalman altered the race of his famous subjects. Ask students to imagine that the pictures are real, that Arnold Schwarze-negger and Queen Elizabeth are black. Then ask why these subjects might be better off passing as the other race. What Stein is saying is that being Native American would not have helped Thompson's situation in the Depression.

Sally Stein's essay considers the questions that surround the production of the image and, in doing so, meditates on Lange's account of how and why she captured the image as well as the larger implications that her selection of subject and scene have for documentary photography. Stein's discoveries about Lange's image—its problematic history within the Farm Security Administration, the way it ignores or misreads the subject's Native American heritage—raise questions about the photographer's intentions and the additional meanings later viewers have found in the picture. As your students read the essay, you might use the example of *Migrant Mother* to discuss how the signs and significance of an image can change over time and across various contexts.

The Nation, January 2005 cover (p. 576)

Students will be able to piece together the meaning of this altered image of Lange's famous photograph from the juxtaposition of the black and white image with the signature blue Wal-Mart vest and the title of the cover story. You might want to ask students what other indications of socioeconomic class they see in this image.

The Nation cover capitalizes on the photograph's status as a document of poverty and hardship but updates the mother's occupation, changing her from a farmworker to a Wal-Mart employee. Interestingly, this new take on the image gives the figure an invented name, which she never possessed for Lange. The name is stamped on her work badge, which associates identity directly with her occupation.

Dorothea Lange, *Eloy, Pinal County, Arizona* (p. 577)

This is another photograph by Dorothea Lange documenting migratory farm labor. The workers frequently traveled like this in caravans. This particular truckload of cotton pickers had just pulled into town in the late afternoon from Arkansas.

In some ways, *Eloy, Pinal County, Arizona* is closer to the standard documentary photograph that Lange's employers at the Farm Security Administration would have expected her to produce. In examining the compositional differences between them, students will see for themselves the ways in which *Migrant Mother* operates more as a symbol than as a document.

• Before they read Stein's essay, you might ask students to look at Lange's famous image, *Migrant Mother* (p. 560), and to freewrite about what the picture means to them. What impressions do they get from the picture? Why do you think this image has become an icon?

• To help students understand Stein's argument, ask them to react to and paraphrase the essay's claims in a reading journal.

• Instead of asking students to take one side or the other on the issue of passing, encourage them to notice how Stein treats the subject, fairly presenting the multiple views. In the end, neither erasing nor broadcasting the migrant woman's ethnicity seems an ideal solution. Ask students to think of modern examples that illustrate Stein's conclusion that we need to "become a society committed to problematizing the historic assumption of normative whiteness" (para. 24).

• How does the picture of Florence Thompson with her family, taken in 1979, compare to *Migrant Mother*? Is it more real for being less iconic? Have students discuss specific choices, especially in the composition of the photograph, as they answer this question.

ADDITIONAL WRITING TOPICS AND CLASSROOM ACTIVITIES

• Have students take another look at the cover of *The Nation* (p. 576), which used Lange's famous photograph to make a statement. After reading Stein's essay, do students see this cover any differently?

• Stein argues that one of the reasons *Migrant Mother* has been so frequently appropriated for other uses is that it was a government-owned image in the public domain. What does the photo's copyright status have to do with its iconicity? Ask students to discuss the broader connections Stein makes between artistic ownership of the image and its status as an icon.

• Once students have read the essay, you can ask them to compare their impressions of the picture before and after reading Stein's work. How do they react to the revelation that this woman is Native American? Can they summarize Stein's complicated argument about Lange's photograph and what it means to our current issues with difference? What are the dangers in "the canonization of this image as mainstream Anglo icon" (para. 21)? How do they react to Stein's argument?

• Stein observes that if Lange's subject in *Migrant Mother* had been identified as Native American, Lange might not have taken the picture, or the picture would not have found wide circulation: "The image's promotion and circulation would have been quite limited. It would have undermined conventional thinking in two ways: It directed attention away from Anglos, and it refused to support the image of Indians as a 'vanishing race'" (para. 17). Ask students to write an exploratory paper about how similar trends may be happening today with certain images and certain people.

CONNECTIONS WITH OTHER TEXTS

• Ask students to think about the photo and Stein's arguments about how it is racially marked in the terms established in Chapter 5, Examining Difference. How does the story of the photo demonstrate racial essentialism? Or how does it challenge essentialism? What does

Stein's redefinition of "passing" add to discussions about racial difference?

•   Have students work in groups to research some other Depression-era documentary photographs. (They can find a useful collection at english.illinois.edu/MAPS/depression/photo essay.htm.) Once they have viewed at least five more photographs, ask them to make some general observations about the style and the effect of Great Depression photography. In their description, they should make specific reference to details of the photographs they have viewed.

SUGGESTIONS FOR FURTHER READING, THINKING, AND WRITING

PRINT

Curtis, James. *Mind's Eye, Mind's Truth: FSA Photography Reconsidered.* Philadelphia: Temple UP, 1989. Print.

WEB

loc.gov/rr/print/list/128_migm.html. The Library of Congress's web page on the series of pictures from which *Migrant Mother* comes. migrantgrandson.com. Thompson's grandson's web site.

Surefire Assignment: Learning by Doing

Jeff Cravello
*California State Polytechnic
University, Pomona*
(Profile, p. 9)

Teaching remedial English or freshman composition at a polytechnic university is, at best, a challenge. Most students come from the practical sciences and view composition as redundant and unnecessary. Using *Seeing & Writing* has helped me confront the students' attitudes and address their legitimate concerns.

Given the word, my students would probably ask for more "praxis" in English classes because most have been exposed to little more than formulary literary analysis throughout high school. Moreover, few have truly been exposed to analyzing images in any medium. My students, when first confronted with their gap in understanding basic images, are quite startled and intrigued. Studying images critically isn't redundant at all. For most, it's quite new.

At the same time, Cal Poly Pomona emphasizes the concept of "learning by doing" from orientation through graduation, and while many of us in the humanities scorn this approach, in a Plato-versus-Aristotle fashion, it certainly does have a place in our pedagogy.

My first step toward learning by doing is presenting the students with the very real task of examining and selecting readings that both interest them and have the potential for producing the best writing. Of course, I could choose the selections from *Seeing & Writing*, but with such variety, there is tremendous freedom of choice. Frankly, we could discuss any set of photographs, ads, or symbols, but in the final

analysis, it is the composition that will be the mark of success or failure. Consequently, the course assignments section of my syllabus is blank.

Generally, given the constraints of a ten-week quarter system, I direct the students to consider three chapters: Chapter 1, Observing the Ordinary; Chapter 6, Confronting Class; and Chapter 7, Taking a Stand. Students are welcome to choose different chapters if they seem more appealing and conducive to writing. Then we begin selecting, through a democratic process, which images and readings in each chapter to tackle. This process both empowers the students and gives them a sense of accountability. They aren't reading what I've assigned, so they can't provide the common excuse of writing poorly because of lack of interest. If Paulo Freire seems to have influenced this approach, he has.

In keeping with learning by doing, I encourage personal investigation into the images and stories, and I recommend that students try to re-create what they've seen or read. For example, most classes will choose Sally Stein's essay on Dorothea Lange's photography. This essay is ripe for a photo assignment. Instead of imagining from afar what Dorothea Lange did, students have the option of using their own cameras and capturing and promoting our own campus community as either exciting, studious, or diverse, as if they were working for our Public Affairs Office.

Once they see through the eye of the camera, they almost inherently understand the daunting task of providing photos that are both accurate and persuasive. They are permitted to stage friends or fellow students for their photos or simply capture whatever the campus presents. Their own photographic journey then becomes another story to be told and compared to Lange's classic work. This becomes the foundation for a comparative analytical essay.

As impressed as I am by their creativity, I emphasize that it is their writing I will evaluate, not their photography or photo-editing talents. The goal of the photo assignment is simply to learn by doing. Invariably, students have a greater connection with their essay responses, whether they relate to Dorothea Lange's *Migrant Mother*, Frank Fournier's *Omayra Sanchez, Colombia, 1985* (Chapter 7, p. 590), or the portrayal of war in the Retrospect in Chapter 7.

As composition instructors, our greatest task is often overcoming the general apprehension or outright fear of writing that most students have. With few exceptions, students who have something concrete to convey from their own experience write more confidently. The seemingly remote stories of photos and photographers become situations students have encountered through attempting the photographic process personally, which opens the door for better written critical analysis and the desire to relate connections and divergences.

7
TAKING A
STAND

How do words and images work together to create an argument? Are some arguments better served by language or by pictures? How is our increasingly visual culture changing the way we communicate with one another about important issues?

As the McQuades write in their introduction, the texts in this chapter "highlight the contested nature of a great deal of thinking in writing" (p. 581). They emphasize the way both language and imagery support arguments. In doing so, they also raise questions central to a very old rivalry between word and image: Which of these sign systems have the closest link to reality? What can words do that pictures cannot, and vice versa? Which is the most effective at referring to the world or at expressing things we can only imagine? As students work through this chapter, ask them to think about how word and image complement each other but also about how each has its separate claims to superiority.

One answer to these questions is that images are more useful in illustrating than in making arguments. However, in their essay "Outlines of a Theory of Visual Argument" (in *Argumentation and Advocacy*, Winter/Spring 2007), David S. Birdsell and Leo Groarke oppose the idea that "images cannot assert; that they are too vague and ambiguous to function as propositions; that they are emotional and never cognitive; that they cannot express negations; and that words have ultimate authority in the realm of argument." Birdsell and Groarke claim that, like verbal arguments, visual arguments must be understood in their context. When they are used to make arguments, images may function as "flags, demonstrations, metaphors, symbols, and archetypes." You might give this list to students and have them discuss how images work in each of these functions, or even ask them to find an example of each.

To get students thinking about the relationship between text and image, have them look at the Portfolio of images that Collaborate created for Amnesty International, the Sierra Club, and Rock the Vote. Ask them how many words could be removed from each ad without changing its meaning. How would the addition of words dilute the effect of each ad? How do text and image complement each other? You might put students into groups to brainstorm responses to these questions.

Though the arguments in this chapter encompass a wide range of topics, each one takes a strong stand on an issue that might bring up differing opinions among students. Whatever their response to the arguments, though, students can learn from the argument techniques employed by authors like Michael Pollan and Steven Johnson. Direct students to pay attention to their particular moves — how the authors incorporate examples, how they cite authorities, or how they anticipate objections, for example — as well as to the content of their argument. This chapter explicitly asks students to consider what *Seeing & Writing* encourages them to do throughout: to become interpreters and critics of information conveyed visually, just as they would of information conveyed in language. It also asks them to reflect on their own reasoning processes: how they gather information and use it to make decisions.

POSSIBILITIES FOR DISCUSSION, REFLECTION, AND JOURNALING

- Ask students to think about "loaded images" and how they are used to make arguments. What images convey a lot of meaning in our culture? How did they arrive at these associations? How do artists or designers play on their meanings?

- During recent conflicts, the military has established specific policies for how to treat images of American soldiers. Have students discuss, for example, the prohibition on showing the coffins of American servicemen and -women. What is the reasoning behind it? What arguments have been made to the contrary?

- The notion that young people are increasingly visual and that verbal skills are on the decline has by now become a cliché. Ask students to discuss this widely held belief. Do they think it is true? If so, where do they see evidence of the change?

- Ask students to consider how technology has changed or will change the way we read images. For example, how does digital video provide new opportunities for news coverage? How does the prevalence of software like Photoshop change the way we evaluate pictures? What technological changes do students see on the horizon?

ADDITIONAL WRITING TOPICS AND CLASSROOM ACTIVITIES

- Have the class, working together, come up with a list of tools that writers use when trying to persuade a reader. Then discuss whether there are equivalent tools for photographers, designers, and visual artists.

- Before getting into these readings and images that "take a stand," ask students to brainstorm about how argument exists in our culture. Where does argumentation take place? What venues are available for people who want to put forward an argument?

- Assign an essay in which students analyze a visual argument in terms of Aristotle's rhetorical framework. That is, ask them to discuss how the image makes appeals to logos, ethos, and pathos. Does one of these appeals predominate? Why?

- Have students do some research on editorial policy at major newspapers for how to deal with controversial images. How do the newspapers make decisions about when to include or omit them? Then ask students to write an argument either for broader inclusion or for more selective editing of photographs that have violent, sexual, or otherwise objectionable content.

Surefire Class: Taking a Stand

Priscilla Riggle
Truman State University
(Profile, p. 18)

The objective of this class is to introduce students to the final chapter of *Seeing & Writing*, which I present as an opportunity to apply the principles with which students are already familiar to current events, images, and topics of special interest to them.

Preparation. Students have been assigned to read the chapter introduction and Stephens's "Expanding the Language of Photographs" (p. 664). They read Bordo's "Never Just Pictures" (Chapter 4, p. 367) and "Reading a Photograph" (Appendix B, p. 741) earlier in the semester; I ask them to quickly look back over those few pages before class.

In-class materials. We begin by looking at a visual text that is familiar but not too personal, Lange's photo *Migrant Mother* (p. 560), which we've looked at earlier in the semester. There are several other examples of Lange's photos, including some with more than one version, available at the Library of Congress Prints and Photographs Reading Room (loc.gov/rr/print/catalog .html). I bring in a few prints for students to look at for comparison purposes. I also bring in photos and video clips of television coverage from the Columbine shootings, the September 11 attacks, and other well-known historical events. Students have indicated early in the semester what events they feel have impacted them the most. We also focus on the photos in the Looking Closer section at the end of Chapter 7, Altering Images.

Analysis prompts for published photos (small groups).

- What audience does each photo seem to be addressing, inviting, or constructing? How can you tell?

- What assumptions does the photo appear to make? What values, beliefs, and attitudes does it seem to hold? What in the photo provides you with this information?

- What message(s) does the photo relay? How so?

- Assuming that the photo frames content with some degree of intentionality, what decisions has the photographer and/or editor made that impact the overall message(s)? What effect on meaning would different decisions have made? (Think of at least three.)

Discussion. The class shares the small-group findings. Connect those findings to the current readings, focusing on how images challenge us and how we can challenge them.

Reading historical events through image. We look at photos and video for each event we've decided to focus on. Adapting the prompts above for looking at published photos, we discuss the extent to which and the ways in which the events are "pseudo-events," and what the consequences of representing events this way are for us individually and culturally.

Target project. In the class period or two following this initial discussion, we spend a good deal of time with the other materials in this chapter. The project students are assigned for this chapter—they have a few weeks to complete it—is to select a still photo, advertisement, or video that somehow relates to a current event, controversy, or issue of public interest. Using editing software (or good old-fashioned manual manipulation), students create at least three versions of their selected image, each telling a slightly (but significantly) different story. Then they write an analysis paper that describes the various choices they have made and the effects of those choices. They pull the project together by drawing a broad conclusion regarding what they've learned about challenging images by completing this activity.

Portfolio: Collaborate (p. 584)

Collaborate/Amnesty International, *Imagine All the People Living Life in Peace; Imagine Nothing to Kill or Die For;* and *You May Say I'm a Dreamer, but I'm Not the Only One*
Collaborate/Sierra Club & Amnesty International, *Defend the Earth*
Collaborate/Rock the Vote, *Yes/No*

The Seeing questions in the text are excellent once discussion gets going. In the Imagine ads, do students look at the top or the bottom first? The "first" may be hard to tease out because we are aware of the difference between the top and the bottom of each ad as soon as we look at the page; however, their reading maneuvers after that might be easier to describe.

POSSIBILITIES FOR DISCUSSION, REFLECTION, AND JOURNALING

• Ask students to record how they make sense of these ads: Where are their eyes drawn first? To the text or to the image? Can they even see the ads as two distinct elements?

• How does "Defend the Earth" evoke pathos?

• What connections are readers expected to make in "Yes/No"? How?

ADDITIONAL WRITING TOPICS AND CLASSROOM ACTIVITIES

• **Image/Writing Assignment:** Ask students to design their own Imagine ad for Amnesty International. Have them find or draw an image and incorporate it with the sky used in the real ads. Then ask them to add a caption and an appropriate John Lennon lyric. Some students may question the project, especially if they feel that they're going to be assessed on the emotionality of their work. In response, you might stress that your focus here is on how well they have learned and applied the strategies needed to create an effective ad like those in Amnesty International's Imagine campaign.

• Ask students to choose the most effective of these five ads and to write an essay that analyzes and explains why and how it works. Suggest that they begin by defining *most effective.* How much of the ad's effectiveness depends on the connection between word and image? If necessary, they could compare and contrast the ad they've selected with the other ads here.

CONNECTIONS WITH OTHER TEXTS

• To help students get a sense of Collaborate's style, ask them to compare these ads with other ads for Amnesty International, the Sierra Club, and Rock the Vote that were not created by Collaborate. They can find other ads on the organizations' web sites (noted below).

• By this point in the book, students have examined numerous ads that do not simply sell a product but make an argument of some kind (even if that argument, ultimately, is "buy this") — as these ads do. Ask students to find an ad in *Seeing & Writing* that sells a product and to compare it with these ads. Do the ads share similar strategies? How are they different in tone?

SUGGESTIONS FOR FURTHER READING, THINKING, AND WRITING

WEB

amnestyusa.org/imagine/. Amnesty's Imagine campaign page.

merseyworld.com/imagine/lyrics/imagine.htm. Lyrics for John Lennon's "Imagine." The rest of the site is a tribute to Lennon, with pictures and interviews.

rockthevote.com/home.php. Other Rock the Vote ads can be found here, at the organization's official site.

sierraclub.org/pressroom/media/. This page on the Sierra Club site provides audio, video, and print ads.

AUDIOVISUAL

Lennon, John. *John Lennon: The Very Best of John Lennon.* Capitol Records, 1998. CD. A great collection of Lennon's music.

Pair: Fournier & Allende (p. 590)

Frank Fournier, *Omayra Sanchez, Colombia, 1985*
Isabel Allende, *Omayra Sanchez*

You might want students to consider Fournier's image before they read Allende's piece. Omayra's face is almost perfectly centered in this photograph. You might ask students how this positioning affects their response to the image. Viewers are separated from Omayra by the branch that perfectly cuts her mouth in two, keeping her silent. You might ask students how this branch, this separation, affects their impression of her situation. Also, her hands seem almost too large in the image, in part because of their whiteness. Ask students how the position of her hands affects their reading. She does not seem threatened, nor does she seem to be holding on for her life. Finally, you might call attention to Omayra's gold earrings; they are a small but poignant detail.

Allende's short essay addresses not just Fournier's photograph but also how images like this one stay with us. The image has taken on special meaning for Allende because she ties it to her own life, especially the time she is spending with her seriously ill daughter. In fact, Allende suggests that Omayra's photo has gained importance over the time she has been at her daughter's bedside because it has come to stand for "endurance and the love of life, and, ironically, the acceptance of tragedy and death" (para. 1).

Allende wants the reader to identify with Omayra on several levels. She gives Omayra a sense of nobility—"She never begged for help, never complained" (para. 1)—and she goes on to describe the elegance of the child's hands. But she doesn't let us forget the real child "stuck between two pieces of wood and the bodies of her brothers," feeling "the cold, the fear, the stress . . . so much in pain" (para. 2). And finally, Allende makes Omayra a personal symbol. In paragraph 4, she writes that she wishes she could hold the girl the way she holds her own daughter. Through Fournier's image, Omayra has become a part of Allende's family and a means for Allende to cope with her daughter's illness.

Allende's essay clearly changes the way in which students look at Fournier's image. It may be useful to remind them that Allende is basing her reading not just on the context of the volcano's erupting but also on her understanding of Colombia. She writes that Omayra was "not very afraid," perhaps because "she walked around hand in hand with death, as most poor people do all over the world" (para. 6). Allende argues that death is frightening only to "people who . . . think that they're going to live forever" (para. 6). Thus, because of her wealth and privilege, Allende has been changed by the image of the dying child in a way that those in Omayra's village could never be.

POSSIBILITIES FOR DISCUSSION, REFLECTION, AND JOURNALING

• Ask students what they believe the image is conveying. Who do they think this child is, and what do they think she is doing? Chances are they will not know immediately that the child is dying.

• Some students, after years of watching Save the Children commercials, may describe Omayra as poor, disadvantaged, even hungry. You might ask them what *within the frame* contributed to their reading of the child. Was it her eyes? the striking bags beneath them? the dirty water?

• What does the position of Omayra's face in this photograph indicate? Does the pitch-black of her eyes, reinforced by her hair and the framing shadows of her face, draw them in or distance them?

• Ask students to think of images they have collected over the years that have become symbols of larger ideas and ideals. You might suggest that they begin with images of events they likely share (e.g., photographs of a birthday party or graduation) or an image with which they are all likely to be familiar (e.g., *The Last Supper*).

• Ask students to consider why certain events stay with them while others disappear from memory. They might discuss the last time they were seriously impacted by an image in a newspaper or on the news—and why.

ADDITIONAL WRITING TOPICS AND CLASSROOM ACTIVITIES

• Ask students to research—online or in the library—the media coverage of Omayra Sanchez immediately following the eruption of the volcano in Colombia and then to write a short essay describing how the event was covered.

• Ask students to write a quick in-class piece that compares their reaction to the photograph of Omayra with Allende's reaction. Was their reaction similar to Allende's? Was it determined as well by a personal loss?

• Allende states that "the wonder of photography is that it does what no words can" (para. 3) and adds that she remembers her life in images. Ask students to use images—family photographs or other images—to remember a time in their life.

CONNECTIONS WITH OTHER TEXTS

• Ask students to identify specific references to Fournier's photograph in Allende's essay. What elements of the photograph does Allende highlight? Why does she choose these particular elements?

• Ask students to write an essay in which they identify the tone of the photograph, supporting their interpretation with evidence from the image. Alternatively, ask them to compare and contrast this photograph with one used to raise funds for a nonprofit organization (CARE, UNICEF, and Save the Children are examples) or to sell children's clothes or toys (for Baby-Gap, Gerber, or Little Me).

SUGGESTIONS FOR FURTHER READING, THINKING, AND WRITING

PRINT

Allende, Isabel. *Paula.* New York: Harper, 1995. Print.

Rodder, John. *Conversations with Isabel Allende.* Austin: U of Texas P, 1999. Print.

WEB

isabelallende.com. This site includes a long Q&A with the writer.

AUDIOVISUAL

Interview with Isabel Allende. National Public Radio, July 26, 1999. Terry Gross, host of NPR's *Fresh Air*, interviews Allende about her book *Paula.*

Michael Pollan, *Farmer in Chief* (p. 597)

At the beginning of the essay, Pollan acknowledges that food might not seem like the most pressing issue, but he argues that food policy is closely tied to some of the most crucial problems America faces today. First, he claims that "after cars, the food system uses more fossil fuel than any other sector of the economy" (para. 3). Thus the goal of energy independence would be furthered by a shift in agricultural methods. Second, food choices are directly related to health and the obesity crisis. As Pollan states, "four of the top 10 killers in America today are chronic diseases linked to diet: heart disease, stroke, Type 2 diabetes and cancer" (para. 4). Furthermore, Pollan forecasts that food security will become an increasingly important determinant of national security.

To provide historical background for the current system, Pollan goes back to the period after World War II, when government policies shifted to encourage "the conversion of the munitions industry to fertilizer" (para. 12). Since then, government policy, which kept grain prices low and supported the conversion to large factory farms, has moved agriculture ever further into what Pollan calls a petroleum-based system. His most important suggestion for the new president is to make policies that move farms back to a solar-based system, one that depends more on natural elements than on chemical fertilizers for its yields. He also argues for a shift from nationwide shipping of agricultural products to regional food systems that link local suppliers with local consumers, a change that would further reduce the amount of petroleum required to feed America. To support both of these changes, Pollan believes that we also need a change in the "food culture" of the country, so that consumers would be more educated about making healthy choices for themselves and for the country.

POSSIBILITIES FOR DISCUSSION, REFLECTION, AND JOURNALING

• Since Pollan's argument is framed as a letter to the future president, you might direct students' attention back to Visualizing Composition: Audience (Chapter 5, p. 439). What is Pollan's purpose in addressing his points directly to the future president, and where in the essay does the audience become most important? What difference does it make that Pollan does not yet know which of the candidates will win? Students will likely note places where Pollan is not just arguing for policy change but also asking directly for swift intervention.

• Ask students to discuss which system their food choices support—petroleum-based or solar agriculture. As a whole, does their community show interest in shifting to local food or smaller farms? What about the food available on campus?

• Once students have understood Pollan's concerns about American food culture, have them think about whether they would add any problems to his summary.

ADDITIONAL WRITING TOPICS AND CLASSROOM ACTIVITIES

• Though "Farmer in Chief" is long and detailed, it is also very carefully organized. If students find the reading dense, you might have them work in pairs or small groups to create an outline of Pollan's points.

• Ask students to research recent attempts by the president (and the first lady) to influence food policy. Then have them write about how the "farmer in chief" is responding to Pollan's requests. Has he made progress? If so, in what ways? If not, why?

• Have students choose an issue important to them and write their own letters to the president. For example, they might address him as "teacher in chief" or "doctor in chief."

• **Image/Writing Assignment:** Have students create a public-service ad that encourages consumers to support the "sun-food agenda." Which of Pollan's arguments for this change in agriculture would be most persuasive, and how would they convey the argument in images?

CONNECTION WITH ANOTHER TEXT

• Ask students to take another look at Annie Leonard's web site The Story of Stuff, from which a screen shot was featured in Chapter 1, Observing the Ordinary (p. 124). Then have them create visual representations, similar to the ones featured on The Story of Stuff, of one of the systems Pollan describes—perhaps the way our current agricultural system inputs petroleum to increase yield or the way regional food systems would decrease shipping distances. Students should feel free to use very basic sketches—the point is to show a compli- cated series of relationships or steps through visual means.

SUGGESTIONS FOR FURTHER READING, THINKING, AND WRITING

PRINT

Pollan, Michael. *In Defense of Food.* New York: Penguin, 2008. Print.

————. *The Omnivore's Dilemma.* New York: Penguin, 2006. Print.

WEB

michaelpollan.com. The writer's web page pro- vides biographical information as well as links to resources about sustainable eating.

AUDIOVISUAL

youtube.com/watch?v=TQPN1O03z8I/. Pollan gives an eighteen-minute speech that imag- ines life from the view of a plant.

Portfolio: World Wildlife Fund (p. 616)

The three World Wildlife Fund ads are both comical and poignant in their use of the visual tropes of homelessness to comment on wildlife habitats endangered by global warming. A polar bear slumps in an alley, an adult and baby penguin stand around a fire in an oil drum, and a seal sleeps on a bench beneath a sheet of newspaper. Besides the surprising juxtaposition of wild animals in urban spaces, the ads have a realistic feeling created through the use of details to characterize stark cityscapes. Graffiti on the walls, litter on the ground, closed-up shop win- dows and doors, and a fleet of trash dumpsters all suggest the largely hidden parts of the city to which the homeless are confined. Because these situations are so familiar from movies and television shows that portray homeless people, the ads manage to convey a great deal of information using very few words.

POSSIBILITIES FOR DISCUSSION, REFLECTION, AND JOURNALING

• Have students discuss the design of the text in the ads. Why is the "You can help" slogan set off on a separate background? What does the texture of this background or the appearance of the text convey?

• Ask students to discuss the actions the ads direct readers to carry out. How closely tied are they to the images of the polar animals? What other images could the designers have used to support the text at the bottom of each ad?

ADDITIONAL WRITING TOPICS AND CLASSROOM ACTIVITIES

• Have students write about their personal reaction to the ads. Was their first impulse to laugh? Did the images make them sad? What emotional response do they think the ads are meant to provoke? Have groups of students compare thoughts on these questions.

• The ads play on familiar tropes of homeless- ness. Ask groups to discuss why these tropes are familiar and what they signify. What parts of the ads immediately link the plight of the animals to the problems of the homeless in our cities?

•   Ask students to write a press release to announce the WWF's new ad campaign. How would they express, in relatively concise language, the goals of this series of ads? Where are the ads going to appear, and who is their target audience?

•   These ads use the imagery of a social problem (homelessness) to comment on a different problem (global warming and its effect on habitat). Ask students to create their own ads using this method. That is, they should comment on one problem by metaphorically comparing it to another.

•   While these images are captivating, they do not have the simplicity of the WWF's emblematic panda logo, which appears on the bottom of each ad. Challenge students to reimagine one of these ads as a logo. What would have to change about the image?

CONNECTIONS WITH OTHER TEXTS

•   Direct students to Visualizing Composition: Metaphor (Chapter 6, p. 558). What metaphors are being employed in these ads? What other metaphors could students imagine to explain the dangers of global warming?

•   The three ads use color in a limited way. Ask students to discuss why the designers chose this color palette. What mood does it create? How does it direct the viewer's attention? Ask students to choose another image from *Seeing & Writing*, either in black and white or in color, and have them write a comparison-and-contrast essay comparing the use of color in these ads to the use of color in the image they chose.

SUGGESTIONS FOR FURTHER READING, THINKING, AND WRITING

WEB

panda.org. The World Wildlife Organization's home page provides information on the organization and all that it does.

AUDIOVISUAL

youtube.com/user/WWF#play/all/. The World Wildlife Organization's YouTube channel.

Surefire Assignment: Artist Editions

GAY LYNN CROSSLEY
MARIAN UNIVERSITY

The most significant acts of composition I've witnessed have grown out of projects for which students have composed as writers through visuals. One such project is the artist edition. The artist edition requires students to present a portfolio as a three-dimensional tactile experience for readers. In the process of determining the ways they want readers to experience their writing, even to approach their writing, students come to see themselves as writers in rich and challenging ways. Where once stood students trying to complete a required writing course, writers emerge.

Students learn of the artist edition assignment within the first two weeks of class. Typically I include in my writing courses the study of relationships between form and content. Students practice and reflect on forms ranging from thesis-driven, to what Paul Heilke calls "chronologic," to mosaic. Once students have submitted their first essay, I give them the following handout.

ASSIGNMENT FOR ARTIST EDITION

During finals week, you will submit an artist edition of three selected and revised essays you've written this semester as well as a preface (see below). With this assignment, I challenge you to assume creative control over the presentation of your work. Work to arrive at a presentation that will enrich or reinforce the meaning of your work while also sharing your views toward writing and/or writers and/or readers.

To get started, as you make final decisions about which essays to include in your artist edition, spend time thinking about the following question: How do I want readers to approach/experience my essays and why? As your ideas develop, consider the following questions to help you determine specific elements of your edition:

1. What medium best represents the feeling, themes, or ideas I want people to associate with my work?

2. Given the nature of my essays and the ideas they speak to, what kind of paper/material will I use to present my texts?

3. How will I "bind" my edition, and what binding choices would best suit the content or nature of the writing included?

4. How can the "cover" of my edition reflect something about the work I've included?

5. What personal or cultural artifacts (such as photographs, illustrations, artwork, leaves, cereal boxes, advertisements, articles of clothing, objects) do I want to include in the edition, in light of what my writing is saying to others?

6. In what order should my essays appear? What is the significance of that order?

Your decisions about presenting your work should not be divorced from a message you hope people take from the writing included in the portfolio and the experience you want readers to have in reading it. The presentation of your work should contribute to what your writing has to say to others.

ASSIGNMENT FOR THE PREFACE

A preface, in its most generic sense, is a short introduction. For our purposes, the preface to your artist edition should introduce the essays as well as you, the writer of that work—not you the person born on September 23, 1978, in Atlanta, Indiana, the only child of Linda and Bob, but you the *writer*, someone who has crafted something to say to other people through the written word, and someone who has the experience necessary to talk with others about the nature, struggle, and joy of writing. The preface must be, at a minimum, the equivalent of four double-spaced pages.

A challenge of writing a preface, given all that you could write about, is to determine *what you most want to tell others about your work as a writer and the writing you're about to share with us*. Search for connections/parallels between what your essays have to say and what you know, have experienced, and appreciate about writing (whether the writing in your edition or writing in general). To help you search for these parallels, consider the following questions:

1. Why have I chosen these three essays for my edition? What do my selections say about what I value in my writing, what I've worked to achieve in my writing, what I want to say to others through writing?

2. Why have I ordered these three essays the way I have? Why *is* the first essay the first one? What does the order say about my project as a writer, what I hope people think about as they read through my essays?

3. What is my attitude toward these essays, to me as a writer, to writing in general, and to the work in this artist edition? Does my attitude speak to a significant understanding, view, image of myself as a writer and my writing?

4. Does the way I address, explore, and discuss the subject in my three essays say anything significant about me as a writer, my concept of writing, and what I value about writing?

Introducing the Assignment

Because the assignment intimidates many students at first, I put much effort into explaining that the assignment does not require artistic talent. What it does require is a thoughtful and well-executed presentation and experience for readers. A successful edition is not complicated, slick, or fancy, but is simply meaningful.

Then I emphasize that the key to performing this assignment well is resisting any temptation to create a slick package that distracts from the writing itself. Students will have a chance to explain to me in writing (usually an informal in-class writing) what informed their decisions. In essence, I reproduce the questions on the original assignment and ask students to explain what meaning they want the artist edition to share with readers and then to discuss in detail the choices they made in order to share that intended meaning.

Artist Exhibitions

The first semester I began a writing course with the artist edition, as students began sharing and workshopping their plans, they asked for time to see everyone's editions. Consequently, we held an Artist Exhibition during finals week and invited students, faculty, and administrators from across the college to attend.

No matter how simple or complicated the editions have been (or how involved the exhibitions), each semester, when I walk through the exhibition eavesdropping on students talking about their writing with earned authority and answering questions about the content of their essays, I am stunned at the transformations I see. And each semester, when I sit at my dining room table with a cup of coffee before me, my breath is taken away.

Michael Lewis, *Serfs of the Turf* (p. 621)

In "Serfs of the Turf," Lewis challenges the widely held opinion that the amateur status of college football benefits the players, as well as the schools for which they play. Instead, he argues, college football puts players in a disadvantageous position: "Everyone associated with it is getting rich except the people whose labor creates the value" (para. 5). By calling them "serfs" in his title, Lewis compares the NCAA rules that regulate amateur play to a feudal system in which the workers never own the land but owe all of their work to their lords. Lewis debunks a few myths: (1) that college sports aren't already commercialized and (2) that college players go to school for an education rather than to make their way into professional sports. Both of these, he argues, are clearly untrue to any observer of the sport.

In making his argument, Lewis is careful to separate sports teams, which can be hugely profitable, from the nonprofit universities with which they are linked. The connection with the university has long benefited college teams, but Lewis believes we should question their status: "Why are these enterprises that have nothing to do with education and everything to do with profits exempt from paying taxes? Or why don't they pay their employees?" (para. 4). He suggests that we can't deal with these questions honestly until we can see the sport clearly.

POSSIBILITIES FOR DISCUSSION, REFLECTION, AND JOURNALING

• Ask students to come up with examples to support Lewis's statement that "college football is already commercialized" (para. 8). Where do they see evidence of the sport's profitability? They might even look to news stories to find recent debates about money in college sports.

• Is it true that college players are getting an education only as a pretense? Have students discuss Lewis's arguments that learning is not the point. He lists several reasons why this is true. Which do students find most convincing?

ADDITIONAL WRITING TOPICS AND CLASSROOM ACTIVITIES

• Have students work together to create graphic representations to convey Lewis's point about how players get left out of a college team's earnings. How would they represent where team profits go now? How does Lewis say the picture would be different if the players were paid for their skills?

• Ask small groups to research the economic conditions of other college sports. For example, how much revenue do basketball teams bring into schools? Do students see some of the same problems Lewis identifies operating in other sports?

• Ask students to write a memo to the president of their college or university about the economic status of sports teams. They might cite Lewis as a source in arguing for a new approach to college teams. Or they might write about the benefits of the current system.

- In commenting on the players' economic status, Lewis raises some important questions about class in this essay. Ask students to write about his observations using the lens of class they employed with the readings for Chapter 6, Confronting Class. What does college football reveal about class relations?

SUGGESTIONS FOR FURTHER READING, THINKING, AND WRITING

WEB

newnewjournalism.com/bio.php?last_name= lewis. This site provides biographical information for Lewis as well as a list of the books and articles he has written.
thenewnewblog.com. Michael Lewis's blog.

Clay Bennett, *Wiretaps and Privacy Rights* (p. 625)

Bennett's cartoon plays with scale, both enlarging the everyday object to give it monumental importance and shrinking the figure of the government official to make him seem secretive and hidden. The almost pop-art enlargement of the phone and the realistic shading with which Bennett renders it contrast to the more cartoonish figure of the NSA spy hiding inside the phone. The spy wears the hat and trenchcoat of an old private eye, and his suspicious glance suggests the covert nature of his operation. The cartoon comments on the feeling many Americans experienced, after hearing revelations about the dubious legality of wiretaps, that we might be more constantly under surveillance than we know.

POSSIBILITIES FOR DISCUSSION, REFLECTION, AND JOURNALING

- Compared to many editorial cartoons, this one is fairly minimalist. Ask students how this style works to convey Bennett's point. How would the cartoon change if Bennett used text or introduced more people into the scene he draws?

- Have students discuss the figure of the NSA employee visible in the phone. How does Bennett portray him? What do they gather from the details of his clothing or the expression on his face?

ADDITIONAL WRITING TOPICS AND CLASSROOM ACTIVITIES

- Ask students to find another cartoon on Bennett's web site with which to compare this one on wiretaps. They should consider his style of drawing as well as the rhetorical moves he uses to make his points. Do they see common methods in both cartoons?

- Ask students to do a close analysis of Bennett's choices for this cartoon. For example, why does he choose an old-fashioned phone receiver? How would they describe the way he draws and shades the phone? Is the man inside drawn differently or in the same style? And what information does Bennett choose to convey about him?

- Based on this cartoon, what argument is Bennett illustrating about wiretaps? Have students write a paper in which they agree or disagree with Bennett, and have them include one or more outside sources that support their argument.

CONNECTIONS WITH OTHER TEXTS

• Have students go to pulitzer.org/works/ 2002-Editorial-Cartooning/ and look at the portfolio of images for which Bennett won a Pulitzer Prize. Then ask them to put themselves in the position of the jury for the award and to write a review of the cartoons. Which stand out most and why? Why is this a winning portfolio?

• Direct students to the American Political Science Association's web site at apsanet.org and have them find the interview with Bennett on the state of editorial cartoonists in the profession and the challenges to journalism in general. Have them read the interview and then write an essay on the value of editorial cartoons, citing Bennett's work as an example.

SUGGESTION FOR FURTHER READING, THINKING, AND WRITING

WEB

claybennett.com. The artist's web site provides biographical information and other examples of Bennett's work.

Steven Johnson, *Watching TV Makes You Smarter* (p. 627)

Looking closely at the world of pop culture, Steven Johnson argues that, far from being cognitive junk food, TV shows have put increasing demands on their audiences in terms of structure and content. *The Sopranos* and *24* typify shows that illustrate what Johnson terms "the Sleeper Curve"—the surprising shift in what makes "quality" entertainment.

One thing that has changed a great deal in the television shows of the last decades is that clear and comprehensible moral worlds, once the standard, are now almost absent from acclaimed TV dramas. Instead, viewers are asked to sympathize with a Mafia don or to try to understand the difficult decisions of government officials dealing with threats of terrorism. As Johnson says, "the morals of the stories have grown darker and more ambiguous, and the anti-heroes have multiplied" (para. 4). He also argues that shows emphasize social factors more now, so viewers have to constantly track the shifting relationships among a network of characters.

Most important of all, according to Johnson's case for the benefits of television, is the way shows now refuse to orient their viewers. Often the audience is asking not "How will this turn out in the end?" but "What is happening right now?" (para. 19). Ultimately what Johnson finds in current TV shows is a lesson about the human mind: "It may be drawn toward the sensational where content is concerned—sex does sell, after all. But the mind also likes to be challenged; there's a real pleasure to be found in solving puzzles, detecting patterns or unpacking a complex narrative system" (para. 32).

• Johnson's argument is based on the premise that complexity is better than simplicity. Ask students in what ways this is true. Is it ever not the case? Are there instances in which we learn from simplicity?

• Many people interested in gaming, including the film director Guillermo del Toro, have predicted that we will soon see the *Citizen Kane* of video games. Do students agree that this is the case? What do they think Johnson would say? What would characterize the *Citizen Kane* of games?

ADDITIONAL WRITING TOPICS AND CLASSROOM ACTIVITIES

• Have students chart an episode of their favorite show, using Johnson's charts as models. What do the visual representations say about the plots? Was creating the charts difficult or relatively easy?

• Ask groups to list their favorite TV shows. Which shows would Johnson designate as smart shows, and which wouldn't fall into that category? How would students defend the shows that aren't cognitively challenging?

• At the beginning of this essay, Johnson compares the show *24* to *Middlemarch*. Ask students to reflect on the pleasures of reading a novel, especially a long one like Eliot's. How are these pleasures similar to the pleasures of watching a drama like *24*?

• **Image/Writing Assignment:** Johnson describes the "Sleeper Curve" in terms of narrative media — shows and games that represent events unfolding over time. Could a similar theory be applied to static visual images such as paintings or photographs? Ask students to find an image that they think is cognitively challenging and then to discuss whether Johnson's terms help them to explain why.

CONNECTIONS WITH OTHER TEXTS

• Based on his photograph reprinted in the text (Chapter 1, p. 45), do students think that Matthew Pillsbury would agree with Steven Johnson? Have them write an essay in which they explain why or why not.

• Have students look at the How Class Works Portfolio (Chapter 6, p. 540). Then have them take a survey of the television habits of their friends and family. Using the charts and graphs from the How Class Works Portfolio as a reference, have students make a chart that shows the results of their survey. Are they able to find any correlation between people's race and the television shows they watch? Does a person's gender affect the television shows he or she watches?

SUGGESTIONS FOR FURTHER READING, THINKING, AND WRITING

PRINT

Johnson, Steven. *Everything Bad Is Good for You: How Today's Popular Culture Is Actually Making Us Smarter*. New York: Penguin, 2006. Print.

WEB

stevenberlinjohnson.com. Johnson's blog.

Surefire Assignment: Reality vs. Make-Believe

Ann Parker
*Southern Polytechnic
State University*

This assignment originated in my second-semester freshman composition course. It is the second portfolio in a series of three, and it satisfies the requirement for a research component. Here the students are actually writing an I-Search paper that incorporates personal research, field research, and traditional library research. We also use film, in this case *The Truman Show*, starring Jim Carrey, as a resource for ideas for this paper. The topic of the portfolio and the subsequent final research project is Reality vs. Make-Believe. In other words, how do we decide what is real and what is not in today's mediated society?

I tell students that their topic should be something they are interested in that will fulfill a need in their lives rather than my notion of what would be good for them to pursue.[1] In other words, I ask them to consider how they are living their lives. Are their lives "real"? Can they make a difference to someone else or to themselves by examining how society defines *reality*?

A large part of this portfolio is our examination of *The Truman Show* and the ideas it presents on the topics within the framework of this project. The film addresses cultural and personal perceptions of truth and fiction as well as the way society lives vicariously through mediated perceptions of reality. When reality is reinterpreted by the media, as it is in *The Truman Show*

and on reality television shows today, how skewed do our own interpretations of reality become?

I ask students to include traditional Internet and library research, field research, and photography in this final project for various reasons. Because we use *Seeing & Writing* as our textbook, much of our discussion throughout the semester deals with how we interpret what we *see*, literally, figuratively, and in the media, and how we report on that in writing. I also ask students to visit a place related to their topic, to take notes and pictures, and to get an idea of how the people involved in this place react to the topic at hand. Students are required to take photographs of their subject to help their readers see how they are interpreting this reality. This gets them off of the campus and into the real world, something essential to deciding what is real and what isn't.

Some of the Reality vs. Make-Believe topics that my students have explored are the following:

1. The evolution of evolution

2. How college is portrayed in the media (fun, sex, free time) versus the realities of being a college student

3. Growing up as a gang member versus the way gangs are portrayed in the media

4. Choosing a major (the realities of the job versus students' perceptions of it)

5. Living life as a gay man versus the public's perception and the media's portrayal of gays

6. Living in the United States versus living in India (Which life is more real?)

---

[1] This suggestion comes from Ken Macrorie's *The I-Search Paper* (Portsmouth, N.H.: Boynton/Cook, 1988; print), page 62.

7. The realities of teen parenthood versus the media's portrayal of teen parenthood

8. Teen attitudes toward sex versus the media's portrayal of those attitudes

9. The point at which someone loses touch with reality because his or her life is consumed with playing electronic games

In addition to the Macrorie book noted above, you might be interested in exploring Josh Luukkonen's "Relevancy in the Classroom: Bringing the Real World into School" (*Classroom Notes Plus*, October 2003, pp. 8–10).

James Rosenquist, *Professional Courtesy* (p. 640)

This painting presents two hands, each holding a gun pointed directly at the other, against a red background. Before students read Rosenquist's words in the headnote, you might ask them to freewrite about their reaction to the painting. Then ask them to share their writing with the class. Some students might say that they feel as though they are part of the painting because the gun in the foreground seems to extend from the viewer's position. If students have difficulty understanding the positioning of the guns, ask them how the painting would be different if the guns were presented horizontally, extending from the sides of the painting.

POSSIBILITIES FOR DISCUSSION, REFLECTION, AND JOURNALING

• Do students see the painting as a "stark look and confrontation of a handgun" (p. 641)?

• Ask students whether they sense Rosenquist's intention to make viewers "question the idea of who really is the target" (p. 641).

• How does the title affect students' reading of the painting? (For further discussion of the title, you could direct them to the second Writing question on p. 641.)

• How do students read the red background? Does it suggest urgency? blood?

• Ask students why they think Rosenquist shows just the hands of the figures holding the guns. Would faces distract us from the guns? Would we attempt to attach a motive to a face?

ADDITIONAL WRITING TOPICS AND CLASSROOM ACTIVITIES

• Ask students to use Rosenquist's painting as one example in an argument essay about whether images can inspire change in society.

• Ask each student to create a different title for the painting and to write a brief essay that explains how that title would affect the painting's meaning.

• Some students might take issue with Rosenquist's statement that "young people are confused by the way guns are depicted in the movies and on television" (p. 641). Have students write an essay that explains why they agree or disagree with the artist.

CONNECTION WITH ANOTHER TEXT

• Rosenquist is concerned about the pervasiveness of guns in our society. Ask students to discuss the gun as an American icon. What images would they use to show the gun as an icon?

SUGGESTIONS FOR FURTHER READING, THINKING, AND WRITING

PRINT

Goldman, Judith. *James Rosenquist*. New York: Viking, 1985. Print.

WEB

artcyclopedia.com/artists/rosenquist_james .html. Artcyclopedia's web page on Rosenquist.

Robert Unell, *The Kansas City Star, 2007* (p. 642)
Wayne Stayskal, *I'm Taking a Poll, Sir* (p. 643)

Unell's cartoon places gun control in the bull's-eye of the target, but surrounding it are several other changes that, this cartoon argues, would help to prevent shootings like those at Virginia Tech. You might have students discuss each of the factors Unell includes on this target. How were each of these missed in the case of Virginia Tech or other high-profile shootings? While Unell focuses on the complexities behind the issue of gun control, Stayskal uses irony to break down arguments. In his cartoon, the two armed homeowners suggest the naïveté of the pollster and, by extension, of the gun control movement.

POSSIBILITIES FOR DISCUSSION, REFLECTION, AND JOURNALING

• Ask students to discuss how they read political cartoons. How does their approach to these editorial pieces differ from the way they read cartoons in the funny pages? Where do political cartoons appear in the paper? How does the style of illustration they use compare to other cartoons?

• Have students discuss which of these two cartoons is more effective and why. Which is more visually striking? more thought-provoking?

ADDITIONAL WRITING TOPICS AND CLASSROOM ACTIVITIES

• Ask students to work together to research other editorial cartoons about gun control. Have them compare the methods these other cartoons use with those used in Unell's and Stayskal's cartoons.

• Choose an issue relevant to the campus or local community. Divide the class in half and ask each half to brainstorm ideas for cartoons that would support one side of the issue.

• Ask students to construct a written argument to accompany each of the two cartoons.

What would they identify as the main points of each? What is the purpose of each? That is, what goals is each cartoon trying to accomplish?

• **Image/Writing Assignment:** Assign a report in which students consider an editorial cartoon in the context of the whole newspaper. Ask them to choose a cartoon from a recent issue of a newspaper and then to read the entire issue. Are there other stories or cartoons on the same subject? What subjects do the other Op-Ed pieces consider? What were the front-page headlines for that day? Does this context help them understand the goals of the cartoon?

CONNECTIONS WITH OTHER TEXTS

• Ask students to bring in a cartoon that also deals with gun control from their local paper or from an online news source. Then have them write an essay that compares their cartoon with Unell's and Stayskal's. What part does geography play in the cartoons? Do the cartoons give a clue to the political climate of the news source's state?

- Have students reread Pollan's "Farmer in Chief" (p. 597) and then ask them to create a political cartoon that would best represent one of the arguments from his letter.

- Have students look at the World Wildlife Fund ads (p. 616) and ask them to consider the importance of text in a political cartoon. Have them redesign Stayskal's cartoon without the text.

SUGGESTIONS FOR FURTHER READING, THINKING, AND WRITING

PRINT

Brooks, Charles, ed. *Best Editorial Cartoons of the Year: 2009 Edition*. Gretna, LA: Pelican Publishing, 2009. Print.

Cagle, Daryl, and Brian Farrington, eds. *The Best Political Cartoons of the Year, 2009 Edition*. Toronto, Ontario: Que Publishing, 2009. Print.

WEB

editorialcartoonists.com/cartoonist/profile.cfm/UnellR/. The Association of American Editorial Cartoonists has a profile of Robert Unell and links to some of his most recent cartoons. It also has a section devoted to educators using cartoons in the classroom.

gocomics.com/explore/editorial_lists/. Wayne Stayskal is featured on the GoComics list of cartoonists. Simply scroll your cursor over his name for a brief profile to appear, and click his name to view Stayskal's daily comic strips.

xroads.virginia.edu/~MA96/Puck/part1.html. The American Studies Department at the University of Virginia offers "A Brief History of Political Cartoons."

Rev. John P. Minogue, *The Twentieth-Century University Is Obsolete* (p. 644)

In this essay, Minogue offers a detailed analysis of a new phenomenon that many in academia have dismissed offhand: for-profit universities offering degrees that students can complete entirely online. While many question the value of such degrees, Minogue argues that they serve a real need in our "Knowledge Age" and that, moreover, they are better able to adapt to the rapidly changing needs of job seekers: "Since they do not carry tenured faculty, they can rapidly jettison disciplines of study that do not penetrate market" (para. 7). Minogue argues that the criteria on which people choose colleges are not always well suited to current demands of employers. They may be motivated less by outcomes than by "brand name" or by "an instinctual and irrational desire" to succeed in a traditional liberal arts school (para. 10). These desires can lead students and parents to spend much more for an education that might not serve them well in their working lives. These problems are compounded by the fact that "state funding is not keeping up with inflation or enrollment growth, forcing higher education institutions to rely more on tuition and donations" (para. 14). The changing needs of people looking for jobs, as well as the challenges to state-supported education, show why for-profit universities are playing an increasingly important role for students.

POSSIBILITIES FOR DISCUSSION, REFLECTION, AND JOURNALING

• What preconceptions do students have about online degrees or for-profit universities? Are these notions fair? Are attitudes about these forms of education changing?

ADDITIONAL WRITING TOPICS AND CLASSROOM ACTIVITIES

• Ask groups to create a timeline that visually represents the evolution of universities Minogue describes in paragraph 2. In addition to the milestones he points out, ask them to find the date on which their own university was founded and the dates of any significant changes in the course of its "evolution."

• Have students work together to create a chart that compares a traditional university with a for-profit university on categories they think are important. For example, they might look up tuition prices, number of majors offered, and percentage of students who live on campus.

• Ask students to write an essay that responds to Minogue's argument. They might quote his points in order to support his argument for the benefits of for-profit universities, or they might take issue with his apparent dismissal of conventional liberal arts education.

• Minogue thinks of the university primarily in economic terms. Have students write a close analysis of his economic language. Does thinking only in terms of the market leave anything out of his assessment?

CONNECTION WITH ANOTHER TEXT

• Ask students to think back to Visualizing Composition: Metaphor (Chapter 6, p. 558).

Then have them discuss the metaphor Minogue uses at the beginning of his essay. How does the reference to DNA and evolution help him make his point about universities? What other metaphors does he use in the course of the essay?

SUGGESTIONS FOR FURTHER READING, THINKING, AND WRITING

PRINT

Altbach, Philip G., and Patty McGill Peterson. *Higher Education in the New Century: Global Challenges and Innovative Ideas*. Rotterdam, Netherlands: Sense Publishers, 2008. Print.

Geiger, Roger L., Carol Colbeck, Roger L. Williams, and Christian K. Anderson, eds. *Future of the American Public Research University*. Rotterdam, Netherlands: Sense Publishers, 2007. Print.

Thelin, John R. *A History of American Higher Education*. Baltimore, MD: Johns Hopkins UP, 2004. Print.

Vest, Charles M. *The American Research University from World War II to World Wide Web: Governments, the Private Sector, and the Emerging Meta-University*. Berkeley: U of California P, 2007. Print.

Zemsky, Robert. *Making Reform Work: The Case for Transforming American Higher Education*. Piscataway, NJ: Rutgers Press, 2009. Print.

WEB

chronicle.com/section/Home/5/. The *Chronicle of Higher Education*'s web site publishes

AUDIOVISUAL

Declining by Degrees: Higher Education at Risk.
PBS Home Video, 2005. DVD.

Susan Sontag, *Regarding the Pain of Others* (p. 650)

Sontag's piece may be difficult for students because it does not make a thesis statement and then develop it. Certainly the work is more exploratory than many of the verbal texts students have studied in the textbook, but Sontag's writing does not meander. As you discuss the piece, point out the transitions she uses and how one idea or paragraph logically leads to the next.

Some students may resist Sontag's final paragraph, feeling that she is bashing America when she describes the failure to establish a museum "chronicling the great crime that was African slavery in the United States of America." If so, redirect the discussion by asking how an absence of slavery images hides the issue. Would slavery be a more potent topic in Americans' minds if there were photographs to "illustrate as well as corroborate" (para. 7) the facts? And what does this say about the function and power of images?

POSSIBILITIES FOR DISCUSSION, REFLECTION, AND JOURNALING

• Ask students to list the different things that photographs do according to Sontag: beautify, uglify, invite an active response, accuse, alter conduct, shock, testify, illustrate, corroborate, make reference, construct and revise the past, stipulate, commemorate, and more. As they name the various functions, put them on the board. Then go through them, asking students not only for Sontag's specific thoughts on each function but also for their experience of photographs that serve that function. Discussing the essay in this way should give the class a thorough understanding of Sontag's thinking.

• Sontag states: "Poster-ready photographs — the mushroom cloud of an A-bomb test, Martin Luther King, Jr., speaking at the Lincoln Memorial in Washington, D.C., the astronaut on the moon — are the visual equivalent of sound bites" (para. 9). You could project these images on a screen, or you could ask students to look again at the many "poster-ready photographs" in the text — the flag raising on Iwo Jima (Chapter 3, p. 308), the flag raising at Ground Zero (Chapter 3, p. 312), Dorothea Lange's *Migrant Mother* (Chapter 6, p. 560), the war pictures in this chapter. Or you could have students bring in copies of photographs they feel are "the visual equivalent of sound bites." Ask them why these pictures — and not others — have become important. Why do we embrace the stories they tell? What "predictable thoughts [and] feelings" (para. 9) do they evoke? Some students might wonder what Sontag is really saying. Does she mean that these images are somehow wrong? that we should replace them with others? Or is she simply describing a reality so that we can be aware of it?

ADDITIONAL WRITING TOPICS AND CLASSROOM ACTIVITIES

•   Ask students to freewrite about the functions of memorial museums. Some may say that the purpose of a memorial museum is to remind us never to do it again. Yet despite several exhibits on the West Coast relating to the internment in this country of Japanese Americans during World War II, the U.S. government is once again holding people on suspicion alone, this time at Guantánamo Bay. What power do memorials hold if we forget or ignore their message? And what if the act behind the memorial is in dispute? Japan's memorial to the devastation of Hiroshima is a moving, powerful reminder never to use atomic bombs again; yet some Americans argue that the bombings of Hiroshima and Nagasaki were necessary to end World War II. This is a complex question, and you may want students to turn their focused freewrites into thoughtful, researched essays.

•   **Image/Writing Assignment:** Have students research a historical event and the photographs most commonly associated with that event, analyzing how the photographs tell the story. Have these photographs become collective memory? collective instruction? How?

CONNECTIONS WITH OTHER TEXTS

•   Speaking about the visual power of photographs, Sontag states: "Photographs lay down routes of reference, and serve as totems of causes: Sentiment is more likely to crystalize around a photograph than around a verbal slogan" (para. 8). Discuss the Amnesty International ads at the beginning of this chapter. How effective would these ads be without the black and white photographs?

•   Ask students to consider Lange's *Migrant Mother* (Chapter 6, p. 560) in light of Sontag's comment about collective instruction: "What is called collective memory is not a remembering but a stipulating: that *this* is important, and this is the story of how it happened, with the pictures that lock the story in our minds" (para. 9).

SUGGESTIONS FOR FURTHER READING, THINKING, AND WRITING

PRINT

Sontag, Susan. *On Photography*. New York: Picador, 2001. Print.

———. *Regarding the Pain of Others*. New York: Farrar, 2003. Print.

WEB

auschwitz-muzeum.oswiecim.pl/html/eng/start/index.php. Poland's Auschwitz Memorial and Museum site.

buchenwald.de/index_en.html. Germany's Buchenwald Memorial site. If anyone doubts that a country would choose to highlight its dark history with a museum, this detailed site is a stunning reply.

civilrightsmuseum.org. The National Civil Rights Museum web site.

science.co.il/Holocaust-Museums.asp. A global directory of Holocaust museums.

susansontag.com. Susan Sontag's web site.

ushmm.org. The United States Holocaust Memorial Museum web site.

Retrospect: Picturing War (p. 656)

Famous pictures from wars are collected in this Retrospect. The key question may be why these photographs have become famous. In pursuing an answer to that question, you'll want to raise other questions to help students move beyond circular responses ("They're famous because people like them") and easy answers ("They're famous because they capture important events"). Be insistent: Of all the war photographs that have been taken, why do these stand out? Why do you think they were published in the first place? What narratives do they tell? What do they support or challenge?

The first photograph in the Retrospect, *Home of a Rebel Sharpshooter*, was staged by the photographer: It does not capture a sharpshooter; an infantryman's body was found on a hillside and moved to this den. The gun placed near the corpse was not used by a sharpshooter[1]; it was probably one of Alexander Gardner's props. Still, the photograph is effective.

The next two photographs, *The Men of the 308th, the "Lost Battalion"* and *Omaha Beach*, were not staged. The first, from World War I, captures the six hundred men of the "Lost Battalion" as they disembarked in France in April 1919. Several months later these six hundred soldiers would face overwhelming odds in a five-day fight in the Argonne Forest against German battalions with more men and more supplies. The battalion lost nearly four hundred men before reinforcements arrived. The photograph is powerful even without the knowledge that two-thirds of the troops would die.

Robert Capa's pictures of the D-day invasion have come to define that day. *Omaha Beach* captures American soldiers taking cover from German fire in the shallow waters off Normandy.[2] One of the reasons Capa's pictures became famous is that they actually show combat on one of the most important days leading up to the Allied victory in World War II. Some students may imagine scenes (or maybe cannot help but recall scenes) from *Saving Private Ryan* as they look at this photograph.

The rest of the photographs in the Retrospect have strikingly different tones. In *Greenhouse Dog*, the setting seems ridiculous: Relaxing in beach chairs, observers wear oversize goggles (and hopefully a ton of sunscreen) to watch the testing of an eighty-one-kiloton nuclear device. During Operation Greenhouse,

---

[1] For a brief description of how *Rebel Sharpshooter* was staged and a discussion of other staged war photographs, see Susan Sontag's book *Regarding the Pain of Others*. A selection from another section of the book begins on page 650.

[2] The V-shaped structures in the water were called *Czech hedgehogs*; they were steel obstacles the Germans had set along the beach to prevent the Allied troops from advancing.

four nuclear devices were detonated on Enewetak Atoll in the Pacific Ocean, tests that led to the development of thermonuclear weapons.

Nick Ut's *Children Fleeing a Napalm Strike, Vietnam* may be the most familiar of these photographs to students. You might remind students that even though this is a live-action photograph, Ut could have framed it differently as he shot it (zooming in on the soldiers, for example) or cropped it for a different effect later.

Jean-Marc Bouju's *Iraqi Man at a Regroupment Center for POWs*, winner of World Press Photo 2003, shows a hooded Iraqi war prisoner holding his son. The child, who was with the man when he was captured, was brought with him to the regroupment center. According to Bouju, the soldiers at the center were not told much of anything about the prisoners when they were brought in; one of the American soldiers cut the prisoner's plastic handcuffs and let him console his crying child.

POSSIBILITIES FOR DISCUSSION, REFLECTION, AND JOURNALING

• To help students see why *Home of a Rebel Sharpshooter* works, ask them to consider how specific changes might affect their reading of it: What if they couldn't see the soldier's face? What if the sky had been cropped out of the picture? What if more than one body was shown?

• Ask students to explain why they think *The Men of the 308th, the "Lost Battalion,"* is considered a powerful photograph even without the knowledge that two-thirds of the troops would die. Is there something about seeing troops in preparation, massed together safely for the last time? How does the knowledge of what happened to these men in the Argonne Forest affect students' reading of the picture?

• How does the portrayal of American soldiers differ in *Children Fleeing a Napalm Strike, Vietnam*? Ask students to consider the placement of soldiers in this picture, with the children running toward the viewer, away from the soldiers. What does this say about the role of the viewer in the war?

• How does the razor wire encircling the foreground affect the image *Iraqi Man at a Regroupment Center for POWs*? Ask students to consider what they know of the story behind the photograph. What if Bouju had captured the child in motion, running to his father, or the moment when the American soldier released the prisoner's hands, or the inevitable moment when the child was taken away? What message(s) do students read into this specific photograph?

ADDITIONAL WRITING TOPICS AND CLASSROOM ACTIVITIES

• Ask students to research the pictures before you discuss them in class, or you could put students into pairs to research the photographs in class. They can find a wealth of information about each of these images online. In their research, students may come up with information that can lead to fascinating discussion. For example, some students may find that *Home of a Rebel Sharpshooter*, a celebrated Civil War picture, is actually a fraud. Or students may discover different captions for *Iraqi Man at a Regroupment Center for POWs*. What does each caption suggest about its writer's bias?

• Ask students to freewrite about the most disturbing images of war they have seen and the sources (documentaries, photographs, films) of those images.

• Ask students to watch a recent war film. What seems to be the filmmaker's point of view on this war? on war in general? If students are interested, have them watch several films about the same war — *Casualties of War*, *Platoon*, and *Full Metal Jacket* on Vietnam, for instance. Or they could examine several films that treat a number of different wars: How does the treatment of war in *Saving Private Ryan* or *The Thin Red Line* compare with the treatment of war in *Braveheart*, *Troy*, or *Kingdom of Heaven*?

CONNECTIONS WITH OTHER TEXTS

• Ask students to find other war photographs and to bring them to class. Put the students into groups to look at one another's photographs. Ask each group to decide on one photograph to include in the Retrospect in the textbook. Why should it be added?

• Ask students to look back at Joe Rosenthal's photograph *Marines Raising the Flag on Mount Suribachi, Iwo Jima* (Chapter 3, p. 308). How does it compare with Capa's image of the troops taking fire on Omaha Beach? Why do students think the McQuades chose Capa's image for this Retrospect instead of Rosenthal's?

SUGGESTIONS FOR FURTHER READING, THINKING, AND WRITING

PRINT

Frassanito, William. *Gettysburg: A Journey in Time*. New York: Scribner's, 1975. Print. Provides an impressive analysis of *Home of a Rebel Sharpshooter* as well as other Civil War photographs.

WEB

ap.org/pages/about/pressreleases/pr_021304 .html. Bouju talks about the photograph he took of the Iraqi man holding his son.

digitaljournalist.org/issue0008/ng2.htm. Nick Ut recalls the events surrounding his famous photograph.

memory.loc.gov/ammem/cwphtml/cwpcam/ cwcam3.html. The Library of Congress maintains an archive of Civil War photographs. This page from the LOC's web site examines the *Home of a Rebel Sharpshooter* photograph.

skylighters.org/photos/robertcapa.html. An excellent overview of Capa's D-day photographs.

AUDIOVISUAL

The Lost Battalion. 92 min. 2001. DVD. Distributed by A&E Home Video. A movie based on the real events surrounding the Lost Battalion during World War I.

Surefire Assignment: Critical Synthesis of Visual and Textual Meanings

Jon Lindsay
*Southern Polytechnic
State University*

This class assignment is intended to blend the ideas presented in *Seeing & Writing 4* to weld them together in a way that unites several chapters and explores their ideas, connectivity, and relationship. The challenge is to find connection and inter-relationship in a way that creates/reflects identity. This assignment is about synthesizing the expressed ideas of several authors, photographers, and students' experiences into one overarching idea.

Usually, this assignment is conducted as the final in a series of assignments in which we have reviewed various chapters of the text and accomplished assignments that tie them together. This work will have already shown students the interrelationship of ideas through a visual-personal-textual perceptual process. The assignment sequence stresses unifying the chapters of the text by seeking overarching ideas and meanings.

THE ASSIGNMENT

1. Read the following:

   • K. C. Cole, "A Matter of Scale" (Chapter 1, p. 85)

   • Annie Dillard, "Seeing" (Chapter 1, p. 96)

   • Eudora Welty, "The Little Store" (Chapter 2, p. 147)

   • Ethan Canin, "Vivian, Fort Barnwell" (Chapter 3, p. 242)

   • Retrospect: Picturing War (Chapter 7, p. 656)

   • Appendix B (p. 736)

2. Then, for each of the above selections, write a short summary, a reflection, and a short personal experience that relates to the idea you see in the reading/photo.

3. Synthesize the summaries, reflections, and personal experiences. Think critically, seeking a common association that unites the essays and photos.

4. Write an essay based on your critical thinking about the ideas generated from the above activities. Your essay should make sense of, interpret, and come to an understanding of the world around you and your place in it; the synthesis should relate to life, human nature, and "the truth" as you see it. Share your sense of meaning with others through your detailed and critical seeing and writing.

5. Illustrate your essay with your own photo/artwork that enhances the meaning of your idea; the illustration should not be "for art's sake" but should make a meaningful contribution to your text.

This assignment may take one or several class sessions to complete, depending on your objectives and time. For example, each activity can be a separate class to emphasize the writing process, or the activities can be combined into fewer classes; reading aloud and discussion at each activity can enhance the process. Sharing and discussing through peer reviewing is encouraged. Instructors can substitute any of the reading/visual materials in *Seeing & Writing 4*, as desired. The ones listed above are only suggestions.

For further consideration, the entire process can become a multistage research project that includes researching each author/photographer/subject and integrating the researched knowledge into societal, communal, cultural, or generational investigations (this can even be done as an ethnographic study). Students should select a minimum of five sources from various chapters of the textbook as the basis for their work, and they should include some number of related additional essays/photos they find through their research. Original writing/photos are encouraged. The length of the assignment can be modified to fit time requirements by adding or deleting various pieces of the assignment. Drafts that are peer reviewed can also be included as part of the writing/research process. Besides the written product, students may be required to present their work via other media methods, such as a script based on their work presented via YouTube. Oral presentations that include visual media support for their work are also encouraged.

Looking Closer:
Altering Images

While Chapter 7 offers students many opportunities to consider how images can be used to make arguments, the essays and images grouped here ask them to think about an ongoing argument regarding the nature of imagery. As digital manipulation of photographs becomes increasingly popular, viewers of photography also become increasingly savvy about potential alteration. There is even a slang term, *fauxtography*, to refer to doctored images. Viewers have certainly grown savvier about the pictures they see in the popular media. However, many observers of photography and especially photojournalism have called for clearer guidelines about when to use altered images and how to indicate the changes. The essays and images in this section offer several different answers to how this reevaluation might be accomplished.

Mitchell Stephens, *Expanding the Language of Photographs* (p. 664)

Stephens mentions three examples of digitally altered news photos: Tonya Harding skating with Nancy Kerrigan in *New York Newsday*; the repositioned pyramids in an issue of *National Geographic*; and Governor Ann Richards riding a Harley in *Texas Monthly*. Stephens does not accept that altering news photographs is like lying; instead he suggests that altering news photographs is necessary for the evolution of photojournalism. He argues that photographs are altered from the outset by photographers' choice of angles, filters, contrast, and depth of field. Digital altering, then, does not render them more subjective than they already are. He draws a comparison to language, to the use of verb tense and form to refer to what could be there but is not there now; and he suggests that photographs should be allowed the same conditionality as long as their alteration is clearly labeled as such.

Stephens asserts that altered photographs "will allow us to peek, however hazily, into the future: showing not just how Harding and Kerrigan might look together on the ice but how that new building might change the neighborhood" (para. 9). He thinks the assumption that photographs represent reality has always been "something of a misperception" and that "if we are to take advantage of the great promise of digital technology, we'll have to wise up" (para. 14).

George Hunt, *Untitled* (p. 668)

Hunt's *Untitled* demonstrates how photographs have always been manipulated, even before it was possible to alter them digitally. Here we see the fiction used to create the "truth" of a Kwakiutl woman and her weaving. The backdrop is being held up to create a better picture of the woman at her task. Is the photograph less true for being staged? Is it less authentic than an unstaged photograph would be?

John Long, *Ethics in the Age of Digital Photography* (p. 669)

In this essay, Long discusses how unethical changes to photographs have damaged journalism's credibility. He refers to some of the same examples mentioned by Stephens, but he takes the opposite view: "No amount of captioning can forgive a visual lie. In the context of news, if a photo looks real, it better be real" (para. 22). His contention that fake photographs leave actual copy that can be mistaken for the real thing is borne out by the fact that the Associated Press actually ran the doctored photograph of Ann Richards on a motorcycle without realizing it was a fake.

Some argue that technical changes, changes "that make the photo more readable," are "neither ethical nor unethical" (para. 24). Long does not agree. He acknowledges that "Essential changes change the meaning of the photograph, and Accidental changes change useless details but do not change the real meaning" (para. 25). But he insists that any change in content is wrong. Changes diminish the power of the photograph to capture a moment as it happened. "Real photos," he writes, "can change the hearts and minds of the people. . . . They are powerful, and they get their power from the fact that they are real Moments captured for all time on film" (para. 37).

Hoax Photograph (p. 677)

The first image is Lance Cheung's helicopter; the second is Charles Maxwell's shark jumping out of the water. In the third, the two images have been spliced together and edited to make what circulated via e-mail as *National Geographic*'s "THE Photo of the Year." In their essays, both Stephens and Long discuss the consequences of professional journalists' altering of photographs. But what does it mean when anyone with a computer and off-the-shelf software can manipulate images?

Barry Blitt, *The Politics of Fear* (p. 678)

Blitt's cover for *The New Yorker* caused a stir several months before the 2008 presidential election. Blitt says that he meant the drawing as a satire of overblown suspicions about the political leanings of Barack Obama and his wife Michelle Obama. The former is depicted in clothing that links him to radical Islam, while the latter has the Afro hairstyle and camouflage pants of a 1960s-era black nationalist. The cartoon imagines an Oval Office in which Osama bin Laden's portrait has a place over the fireplace, in which we see an American flag burning.

Some viewers of the image missed Blitt's satirical intent and found the image shocking and even offensive. One question you might ask students is how they read the illustration now that the election has been decided. Does the cover read differently in hindsight than it did during the heat of the campaign? You might also have them discuss why Blitt combines these two fears about the Obamas—their links both to Islam and to radical advocates for civil rights in the United States. Do the two have much in common?

Virginia Postrel, *The Politics of the Retouched Headshot* (p. 679)

Postrel's essay offers an interesting counterpart to Stephens and Long by showing how ubiquitous photo retouching is, not just for fashion models but also for public figures like Sarah Palin. Fox's criticism of the *Newsweek* photo suggests that altering photos is now de rigueur and that the failure to touch up Palin's face carries a political message. In order to examine claims about the photo, Postrel looks to the tradition of portraiture, in which the goal of representing the subject's essence is arguably more important than strict accuracy. She opposes the "reasoned image" with the portrait, which is selected out of many possible views to flatter the subject. Given this objective, are objections to Palin's portrait (which Postrel is quick to point out is actually quite attractive) fair?

Rankin, *Bootiful* (p. 682)

These two images present the before-and-after digital alteration of a face. Rankin's work moves the discussion of digital alteration from constraints on news photographers to constraints on individuals and the very personal choice of the face they want to present to the world. Is there a point at which even this kind of alteration becomes unacceptable?

POSSIBILITIES FOR DISCUSSION, REFLECTION, AND JOURNALING

• How does the ready availability of technology complicate the truthfulness of images? And how does our awareness of digital enhancement, our knowledge of special effects from TV and the movies, complicate our reading of images? Has the role of viewer changed since George Hunt staged his photograph? Can we trust our eyes? Should we?

• Both Stephens and Long refer in their essays to *Texas Monthly*'s cover, which placed the head of Governor Ann Richards on a model's body. However, the two writers take very different stances on how the cover was received. Ask students to discuss this difference of opinion and what underlies the writers' different judgments.

• Can and should portraits of political figures be chosen using the same criteria that you would use to choose pictures for a personal photo album?

ADDITIONAL WRITING TOPICS AND CLASSROOM ACTIVITIES

• Ask students to use Photoshop to alter one of their own photographs. When they present the photos to the class, see whether the other students are able to detect the changes.

• Ask students to draft an essay analyzing the photographs they find in a national or local paper. What elements in the photographs indicate that they are real? What elements suggest that they are not real? Ask students to examine the photographs and imagine alternative versions of them and how such versions might change the story.

• Ask students to watch a documentary on television. Then have them list and explain in an essay the elements of the show that were staged and those that were not. For example, what role did the people play? Were any of them actors? How was the story presented visually? Had the film been shot recently? Or did the documentary make use of old footage? Were the cameras visible? Was there voice-over narration, or did the images speak for themselves?

• At the beginning of this chapter, the McQuades quote Neil Postman: "'We are now a culture whose information, ideas, and epistemology are given form by television, not by the printed word'" (p. 582). Ask students to write about how the pieces in this Looking Closer section support and challenge Postman's claim.

CONNECTIONS WITH OTHER TEXTS

• Ask students to consult the *Oxford English Dictionary* for definitions of the word *ethics*. Discuss with them the original meaning of the word, and have them apply it to the texts in this section. To what extent are these representations ethical or not?

• Bring in copies of the *National Geographic* or another magazine, and ask students to examine the photography and evaluate its authenticity. How do the qualities of these photographs

differ from the many advertising photographs shown in the textbook?

SUGGESTIONS FOR FURTHER READING, THINKING, AND WRITING

PRINT

Anonymous. "Magic (Airbrush Art)." *The New Yorker*, February 3, 1992: 24+. Print.

Edwards, Elizabeth. *Anthropology and Photography, 1860–1920*. New Haven: Yale UP, 1992. Print. Includes an essay on George Hunt and his work.

Stephens, Mitchell. *The Rise of the Image, the Fall of the Word*. New York: Oxford UP, 1998. Print.

WEB

museumofhoaxes.com/tests/hoaxphototest.html. The Museum of Hoaxes has four pages that test one's ability to tell a real photo from a hoax. Many of them are obvious hoaxes, but some are surprisingly true. This site could be useful, especially if students tend to oversimplify people's gullibility.

AUDIOVISUAL

A Brief History of Time. 84 min. NTSC, 1992. VHS. Distributed by Paramount Studios. Director Errol Morris is a master of riding the thin line between documentary and fiction film. His production values are pure Hollywood, but in this movie his focus is on making Stephen Hawking and his complex scientific theory comprehensible to the audience —a wonderful marriage of science and art.

The Matrix. 136 min. 1999. DVD. Distributed by Warner Studios. Performers include Keanu Reeves and Laurence Fishburne. A technological thriller that raises questions about the future of virtual reality and the role of ethics in representation.

Surefire Assignment: Participatory Writing in the Network Society

Iraj Omidvar
*Southern Polytechnic
State University*

One of the most remarkable features of the unrest in Iran was the massive flood of digital communication from Iranians with access to the Internet, cell phone text messaging, and digital camera capabilities. Not only professional journalists but also "citizen journalists" searched, assessed, and conveyed reliable, authoritative, and otherwise responsible information. Persian- and English-language as well as bilingual blogs were covering and processing the news so rapidly and thoroughly that they became part of the news. Social networking sites came to be recognized as potentially potent political forums, allowing people who at other times would remain consumers of news to become powerful participants not just in collecting and processing the news but in creating it as well.

I have come to accept that our students live in an information environment that is in significant ways different from the environment students lived in only a decade ago. The new environment requires the creation, processing, and distribution of information, and the skills that go along with these activities. One of the exciting features of this environment is that the reporting of the information and then its analysis, repackaging, and redistribution help shape not only the information environment but sometimes the social phenomenon itself. In other words, here communication helps participants not only to understand but also to change the world, or, as the chapter puts it, to take a stand. In this environment, the types of

reading and writing students engage in are different from the kinds of reading and writing students traditionally engaged in, and the critical reading and writing education that students bring to bear on their activities must be adjusted accordingly. In my composition classes, I now try to create reading and writing environments that students increasingly encounter in their daily lives and activities. Below are some of the ideas I have been trying in my classes. I sometimes build two or more of them into larger units.

1. First, I ask my students to explore the potentials and limitations of "comments" sections accompanying news stories on reputable online news web sites. Students examine and evaluate the ways in which several sites channel reader comments. For example, some sites post any and all comments, while others strictly moderate this forum. Some require readers to register, and some are rather strict and thorough in terms of the information they collect during registration. Some offer opportunities for readers to vote on and write responses to other comments. Some permit the comments to be sorted by the number of votes. Some select particularly relevant or useful comments (Editors' Choice), and readers can sort comments according to the editors' selections.

   After having been introduced to rhetorical concepts, students can evaluate effective and ineffective reader comments. And in preparation for reporting on their findings, they participate in writing comments at various venues and assess the results.

2. Students can also explore and evaluate editorial videos. Students combine an

exploration of photos and clips with the concepts surrounding purpose, context, and audience to evaluate such editorials.

3. A news area whose importance as a source was a constant topic of debate and discussion during the unrest in Iran was text messaging, especially a variation of it on the communication venue Twitter. This form of communication has extraordinary features (possibilities and limitations) and can be a powerful tool for studying language use. Some of its elements are particularly suited to the application of some venerable concepts in literary studies: the aphorism, the epigram, the metaphor, the haiku, the nursery rhyme. Tweets have also been criticized for the misinformation that they intentionally or inadvertently spread. Assignments can range from examining the possibilities and limitations of this form of communication, to writing terse messages/poems, to exploring the meaning and conciseness of messages.

4. Students can pursue a controversial, ongoing event for all or part of a semester and examine news sources that participate in the making, processing, and distribution of the news, such as social networking sites, blogs, photo- and video-sharing sites, news aggregator sites, and traditional news media with a strong online presence. Students keep a blog of their ongoing discoveries and reflections and then end the semester with an essay synthesizing their efforts. Alternatively, students can examine the range of news coverage sites and collect information by identifying and participating in online networks covering local or other events and contributing to the creation, processing, and distribution of the news.

5. Students can spend time observing social networking sites—from Facebook to computer game forums—to classify the types of sites that are created, their appeal to various audiences, the means by which certain sites and activities become very popular, and the way in which various people choose to present themselves. The contexts, purposes, and audiences of these sites cover practically the entire spectrum of communicative acts. The forums, for example, can be for people who are trying to gather information about illnesses or government or corporate services. Assignments can require students not only to identify and analyze sites that provide answers to questions of immediate importance to their social lives but also to analyze them and to contribute to their creation in order to help other people.

Appendix

The theoretical texts chosen for the Appendix address the two areas that *Seeing & Writing* highlights in composition instruction: sharpening students' abilities to read and write about images (Berger), and identifying connections and differences between the verbal and visual dimensions of American culture (McCloud).

John Berger, *Ways of Seeing* (p. 690)

Berger's essay can be used as a lens through which to reexamine any visual selection in the book.

POSSIBILITIES FOR DISCUSSION, REFLECTION, AND JOURNALING

• You could begin by asking the class to analyze the first sentence of this piece: "Seeing comes before words."

• How might students rethink their interpretations of images in the book after reading Berger's piece? Ask them to refer to specific selections in the book.

ADDITIONAL WRITING TOPICS AND CLASSROOM ACTIVITIES

• Paragraph 43 (on reproduction) is an especially important—and provocative—passage to teach. Ask students to apply Berger's discussion of image reproduction to *Seeing & Writing*.

• Ask students why they think the textbook reproduces such a huge variety of visual selections—some difficult, some pleasant, some familiar, some new.

• Have students write an essay in which they explain how reproducing images in a textbook is different from reproducing images on a T-shirt, in an ad, or in a poster.

CONNECTIONS WITH OTHER TEXTS

• Have students compare John Berger's discussion of photography (para. 8) with the discussion by Susan Sontag (Chapter 3, p. 304).

• Ask students to do some basic research on how Andy Warhol created his famous paintings of Elvis Presley or Marilyn Monroe. What might Berger say about art that takes reproduction as a subject?

SUGGESTIONS FOR FURTHER READING, THINKING, AND WRITING

PRINT

Berger, John. *About Looking*. New York: Pantheon, 1980. Print.

———. *Another Way of Telling*. New York: Pantheon, 1982. Print.

courses.washington.edu/englhtml/engl569/
berger/bergersup.html. This University of
Washington site contains digital images of
the paintings in Berger's essay as well as a
link to the Benjamin essay he mentions as
a source.

Scott McCloud, *Show and Tell* (p. 138)

If John Berger delves into reading visual images, the selection from Scott McCloud
speaks to the changing differences in—and significance of—cultural roles.
McCloud's piece would serve as an excellent instructional companion to any
one of the Pair selections in *Seeing & Writing* (all come shortly after the chapter introductions). This selection from McCloud provides a lens through
which to continue any comparison of a verbal and a visual representation of a
similar theme.

POSSIBILITIES FOR DISCUSSION, REFLECTION, AND JOURNALING

• Ask students to discuss the differences between *showing* and *telling*.

• How do the Pair selections in *Seeing & Writing* demonstrate not only similarities but also
differences?

• Have students consider the specific compositional strategies Berger and McCloud have
employed to convey their points.

SUGGESTIONS FOR FURTHER READING, THINKING, AND WRITING

PRINT

McCloud, Scott. *Reinventing Comics: How Imagination and Technology Are Revolutionizing an
Art Form*. New York: Perennial, 2000. Print.

ADDITIONAL WRITING TOPICS AND CLASSROOM ACTIVITIES

• Have students write an essay in which they
argue for or against the proposition that images
have replaced words in importance in contemporary American culture.

• Using McCloud's piece as an example, ask
students to freewrite about which topics are
best suited to the medium of comics.

WEB

bookslut.com/features/2003_10_000772.php.
An interview with Scott McCloud about the
impact of digital technology on comics.

CONNECTIONS WITH OTHER TEXTS

• Ask students to explore the notion that "the
medium is the message" in both Berger's and
McCloud's selections.